THE PHENOMENON
OF REVOLUTION

D0107835

DAVID FELLMAN
Vilas Professor of Political Science
University of Wisconsin-Madison
Advisory Editor to Dodd, Mead & Company

THE PHENOMENON
OF REVOLUTION

Mark N. Hagopian

American International College

DODD, MEAD & COMPANY
New York   1975

ISBN 0-396-06938-X

Library of Congress Catalog Card Number: 73-21167

Printed in the United States of America

DESIGNED BY JEFFREY M. BARRIE

Second Printing

ACKNOWLEDGMENTS

I gratefully thank the following publishers for permission to quote from their books:

Addison-Wesley Publishing Co. for Gardner Lindzey, ed., *Handbook of Social Psychology*
(1954 ed.).
Basic Books for Lewis Feuer, *The Conflict of Generations*.
The Bobbs-Merrill Co. for J. E. Connor, ed., Lenin: *On Revolution*.
Harcourt Brace Jovanovich for Karl Mannheim, *Ideology and Utopia*.
Harper & Row for Eric Hoffer, *The True Believer;* and for George Pettee, *The Process of
Revolution*.
Harvard University Press for Mark Seldon, *The Yenan Way*.
Holt, Rinehart and Winston for H. A. Taine, *The Ancient Regime*.
Humanities Press, for Sidney Hook, *The Hero in History*.
International Universities Press for Gustav Bychowski, *Dictators and Disciples*.
Oxford University Press for H. Gerth and C. W. Mills, *From Max Weber: Essays in
Sociology*.
Prentice-Hall Inc. for Crane Brinton, *The Anatomy of Revolution*.
Princeton University Press for Ted R. Gurr, *Why Men Rebel*.
University of California Press for Franz Schurmann, *Ideology and Organization in
Communist China*.
The Viking Press for Hannah Arendt, *On Revolution*.
Yale University Press for Samuel P. Huntington, *Political Order in Changing Societies*.
Xerox College Publishing for R. M. MacIver, *Social Causation*.

To *Alice and Berj*

PREFACE

My main goal in *The Phenomenon of Revolution* is to attempt a summary statement of what is known and what is unknown about the revolutionary process a generation and better after the classics of Edwards, Pettee, and Brinton. Three chief considerations prompt a reappraisal of our knowledge of revolution at this time. Perhaps the most important is the reality of revolution itself. The experience of China, Viet Nam, and Cuba with their reverberations in thought and action suggest a reexamination of many generalizations about revolution derived from the three great Western revolutions in England, France, and Russia. The sum total of these generalizations have solidified into a sort of conventional wisdom about revolution. The approach taken in this book towards this body of thought will be critical, but not iconoclastic. Edwards, Pettee, Brinton, and others have produced an intellectual scaffolding of revolutionary theory, a good portion of which remains standing despite the rude storms of the last three decades.

My second stimulus is provided by advances made in the social sciences over the same period. Unfortunately, for a time the price paid for increased rigor and sophistication in the several disciplines of political science, history, anthropology, sociology, psychology, and economics has been a division of labor that has bordered on isolation and fragmentation. But it is precisely topics such as revolution which require a multilateral approach that can pave the way towards greater unity in social science. Since I cannot assume that all readers have a general familiarity with key concepts in the several social sciences, I have been forced into considerable definition of terms and conceptual analysis.

The third consideration prompting a reappraisal of our knowledge of revolution is a matter of change in climates of opinion. Much of the academic social science of the 1950's was concerned with themes such as the "end of ideology," the requisites of "pluralistic democracy," and the notions of political stability and social equilibrium. There is nothing wrong with such concerns, provided they do not, as they did for a while, obscure the other aspects of man's political life. Growing political unrest punctuated sometimes by violence in the middle and late 1960's has helped to restore a balanced awareness of both the stability-equilibrium side of politics and the instability-conflict side of it.

The Phenomenon of Revolution aims to be a critical synthesis of research, concepts, and theories of revolution. Though it is something less than a didactic monograph with a tightly integrated theory of revolution, it is something more than a "survey of the literature." While I take a stand on most of the issues raised, I have tried to give opposing viewpoints their day in court. I have conducted fairly substantial historical research on the actual practice of revolutions to see if and how much they confirm (or disconfirm) both the claims of revolutionary ideologies and the claims of the conventional wisdom of revolutions. Though my research is not a major concern of this book, I frequently discuss particular revolutionary experiences and episodes in order to exemplify or elaborate some proposed revision in the conventional wisdom of revolution (i.e. with regard to the stages of revolution and to the problem of revolutionary leadership). Though this procedure might disrupt the symmetry of certain chapters and sections, the alternatives were either a much more ponderous volume or a briefer, but highly abstract, monograph. I preferred a middle approach.

Finally, I would like to express my thanks to Professors Samuel P. Huntington and James C. Davies, who read the manuscript and whose substantive and procedural suggestions have markedly improved the end result. At a somewhat different level of involvement, certain of my colleagues at American International College have helped to strengthen various aspects of this book. In particular, Professors Robert Lowrie, Robert Bohlke, Theodore Belsky, and Robert Markel have made my task easier. None of the above naturally bear any responsibility for the remaining deficiencies of *The Phenomenon of Revolution*. Professor Richard Sprinthall's help was more evident in the general problems of academic authorship. I would also like to thank the Administration of American International College, especially Vice-President John Mitchell, for granting me help essential to the completion of the manuscript. Mrs. Ruth Temple typed the bulk of the final manuscript with speed and skill. Last, I owe much to William Oman, Genia Graves, and their associates at Dodd, Mead & Company. Their faith, good faith, and professional skill are surely out of the ordinary.

MARK N. HAGOPIAN

CONTENTS

List of Figures

THE PHENOMENON
OF REVOLUTION

I

WHAT REVOLUTION IS NOT

A revolution is an acute, prolonged crisis in one or more of the traditional systems of stratification (class, status, power) of a political community, which involves a purposive, elite-directed attempt to abolish or to reconstruct one or more of said systems by means of an intensification of political power and recourse to violence. While the full analysis and defense of this concept of revolution will be the concern of Chapter III, some immediate clarification is necessary to see more clearly why phenomena such as coup d' etat, revolt, and secession differ from true revolution.

The stress of this definition on acuteness and prolongation of crisis underscores the utter seriousness, and hence the relative infrequency, of the revolutionary situation. "Crisis" is one of the most abused words in the social sciences, for in any relatively complex society, some part of that society is always undergoing an ostensible crisis. All sorts of dramatic, even bizarre disturbances unsettle the surface of society; and yet, like the ripples caused by a stone cutting through the surface of a still pond, they do not leave permanent traces. Not so with revolution; even abortive or unsuccessful revolutions have a more or less permanent impact on society. Societies almost always contain a measure of critics, malcontents, deviants, and idealists who repudiate the status quo; but only on rare occasions does the aggregate discontent reach a level incompatible with the existing order. Revolutionaries cannot really create a revolutionary situation. They can only hope to exacerbate it and thus profit from it.

The separate mention of economic (class), status, and political (power) systems of stratification is intended to reflect an awareness of the various complex forms of social structure encountered in societies undergoing revolution. This complexity is in turn translated into the extreme complexity of the origins, protagonists, and course of each particular historical revolution. Separation of the three systems of stratification further implies that the "stakes" of one revolution may differ somewhat from those of the next. Revolutions vary in intensity as they aim to overturn or abolish one, two, or three stratification systems.[1] Some revolutions are therefore "more revolutionary" than others. The term "political community" in our definition of revolution is employed to show that a revolutionary crisis eventually engulfs an entire society and is not a merely local affair. Revolution thus differs in *scope* as well as intensity from other forms of sociopolitical change and violence.

The second part of our definition establishes that revolution is not merely negative; it involves "a purposive, elite-directed attempt to abolish or to reconstruct one or more of [the stratification] systems. . . ." The term "purposive" here implies that some sort of revolutionary ideology exists which does three things: (1) it provides an indictment of the old regime by spelling out what is wrong with it and why; (2) it conveys the idea that a future or possible society is enormously superior to the existing one, either by a detailed blueprint or plan (a utopia) or by vague hints or suggestions about the postrevolutionary order; (3) less commonly, though increasingly as we approach the present epoch, the revolutionary ideology offers strategic principles for attaining and retaining power in the hands of the revolutionaries. Thus, ideology infuses a sense of direction and purpose to revolution that is often lacking to coups, revolts, and secessions.

Elite-direction is an important characteristic of revolution whose exact importance is a matter of grave controversy. Here, we can only didactically state how important the role of leadership is in all stages of a revolution. Without strong leadership the very complexity of goals, aspirations, and motivations characteristic of a revolutionary situation could easily degenerate into a Hobbesian war of each against all. Thus, the really distinctive work of the revolution—the attempted restructuring or destruction of one or more of the stratification systems—cannot get very far without resorting to effective leadership.

The means employed by revolution as well as its goals distinguish it from other forms of political and social change. In fact, critics of revolution have often attacked its methods and measures rather than its long-term objectives. The emphasis in our definition upon intensification of political power and recourse to violence illustrates what some concepts of revolution either neglect or underestimate: that revolution is a political phenomenon. Its political dimension figures both with respect to goals and to means. The goal of a revolution in fact may be a new political order, while political methods are unavoidable no matter what the stakes of revolution may be. This double importance of political power gives it some claim to being considered the most important, though not the exclusive, factor involved.

Finally, our definition of revolution considers recourse to violence as essential rather than accidental to it. The magnitude and the abruptness of change involved in revolution always produces violence in some form. Revolution must be distinguished from reform, however radical, and from long-term evolutionary developments such as the so-called industrial revolution and the growth of certain religious movements. The factor of violence helps to do this.

It was stated that our definition of revolution would help to distinguish it from phenomena such as coup d'etat, revolt, and secession. These have often been confused with revolution, and understanding why this has happened is itself instructive. Revolution, coup d'etat, revolt, and secession are by no means exclusive categories. There are coups within revolutions as well as coups having nothing to do with them. A revolution may be sparked by or engender one or more revolts. A secessionist movement may or may not be revolutionary. What follows, however, in the rest of this chapter is for the most part an analysis and classification of "pure" (i.e., nonrevolutionary) coups d'etat, revolts, and secessions. The discussion will develop what Max Weber termed "ideal types" [2] of the phenomena in question.

COUP D'ETAT

The term "coup d'etat" means literally a blow at the state (i.e., a sudden attack on the government). More broadly, it connotes the sudden expulsion of the existing governmental leadership (kings, presidents, regents, etc., along with their followers), or alternatively the sudden and drastic overturning of the existing balance of institutional power in favor of the executive. *Simple* or *pure* coups d'etat are quite restricted in their overall objectives: replacement of the incumbent ruling clique, change of controversial foreign or domestic policies, and more ambitiously a certain institutional reshuffling. Although the goals of simple coups vary considerably, they do not seek to reconstruct the country's fundamental political, social, and economic institutions. Most historical coups have been rather mild affairs usually, though not always, involving a minimum of bloodshed and a speedy return to normalcy. It is true that the new ruling clique may consolidate its often shaky grip on power by "mopping up" whatever belated resistance partisans of the deposed oligarchy can offer or by making concessions to strategically important groups. Nevertheless, the scope and intensity of change is quite limited, and we must not be fooled by the sometimes flamboyant rhetoric of the new government. In short, the stakes of the simple coup are generally power as an end in itself coupled in certain cases with shifts in the day-to-day pattern of policy and administration.

Differing drastically from simple coups are both revolutionary and counterrevolutionary coups. The revolutionary coup takes two forms: (1) coups that initiate a revolution, (2) coups that occur during the revolution. In the revolutionary coup the stakes are much higher than a simple replacement of personnel or minor modifications of existing institutions. The coup in this context is merely the surface manifestation of much deeper currents of change. In fact, with coups initiating true revolutions the leaders of the coup may be ignorant of the significance of the process that has brought them, perhaps momentarily, to power. Moderate reformers often find their governments serving as the prelude to events that soon overwhelm them.

Coups during revolutions occur after a professedly revolutionary government has been established, and they replace one faction of revolutionaries with another favoring different policies. In fact, some theorists of revolution view these coups as marking transitions between phases of a predetermined pattern of revolution. Whether or not these claims hold up will be discussed in Chapter IV. In any case, radicals do overthrow moderates and sometimes vice versa during revolutions.

Counterrevolutionary coups are launched to forestall an incipient revolution or to overthrow one that has achieved a measure of success. An important difference between the simple coup and the counterrevolutionary coup is seen when the coup does not immediately succeed. When a counterrevolutionary coup aborts, it is often followed by a bitter civil war (Spain,1936). The simple coup generally either succeeds or fails quickly, thus sparing the country some of the worst ravages of protracted civil strife. Since they are parts of larger wholes, however, further discussion of revolutionary and counterrevolutionary coups must be postponed to later chapters.

Before tackling the specific varieties of the simple coup d'etat, several general remarks are in order. One student of the coup d'etat has pointed out three conditions influencing the outcome of any coup d'etat: "the sympathies of the nation's armed forces, the state of public opinion, and the international situation." [3] These factors must be weighed first of all by the conspirators—coups are by their very nature conspiratorial—and then by those who analyze the causes of the success or failure of any given coup. Given the widespread occurrence and diverse character of coups, it might seem hazardous to rank these three variables in order of importance. Nevertheless, it seems that the state of mind of the military (or other security forces) takes precedence in most cases, because force is at the very heart of the coup d'etat. Active complicity or even benevolent neutrality of the military enormously enhances the chances of any given coup. It is difficult, indeed, to imagine a coup succeeding against the wishes of a strong military establishment resolutely united in support of the existing government. As a qualification Edward Luttwak suggests that the "forces relevant to a coup are those whose locations and/or equipment enables them to intervene in its locale . . . within the 12–24 hour timespan which precedes the establishment of its control over the machinery of government." [4] A divided military, however, changes the situation, perhaps to the extent of allowing the architects of the coup to profit from the stalemate and seize power.

The "state of public opinion" as an expression requires some qualification, because in some societies the politically relevant public or "political nation" is a tiny proportion of the adult population, while in others it is quite numerous. In the former case vast masses of the populace are utterly indifferent as to which clique of "notables" happens to be in power.[5] With these stipulations, we can place public opinion second on the list of important conditions. The international situation is usually the least significant variable of the three, as foreign powers are often confronted with the accomplished fact of a new government, with which they must somehow come to terms. However, there are situations in which the international situation becomes the determinant factor in the fate of the coup. In many cases the coup is engineered under the auspices or with the knowledge of a foreign power. Thus the role of the outsider and his own foreign relations can overshadow the domestic situation. In other cases the crucial question is whether the coup will be tolerated for long by outside powers. Some coups encounter serious international hostility expressed in terms running from diplomatic pressure to direct military intervention. Many coups have failed through the unfavorable influence of one, two, or three of these considerations; and many more have been left at the planning stage because of a bad prognosis.

A related consideration concerns the degree of political-administrative centralization of the target country. The existence of a capital city that is the political and even the economic-cultural hub of the state makes the ultimate success of a coup technically easier. In a decentralized situation, coordination of actions against a variety of pressure points enormously complicates the logistics of the coup. In such a context success of the coup in the capital city may still leave the total victory of the coup far from accomplished.

A final general distinction concerns whether the makers of the coups come from within or from outside the formal governmental structure (i.e., whether or not they are officeholders). One authority has defined the problem out of existence by understanding coup d'etat as a "change of government effected by the holders of government power in defiance of the state's legal constitution." [6] This conception, which is heavily influenced by the executive coups of Napoleon I and Napoleon III, gravely restricts the meaning of coup d'etat and leaves us with a host of military and paramilitary seizures of power that are apparently unclassifiable. However, the extragovernmental or intragovernmental origin should not be decided by definition. Coups can be attempted from within the governmental structure (e.g., executive coups); or from outside of it (e.g., paramilitary coups); or by groups who are in some respects within it and in other respects outside it (e.g., military coups).

Palace Revolutions

Palace revolution is problably the least complex and easiest to understand of simple coups. The very term implies that the classic form of palace revolution occurs in a monarchy, whether the ruler's official title is king, emperor, sultan, caliph, or whatever. In one type of palace revolution the ruler is forced to abdicate the throne to a rival or is killed and the rival assumes the throne immediately or shortly thereafter. The rival may be a close relative (brother or half brother), a distant one with some claims to the throne, or someone hailing from a rival house with royal pretensions. The political dramas of Shakespeare portray as well as any history the kind of intrigue and grisly violence that palace revolutions sometimes involve. Understandably the military often participates, though not to the extent nor with the objectives that would qualify palace revolutions as military coups. The military may be split into factions favoring the reigning monarch and the pretender or usurper, respectively. While the stakes in such cases seem to be the personal power of an individual or a small coterie, a policy dimension may be involved. Foreign powers, for example, may be interested in ousting a particular ruler and installing one more congenial to their interests. One suspects that foreign intervention would loom larger in the history of palace revolutions, if all the facts were available. Similarly, domestic groups may give active or tacit support to a conspiracy against the throne.

A second type of palace revolution finds the monarch threatened by a legally subordinate official. This servant of the king (or his predecessors) has made himself indispensable to the often incompetent ruler (or his forebears). The king may, in fact, be a virtual prisoner in his own palace, and here the expression "power behind the throne" assumes a literal significance. The transition of power from the legal ruler to the official can take place all at once, or in more or less lengthy phases. In the latter case, the official—prime minister, grand vizier, mayor of the palace, etc.—first takes *de facto* power out of the hands of the monarch, who thus becomes a more or less conscious puppet. In time, however, the facade of the powerless monarchy may be cast down, and the real power holder becomes the titular ruler as well. There is no driving necessity to take this final step, and the contrast between the shadow and substance of power can be maintained for generations.[7]

Executive Coups

Executive coups vary in form and significance. The most blatant form occurs when the chief executive of a republic abolishes the existing constitution and proclaims himself king or emperor with the intention of founding a dynasty. Most executive coups, however, fall short of changing the official form of government. In Latin America, for example, *continuismo*, or the unconstitutional and indefinite prolongation of a president's term of office, constitutes a favored type of executive coup. Executive coups also occur when a chief executive tires of opposition stemming from the legislative branch. In this instance he either disbands, purges, or forcibly coerces the legislative assembly or replaces it with one that is handpicked. In some cases a veneer of legality is preserved, though usually with the "suspension" of certain constitutional guarantees.

Executive coups must not be confused with "constitutional dictatorship." [8] The latter is a *temporary* expedient whereby the executive assumes extraordinary powers with the consent of the legislative in order to deal effectively with grave national emergencies such as war, insurrection, or economic collapse. In such a case it is understood by all that the concentration of powers in the executive will last no longer than the crisis that necessitated it. Accordingly, many constitutions even have an emergency clause which stipulates certain conditions and procedures for invoking constitutional dictatorship. However, experience has shown that defining the nature and duration of an emergency is a potent cause of political discord. Furthermore, it is easy to see that the concentration of powers in a period of constitutional dictatorship affords an excellent base of operations for a full-fledged executive coup.

Military Coups

While the military plays a role in many palace revolutions and executive coups, we must reserve the term "military coup" for those coups in which the military is the prime mover of events. The military coup can lead to direct military rule (nowadays styled as a military "junta") or to civilian rule under the sufferance of the military. In the second case the military withdraws to a position of surveillance ready to act if the civilian government displeases them too much or too often. Taking their cue from the infamous Praetorian Guard of the later Roman Empire, recent scholars have extended the terms "praetorianism" or "praetorian state" to describe societies whose structural weaknesses make the military coup a "normal" method of leadership and policy change.[9] In the praetorian state, force, usually in the form of the military coup, is both the first and last resort of the discontented and the ambitious. To say that politicians and the military are venal and corrupt in the praetorian setting is to apply standards that really have little meaning there.

In some contexts the military becomes an important part, if not the vanguard, of a newly politicized middle class, which is increasingly discontented with the old oligarchy. The military coup which overthrows oligarchy and which responds to middle-class demands for change and participation can be termed a *reform* coup. A reform coup is situated midway between the low-stakes coup of the oligarchical period and the all-or-nothing coup which begins an authentic revolution. Governments set up by reform coups undertake orderly social reform without launching a full-scale attack on the existing order. However, these governments may still be plagued by military coups. Some of these coups are anticipatory, because they assay the strength of the old regime.[10] In the *breakthrough* coup, the reform-minded military itself takes power. Often the more radical and impatient officers engineer a further *consolidating* coup, which decrees reforms intended to prevent any relapse into the old order. However, the opposite may occur in the case of a *conservative* coup "carried out by a combination of military and upper-middle-class or oligarchical elements. They attempt to put the brake on change, but they are seldom able to undo it." [11]

From this brief sketch one can appreciate the wide diversity of forms and objectives that mark military coups. In traditional polities the social content of the military coup is almost nonexistent. When the middle class has risen to some prominence, the social content can be either "conservative" or "progressive." In mass praetorianism it is generally the former. In short, the significance of the military coup varies according to the social and historical circumstances involved. Though the military coup is usually nonrevolutionary, the so-called consolidation coup—in which the more radical officers oust their former partners, the moderates—takes on many of the characteristics of authentic revolution.[12] If this indeed is the case, the military character of the coup recedes to a place of secondary importance in the face of the unfolding of a genuinely revolutionary dynamic.

Paramilitary Coups

A paramilitary group or formation can be loosely described as a private army; it is an armed, drilled, uniformed, officered, semipermanent fighting force outside the state's official military establishment. Often it is a part of a wider political movement or party which aims at the seizure of power. In certain cases a paramilitary formation can achieve a semiofficial status by being more or less covertly paid, provisioned, or supported by government officials. And should the parent movement take power, the paramilitary formation may end up incorporated into the nation's armed forces. Twentieth-century paramilitary formations have often distinguished themselves by the color of their uniforms: Hitler's Brown Shirts, Mussolini's Black Shirts.

Much of the activity of paramilitary groups consists of harassing political opponents (who often have their own formations) and defending the "movement" from attacks and counterattacks. These encounters can reach the level of pitched battles involving heavy casualties. On occasion, however, the group will play for higher stakes and attempt to seize political power by means of a coup d'etat. The German term "putsch" is often used to identify such situations, because of the large number of paramilitary organizations and coups that characterized German history immediately after World War I. Conditions of massive, rapid demobilization of thousands of regular army officers and men are extremely propitious for the development of paramilitary formations. The soldiers have known no other life than the military for several years and have extreme difficulty in reintegrating themselves into the civilian society. Add to this picture serious economic disarray and violent political conflict, and the likelihood of paramilitary groups increases proportionally. If the political right is the first to form such groups, the political left is almost compelled to follow suit, or vice versa. Paramilitary coups from either side of the political spectrum rarely succeed in taking power on their own initiative. The regular military forces often intervene against them as an unwanted competitor or simply because of loyalty to the existing regime. In some cases the political basis and support of the group is so slight that even if they expel the legal government, their victory is short-lived. A general strike was sufficient to overwhelm the Kapp putsch in Berlin in 1920.

REVOLT

Revolt is the second great class of violent political phenomena to be distinguished from revolution. Like coup d'etat it is often involved in the course of revolution and complex forms of revolt show considerable resemblances to revolution. Revolt can take one of five "pure" forms: jacqueries and peasant revolts, urban mobs, nativism, millenarianism-messianism, and aristocratic revolts. Actual historical revolts, however, can involve from one to five of these forms; this produces strange political alliances as well as difficulties for the student. Before tackling the five pure forms, however, we must strive to understand how revolt in general differs from revolution in general.

Jacques Ellul has cleared the way for us by pointing out some false or uninteresting criteria of distinction.[13] First, the *success-failure dichotomy*, wherein revolution is success and revolt failure, is trivial because it does not allow us to differentiate phenomena whose goals, development, and historical significance are not the same. The term "abortive" should be used to designate revolutions, coups, revolts, or secessions which fail to attain their immediate objectives. Second, the *level of violence measure*, whereby revolution is supposedly more violent than revolt, conflicts with the fact of the extreme bloodiness of numerous historical revolts. Third, the *amplitude measure*, which sees revolution as nationwide and revolt as localized, is belied by the wide geographical extent of many revolts. Fourth, the *different socioeconomic results* of revolt and revolution are a less attractive contrast than appears at first glance, according to Ellul, because "certain revolutions have not had profound economic or sociological results"—that is, their results have been largely confined to the political realm. These criteria are false because they are essentially quantitative (i.e., they move along a single scale or continuum from less to more of something—success, violence, area, results). Revolt has less of the privileged factor, revolution more.

The differences between revolt and revolution, however, are qualitative—marked by differences in kind, not just in amount. Furthermore, the differences move along several distinct planes, which as we shall see makes the construction of a continuum from revolt to revolution more complicated than is sometimes thought. The most essential differences between the two are (1) the stakes of the uprising, (2) the function of ideology, and (3) the role of leadership. We have argued that the stakes of revolution are the abolition or reconstruction of one or more of the systems of stratification in society. In simple revolt none of these systems as structures is threatened by serious attempts at reconstruction, let alone by complete abolition. Revolts are virtual prisoners of the reigning set of social values, and therefore cannot mount a full-scale attack on the institutionalized systems of stratification that are both cause and effect of these values. The short-run impact of revolt on the structure and function of social and political institutions is therefore indirect and marginal.

What then is revolt all about? Following Camus, we can say that the essence of revolt is the angry, violent expression of the refusal of an individual or a group to continue in its present condition. To the rebel the existing situation and the prognosis for the future appear intolerable. As Camus has stated: "The movement of rebellion is founded simultaneously on the categorical rejection of an intrusion that is considered intolerable and on the confused conviction of an absolute right which, in the rebel's mind, is more precisely the impression that he has the right to. . . ." [14] Hunger, rising prices, taxes, military impressment, arbitrary government, wage cuts, withdrawal of privileges—all can light the fuse of revolt. The rebel has become desperate, and his despair moves him to strike out against those things and people he holds responsible for his condition. Violent protest, revenge, primitive justice, and emotional release are the main motive forces of many revolts.

The rebel is incensed by the way society or his corner of it is operating. But his indictment of it is highly personalistic; he is a devotee of the "devil" theory of politics, which holds that certain "bad men" are accountable for the evils plaguing him. The implication is that destruction, or at least removal, of them will end the time of troubles. A revolt needs scapegoats and finds them in individuals ranging from the lowliest tax clerk up to the cabal of notables surrounding the throne.

Revolt cannot be satisfied with sociological analyses, nor "with abstract objects responsible for misery (the State), nor with far-off and mythical personages (the King), nor with more or less hazy groups (a class, for example). Revolt lives in the immediate: it is in the immediate that it needs someone accountable: it is *here* that it brings accusation against someone." [15] It is the very concreteness and specificity of revolt that prevent it from calling the social order as a whole into question. It is concerned with men and measures, not with fundamental institutions. This is what separates it from revolution. Revolt then "is an act of social surgery; it is intended to cut out one or more members who are offending against the joint commitments to maintain a particular social structure." [16]

Revolt therefore has a clearly conservative or even retrograde character. As it does not make the linkage between felt misery or alienation and the basic institutional setup of society, its horizons are limited to bringing things back to an equilibrium which is thought to have existed before things went bad. Certain innovations must be abolished; privileges must be restored; certain evil influences around the centers of power must be eliminated. Once these purifying operations are performed, it is felt that society will return to its true moorings. The violence and elan of revolt should not obscure the fact that what is at stake is renovation rather than innovation. It is important not to absolutize this contrast, however. Some revolts do lead to reforms: it is just that their lasting impact is something less than revolutionary. On the other hand, in the early phases of certain revolutions there is also a certain retrospective or restorative element. Some of the parliamentary leaders in the English Revolution thought to restore a constitutional balance that supposedly existed under Queen Elizabeth. In the French "pre-revolution" of 1787–88, groups friendly to the *parlements,* or special courts, wished to restore their powers and privileges. In the Mexican Revolution of 1910, "return to the Constitution of 1857" was the slogan of certain liberal factions. Nonetheless, the balance between the old and the new is quite different in revolt and revolution.

The limited stakes and backward glance of revolt are associated with its low level of ideology.[17] "A revolt does not have any idea [*pensée*] at the origin; it is visceral, immediate. A revolution implies a doctrine, a project, a program, some kind of theory. . . ." [18] The bases of the revolutionary ideology should ideally have been laid down before the outbreak of the revolution, and should to some extent have formed the mentality of the insurrectionaries. These conditions are lacking in revolts. If a revolt is prolonged, it may develop a certain ideological pretense (or flashes of authentically revolutionary thought may appear on the fringes of the revolt itself), but the "ideology" of revolt generally proves to be a selective accentuation of traditional beliefs. This lack or the weakness of ideology helps to explain why many revolts hesitate and then disintegrate after having routed the forces of order. The revolt simply does not know what to do with its somewhat inadvertently gained power. The rebel leaders lack the sense of direction that an ideology provides. It is no external force which prevents them from proceeding to a reconstruction of society; their paralysis of will stems from their inability to conceive of society in terms drastically different from those dictated by tradition. In many revolts this indecision allows the surviving members of the elite to regroup, counterattack, and ultimately defeat and disperse the rebels. Society, nearly destroyed by the catharsis of violence, returns to the old ways without profound traces of the revolt, although something like a "tradition of revolt" certainly develops in many instances.

The final major point of difference between revolt and revolution consists in the role of leadership. It is not that revolts are leaderless, while revolutions are led. All collective violence involves leaders of some sort. The question is rather the role played by leadership. The leaders of revolts are often skillful tacticians with occasional charismatic qualities. Yet as already indicated, they usually suffer from the lack of a comprehensive project or plan which only a full-scale ideology can provide. Strategy is really possible only in relation to clear-cut goals and the lack of these becomes clearer the more a revolt is prolonged. The leaders of a revolt allow the energy harnessed by the revolt to expend itself in often senseless acts of destruction, whereas the leaders of a revolution are able to impart some coherence to the revolutionary elan and divert some of it to what they consider constructive purposes. In a further difference, the leaders of revolts, especially of jacqueries and urban mobs, are generally "natural" leaders—notables or ordinary individuals who at the time of the revolt display previously unknown talents. The revolutionary elite, on the other hand, has been produced for the most part by a distinctive sociohistorical process. After the development of the modern revolutionary tradition following the French Revolution, the contrast between the professional revolutionary and the traditional rebel leader has become even more pronounced.

Jacqueries and Peasant Revolts

Because of their seeming ubiquity in space and time, peasant revolts present the observer with a bewildering diversity. In order to reduce this diversity to manageable proportions, we will adopt and adapt a recent typology of collective violence, whose categories embrace urban as well as rural violence, small-scale riot as well as full-scale revolt.[19] The first of these categories, *primitive collective violence,* includes such actions as feuds, brawls, and scuffles between members of guilds, communes, and religious congregations, etc. Most examples of this type of violence are quite small in scale and localized in scope. They normally involve members of a natural or "communal" grouping [20] whose overall objectives in the conflict remain hazy and apolitical. Sometimes, however, the violence can spread from its epicenter and engulf, temporarily at least, large areas of a country. The type of peasant revolt that corresponds most to primitive collective violence is the *jacquerie.*

Reactionary collective violence pits "either communal groups or loosely organized members of the general population against those who hold power," and usually includes "a critique of the way power is being wielded." [21] A group engages in this form of violence when it feels deprived of rights that it once enjoyed. The violence is a protest against the loss or threatened loss of these rights and perhaps represents an attempt to recover them. The form of peasant revolt that corresponds most to reactionary violence is the *traditional peasant revolt.*

Modern collective violence involves "specialized associations with relatively well-defined objectives, organized for political or economic action."[22] This type of violence is more likely to leave the confines of a single area and to develop out of originally "nonviolent" manifestations. It differs from primitive and reactionary violence also in that its participants act for the sake of "rights not yet enjoyed but within reach."[23] In other words, their protagonists are "forward looking."[24] The type of peasant revolt that corresponds best to this description 's the *modern peasant revolt*.

"Jacquerie" is a term applicable only to certain kinds of peasant revolt. The term derives from "Jacques Bonhomme," a derisive nickname for peasants employed by French nobles in the fourteenth century; and the original Jacquerie itself was a month-long peasant revolt in north-central France in the late spring of 1358. The peasants had suffered horribly from the ravages of the Hundred Years War (c.1340–1453) with the English. At the time of the Jacquerie the French had undergone several disastrous defeats in the field. The peasants held the nobility largely responsible both for the defeat and the hardships it produced. The country had disintegrated into near anarchy: the throne was in dispute; the bourgeoisie of Paris and their famous leader Etienne Marcel were embroiled in a revolt of their own against the king; bands of brigands composed mostly of soldiers discharged from both armies killed and plundered the peasantry. In this last case the nobles were often implicated or indifferent, although under the feudal system they were supposed to protect the commoners in exchange for certain privileges. All of these conditions contributed to the curtailment of agricultural production and trade, thus provoking the scarcity and misery that so easily strikes a near-subsistence economy.

The peasants' sense of outrage grew so great that a trivial incident was enough to spark thousands of them into action. The revolt spread quickly in those areas most affected by brigandage and shortages. Directed almost entirely at the persons and property of the nobility, the violence of the Jacquerie revealed a sharp cleavage between two communal status groups: the privileged nobility and the underprivileged peasantry. The Jacques struck out viciously at those considered vaguely responsible for their plight; the nobles in their eyes were guilty of a kind of breach of contract in failing to protect them against foreign invader and domestic brigand. As is the way of this kind of uprising, the initial anger cooled down quickly and the blood vengeance was sated, thus revealing its basically negative, vindictive character. Without a real program, without a sense of direction and purpose, without a corps of revolutionary leaders, the Jacquerie soon lost its bearings, began to disintegrate, and was ruthlessly repressed and revenged by the nobility in what has been aptly called *la contre-Jacquerie*.[25]

It would thus seem appropriate to reserve the general term "jacquerie" for peasant revolts characterized by brutal primitive violence,
total lack of a program, and sharp status group or class cleavages. A
jacquerie then is one of the simplest and most elemental forms of
revolt, since the violent refusal to continue the immediate state of affairs and the need for scapegoats seem to exhaust its possibilities. The
jacquerie will erupt more spontaneously than other types of revolt.
Consequently, if a jacquerie is to mount a serious threat—not to persons and their property, but to the existing institutions and social structure—it must be taken over and transformed by a movement of a more
definite political or revolutionary character. This would entail a broad
coalition of oppositional elements and, especially, urban elements. The
Jacquerie of 1358 showed rudimentary signs of going beyond its original narrow limits, but the complex domestic political situation proved
unfavorable to such development.

Traditional peasant revolts, except for the involvement of large
numbers of peasants, differ appreciably from jacqueries. In the first
place, they prove to be far less purely peasant affairs, as the peasants
are in league with various other groups, either against commonly felt
grievances or on a mutual aid basis. Second, the pronounced group
conflict between the peasants and the upper social strata that marks the
jacquerie may be toned down or nearly absent in the traditional peasant revolt. Finally, the level of organization, the quality of leadership,
and the programmatic content (however rudimentary) are more impressive than in a jacquerie.

As these traits characterize many uprisings involving peasants in
seventeenth-century France, debate on their real nature and causes has
raised some theoretical issues having implications for the study of both
revolt and revolution. One school of thought, heavily influenced by
Marxism, tends to offer structural interpretations of traditional peasant
revolts. Their underlying cause, according to this school of thought,
was to be found in the bifurcation of society into exploiting classes and
exploited classes. Revolts were attempts of the exploited peasant masses
and their frequent urban "plebeian" [26] allies to shake off the yoke of
the "feudal" nobility. Although a given revolt may have been triggered
by a new tax striking a particular regional or occupational group, "misery was the principal and real cause of the uprisings. . . . taxes by
themselves did not create this needy stratum [the plebeians] in the
cities. . . . In the countryside, taxes only worked to complete the ruin
of peasants already exploited by the feudal lords." [27] While this analysis
is intended to apply specifically to seventeenth-century France, it serves
as a model for Marxist explanations of peasant revolts on a much
broader scale.

In this outlook, the peasant revolts, with or without plebeian allies, constitute a serious but imperfect challenge to the existing socioeconomic order. While it is true that their resentment spreads from its
original targets, the tax collectors and public officials, to include the
rich in general, the peasants still profess loyalty to the king and by
implication to the state, which, ironically, is the very kingpin of the
social order that oppresses and exploits them. The peasant uprising is
rather like a blind giant who gropes about wreaking havoc without
knowing exactly what he is doing. If this potentially revolutionary force
could be directed into the proper channels, then the existing feudal society would collapse like a house of cards. Leadership of the peasant
revolt thus becomes the crucial variable. When the peasantry throws up
leaders from its own ranks, they usually prove unable to preserve the
movement "from an absolute absence of broad perspectives, from a
certain limitation restricted to local conditions." [28] The urban plebeians
cannot provide the necessary leadership for a true revolution either,
because they develop into a coherent social class only with the rise of
the modern industrial proletariat. The ultimate fate of the peasant
revolt in these conditions rests with the attitude of the bourgeoisie. If it
wishes to captain the movement and push it to its logical conclusion,
then the old order will fall and modern capitalism will be ushered in.
However, if the bourgeoisie is frightened by the aspect of popular revolution and makes common cause with the existing regime, the revolt
cannot pass over into revolution. Similarly, peasant movements are
often denatured when for reasons of military efficiency or through
pure custom, members of the old nobility are placed at the head of the
insurgents. It is idle to expect a scion of the ruling class to help to destroy the social order which makes him what he is.

A more satisfactory understanding of traditional peasant revolts is
rendered by those who look to the specific *conjuncture* of events as well
as to underlying social structures. While not denying the importance of
social structures (i.e., of systems of stratification), this school demands
that structures be put in their proper setting without "transposing
theories, valid perhaps for another epoch and for another type of society," [29] where they do not apply. The "conjuncturalist" approach is
reluctant to view society as a simple dichotomy of classes or class fronts.
Traditional peasant revolts, therefore, are not necessarily uprisings
directed against a landlord class, feudal or otherwise. To understand
each particular revolt and to classify it upon an empirical basis requires
acquaintance not only with the peculiar social structures involved, but
just as importantly an awareness of the rhythms and type of change
operating within each milieu.

The conjuncturalist approach entails a weighting of both *evolu-*

tionary change, such as the growth of the modern state or of modern market relationships, and of *cyclical* change, such as price fluctuations, crop failures, etc.[30] It clearly demonstrates that many peasant revolts are provoked by specific conjunctures of circumstances rather than directly by social inequalities. In other words, the circumstances are the variable factor in the equation, while the structures are parametric. While the social structure may dispose a given group to revolt, it does not explain why this revolt broke out, took this precise form, and met this precise fate. The conjuncturalist outlook is able to show that many peasant revolts are simply one facet, however prominent, of a many-sided uprising including those very strata that simplistic class struggle theories oppose a priori to the peasant masses. Closer inspection of many peasant revolts reveals that "all social groups, or almost all, suffered from those times of war and misery; that there were rebels in all social groups; that the majority of rebels suggest a vertical cleavage of society, with people of all social strata in each of the camps, rebel and government; that the cooperation of social groups seems more fundamental than their opposition." [31] Wherever the communal bonds of province or locality or the personal bonds of fealty transcend status or class differences, a conjuncture of unfavorable circumstances coupled to unpopular government policies will provide the basis for revolt.

Taxation usually is the spark or occasion of the revolt, because in difficult times new or increased taxes damage the vital interests of nearly all segments of society. Landlord and peasant can be in a symbiotic, rather than a purely exploitative, relationship; or at least their interests prove relatively harmonious. At any rate, in many traditional peasant revolts the attitude and involvement of higher social strata range from benevolent neutrality, through incitement and encouragement, up to direct leadership. Consequently, "the movements of peasants and artisans are rarely spontaneous, more frequently provoked by gentlemen, officials, seigneurs." [32] At the very least the "climate of revolt" has been prepared by what can be termed the propaganda of dissident noblemen, clergy, and bourgeois.

What is it then that unites these otherwise disparate elements into a common front of revolt? The answer is to be sought more in the political than in the social realm. More precisely, it can be said of the seventeenth century, the great age of peasant revolts before the twentieth century, that "in difficult economic conjunctures of climatic origin, the great cause of revolts was the development of the state in France and Russia, centralization, uniformization, the reduction of customary local liberties and privileges. . . . In China in a similar conjuncture, it has been the crisis of state provoked by the decline of a dynasty." [33] New "foreign" ways are thrust upon the peasant milieu, threatening the

sanctity of custom and the still real regional identity. Traditional lead
ers and methods of consultation are bypassed in favor of new officials,
new taxes, new regulations, and new standards—all in the name of
"reason of state." The nonrevolutionary character of traditional
peasant revolts comes through clearly in their demands for a return to
the old ways, institutions, and patterns of authority.

Modern peasant revolts are Janus-faced. On the one hand they
reflect the traditional values and structures of peasant societies, and
thus bear a certain resemblance to traditional peasant revolts. On the
other hand the global society has itself changed, which provokes sympathetic changes in the peasant way of life. In this sense the function of
modern peasant revolts differs considerably from their ancestors:

> the peasant rebellions of the twentieth century are no longer simple re-
> sponses to local problems, if indeed they ever were. They are but the pa-
> rochial reactions to major social dislocations, set in motion by overwhelm-
> ing societal change. The spread of the market has torn men up by their
> roots, and shaken them loose from the social relationships into which
> they were born. Industrialization and expanded communication have
> given rise to new social clusters . . . forced by the imbalance of their lives
> to seek a new adjustment.[34]

The modern peasant is in a classic dilemma. The traditional communal
social organization still exists, while its economic functions are increasingly challenged by more production-oriented and impersonal market
relationships. Furthermore, the peasant wants things he has never had
before, but the kind of society that could provide them is very different
from what he knows.

The modern peasants' revolt shares with all forms of modern collective violence a sense of the newness of its demands, but it stops short
of a complete overthrow of traditional society. This seems to confirm
the classic Marxist postulate that peasants cannot launch a real revolution under their own initiative. And yet, many students contend that
peasant upheaval is a necessary though not sufficient condition for
modern revolution. The contradiction is only apparent if one does not
lose sight of the fundamental importance of leadership in determining
the direction of collective violence. The ambivalent nature of modern
peasant revolt makes it more susceptible to being taken over by revolutionary urban intellectuals. They alone can drive revolt out of its original limits and into the maelstrom of revolution.[35] It is immeasurably
more difficult to do this with the backward-looking traditional peasant
revolt.

This catalytic action of outside leadership raises serious questions
about the character of the resultant revolutionary movement—ques-

tions which are not really answered by maintaining that it is a "particularly misleading trick to deny that a revolution stems from peasant grievances because its leaders happen to be professional men or intellectuals." [36] Peasant grievances play a role in nearly all revolutions. The real question is whether the revolutionai y elite which transforms revolt into revolution follows the wishes and/or the long-term interests of the bulk of the peasant masses. The answer to the first point regarding the peasants' wishes is "no." The answer to the second is so complex and filled with moral and ideological overtones as to defy a simple "yes" or "no" categorization. Nevertheless, the term "peasant revolution" remains highly dubious in cases where there is "no indication that the peasants were about to organize effectively or do anything about their problems of their own accord" or where evidence fails to confirm that "peasant villages were in open revolt" before the arrival of urban-based revolutionary cadres.[37] The closest approximation we have of purely peasant movements crossing the divide from revolt to revolution is in anarchistic movements such as that of Nestor Makhno during the Russian civil war.

Urban Mobs

While the term "mob" has a wide variety of largely pejorative connotations, we understand it here more specifically as referring to the "pre-industrial crowd." [38] The classic urban mob has been defined as "the movement of all classes of the urban poor for the achievement of economic or political changes by direct action—that is by riot or rebellion—but as a movement which was yet inspired by no specific ideology; or if it found expression for its aspirations at all, in terms of traditionalism and conservatism. . . ." [39] Early students of the mob in the last century tended to view it as composed exclusively of the *lumpenproletariat* (i.e., the chronically unemployed, idlers, petty thieves, prostitutes, beggars, etc.). Reacting, or perhaps overreacting, against this stereotype, recent students tend to point out the heavy contingent of shopkeepers, artisans, journeymen, and other more or less respectable elements active in the mob. What is certain is the preponderantly lower-class composition of the mob, which also included people by no means on the brink of starvation. Furthermore, the early students had been preoccupied with the irrational, unstable, and indiscriminately destructive character and behavior of the mob, especially in times of revolution. Here too modern students have drawn up a more balanced appraisal with impressive examples of moderation and tactical finesse that do not square easily with berserk irrationality. This is not to deny the high incidence of violence but merely to qualify its character better.

"Destruction of property . . . is a constant feature of the pre-industrial crowd; but not the destruction of human lives, which is more properly associated with the *jacqueries,* slave revolts, peasant rebellions, and millenarial outbursts of the past, as it is with the race riots and communal disturbances of more recent times." [40]

The riots and rebellions of the classic pre-industrial crowd or mob illustrate once again the wide variety of functions and purposes involved in collective violence. Recent theories of politics have attempted to interpret the political process in terms of the "articulation" of interests. Accordingly, a variety of interest groups makes "demands" upon the political system, demands presented either in their raw state or combined and refined ("aggregated") with other demands. It is then up to the authorities to dispose of these demands favorably or unfavorably in the form of decisions or policies. These in turn are weighed by the originators of the demands, who react by offering or denying support to the regime. Whatever the ultimate validity of this approach, the violence of the classic mob fits rather well into it. This type of violence is by no means intended to overthrow or even to threaten the existing social or political system. Rather, it serves as a barometer of the feelings of a strategically located segment of the population. Before the days of popular representation the mob employed violence to communicate its demands to the political authorities. So long as modern ideologies had not disturbed the traditional relationship between the elite of notables and the mob, and so long as the standard of living remained above a certain minimum, the mob was prepared to defend its superiors "with enthusiasm." [41] Should conditions deteriorate, riot was the way the mob recalled its rulers to their "duty." "The threat of perennial rioting kept rulers ready to control prices and to distribute work or largesses, or indeed to listen to their faithful commons on other matters. Since the riots were not directed against the social system, public order could remain surprisingly lax by modern standards." [42] In short, recourse to violence was the normal method of articulating demands, and both sides knew and accepted this fact.

Revolts launched by the classic mob are essentially backward-looking. They do not seek to overturn the existing political and social structure but to return it to its primitive purity. Economic and political changes have disrupted even the lowly position of the mob, and it reacts against further threatening changes. Yet despite the basically conservative orientations of mob revolt, the "social question" often plays a distinctive, though perhaps subsidiary, role. One student of the classic mob has put his finger on a feature whose implications go far in dispelling some of the ambiguities of pre-modern collective violence: "there is the traditional 'leveling' instinct . . . which prompts the poor to seek a degree of elementary social justice at the expense of the rich, *les grands* and those in authority regardless of whether they are government officials, feudal lords, capitalists, or middle-class revolutionary leaders." [43] This explains why it is anachronistic to push the origins of modern collectivist or revolutionary movements too far into the past on the basis of egalitarian overtones in the violence of the classic mob. While a surprising amount of social behavior is elucidated, if not entirely explained, by the rich-poor dichotomy, specific historical conditions may produce countervailing tendencies which retard its full impact. The conservatism of the poor is by no means identical to that of the rich, but the conflict between the two outlooks can remain on the level of immediate interests rather than of general principles. The classic mob revolt is a mode of adjustment between two versions of the same belief system. However, the French Revolution and industrialism will change, though not completely eradicate, this state of affairs.

Nativism

For anyone acquainted with anthropological literature the separation between nativism and millenarianism-messianism in this and the next section may appear dubious. The difficulty is not only conceptual but also historical, "for a given revitalization movement may be nativistic, millenarian, and revivalist all at once. . . ." [44] Nevertheless, not all forms of nativism involve millenarianism or messianism, and some of these latter movements are not nativistic. The classic definition and typology of nativism was developed by Ralph Linton, who defined a "nativistic movement" as "any conscious, organized attempt on the part of a society's members to revive or perpetuate selected aspects of its culture." [45] To qualify as nativistic, such an attempt must take place in a situation of prolonged culture contact and interaction (i.e., during *acculturation*). The external culture appears as a threat to the indigenous culture, which responds by the defense mechanism of the nativistic movement. The factors governing selection of the aspects of the culture to be revived or perpetuated are their *distinctiveness* and *practicality*. Later students have pointed out the extreme ambiguity of the selection process insofar as "avowedly revivalist movements are never entirely what they claim to be, for the image of the ancient culture to be revived is distorted by historical ignorance and by the presence of imported and innovative elements." [46]

Linton himself makes much of two lines of distinction which give rise to a fourfold typology of nativistic movements. Implied in the first distinction, between movements that *revive* and movements that *perpetuate,* is a sense that revivalist movements are of the two by far the more flamboyant, troublesome, and radical. The second distinction concerns means rather than goals of revival or perpetuation. *Magical* nativism invents a magical formula to bring back the golden age of the ancestral past. Special symbols, rites, and often a prophetic or messianic leader emerge as the indispensable means for the community's return to greatness. While Linton sees certain differences between messianic and magical nativistic movements, they are both characterized by "frankly irrational flights from reality." [47] *Rational* nativistic movements on the other hand are free from the exotic and bizarre features of the magical species, because "the culture elements selected for symbolic use are chosen realistically and with regard to the possibility of perpetuating them under current conditions." [48]

With the customary disclaimer against finding "pure" types in reality, Linton offers four basic types of nativistic movement: (1) revivalistic-magical, (2) revivalistic-rational, (3) perpetuative-magical, and (4) perpetuative-rational. Type 1 is the most common; while type 3 is so rare that Linton could cite no example of it. Type 4 is apparently more frequent than type 2.

As nativism is a phenomenon of acculturation, it requires contact between two (or more) cultures. In the two-sided and most common relationship, one of the peoples is dominant and the other dominated. This domination is often not only political, but social and economic as well (e.g., the typical colonial situation). However, an important variable is how both parties, the dominant and the dominated, compare the cultures in question. The dominant people may view its culture as superior or inferior to that of the dominated, and the dominated people can also feel either way vis-à-vis the culture of the dominant people. There can be agreement or disagreement between the two parties on these questions, though disagreement seems the more prevalent situation. Since according to Linton nativistic movements can arise in dominant as well as in dominated peoples, the precise configuration of attitudes of superiority and inferiority will largely determine the nature of nativistic movements that emerge in a given circumstance.

Critics have found Linton's revivalist-perpetuative dichotomy too simplistic. To them it seems to underplay the critical, innovative features of many nativistic movements, and thus they call for a broader typology. One attempt in this line proposes three types of nativism. The first type is called *dynamic* nativism and corresponds to Linton's revivalist nativism, though it lacks the magical and rational subtypes. The second type is *passive* or *adjustive* nativism and involves "passive resistance or apathy to the beliefs, values, and practices that may be imposed or indoctrinated by a dominant society." [49] While a frequently observable phenomenon, passive nativism is not, strictly speaking, a nativistic *movement,* as it lacks organization and perhaps even full consciousness among its participants. However, it can serve as a preliminary stage to the foundation of an organized movement. *Reformative* nativism is the third type, which differs from dynamic (or revivalist) nativism by striving to "attain a personal and social reintegration through selective rejection, modification, and synthesis of both traditional and (alien) dominant cultural components." [50] Reformative nativism differs from Linton's revivalist-perpetuative dualism by its greater receptivity and adaptability to outside influences. The end product differs both from the traditional home culture and the alien external one. The later forms of nativism among the American Indians, for example, seemed to move through the stages of revivalism and apathy to something very much like reformative nativism.

It should be evident that not every type of nativistic movement or response (e.g. apathy) has the same significance for a typology of revolt. Properly speaking, only those movements which attain a degree of organizational coherence and whose objectives conflict with those of the legal government sufficiently to provoke violence and counterviolence would qualify as *nativistic revolts*. It does not matter so much who "fired the first shot"—that is, which side, the government or the movement, initiated the violence. What is important is that the nativistic movement is perceived as a threat by groups close to the central authority or that the latter is viewed as implacably hostile by the movement. This means that the distinction between professedly violent nativistic movements and those practicing nonviolent forms of civil disobedience may not be very significant. The key factors are the militancy of the movement and its attitude towards the government. Nevertheless, it would be misleading, if not meaningless, to describe movements which scrupulously observe the letter of the law as revolts.

A nativistic revolt then expresses the will to break the law and risk violence in order to defend those cultural values it deems sacred. There is little doubt therefore that revivalist (or dynamic) nativistic movements are those most prone to revolt. Passive or adjustive nativism is too fragmented and individualistic to produce *collective* violence. Reformative nativism, while not ruling out revolt, would resort to violence mainly in cases where the representatives of the alien culture either increased their pressures for complete assimilation or conversely tried to repress attempts at cultural synthesis undertaken by native reformers. Either of these two situations can emerge in the typical colonial situation.

Revivalist movements have the greatest potential for violence and revolt because of their Manichean association of all that is good with the ancestral ways (or more precisely, with what they believe to have been the ancestral ways) and all that is evil with the foreign devils and their ways. This tendency is reenforced by the hyperemotionalism characteristic of this type of nativistic movement. It is a short step from exacerbated xenophobia to violence against the detested alien whose very presence, according to extreme movements, is both an affront to God and an impediment to the rebirth of his people. Violent expulsion of the alien becomes thus the rationale for nativistic revolt.

Millenarianism-Messianism

Millenarianism and messianism[51] are forms of revolt that sometimes resemble revolution and have been thus characterized.[52] Millenarianism is the general category of movements which claim to replace the sinful, corrupt, or soon to be destroyed community with one that is directly inspired and informed by a religious rebirth. It promises a perfect society—"a land without evil"—in the sense of realizing the moral and religious commands of the divinity. By rejecting existing practices and rituals, and adopting the "new" discipline of the millenarian movement, the devotees or "adepts" of the millenarian movement guarantee their salvation. While the religious exaltation of millenarianism strikes the eye with its brilliance, it nevertheless is "at the same time religious and sociopolitical" and closely binds the "sacred and the profane." [53] This mixed character of millenarianism differentiates it from purely secular movements.[54]

Controversy exists as to whether or not millenarianism can exist wholly divorced from the Judeo-Christian tradition. The evidence seems to favor an affirmative answer provided that the religious background is active or dynamic and teaches that the individual has "the power to transform the world in which he lives." [55] Religions which are passive or static (i.e., restrict themselves to the contemplation of a changeless or unchangeable ultimate reality) are unfavorable to the development of millenarian sects and movements. Outbreaks of the latter are usually accompanied by strange "orgiastic" practices or rituals, which seek to raise the enthusiasm of adepts to a fever pitch and thus make them more capable of receiving the divine message. One can understand why the established lay and ecclesiastical authorities generally regard millenarian movements with fear and move against them at the first opportunity. Masses of men in a state of religious ecstasy have been known to do the unexpected, if not the impossible.

For our purposes messianism is the most interesting form of millenarian movement. It is characterized by the exalted position of a charismatic leader or messiah over the community of adepts. The claims of the messiah run the gamut from being the spokesman or mouthpiece of the deity to being his direct incarnation. His mission is to lead his followers "unto the paths of righteousness"—in some cases toward a new purified way of life, in others into a final preparatory stage before the catastrophe marking the end of this world and the return to God. The adept owes blind, unquestioning obedience to the messiah because of the holiness of his work. This may include exemption from further compliance with the moral and legal precepts of the traditional order, since obedience is now to the rules of an infinitely higher one. This radicalism largely accounts for attempts to attach the label "revolutionary" to extreme messianic movements.

All messianic movements require (1) a discontented or oppressed collectivity, (2) hope in the coming of a divine emissary, and (3) the belief in a simultaneously sacred and profane paradise. Within these stipulations, however, we encounter a wide range of causes, goals, and behavior. Historians and anthropologists have delineated at least three fundamental types of messianic movement, each corresponding to a somewhat different social and political situation: (1) messianic movements of national liberation, (2) reformist messianic movements, and (3) subversive or "revolutionary" messianic movements.[56] All three types are associated with two fundamental characteristics. First of all, they almost exclusively occur in societies in which the basic form of social structure is the extended family or *clan*. The clan is organized around a patriarch or matriarch and embraces cousins to the second or third degree of removal. The clan also serves as an economic unit and to some extent as a political unit. In a clan-dominated society, class and sometimes status differences are considerably muted as the clan cuts across or, more precisely, cuts vertically through various social strata, especially when dependents, servants, retainers, clients, etc., are included. The clan is held together by basically emotional or "affective" ties. In fact, the very intimacy of intraclan relationships serves as a model for the nascent messianic community. The second major characteristic of these movements is that the societies which host them do not themselves sharply demarcate the secular and the religious realms. Traditional institutions, customs, and mores are infused with a religious significance, which discourages any challenge to them on purely secular grounds. A movement for change, then, will have far greater chances for success if it takes the form of a religious revival.

Messianic movements of national liberation emerge either as the response of a conquered people to their oppressors, as in a typical colonial situation, or as an attempt to reforge a disaggregated national unit and to raise a people back to its glorious heights. Such movements are generally "all-class" movements, in which an entire national or tribal group strives to recapture its lost independence or grandeur. The "social question"—which pits class against class, rich against poor—recedes into the background in the face of the ties of national or tribal unity.

In European movements, the secular and religious aspects of national renewal are inseparable. The messiah is considered a reincarnation of a king or national hero, whose reappearance heralds the dawning of a new epoch for his people. The messianic movement generally exaggerates the religious significance of the returned hero, and the historical basis of his legend becomes overlaid with myth. In the colonial situation, as in modern Africa, the messiah can be a returned tribal king; or when the religious basis is *syncretistic* (i.e., combines indigenous religious lore with traditional Christian themes), the reincarnation of Jesus Christ.

Messianic movements of reform aim to reinvigorate a society undergoing serious disorganization. Here too class differences are less significant than other factors of social malaise. The most productive source of these movements seems to be traditional peasant societies which have become somewhat unhinged from the old way of life. A frequent explanation given for the emergence of messianic movements maintains that external forces such as capitalism, urbanization, or industrialization impinge upon the rural milieu and upset the age-old equilibrium of economic and social life. In this sense, the messianic movement would operate as a combination escapist and rearguard action striving vainly to stave off the results of "progress." While these factors no doubt play a role, certain messianic movements develop for rather different reasons.

All societies—traditional, peasant, tribal, modern industrial —experience two basic forms of social change. The first of these, *evolutionary change,* is unilinear, irreversible, and cumulative. Certain changes occur once and for all; they are unique and their impact cannot be eradicated. Modern technological change is a good example of this kind of change. The second of these forms, *cyclical change*, is periodic, recurrent change. Sometimes such change can be predicted with great accuracy; at other times it is erratically recurrent. Seasons, droughts, famines, plagues, and their social consequences illustrate the principle of cyclical change. While a simple dichotomy is out of the question, there is little doubt that traditional societies are subject more to cyclical change than to evolutionary change, while the reverse seems to be true for modern societies. The proportions of the two forms of change obtaining in a given society affect the likelihood and the configuration of messianic movements.

Messianic movements of reform are often more a response to cyclical than to evolutionary patterns of change, because modern class relationships have not developed and external factors have not had much impact upon the social equilibrium. The disturbance is generated from within and occurs in the realm of social values rather than in the realms of social structure or economic change. The following remarks characterize many messianic movements of reform: "the old peasant solidarity had suffered an eclipse; the traditional family was dissolved, accompanying the reduction of the economic level caused by new taxes and bad harvests. The peasants were going through a period of instability, in which the old models of behavior were no longer followed without others having taken their place. . . . It was the disorganization of the rural world." [57] While external factors certainly exacerbate this type of situation, the collapse of values and norms—what Emile Durkheim referred to as *anomie*—can follow a rhythm of its own.

As a response to the threat of complete social disorganization, the messianic movement functions to restore and revitalize the traditional social order through selective reform. Many of the old values and institutions are accepted by the messiah, his inner circle of disciples, and the broad mass of adepts. Innovation usually proves to be modification of traditional themes rather than outright replacement of them. Since reform, even conservative reform, will clash with existing interests, the messianic movement has difficulty remaining aloof from surrounding political conflicts. When this happens, the movement becomes an "additional element in the circulation of socio-political elites. . . . The messianic movements contribute thus to the renovation of cadres. They [are] movements of reform if we understand by reform the reorganization of institutions, which implies the replacement of leaders no longer esteemed with others who appear more deserving." [58] While the reception of the movement by the surrounding society varies from outright hostility to peaceful coexistence, messianic movements of reform are usually pacific and fight only if attacked. Good relations are especially likely where the authorities recognize the essentially conservative function of the movement and reach a *modus vivendi* with it.

Subversive messianic movements reflect more clearly the themes of class struggle and revolt. They tend to occur in transitional societies poised midway between a traditional society and more modern forms of social organization. Transitional societies are more subject than their predecessors to evolutionary patterns of change and to influences stemming from outside the society; kinship is rapidly being replaced by impersonal class relationships as the predominant form of social structure. The emergence of the social question is reflected in the predominantly lower-class appeal of the subversive messianic movements. These movements make much of traditional Christian themes extolling the virtues of poverty and castigating the corruption and injustice of the high and the mighty. Prophecies that proclaim the complete over-turning of class relationships—"the meek shall inherit the earth"—are especially in vogue. It should cause no surprise then that messianic movements of this type often come to practice forms of primitive communism among the adepts.

Certainly the most radical form of messianism, the subversive movements nevertheless cannot be termed fully revolutionary. Although they are authentic movements of lower-class protest and revolt, they rise up *against* the prevailing direction of change towards a more secularized, industrialized, and centralized society. In short, they reject the very core of values usually associated with the term "progress." They are trapped between two worlds: unwilling to go ahead, but unable to go back. "In their ambiguity they define themselves as revolutionary before the traditional society; however, they remain united to the very tradition which they wish to break." [59] Subversive messianic movements can be interpreted more as the death rattle of an old society than as the birth cry of a new one.

As with nativistic movements, millenarian and messianic movements display a considerable variety, which complicates the task of relating them to revolt or revolution. It would seem that messianic movements of reform are the least likely to develop into full-scale revolts, because of their moderation and their ability to come to terms with the existing authorities in church and state. This tendency is also enhanced by the remoteness of the areas that often host this type of messianic movement. The low salience of horizontal social differences in the movement further limits the potential for violence inherent in latent class or status resentments.

Messianic movements of national liberation will more frequently develop into violent revolt, especially in the case of a subject people which desires independence. As a manifestation of the wish to expel the foreigner, messianic movements in the colonial situation display strong nativistic influences. Very often a vigorous competition develops between the messianic movement and "modern" nationalist groups found among intellectuals. Similarly, messianic movements in times of national decline and disintegration may resort to violence in order to restore the fragmented political unity of a people. In this case the hero-messiah serves as a focus of unity above and beyond the petty sovereignties into which the state has crumbled.

Subversive messianic movements are highly prone to revolt. The combination of sharp social cleavages; a transition to different forms of economy and society; cyclical factors such as famine, climatic disturbances, or plague; and religious enthusiasms contribute to heighten the militancy of this type of messianic movement. The messiah and his adepts deem it their sacred mission to convert those capable of receiving grace and perhaps to extirpate the rest. Violence becomes a ritual of purification which prepares this world for the coming of the millennium. None of the powers that be should be left standing if they in any way obstruct the mission of the messiah.

Aristocratic Revolts

Aristocratic revolts are a frequent feature of Western history from the middle ages to the end of the eighteenth century. Far Eastern history has also experienced them. Although the term "feudal reaction" is often used to describe these revolts, this runs into the problem of loose usage that some historians make of the notion of feudalism.[60] Furthermore, aristocratic revolts can occur in conditions that bear little resemblance to "feudalism," in the proper sense of that term. In short, some aristocratic revolts are feudal in nature; others are not. They must not, however, be confused with attempted coups or palace revolutions or even civil wars that involve rival coalitions of aristocratic houses. Such disputes concern occupancy of or influence over the throne, family feuds, and personal vendettas. However bloody the battles and however impressive the forces arrayed under the rival banners, these factional conflicts lack the substantive issues that characterize aristocratic revolt. Similarly, aristocratic participation in a counterrevolution must be distinguished from true aristocratic revolt. Counterrevolution is aimed against a revolutionary movement; aristocratic revolt moves against a legitimate regime sanctioned by tradition. Accordingly, aristocratic rebels display considerable unease in their new role, especially if the revolt is not quickly terminated by settlement or reconciliation.

Aristocratic revolts are a response to definite social and, especially, political changes. Most often they are violent protests against the centralization undertaken by an absolutist or a modernizing monarchy which wishes to concentrate power in its own hands and to this end erects an impressive bureaucratic or semibureaucratic apparatus staffed in large part by men of humble or non-noble origin. As in France, Russia, and China these new officials are often given noble rank and in some cases have even purchased the offices that automatically confer it. This often brings them and their master, the king, into conflict with the older nobility, which is based upon inheritance and the profession of arms. Status resentment enters the situation as the old nobility feels itself threatened and the very notion of nobility cheapened and debased. The new officialdom, ennobled or not, for its part suffers from a sense of status inferiority and begins to view the ancient aristocracy more and more as arrogant, functionless, and parasitical.

The revolt is often precipitated by the central government's need for increased revenue. War expenditures are the most frequent cause of the financial crisis. To remedy the crisis the government resorts to greater taxation. But this is not all. In the interests of more efficient collection and of revenue stemming from the sale of office, further centralization is introduced along with some halting steps towards modern bureaucratic regimentation. Perhaps not fully aware of the implications of its policies, the government has in effect launched an attack on provincial and local privilege, which in the long run damages the political and economic position of the aristocracy. Politically speaking, a new body of officials with direct links to the capital city takes the place of the aristocracy in administrative, judicial, and even military functions. The aristocrats may or may not be left with the externals and titles of power, but real decision-making power has shifted away from them. Economically speaking, since the aristocracy depends for its subsistence upon certain fees and rents paid by commoners, heavy central taxation of the latter cuts drastically into the wealth normally destined for aristocratic coffers. This situation contributes to the creation of an aristocratically led provincial alliance composed of different social strata against the encroachments of the central power.

Thus, instances of completely unalloyed aristocratic revolts are relatively rare; they are usually parts of more complex uprisings. (Given the values of traditional societies, aristocrats are often found in real or titular command even when the impetus for revolt comes from below.) In authentic aristocratic revolts, however, the aristocracy emerges as the champion of tradition against royal innovation, of special privilege as against legal uniformity. Before modern methods of warfare were developed, military expertise gave the aristocracy a strong position in revolts against the monarchy, which often had to depend on semireliable mercenary forces. Though aristocratic rebels may wish to replace the reigning monarch, they rarely want a republic. They prefer to extract concessions from the monarchy either in the form of a restoration of old privileges or of the creation of new ones in the guise of restoration. Tradition and the customary law of the land are the bulwark of the aristocratic party. [61] Only inadvertently do they develop an ideology that looks towards the future rather than the past. The Magna Carta of 1215, so often represented in the textbooks as the harbinger of modern liberal and democratic conceptions of government, is equally a series of "feudal" concessions wrung from King John of England after a baronial revolt.

SECESSION

Secession involves the breaking off of one part of the state and the proclamation of its independence. It is thus a simple phenomenon which can be associated with various forms of coup d'etat, revolt, and revolution. For this reason discussion of it can be reduced to some general remarks and a classification. Of the four major types of secession, two (regional and colonial) have self-evident geographical connotations, while two (ethnic and religious) less clearly have such connotations. In fact, geography is a necessary but not sufficient condition for a secessionist movement. With ethnic and religious secessions geography still operates because the secessionist group is largely concentrated in one or more areas or because one or more areas are earmarked to be the "homeland" of the group. On the other hand geographical and topographical features do not by themselves determine the emergence of a secessionist movement. There is always a series of economic, cultural, religious, or ethnic differences superimposed upon the geographical base; and it is the ensemble of these interdependent factors, not geography alone, which favors secession.

Regional Secession

A region is geographically distinguished from the rest of a country not only by the lines of latitude and longitude. Climatic, topographical, and floral and faunal differences also serve to accentuate what separates one region of a country from the rest of it. Furthermore, the economic differences that usually follow from these geographical features ultimately affect the political life of a country. Perhaps of even greater significance are the ethnic, religious, and cultural differences that grow up in the environment of a distinctive region, especially a remote one. The interplay of all these elements lends credence to such apparently trivial sayings as "Every country has its South." Thus, two rather banal generalizations can be offered: (1) the greater the regional heterogeneity of a country, the greater the chances for regional secessionist movements; (2) the more distinctive a particular region is, the greater is the likelihood of its producing one or more secessionist movements.

However, the growth of secessionist movements is by no means automatic. Some historical conditions are more favorable for such growth than others. Especially crucial is the development of a nativistic response similar to those discussed above. Elements of a region's population—usually a minority at the outset—become convinced that their region's cultural identity is being overwhelmed by the culture of a more "advanced," or economically, politically, or culturally dominant, segment of the country, which has gotten control of the central government. This dominant segment is held to be using its economic and political power to extend its cultural sway in the guise of a "national" culture. Standardization and "equality before the law" are thinly veiled assaults on the vestiges of cultural diversity in the various regions. The initial response of the self-proclaimed spokesmen of the ostensibly threatened region is not secessionist, but revivalist and autonomist. That is, a group of the concerned attempt to revitalize the sometimes moribund regional culture so as to withstand increasing pressures from the outside. Their efforts are political only to the extent of demanding the return of old or the creation of new regional guarantees against the central government and its policies. At this stage language can play an important role in regional revitalization, as poets and intellectuals begin to publish in regional dialects and languages in the hope of preserving or even of resuscitating them. In fact, the emergence of a literary, as distinct from a spoken, tongue may occur for the very first time. Often, however, the linguistic revival is confined to a small circle of specialists and fanatics, and the detested "national" language continues not only as the leading literary medium but also as the spoken language of the vast majority of the region's population. Paralleling the linguistic revival (or serving in its place) is vigorous historical activity intended to validate the region's claim to special status. Such hard work is sometimes badly repaid as the patent artificiality of certain revivalist movements is clear to all.

The second phase in the growth of a secessionist movement sees the movement leave behind its goals of mere cultural autonomy to become secessionist and professedly nationalist. Acts of terrorism by the more impatient members are frequent, though the movement now builds up an elaborate propaganda machine financed largely by wealthy patrons. Terrorism serves to dramatize to the outside world the oppression or "cultural genocide" perpetrated by the dominant region. It also provokes reprisals which may gain the movement sympathizers and heighten the solidarity of the old guard. But if the secessionist movement is to exceed the small circle of true believers, important political and economic stimuli are usually required. Broad strata in the region must come to think—rightly or wrongly makes little difference—that they are being "exploited" by government policies contrived in the interest of the dominant region. When this occurs the ranks of the movement may increase tenfold or more, and we are faced with an authentic mass movement. If the secessionist spirit becomes sufficiently widespread it is even proper to speak of a "nationalist" movement. Subjective factors of will are as important as the objective factors of language and culture in the development of nationalism.

With growth, however, comes the inevitable price of success. A regionalist movement purports to be an all-class movement above and beyond the ideological conflicts of the day. But the facade of unity soon cracks under the stress of horizontal social differences and the lure of political left and right. Does the worker or peasant have more in common with his counterpart in other regions, even the dominant one, or do the vertical bonds of regional culture and identity tie him to the capitalist or the aristocrat? There are no simple answers to these questions. The right wing sees regionalism or secession as a return to sacred traditions; the left as an opportunity for radical social experimentation.[62] These almost unavoidable cleavages in a secessionist movement can be readily exploited by wily politicians in charge of the central government.

Colonial Secession

Whether or not a colonial secession breeds revolt or even revolution depends in large part on the kind of colonial situation involved. Two fundamental types of colony exist: (1) those in which settlers from the metropolitan country constitute a large, sometimes preponderant, part of the total resident population; (2) those in which a thin stratum composed of civil and military officials, missionaries, trade representatives, etc., confronts an overwhelming native population. Common sense would seem to indicate that secession of the first type of colony is less likely to be revolutionary than of the second type. This conclusion, however, requires a deeper analysis.

According to Louis Hartz, former colonial areas such as British and French Canada, the thirteen American colonies, Dutch and British South Africa, Australia, and Latin America are best understood as "fragments" of a wider European political culture. This is so because the European settlers whose descendants became numerically or sociopolitically predominant in these areas have preserved the social and political beliefs that first crossed the ocean with them, and in some cases caused them to cross it. They are fragments precisely because they have truncated the right-left European political spectrum of aristocratic "feudal" conservatism, bourgeois liberalism, and lower-class radical liberalism, and have adopted one of these ideologies as a complete political culture fixed forever in its basic outlines. "For when a part of a European nation is detached from the whole of it, and hurled out on to new soil, it loses the stimulus toward change that the whole provides. It lapses into a kind of immobility, nor does it matter what stage the past embodies. . . ." [63] The peculiar fragment, since "it becomes a universal, sinking beneath the surface of thought to the level of an assumption" [64] preemptively excludes all challenges from either left or right. The American "way of life," for example, is an elaboration of basically middle-class liberal values; the French culture of Quebec is an intensification of the aristocratic "feudalism" of pre-revolutionary France. Australia reflects the pre-socialist radicalism of Victorian England. Out of the fragment there develops a kind of nationalism that is "conservative" in the sense of resistance to change, although the nationalist rhetoric will be liberal, feudal, or radical as the case may be.

As the total victory of one of the European ideologies is assured before colonial claims for autonomy or secession are aired, secession itself may be made superfluous by a series of concessions spread out over decades, or as with the United States and Latin America a violent and bloody "war of independence" will not be authentically revolutionary. This follows because "fragmentation by its very nature precludes social revolution." [65] Revolution stems from deep-seated social and ideological differences, which is precisely what the fragment prevents from developing among the dominant community. In the American case liberal and middle-class values had so infected all white colonial strata that secession did not really become revolutionary. No doubt there were significant reforms and changes as any protracted and bitter war will generally produce. But despite the large-scale emigration and transfers of property and despite the impulse and example given to European revolutionaries, the American "Revolution" retained too much of colonial institutions and practice to reach genuinely revolutionary dimensions. In Latin America most Spanish and Portuguese colonies had achieved independence in the first half of the nineteenth century in ways that left the bulk of social institutions intact. Although Latin American history is replete with revolts and coups d'etat, it has had to wait for the twentieth century for authentic revolutions.

While the fragment cultures mentioned above, aside from endemic racial strife, had developed into more or less viable nations before secession, this development was not the rule with the areas that were decolonized in postwar Asia and Africa. There strenuous nation-building efforts were necessary both during and after the struggle for independence. The bitter truth is that throughout the third world there abound "nationalists without a nation" (i.e., the true nationalists before as after independence are a small, middle-class, Western-educated elite composed in the main of intellectuals, professionals, and the military). Nevertheless, the bulk of the population with deep roots in the traditional tribal or communal social order shares with the nationalist elite a desire to be rid of the imperial rulers, though this is less universal than might be thought. While it is important to "distinguish between early instinctively defensive reactions, in which xenophobia played a part" (i.e. nativism) and "the later nationalisms whose aims, structures, and leadership reflect the new trends," [66] it is a mistake to make rigid phases out of these two aspects of anticolonialist sentiment. In many cases traditional values and institutions have proven highly resistant to reforms, whether of colonial administrators or nationalist elites. This is part of the reason why Afro-Asian nationalist movements have tended to be more revolutionary than those in the European fragments. They have had to contend with a greater amount of regional, tribal, caste, ethnic, religious, and other forms of particularism in their attempts to build nations. The greater the obstacles, the greater the efforts required to surmount them.

The whole issue is complicated by the fact that though the nationalists wish to build nations where none existed, there is little agreement as to what a nation is and consequently no settled recipe of how to make one. After stating that a nation is a "community of people who feel that they belong together in the double sense that they share deeply significant elements of a common heritage and that they have a common destiny for the future," [67] one enters the troubled waters of controversy. If one wishes to understand nationalism as more than a widespread subjective feeling and to enumerate an objective *syndrome* of the nation, he immediately encounters objections. Language, territory, culture, religion, economics—rank orderings of these and other factors have foundered in the shoals of too many "exceptions to the rule." Rupert Emerson, however, has provided us with an "ideal type" of the nation which involves a "single people, traditionally fixed on a well-defined territory, speaking the same language and preferably a language all its own, possessing a distinctive culture, and shaped to a common mold by many generations of shared historical experience." [68] The closer a colony approaches this model, the less is the likelihood of its requiring full-scale revolution to build the nation as the complement for a newly independent state. Thus, it is not merely the intransigence and repressiveness of the colonial power which determines the moderation or extremism of the secessionist movement. In fact, intransigence and repressiveness under certain conditions have been able to contain, if not to eradicate, secessionist movements whether of a nativistic or even a properly nationalist orientation.

Nevertheless, the nature of colonial administration does affect the possibilities of revolutionary secessionism in other ways. For example, indirect rule as practiced by the British encourages or allows the persistence of those narrow tribal, local, or regional communities which have proven so much of an impediment to the growth of modern nationalist sentiment. While the direct rule associated especially with French colonialism failed to assimilate the colonial masses to French civilization, it did break down certain pockets of resistance to the eventual nationalist appeal. [69] If other factors did not upset the symmetry of the equation, we could even conclude that the legacy of indirect rule is conducive to revolutionary nationalism, while that of direct rule provides more of a basis for gradualism. With indirect rule the colonial power is plagued with annoying, but not really threatening, nativistic revolts. However, when independence comes, the nativism of the traditionalist segments of society runs into the nationalism of the westernized elite. This clash is not really averted by the nationalists' proclamations of offering the best of both worlds, because for the most part the nationalists have "appeared unconcerned to preserve more of the ancient heritage than seemed compatible with a Western-style rebuilding of their societies." [70] It is out of this kind of predicament that revolutions are born.

Ethnic Secession

A classic definition of ethnic groups or communities stipulates that they are groups "bound together by common ties of race, nationality, or culture, living together within an alien civilization but remaining culturally distinct. They may occupy a position of self-sufficient isolation or they may have extensive dealings with the surrounding population." [71] They are "groups" in the hard sense of the term (i.e., they are "communities" with a common consciousness following certain norms of behavior). The most basic form of ethnic group is the racial minority and next is the national minority, but sociologists nowadays tend to employ the term "ethnic group" to designate almost any culturally distinct minority. Religion and economic interest may under certain conditions operate to maintain the solidarity of an ethnic group.

While an ethnic group can be so heavily concentrated in one region as to make it sometimes difficult to distinguish ethnic from regional secessionist movements, many ethnic groups which are vulnerable to secessionist appeals find themselves scattered unevenly throughout a country and perhaps across its borders. Perhaps also there is a "colony" of the ethnic group in the larger cities or towns. Often members of the group suffer discrimination at the hands of the dominant group or groups. They may even be restricted by law and custom to certain, often low-status, occupations; and they do not enjoy all the rights and privileges of the ordinary citizen or subject. (In certain instances, however, they do enjoy particular privileges denied to others.)

The likelihood of concerted action such as secession or even revolt depends upon the peculiar constellation of cultural, religious, economic, and political factors involved.

While the offensive and the defensive are never unequivocally demarcated in political conflict, we can say that ethnic secessionist movements can be roughly divided into defensive and offensive categories. Defensive movements are reacting to the central government's policies of repression or forced assimilation. The geographical dispersal of many ethnic groups may prove a strategic disability to a defensive movement, as the government can press its attack employing the maxim of divide and conquer. Defense, save in cases of outright genocide, is easier where the ethnic group is concentrated in several areas. Offensive secessionist movements occur (though this is difficult to measure) when the ethnic minority enjoys full or near equality before the law, but succumbs to a wave of nationalist sentiment perhaps originating in an already existing "fatherland." The offensive posture of the secessionist group may even be enhanced by having clusters of its members scattered throughout the country.

In most cases, however, geographical dispersion would seem to make full secession the last resort of the embattled ethnic group. We may thus speak of the existence of a minimal and a maximal secessionist program for the group. The minimal program aims to remove the legal and customary disabilities of the group by peaceful means; cultural autonomy is also a frequent goal. The maximal program involves a full secessionist movement aiming either at the partition of the country leading to an independent state, or to unification with the fatherland or with a friendly protector.

Religious Secession

Religion provides the final major basis for a secessionist movement. A religious community which is wholly different from the dominant one or which represents a schism within the same religion may opt for secession to secure free expression of the cult or to cut itself off from contaminating contact with infidels, heretics, or apostates. Religious secessions and secessionist movements run into the same problems as ethnic movements with the difference that, save for religion, the faithful may be identical to the rest of the population. Here too government policy and popular attitudes may determine the offensive or defensive character of the secessionist movement. The most serious problem that religious secession raises for the student is the one raised whenever religion becomes intertwined with social and political conflict: is the religious element determinant or derivative in the conflict?

In other words, is it burning religious ardor which inspires some men to attack the persons or beliefs and interests of their compatriots, or do conflicting sociopolitical interests and beliefs assume a religious mantle in order to more effectively mobilize the passions of men?

An answer to this question valid for all times and places is impossible to give. In each historical situation there is a balance between the two sets of factors, religious and nonreligious, which can tilt to either side. Sometimes the religious factor predominates; sometimes it is camouflaged; sometimes there is a rough balance. The difficulty emerges because respectable historians who interpret the same conflict are wont to offer any number of different appraisals. We can see this happen in regard to so-called French Wars of Religion in the last four decades of the sixteenth century. (There were overtones of secession in different phases of the conflict.) While most interpreters of this stormy period of French history agree that religious and sociopolitical factors are interwoven in the rise and fall of French Protestantism, many lay greater stress upon the one as opposed to the other factor. For J. W. Thompson, "Although the purposes of the Huguenots were clandestinely more political than religious, it was expedient to cloak them under the mantle of faith." [72] Other historians treat the question of religious versus sociopolitical factors in terms of distinct phases, whereby an originally religious movement is either constrained to become a politico-military force for "defense" of the faith or political dissidents come to seize upon the religious movement as an apt vehicle for basically secular objectives.

While it is not our purpose to decide this issue, it seems as much a mistake to reduce religious motives to the status of rationalizations as it is to neglect the social, economic, and political factors that contribute to the growth of religious movements, secessionist or otherwise. At the very least we can agree that "every great religious or spiritual movement is likely, sooner or later, to take a political direction. It will associate itself with the aspirations and the grievances of classes which are on the rise or which are oppressed. . . ." [73] We would only add that social strata on the decline in terms of wealth, status, and political power are also vulnerable to the appeal of a new religious dispensation. In any case, a secessionist movement which involves religion can be denied its authentically religious character only after serious historical investigation. Religion can produce vertical cleavages in society cutting across, as in sixteenth-century France, more normal bases of stratification: "Religious belief alone, no matter whether it was held with fanatic conviction or for political expediency, could bring together the divergent interests of nobles, burghers, and peasants over areas as wide as the whole of France." [74]

CONCLUSION

We have examined three political phenomena—coup d'etat, revolt, and secession—which are sometimes associated with and often
mistaken for genuine revolution. We have furthermore seen that they
can exist discretely without the remotest connection with revolutionary
change. In each case we have elaborated a typology enumerating the
pure or nonrevolutionary manifestations of these three forms of violent political conflict. However, we have not lost sight of the fact that
revolutions sometimes develop out of coups, revolts, and secessions. It
is relatively easy to distinguish the most elementary types of the three
phenomena from revolution; the boundary separating the highly complex forms from revolution becomes precarious and contentious. Nevertheless, if we keep asking ourselves questions about the stakes of a
particular insurrection (i.e., about its objective impact on the existing
systems of stratification, about the role of ideology in the orientation of
the movement, and about the kind of leadership at its head), some of
the confusion can be dispelled. Understanding what revolution is not,
is crucial to fully understanding what it is.

Coup d'etat, a ubiquitous form of leadership change, can occur almost imperceptibly or it can herald the beginning or ending of a revolutionary time of troubles. The low stakes of the simple coup d'etat, its
frequent ideological vacuum, and its leaders who differ only in name
from those in charge of the previous government should make it easy
enough to distinguish most coups from the epoch-making cataclysms
called revolution.

Likewise simple revolts arising from intolerable decline in living
conditions, or from the loss of traditional privileges or of cultural identity, raise no great difficulties of differentiation. When a movement repudiates a significant portion of the traditional values and institutions
in the name of a millenary vision, it is tempting indeed to call it revolutionary. Yet such movements are characteristically limited to a single
region or sector of society, whereas a true revolution affects the global
society. Since many millenarian and messianic movements turn out to
be more moderate than appears *prima facie*, the most we can accord
them is the title *protorevolutionary*. The real difficulty occurs with complex revolts such as the Fronde in France from 1648–53, which has
been variously interpreted as an abortive bourgeois revolution, a "plebeian" uprising of peasants and artisans, a "feudal reaction" of the aristocracy, and so on. More circumspect historians distinguish an earlier,
more "bourgeois" phase in this revolt from a later, more "aristocratic" one (the Fronde of Princes). Since the Fronde occurred during
the height of the cross-channel English Revolution, some historians

have seen a kind of revolutionary contagion at work. Although a revolution can be largely understood as a convergence of several more or less discrete patterns of revolt into a single composite movement, the elements of the Fronde remained too disparate, too provincial, and too committed to existing political and social institutions to qualify the ensemble of their efforts as a revolution. This illustrates a general principle which can be ignored only at great risk in the study of revolution, indeed in the study of politics in general: speaking of a political or a social movement in the singular should not blind us to the fact that that very movement is the resultant of political, social, economic, and psychological factors which are often discrete, disharmonious, and sometimes contradictory.

Our analysis has also implied that revolts are often *endemic*, while revolutions are *epidemic*. Something is endemic when it is peculiar and recurrent in a given territory; while it is epidemic when it spreads suddenly and extensively. In the seventeenth century, peasant revolts were endemic to many parts of Europe, while the great French Revolution seemed to break out all of a sudden, despite the prescience of a handful of observers. While both revolt and revolution are produced by the interplay of structural and conjunctural forces, the former comes to be considered an ordinary occurrence in certain conditions. Revolution is by definition extraordinary.

Secession, we have seen, cuts across the distinction between revolutionary and nonrevolutionary politics. While secession implies a "transfer of sovereignty," it can occur with a minimal disturbance of traditional political, economic, and social institutions. When colonials or other secessionists merely step into the shoes vacated by their former rulers without otherwise altering political relationships, it is improper to speak of revolution. A secession is likely to become revolutionary when the secessionists are confronted with the enormously difficult task of building a nation.

If we have seen what revolution is not and thus have glimpsed what it is, a survey of some of the major ways in which theorists and historians have conceived of revolution will take us still closer to our destination. This is the concern of Chapter II.

NOTES

[1] See Chapter III for a classification of revolutions according to their intensity.

[2] Max Weber wrote that "an ideal type is formed by the one-sided *accentuation* of one or more points of view and by the synthesis of a great many diffuse, discrete, more or less present and occasionally absent *concrete individual* phenomena, which are arranged according to those one-sidedly emphasized viewpoints into a unified analytical construct.

. . . In its conceptual purity, this mental construct . . . cannot be found anywhere in reality. It is a *utopia*. Historical research favors the task of determining in each individual case, the extent to which this ideal-construct approximates to or diverges from reality. . . ." *The Methodology of the Social Sciences* (New York: The Free Press, 1949), p. 90.

[3] D. J. Goodspeed, *The Conspirators: A Study of the Coup d'Etat* (New York: Viking Press, 1962), p. 210.

[4] Edward Luttwak, *Coup d'Etat* (Greenwich, Conn.: Fawcett Publications, 1969), p. 62.

[5] In fact, one student of the coup goes so far as to make it a rule or precondition for a coup's success that "the social and economic conditions of the target country must be such as to confine political participation to a small fraction of the population." Luttwak, *Coup d'Etat*, p. 24. However, this seems excessive in the light of those successful coups in which political mobilization of the masses is fairly well advanced.

[6] Henry R. Spencer, "Coup d'Etat," in *The Encyclopedia of the Social Sciences*, IV, p. 508.

[7] As is the case with the Shogunate in Japanese history.

[8] Clinton Rossiter, *Constitutional Dictatorship* (New York: Harcourt, Brace & World, 1963).

[9] According to David Rappaport the modern praetorian state is characterized by (1) a lack of consensus as to the form and functions of government, (2) prevalence of "raw" considerations of power and wealth over public needs, (3) a small extremely wealthy oligarchy confronting a "large poverty-stricken mass," and (4) a low level of institutionalization of political and administrative structures. "A Comparative Theory of Military and Political Types," in *Changing Patterns of Military Politics*, ed. Samuel P. Huntington (New York: The Free Press, 1962), pp. 71–101.

[10] Samuel P. Huntington, *Political Order in Changing Societies* (New Haven: Yale University Press, 1970), p. 204.

[11] Samuel P. Huntington, "Patterns of Violence in World Politics," in *Changing Patterns*, p. 36.

[12] Huntington, *Political Order*, p. 204. See below, Chapter VII, "Elites," for a discussion of the revolutionary potential of the "military intelligentsia."

[13] Jacques Ellul, *Autopsie de la révolution* (Paris: Calmann-Levy, 1969), p. 50.

[14] Albert Camus, *The Rebel* (New York: Vintage Books, 1956), p. 13.

[15] Ellul, *Autopsie*, p. 27.

[16] Chalmers Johnson, *Revolutionary Change* (Boston: Little, Brown, 1966), p. 136.

[17] As with so many terms in social science there unfortunately is no settled definition of "ideology." We can, however, speak of two general tendencies that embrace most definitions: (1) "loose" concepts of ideology can be understood roughly as equivalent to "belief system," so that any congery of political beliefs that is at all coherent becomes an ideology; (2) "tight" definitions of ideology demand a much higher degree of logical coherence, more explicit treatment of political themes, a polemical awareness of competing "ideologies," and a distinct philosophical pedigree before a belief system can be called an ideology. For the present, Carl J. Friedrich's definition of ideologies will serve our needs: "Ideologies are action-related systems of ideas. They typically contain a program and a strategy for its realization, and their essential function is to unite organizations which are built around them. . . . Ideologies are sets of ideas related to the existing political and social order and intended either to change it or defend it." *Man and his Government* (New York: McGraw-Hill, 1963), p. 89.

[18] Ellul, *Autopsie*, p. 56.

[19] Charles Tilly, "Collective Violence in European Perspective," in *Violence in America: Historical and Comparative Perspectives*, ed. Hugh D. Graham and Ted R. Gurr (New York: Bantam Books, 1969), pp. 4–45.

[20] *Communal* as opposed to *associational* groupings is a fundamental sociological distinction. Following Max Weber, "A Social relationship will be called 'communal' if and so far as the orientation of social action . . . is based on the subjective feeling of the parties whether affectual or traditional, that they belong together. A social relationship will be called 'associative' if and in so far as the orientation of the social action within it rests on a rationally motivated adjustment of interests or a similarly motivated agreement, whether the basis of rational judgment be absolute values or reasons of expediency." *The Theory of Social and Economic Organization* (New York: The Free Press, 1964), p. 136. "Communities" then include such groups as clans, ethnic groups, tribes, castes, and some local communities. "Associations" would embrace self-interest groups such as trade and labor federations, veterans or professional groups, or "cause" groups opposed to war, capital punishment, and the like.

[21] Tilly, "Collective Violence," p. 16.

[22] *Ibid.*, p. 24.

[23] *Ibid.*, p. 36.

[24] *Ibid.*, p. 24.

[25] Simeon Luce, *Histoire de la jacquerie* (Paris: Honore Champion, 1895), p. 160.

[26] The term "plebeian" in Marxist parlance includes small artisans, journeymen, occasional laborers, ex-peasants in towns, beggars, and the riffraff that Marx called the *lumpenproletariat*. See Boris Porshnev, *Les soulèvements populaires en France de 1623 à 1648* (Paris: S.E.V.P.E.N., 1963), p. 269.

[27] *Ibid.*, p. 268.

[28] *Ibid.*, p. 85.

[29] Roland Mousnier, *La plume, la faucille, et la marteau* (Paris: Presses Universitaires de France, 1970), p. 373.

[30] See "Millenarianism-Messianism" below and Chapter IV for further analysis of this problem.

[31] Roland Mousnier, *Fureurs paysannes: les paysans dans les révoltes du XVIIe siècle* (Paris: Calmann-Levy, 1967), p. 322.

[32] Mousnier, *La plume*, p. 382.

[33] Mousnier, *Fureurs paysannes*, p. 350.

[34] Eric R. Wolf, *Peasant Wars of the Twentieth Century* (New York: Harper & Row, 1969), p. 295.

[35] This seems to explain what happened to the peasant revolt of Emiliano Zapata during the Mexican Revolution of 1910. The character of Zapata and of the movement he led betray the backward glance, provincialism, and narrow-mindedness of traditional peasant revolts. Revolutionary ideology and leadership came from leftist semianarchist intellectuals such as Manuel Palafox and Antonio Diaz Soto y Gama. See John Womack, Jr., *Zapata and the Mexican Revolution* (New York: Vintage Books, 1969). For a rather different interpretation of the Zapatista movement and its ideology, see Robert P. Millon, *Zapata: The Ideology of a Peasant Revolutionary* (New York: International Publishers, 1972).

[36] Barrington Moore, *Social Origins of Democracy and Dictatorship* (Boston: Beacon Press, 1968), p. 480.

[37] *Ibid.*, p. 221.

[38] George Rudé, *The Crowd in History 1730–1848* (New York: John Wiley, 1964), Introduction.

[39] E. J. Hobsbawm, *Primitive Rebels* (New York: W. W. Norton, 1965), p. 110.

[40] Rudé, *The Crowd in History*, p. 255.

[41] Hobsbawm, *Primitive Rebels*, p. 116.

[42] *Ibid.*

[43] Rudé, *The Crowd in History*, p. 224.

[44] Anthony F.C. Wallace, "Revitalization Movements," *American Anthropologist*, LVIII (April, 1956), p. 267.

[45] Ralph Linton, "Nativistic Movements," in *Reader in Comparative Religion*, ed. W.A. Lessa and E.Z. Vogt (Evanston, Ill.: Row, Peterson, 1958), p. 467.

[46] Wallace, "Revitalization Movements," p. 276.

[47] Linton, "Nativistic Movements," p. 468.

[48] *Ibid.*, p. 469.

[49] Fred W. Voget, "The American Indian in Transition: Reformation and Accommodation," *American Anthropologist*, LVIII (April, 1956), p. 249.

[50] *Ibid.*, p. 250.

[51] "Millenarian" as well as the Greek-derived "chiliastic" refer literally to a thousand years: they connote movements that proclaim the "millennium," the thousand-year holy kingdom that figures in certain prophetic writings and traditions. "Messianic" refers to the ancient Hebrew prophecy of a hero-leader who would restore the Jews to greatness, and hence to any such savior or redeemer.

[52] The term "revolutionary" is applied to certain messianic movements in Norman Cohn, *The Pursuit of the Millennium* (New York: Oxford University Press, 1970), p. 201; and in Maria Isaura Pereira de Queiroz, *Historia y etnologia de los movimientos messianicos*, Span. ed (Mexico City: Siglo XXI Editores, 1969), p. 65.

[53] Pereira de Queiroz, *Historia*, p. 20.

[54] "Eschatological" and "apocalyptic" are terms often associated with millenarian and messianic movements. The former refers to the end of the world through divinely ordained catastrophe; the latter connotes prophetic revelations of an eschatological character.

[55] Pereira de Queiroz, *Historia*, p. 20; and Hobsbawm, *Primitive Rebels*, p. 58.

[56] Pereira de Queiroz, *Historia*, Part II, Chaps. 2–4.

[57] *Ibid.*, pp. 95–96.

[58] *Ibid.*, p. 121.

[59] *Ibid.*, p. 161. Such an interpretation is found in Vincent Shih's analysis of the great Taiping Rebellion in China in the third quarter of the nineteenth century. While recent interpretations, especially in China, contend that the Taiping upheaval was an authentic, though abortive or defeated, revolution, Shih insists on the contrary, that though "there were certain ideas borrowed from Christianity and the West which held a genuine possibility of bringing about a real revolution," such an outcome was "nullified when, because of years of indoctrination in the traditional outlook, the Taipings were unable to perceive Christian ideas except through the colored glasses of traditional concepts." Vincent Y.C. Shih, *The Taiping Ideology* (Seattle: University of Washington Press, 1972), p. xv.

[60] The French historian Marc Bloch has pointed out the necessity of distinguishing the notion of feudalism from that of manorialism—or, we might add, from seigneurialism. Manorialism, while an important economic aspect of feudal society, both preceded and survived it. According to Bloch the basic features of Western European feudalism include "a subject peasantry; widespread use of the service tenement (i.e., the fief) instead of a salary . . . ; the supremacy of a class of specialized warriors; ties of obedience and protection which bind man to man and, within the warrior class, assume the distinctive form called vassalage; fragmentation of authority—leading inevitably to disorder; and, in the midst of all this, the survival of other forms of association, family, and State." *Feudal Society*, Vol. II (Chicago: University of Chicago Press, 1966), p. 442. Seigneurialism would thus be a nonfeudal manorial society in which many "survivals" and traces of feudalism could still be found.

[61] A main stratagem here is to lay all blame for conflict on the "king's wicked ad-

visers." Joel T. Rosenthal states: "In this way the barons opposed the king and yet avoided a decisive clash with the theoretical basis of medieval kingship. Furthermore, by attacking wicked advisers the barons not only took cognizance of the political and administrative developments of the medieval state, but they sought as a class to control these innovations and to govern the state which created them. Lastly, the attack on the wicked advisers was a ritualized form of rebellion and, therefore, a conservative one. This was most important, because the aims of the barons always had to be quite limited—to destroy the King was to destroy the basis of their own authority." "The King's 'Wicked Advisers' and Medieval Baronial Rebellions," *Political Science Quarterly*, LXXXII (December, 1967), p. 597.

[62] Raymond Carr, *Spain 1808–1939* (Oxford: Clarendon Press, 1966), Chap. 13.

[63] Louis Hartz, *The Founding of New Societies* (New York: Harcourt, Brace & World, 1964), p. 3.

[64] *Ibid.*, p. 5.

[65] *Ibid.*, p. 73.

[66] Rupert Emerson, *From Empire to Nation* (Boston: Beacon Press, 1963), p. 204.

[67] *Ibid.*, p. 95.

[68] *Ibid.*, p. 103.

[69] *Ibid.*, p. 121.

[70] *Ibid.*, p. 206.

[71] C. Ware, "Ethnic Communities," in *The Encyclopedia of the Social Sciences*, V, pp. 607–13.

[72] See J.H.M. Salmon, ed., *The French Wars of Religion* (Boston: D.C. Heath, 1967) for a sampling of the diversity of opinion on these issues. Thompson's thesis appears on pp. 4–5.

[73] E. Armstrong, *The French Wars of Religion: Their Political Aspects* (London: Percival & Co., 1892), p. 1.

[74] H.G. Koenigsberger, *Estates and Revolutions* (Ithaca, N.Y.: Cornell University Press, 1971), pp. 225–26.

II

CONCEPTS OF REVOLUTION

In this chapter we will survey some of the leading concepts of revolution which have operated in historical and philosophical studies of revolution as well as in the minds of revolutionaries themselves. One can legitimately ask what all the bother is about. Let each define revolution as he sees fit and let us judge instead the results of his work! Or let us forget about the problem of definition altogether and proceed to more specific problems to which research can bring more enlightenment than sterile disputes over words! Such attitudes have in fact characterized studies of revolution. Crane Brinton, for instance, in his brilliant classic *The Anatomy of Revolution* rejects the need to become overly precise in defining what a revolution is. He considers it more fruitful to select four revolutions (the English, the American, the French, and the Russian), study them attentively, and report whatever tentative similarities or "uniformities" they might betray. "It should be very clear," he writes, "that not all revolutions past, present, and future will conform to the pattern here drawn. Our four revolutions are not necessarily even 'typical' in the sense the word 'typical' has for literary critics or moralists." [1] This however is modesty become a fault, and study of Brinton's book would show that his claims are considerably more ambitious than he indicates. Similarly a more recent study asserts that "we shall attempt no new definition of revolution in this work. We are content to leave the question open-ended." [2]

Yet the root problem is not so easily shrugged off as this. Brinton implies that his four revolutions are such because they are called by the same name and because he finds some of the uniformities that he seeks. From the standpoint of the present study, however, the American Revolution does not belong in the list—which Brinton implicitly acknowledges by recurrent qualifications about this or that idiosyncratic feature of the War of Independence. Had he developed a fairly rigorous definition beforehand, he might have reached conclusions different from those produced by an otherwise fruitful conceptual scheme. Clearly an approach that classifies certain phenomena together which do not belong together will risk a distorted or incoherent analysis. The working definition of revolution that a social scientist employs, stated or not, affects his study from beginning to end. If he is interested in the causes of revolution and his concept of revolution is basically economic, then he tends to investigate mainly, if not exclusively, the economic condition of the pre-revolutionary society. If, on the contrary, he conceives of revolution as an attempt to build a perfect society or utopia, he will devote considerable energy to surveying the "intellectual origins" of the revolution. The search for the leading protagonists or for the stages of revolution acquires a different focus according to how one understands revolution in general.

The concepts of revolution that follow are by no means all there are. However, they are highly influential concepts and roughly demarcate the ways in which students of revolution approach their subject. Nearly all of them hearken back to the great French Revolution in one way or another—raising a problem of overgeneralization that we will encounter in several contexts throughout this study. Nor are these concepts necessarily mutually exclusive; in fact, on several occasions the fundamental thrust of a particular concept of revolution has been exaggerated below in order to distinguish it more clearly from the others. All of them have much to recommend them and have left their traces in the concept of revolution introduced in the last chapter and elaborated in the next.

REVOLUTION AS ECONOMIC CATACLYSM

Technology and the Dialectic

The concept of revolution as economic cataclysm is inseparably associated with the philosophy of Karl Marx.[3] His concept can only be understood within the context of his general philosophy, known alternatively as dialectical or historical materialism. Materialism of any type is a philosophy that contends that the ultimate reality in the universe is matter in motion. Classical Greek materialism, upon which Marx wrote his doctoral dissertation, claimed that the world was composed of tiny indivisible material particles called atoms. These atoms combine in countless ways producing all the myriad forms of experience that man (himself made of matter) encounters in the world. Marx felt, however, that the insight of classic materialism was incomplete and incapable of explaining the manifold processes of change in nature and history. He found the missing aspect in the notion of the dialectic, as formulated by the great German idealist philosopher Georg Hegel. The dialectic purports to explain the presence and the forms of change in the world: why new things emerge and why the universe is orderly rather than completely chaotic. In Marx's adaptation of the dialectic, nature becomes historical and history becomes part of nature; they are parts of one and the same process. The dialectic then is a first principle and as such cannot be explained by some further principle. We can only ask how it operates to produce our world.

The motive principle of the dialectic is found in the opposites or *contradictions* that nature inexhaustibly and unfailingly produces. Each given state or condition of things (a "thesis") produces its opposite or contrary (an "antithesis"). The resultant contradiction, however, is creative rather than destructive, because thesis and antithesis do not annihilate each other. Nor do they remain like two equally strong tug-of-war teams in a condition of perfect balance. Rather, at a given point the tension between the thesis and antithesis breaks down and a third condition called the "synthesis" emerges, which in turn becomes a new thesis and so on. The synthesis has in a sense both preserved and annulled the two previous conditions: thesis and antithesis no longer exist in their pristine form although the synthesis contains them, so to speak, as ingredients. Thus the new is never entirely new and the old is never wholly destroyed. However, what is of great importance in the dialectic for Marx's concept of revolution is that the final breakdown of the old system of contradictions is drastic and abrupt, occurring in what Hegel called the "nodal point." An example would be water suddenly boiling at 212°F. and not before. Although the contradictions may gradually "mature" by becoming more serious and acute, the final transition to the next stage is not a simple growth or evolution, but a "qualitative" leap.

Historical materialism applies the dialectic to the study of human history and society. In this application it can be considered a form of economic determinism.[4] Economic determinism holds that the fundamental motivations and forces determining social relationships derive ultimately from economic factors. This outlook can range from the rather vulgar forms implied in maxims such as "money talks" or "everyone has his price," to highly sophisticated conceptual schemes such as those of Marx and certain of his followers.

Marxism begins its analysis of society by distinguishing between its "superstructure" and its "substructure." The superstructure comprises the religion, philosophy, moral codes and customs, political organization, legal systems, and the literary and artistic life of a society. The substructure is the economic system or, more precisely, the system of production and exchange. According to Marxism, the substructure in the last analysis determines the basic content and contours of the superstructure. The economic system is primary, while the political, moral, legal, cultural, and religious systems are secondary. This relationship between the two levels of social reality exists because in the time since the demise of "primitive communal society" and before the advent of future communism a minority group called the *ruling class* owns and hence controls the means of production and exchange in its own narrow interest. The entire superstructure by both dissimulation and justification serves to secure the ruling class's monopolistic advantage. Furthermore, the normal role of the state is to act as "executive committee" of the ruling class by keeping the other social classes in check. Religion can become an "opiate of the people" by directing their attention away from the exploitation and injustice of this world to the paradise of the next and by preaching the virtues of poverty, meekness, and resignation. Literature likewise becomes a hymn of praise to the existing order. In other words, all of mental culture functions as an "ideology" that beclouds the awareness or "consciousness" of the masses and produces instead a "false consciousness." So long as this false consciousness remains intact, the ruling class cannot be overthrown. In short, "The ideas of the ruling class are in every epoch the ruling ideas: i.e. the class, which is the ruling material force of society, is at the same time its ruling intellectual force. The class which has the means of material production at its disposal, has control at the same time over the means of mental production, so that thereby, generally speaking, the ideas of those who lack the means of mental production are subject to it." [5]

Nevertheless, according to Marxism, all ruling classes meet with the same fate: they are overthrown. Because each ruling class as a class is bound up with a particular economic system, it rises and falls with that system. What ultimately determines the outcome is technology—a term roughly equivalent to what Marx called the "productive forces" of society. In this connection Marx makes two assumptions crucial to his concept of revolution: (1) technological advance is in the long run irreversible; and (2) the adaptability of ruling classes to changed economic (i.e., technological) conditions is strictly limited. Technological progress, therefore, produces the obsolescence of ruling classes. At the beginning of each historical epoch [6] the ruling class is the champion of economic progress and as such is an agent of progress. But sooner or later (depending on the level of technology already attained) technological advance outstrips the capacity of the ruling class to lead this development or even to contain or reverse it. The ruling class and the whole superstructure created in its image increasingly becomes a burden to further advance and the contradiction between the system of ownership and the system of production becomes acute. However, "no social order ever perished before all the productive forces for which there is room in it have developed; and new, higher relations of production never appear before the material conditions of their existence have matured in the womb of the old society itself." [7]

Class Struggle and Revolution

In Marxist theory class struggle exists wherever there are classes, but the forms it can take vary enormously. Rudimentary forms of class struggle such as purely economic strikes or isolated acts of violence are barometers of the intensity of class struggle at any given moment. The number of classes in a society can be several, yet with respect to the death and birth of economic systems the leading protagonists are always two: the ruling class and the "challenger" class. As we have seen, the ruling class is the product of a particular economic system which is constantly and increasingly undermined by technological development. The other side of this process involves the rise of a new class whose very existence is bound up with the future (i.e., the new economic order gestating within the old). In the first days of its ascent the challenger class poses no serious threat to the established order; it is too weak and has no real consciousness of its distinctive historical role. Later, the ruling class (or a portion of it) perceives the threat of the challenger but is powerless to counter it, because the economic system can no longer function without its contribution. In this sense every society does produce its own gravediggers by producing the class that will ultimately overthrow it.

The contradictions within a society reach their highest intensity on the eve of revolution. For example, the social strata between the ruling and challenger classes are wiped out or are forced to take sides. They generally side with the class of the future. Acute economic disarray (e.g., more frequent and steeper business cycles) also betokens the intensification of contradictions. At a given point the challenger class, momentarily representing the interests of the whole society, rises up and seizes political power. This seizure is bound to be violent, although Marxists dispute over texts as to whether Marx foresaw a possibly peaceful path for revolution under certain optimum conditions. Engels in a somewhat polemical remark nevertheless seems to follow the logic of Marxism when he wrote that "[a revolution] is the act whereby one part of the population imposes its will upon the other part by means of rifles, bayonets, and cannon—authoritarian means, if such there be at all; and if the victorious party does not want to have fought in vain, it must maintain this rule by means of the terror which its arms inspire in the reactionaries." [8] Yet it is not merely tactical considerations that introduce violence as an essential component of the Marxist idea of revolution. The Hegelian notion of the abruptness of dialectical change in the so-called nodal point predisposes towards considering violence as a necessary feature of revolution. So much of "epoch-making" significance is compressed into such a brief period, it is difficult to imagine how violence could be avoided.

Superficially then, the function of revolution is to depose one class and bring another one to power. More profoundly, revolution marks the transition from one type of economy to another, from one epoch in man's history to another. However, as Engels has pointed out, a crucial distinction must be made: "All revolutions up to the present day have resulted in the displacement of one definite class rule by another; but all ruling classes up to now have been only small minorities in relation to the ruled mass of the people. One ruling minority was thus overthrown; another minority seized the helm of state in its stead and refashioned the state institutions to suit its own interests." [9] In other words, all revolutions up to the proletarian revolution have simply replaced one ruling minority for another. The role of the people—that is, the majority of the poor or "plebeian" elements—in a revolution can vary from indifference to tacit support up to active aid of the key revolutionary class. In the great French Revolution, for example, "the 'have-nothing' masses of Paris, during the Reign of Terror, were able for a moment to gain the mastery, and thus to lead the bourgeois revolution to victory in spite of the bourgeoisie themselves." [10] In cases such as this the masses go beyond the immediate scruples or reluctance of the emergent ruling class without, however, being able to set up a truly democratic regime. It is thus the masses who often do the "dirty work" of revolutions. Just as often they are repaid with ingratitude, even betrayal, as the new ruling class at the moment of victory or soon after takes repressive measures against its former allies.

This is the conceptual scheme in which Marxist historiography places the great revolutions of modern times. Thus, the period from the Protestant Reformation in the early sixteenth century to the revolutions of 1848 witnesses the destruction of feudalism and the establishment of modern capitalism. According to Marx:

> The Revolutions of 1648 and 1789 were not *English* and *French* revolutions; they were revolutions of a *European* pattern. They were not the victory of a *definite* class of society over the *old political order;* they were the *proclamation of political order for the new European society*. The bourgeoisie

was victorious in these revolutions; but the *victory of the bourgeoisie* was at that time the *victory of a new order of society*, the victory of bourgeois property over feudal property, of nationality over provincialism, of competition over the guild. . . .[11]

If we follow the Marxists, then we must interpret the English and French revolutions as the work of the urban capitalist middle class and its allies from above and below. On the eve of these revolutions capitalism had developed as far as it could within the framework of "feudal" restrictions, regulations, and sociopolitical relationships. Capitalism had to burst these bonds in order to liberate the productive forces it contained. The cry for liberty in these revolutions reflected capitalism's need for free trade and free labor. The true nature of these revolutions is thus to be sought in economic cataclysm, although the narrowly political aspect of the conflict seems to be paramount. Appearance, however, is no substitute for reality, since "all political struggles are class struggles, and all class struggles for emancipation, despite the necessarily political form—for every class struggle is a political struggle—turn ultimately on the question of *economic* emancipation." [12] There can thus be no *social revolution* without a *political revolution*.

Differing radically from previous minority revolutions is the incipient proletarian revolution, because the industrial working class is either itself a numerical majority or represents one. Even more significant is the goal of the proletarian revolution: the abolition of classes. However this aspect of Marxist theory is not of direct interest to us here. What concerns us is the place of misery and spontaneity in the modern revolutionary situation. Marx felt that the proletariat was the revolutionary class *par excellence* because its life conditions embodied all the malaise of modern society. Only this class would develop the full consciousness of the moral bankruptcy of capitalism. Through its very life situation, "through urgent, no longer disguisable, absolutely imperative *need*," the proletariat "is driven directly to revolt against that inhumanity. . . ." [13] Marx estimated that the lot of the working class would worsen as capitalism developed: unemployment would rise, wages and living conditions would fall. Nevertheless, it is through misery that liberation (i.e., revolution) must come. The relationship of misery and revolution, rather than the accuracy of Marx's predictions, is of theoretical interest here. Marx implies that mankind as embodied in the proletariat can sink only so low when it suddenly becomes conscious of its plight, spontaneously forms a movement and party, and organizes a full-scale revolution. By offering such a viewpoint Marx took sides in an argument that will recur in different ways throughout the course of this book.

The Marxist concept of revolution as economic cataclysm suffers from an excessive preoccupation with class struggle as an economic phenomenon. Economic stratification is emphasized to the point of neglecting or confusing the role of other forms of stratification. Revolutions are too complex and too unique to be reducible to a facile formula such as bourgeois or proletarian revolution. Are the Netherlands Revolt at the end of the sixteenth century, the English Revolution in the middle of the seventeenth, the French Revolution at the end of the eighteenth, and the central European revolutions in the middle of the nineteenth, all more or less faithful editions of one and the same "bourgeois revolution"? Marxist historiography answers in the affirmative. For now, the words of a recent historian well represent the rejoinder implied in later chapters: "But there is not, in fact, any model pattern of a bourgeois revolution, and while the investigation of analogies can be the most illuminating, there are far more differences between the English and French revolutions than similarities." [14]

REVOLUTION AS CIRCULATION OF THE ELITE

The Rise and Fall of Elites

Revolution as circulation of the elite receives its best-known formulation in the works of the Italian economist and sociologist Vilfredo Pareto (1848–1923). According to Pareto every human society is divided into an elite and a nonelite. The elite (sometimes termed "aristocracy," especially in Pareto's earlier works) is a composite category consisting of all the most able and talented individuals in the various branches of human endeavor. Thus the elite of a society is the sum total of all those who excel, regardless of the moral status of their area of expertise. However, actual human societies being imperfect organisms, they fall short of according the "proper" social position to the members of this elite or "natural aristocracy." In other words, the higher positions in the hierarchies of wealth, power, and status are not always or completely occupied by people who "belong" there. The width of this gap varies enormously over time and between societies. If the gap is narrow (i.e., most of the people in elite positions are intelligent, energetic, and competent), the social equilibrium manifests extreme stability. If the gap widens too much and the ruling elite or aristocracy proves effete and incompetent, various forms of instability including revolution will occur. "By a law of great moment, which is truly the principal cause of many historical and social facts, these aristocracies do not last, but are continuously renovated and in this way there occurs a phenomenon which can be called *circulation of aristocracies.*" [15]

Human society fluctuates between the two extremes of a completely closed and a completely open society, which themselves are never encountered in reality. A completely open society would in effect reconstitute itself every day as a perfect social mobility or circulation of the elite would proceed without interference from considerations of past achievements, wealth, or status. A completely closed society, which caste systems such as those of ancient India approach but never really reach, would assign individuals their social position from cradle to grave. Barring these two unrealistic solutions, human society is still confronted by a dilemma: social utility demands the utmost competence in the elite, as well as a measure of stability. Unfortunately, the scheme that would continuously reinvigorate the elite with new elements without disturbing social stability has not as yet been discovered. Some societies have for an extended period run upon a kind of golden mean between stability and change, but Pareto doubts that they can be successfully emulated.

At any rate, circulation of the elite will occur because it must, and it will take one of two forms. The more normal method can be termed "piecemeal circulation," though Pareto did not himself employ this phrase. Here the decadent elements of the old elite are gradually and almost individually replaced by more vigorous recruits from below. Unfortunately, for both social stability and for the incumbent elite, circulation frequently slows down to a point where the elite becomes more and more a closed caste which haughtily rejects the new men who wish to enter its ranks. Pareto states: "It is not only the accumulation of inferior elements in a social stratum that is harmful to society, but also the accumulation in the lower strata of elite elements which are prevented from rising. When simultaneously the upper strata are full of decadent elements and the lower strata are full of elite elements, the social equilibrium becomes highly unstable and a violent revolution is imminent." [16]

Violent revolutions in the Paretian conception are the reverse of erratic catastrophes; as a form of circulation of the elite they exercise a vital social function. For if circulation is not achieved in either piecemeal or revolutionary fashion, society will *die* (i.e., it will lose its national independence or simply disintegrate). Accordingly Pareto is willing to excuse much of the violence and terror of revolutions because they are merely "external symptoms indicating the advent of strong and courageous people to places formerly held by weaklings and cowards." [17] To a degree Pareto's is a "success philosophy" in reverse; for if the old elite is decimated by the new one and its allies, it simply gets what it deserves. Any elite worthy of the name would have avoided such a fate, if necessary, by striking first.

A revolution, then, is a method of unclogging the channels of social mobility. Pareto offers more than this simple conclusion. His most cogent and concise sketch of the revolutionary situation is found in his *Manuale di economia politica*, where he divides the old or established elite into two segments. One of these, as it still displays the will and capability of defending its position by force,[18] must be presumed still worthy of rule. The other segment has become softened and corrupted especially by what Pareto calls "humanitarian sentiments." It lacks the stomach for a straight fight and spends its time in gratuitous outpourings of sympathy for the plight of the lower strata. The nonelite must be similarly divided into (1) a small minority or "counterelite" of vigorous individuals who seek either to mix with the old elite or to supplant them, and (2) the more or less powerless and mediocre mass which constitutes the vast majority in any society. The characteristics and interplay of these four elements determine the exact outcome of a revolutionary situation. The simplicity of this picture is somewhat complicated by deception and by the fissions and fusions of alliances. Neither the old elite who want to retain their hegemony nor the counterelite who want to take it over can afford to admit their true intentions. Since they are minorities, they both need allies and supporters among the masses of the nonelite to act as rank-and-file troops for an army they lead. To obtain this help they resort to a variety of stratagems designed to show that they are selflessly dedicated to the welfare of the majority. Especially adept is the counterelite in disguising its true objectives by talk of liberty, equality, and fraternity. Quite often the outcome of an attempted revolution depends upon which side succeeds in seducing the masses by its more or less mendacious promises. This is not to say that the masses never benefit from the revolutions which often cost them dearly. Sometimes they directly benefit by immediate improvement in their living conditions; almost always they indirectly benefit because the new elite is more competent than the old. Nevertheless, these benefits are side effects and not the real stakes of the revolution, which concern rather who is going to rule the society. Since power remains in the hands of a minority after as before a revolution, Pareto somewhat cynically concludes that the "replacement of certain politicians by others has been the sole appreciable result of many revolutions." [19]

The simplicity of the revolutionary situation is also disturbed by the secession of a part of the old elite. Moved in some cases by conviction, in others by ambition and greed, these "traitors to their class" readily assume leading positions in the revolutionary movement. "In fact nearly all revolutions have been the work not indeed of the mass, but rather of the aristocracy and especially of the decadent part of the aristocracy. . . . Aristocracies usually end by suicide." [20] In these cases certain individuals have saved themselves at the expense of their former associates. While there is a certain similarity between the Paretian and Marxian conclusions that small minorities have been the ultimate and chief beneficiaries of historic revolutions, Pareto is scornful of the idea that any revolution, proletarian or otherwise, can turn out differently.

Lions, Foxes, and Social Change

In his *magnum opus, The Treatise on General Sociology,* Pareto works his basic concepts of elite circulation and revolution into a more elaborate conceptual framework. He argues that the social equilibrium (if we neglect factors stemming from outside the society) is the resultant of the interaction of four sets of variables: (1) *social heterogeneity,* which refers to the inequalities amongst men that give rise to elites, their circulation, etc.; (2) *interests,* which are the basically economic motivations so important in modern political conflicts; (3) *residues,* which are deep-seated expressions of sentiments or near-instincts that influence human behavior under a wealth of different forms; (4) *derivations,* which are the pseudorational manifestations of the residues, taking the form of moral, religious, and philosophical beliefs, doctrines, and ideologies. For present purposes little more need be said about social heterogeneity and interests because Pareto fashions a social psychology of political power in terms of the residues and derivations. Derivations, as the very terminology implies, depend upon the residues; and despite the logical form in which they are cast are utter nonsense from the scientific point of view. Religious beliefs and doctrines serve Pareto as the purest example of derivations. When he wished to underscore the scientific or "logico-experimental" worthlessness of certain political ideologies, he uses phrases such as "the religion of progress" or "the Goddess Democracy," etc. Like Marx, Pareto is concerned to "unmask" ideologies, but his frame of reference is psychological rather than economic.

It is in his reliance upon the residues, however, that Pareto develops a typology of political personality encompassing the problem of revolution. The complete list of residues includes six basic classes, five of which are broken down into subcategories: Class I, Instinct for Combinations; Class II, Persistence of Aggregates; Class III, Need of Expressing Sentiments by External Acts; Class IV, Residues Connected with Sociality; Class V, Integrity of the Individual and his Appurtenances; Class VI, the Sex Residue. While all of these are conceivably relevant to a psychology of politics, Pareto concentrates on classes I and II. Class I residues produce the desire and the skills for manipulating men and affairs. Someone highly endowed with these residues is crafty, cunning, and clever—in short, a wheeler-dealer. In politics, compromise, bargaining, and negotiating are his strong qualities. In economics, he is a "speculator" who risks his fortune on the basis of his quick wits. This type of person excels in activities requiring high intelligence, adaptability, and strategy; but when brute force is required, he is almost useless. Following Machiavelli, Pareto calls him the *fox*. Class II residues, on the other hand, predispose one towards firm loyalty and attachment to the group. The individual characterized by them is generally dull and slow-witted. However, there is no one better in a fight. This type of individual will defend the interests of his group (class, church, or nation) returning blow for blow to his adversaries. His economic counterpart is the rentier who conservatively sits back and clips his coupons without risking what he already has. Pareto calls this type of person the *lion*.

An elite could remain in power indefinitely if it could discover and maintain the correct ratio of lions to foxes in its ranks. The balance of residues, therefore, becomes the crucial factor in determining social stability. The contingent of foxes in the ruling elite would perform those political functions where skill, finesse, or dissimulation are needed, while the lions would deal with problems in which more bellicose qualities prevail. As we have already seen, it is virtually impossible to avoid change in the character of an elite. In time the balance of types within the elite is upset in favor of the foxes, which in turn causes a buildup of lions in the nonelite. Thus, "the differences between the governing class and the subject class become gradually accentuated, the combination-instincts tending to predominate in the ruling class, and the instincts of group-persistence in the subject class. When that difference becomes sufficiently great, revolution occurs." [21] What actually happens is that the old elite, now composed almost exclusively of foxes, is not only incapable of defending its privileged position by force, but is itself half-converted by the platitudes of equality and democracy that previously served only to disguise its rule. The counterelite, in which lions outnumber foxes, has no such fear of spilling blood to reach its goals. At the appropriate moment the revolution breaks out and the counterelite takes power ostensibly in behalf of the whole people. The new regime usually ushers in a period of prosperity, though the democratic rhetoric of the revolutionary period is forgotten or perverted. In time the balance between lions and foxes will again tilt to one side and the revolutionary cycle will begin anew.

While Pareto's concept of revolution corrects the one-sidedness of the Marxian conception, it is not free of difficulties. The very notion of the elite is somewhat equivocal. It seems to be first and foremost a political category distinguishing those having political power from those that do not. Unfortunately, Pareto fails to relate political stratification to the other forms based on wealth and status. He does speak of the governing elite and the nongoverning elite; but the distinction is vaguely articulated and plays little role in his discussions of revolution, where the elite is treated *en bloc*. Is it simply that wealth and status automatically accrue to the holders of political power? Or does political power accrue to those with wealth and status? Or does the answer to this question vary from society to society? Pareto's notion of the elite helps little in these questions so important in understanding the meaning of revolution. The next chapter will attempt to salvage the notion of elite for the study of revolution.

REVOLUTION AS STRENGTHENING
OF THE STATE

In his great work, *Democracy in America*, Alexis de Tocqueville (1805–59) interpreted the course of modern history in terms of the leveling of social differences. In his later study *The Old Regime and the French Revolution*, he presented the less conspicuous side of this movement as the development of the modern centralized state. However, in his interpretation of the French Revolution Tocqueville did not restrict himself to analyzing the increase of state power. In addition, he pointed out the quasi-religious nature of the revolution, the importance of social stratification among its causes, the role of intellectuals in preparing the emergence of the revolutionary situation. All of these aspects are permanent contributions to the general study of revolutions. Here we are concerned with only one aspect of his picture of the nature of the Revolution, the strengthening of the state. Though Tocqueville took pains to emphasize the uniqueness of the French Revolution, his disciples have for a century extended and applied his insights to all revolutions.

For Tocqueville the revolution was not an accidental or fortuitous event. It was the likely, if not fatal, outcome of a sequence of events and changes in French society spread over hundreds of years. It was both a social and a political revolution. Its social aspect, not our prime concern here, consisted in the eradication of the remnants of medieval society, which had become emptied of their former significance. The revolution achieved by violent and drastic measures what America had accomplished by evolution: the promotion of a general equality of rank amongst all citizens. Politically speaking, the permanent achievement of the revolution, above the rhetoric and the terror, was "to increase the power and the rights of the public authority." [22]

It is not that Tocqueville believed that the revolution created centralization (his term for strengthening of the state) *ex nihilo*. On the contrary, centralization was a policy followed by the French monarchy from the late middle ages. All the famous kings' ministers of the seventeenth century—Richelieu, Mazarin, and Colbert—were devotees and practitioners of the centralized, bureaucratized regime known as absolute monarchy. In an uneven process taking many generations, the central government succeeded in concentrating the administrative, legal, economic, and cultural life of the country in Paris. "Nothing indicates that in order to operate the difficult work the government of the old regime had followed a plan profoundly thought out beforehand. It had abandoned itself to *the instinct which leads every government to wish to direct all matters by itself. . . .*" [23] (Italics mine.) By the time of the revolution the king's government had made a sham out of provincial autonomy and had divested the territorial aristocracy of real administrative-political functions so that only its privileges remained as insult and injury to the lower orders. Thus, much of the paraphernalia of medieval social and political institutions remained formally intact, though as complete anomalies in the modern system of administrative routine. The glaring contrast between the two forms seemed rather like a "contradiction" in the Marxist sense.

Quite simply then, the political function of the revolution was to complete and perfect the work of centralization begun by the absolutist kings of France. "If centralization did not perish in the revolution, it is because it was itself the beginning of this revolution and its sign. . . ." [24] This result is obscured by the apparently destructive and radically innovative nature of the revolution. Tocqueville warns us to look at what was really happening in those times of enthusiasm and excitation: it was not the old regime *en bloc* that was destroyed and replaced during the revolution. Instead, it was the feudal and aristocratic anachronisms which the old regime itself tried unsuccessfully to eliminate that were the target of the revolutionaries. Centralization itself was far too deeply embedded in French life for even a revolution to uproot. "The men of 1789 had overturned the edifice but its foundations had remained in the very soul of its destroyers, and upon these foundations one could suddenly raise it up and build it more solidly than it had ever been." [25] From this point of view, Tocqueville argued, we can see how the revolution continued as well as disrupted the course of French history, or at least how it was a parenthesis separating two phases of the same long-term development.

Although in its last years the old regime had been subjected to a crescendo of criticism by those whom we would today call intellectuals, their very plans and projects of reform bore the imprint of the monarchy's taste for centralization. When the revolution broke out, it could only deepen the ruts carved out by the monarchy. Furthermore, the very destructiveness of the revolution had merely cleared the way for the hypercentralization of the Napoleonic Empire: "from the very entrails of a nation which had just overturned the monarchy we see suddenly arise a power more extensive, more elaborate, more absolute than that exercised by any of our kings." [26]

The wider implications of Tocqueville's ideas have been developed by recent theorists. Bertrand de Jouvenal has suggested that the basic meaning of all revolutions is found in "an accretion of Power's weight." [27] He emphasizes more than Tocqueville the essentially tragic nature of revolutions. Revolutionaries have always believed that they have risen up against oppression and tyranny. Their conscious goal has been the realization of the heroic triad of the French Revolution: liberty, equality, and fraternity. And yet, the end result of every revolution has been a state power beyond the wildest dreams of the rulers of the old regime. Evidently the intentions of the actors in the revolutionary drama have little to do with its unfolding, although many historians have been captivated by their declarations and rhetoric. To Jouvenal, "the Cromwells and the Stalins are no fortuitous consequence, no accidental happening, of the revolutionary tempest. Rather they are its predestined goal, toward which the entire upheaval was moving inevitably; the cycle began with the downfall of an inadequate Power only to close with the consolidation of a more absolute Power." [28] Paradoxically, the revolutionary's obsession with destroying tyranny only succeeds in toppling a regime suffering more from a deficiency of power than an excess. This pattern is typical of all revolutions, although the Russian Revolution strengthened power more efficiently than the French, which in turn had gone further than the English.

Taking up where Jouvenal left off, Jacques Ellul insists that although revolutions begin against the state—or "against history," for the modern state is the product of history—they end by pushing the state to the limits of totalitarianism and sometimes beyond. The pre-revolutionary state has itself grown considerably; but it contains certain irrational, inefficient, and anomalous features. "What man suffers from is the incoherence of an organism which restricts him because it is at the same time powerful and clumsy." [29] For this reason revolution is best understood as *"the crisis of the growth of the state."* [30] The revolution soon gives up its antistate animus and elaborates a more rational and efficient structure which penetrates society much deeper and in more ways than the old state. While Jouvenal stresses the personal rule of the autocrat (Cromwell, Napoleon, Stalin) as the chief result of the revolution, Ellul argues that personal dictatorship is secondary to the "institutional mutation." [31] A disillusioned portion of the original revolutionaries (and historians who sympathize with them) will understandably reproach the revolutionary elite for "betraying" the revolution by perfecting the apparatus of the state instead of dismantling it. Yet, without this "betrayal," the revolution would degenerate into anarchy or be overthrown by the counterrevolutionaries. As in the case of the Russian Revolution "the withering away of the state" anticipated by the first generation of revolutionaries is postponed indefinitely.

Conceiving revolution as strengthening of the state offers advantages as well as disadvantages to the student. There is little doubt that the state is permanently strengthened by revolution, even if "restorations" of sorts do occur, as in England and France. At the height of the revolutionary civil war more power is concentrated in fewer hands than ever before. In this case as in so many others there can never be a full return to normalcy. Nevertheless, the strong emphasis on the strictly political dimension of revolution, however useful as a corrective to excessively economic or "structuralist" theories, can easily become itself exaggerated. Its exponents seem to share the nineteenth-century liberal mistrust of political power in all forms. This causes them to focus too narrowly on one aspect of a very complex and variable picture. Political realism as a doctrine tends to overestimate considerations of raw power and to minimize the role of ideology in politics. Its key precept, to check word against deed, though it must never be forgotten, must not be converted into a dogma denying all efficacy to ideologies and beliefs. This is especially so in the case of revolution. At the very least ideology can strongly influence the ways in which revolution strengthens the state and the kinds of institutions that emerge from it. Tocqueville saw this more clearly perhaps than some of his modern disciples.

REVOLUTION AS CRISIS OF
POLITICAL MODERNIZATION

Revolution as crisis of political modernization has been most cogently argued by Samuel P. Huntington. In Huntington's view political modernization as distinct from other forms of modernization [32] refers to the political mobilization (or "politicization") of groups previously outside the circle of political participation. Groups and strata which were traditionally ignorant of or apathetic about politics rapidly develop an awareness that political life is their affair and that decisions made by the central political authority affect their lives. They furthermore feel that they can or should be able to somehow influence and participate in these decisions on a more or less regular basis. In short, political modernization involves the democratization of political consciousness, if not of political institutions. Political development on the other hand refers to "the creation of political institutions sufficiently adaptable, complex, autonomous, and coherent to absorb and to order the participation of these new groups and to promote social and economic change. . . ." [33] While the emergence of these groups is due to long-range social and economic factors, the problem of what to do with them is eminently political.

If the existing institutions are resilient enough to bear the strain of the explosion in participation or if incumbent elites are capable of timely and appropriate reform, revolution will not occur. Nor is revolution likely in completely traditional societies immune to social and economic modernization or in modernized societies where institutional changes have kept pace with each new wave of broader participation. The most fertile ground for revolution is found in "societies which have experienced some social and economic development and where the processes of political modernization and political development have lagged behind the processes of social and economic change." [34] Revolution becomes more likely as the gap between the level of political modernization and the level of political development widens. A revolution then is a rapid, drastic, and violent closing of this gap. To accomplish this a revolution "involves the destruction of the old political institutions and patterns of legitimacy . . . , the redefinition of the political community, the acceptance of new political values and new concepts of political legitimacy, the conquest of power by a new, more dynamic political elite, and the creation of new and stronger political institutions." [35]

While such a comprehensive listing touches upon several of the concepts of revolution discussed in this chapter, Huntington subordinates them to his emphasis on political participation. "In theory, every social class which has not been incorporated into the political system is potentially revolutionary." [36] However, a revolution is more than the collapse or overthrow of unresponsive institutions; it includes a second phase dedicated to the "creation and institutionalization of a new political order." [37] It is according to the results of this second phase that we judge the success or failure of a revolution. A successful revolution is one that has created political institutions able to handle the increased load of broadened political participation.

Because they have already created such institutions, Huntington concludes that the Western democratic states and the communist states are relatively immune to revolution. In their different ways the Soviet and the American political systems, for example, have successfully dealt with the problems of political modernization and political development. Thus, modern revolutions will tend to occur in underdeveloped or transitional societies. It is there that the participation crisis is most acute. Two groups in particular play a crucial role in determining the onset of a revolutionary situation: *middle-class groups* in the cities, and the *peasantry* in the countryside. The middle class includes intellectuals, civil servants, army officers, teachers, lawyers, engineers, technicians, entrepreneurs, and managers. For Huntington they are the revolutionary class *par excellence,* although some segments are more revolutionary than others. The intelligentsia is "the most active oppositional group within the middle class; and the students are the most coherent and effective revolutionaries within the intelligentsia." [38]

However, the cities where the middle class is based are urban islands in a rural sea; the vast majority of the people remain peasants. Urban discord then is a necessary but not sufficient condition for revolution. "The role of the city is constant: it is the permanent source of opposition. The role of the countryside is variable: it is either the source of stability or the source of revolution." [39] The cities can be a hotbed of revolt and coup d'etat. They can overthrow governments, but without the linkup to a rural movement no authentic revolution can develop. A tradition-bound peasantry can prove to be a bastion of order to the extent of denouncing or even killing urban-based revolutionaries sent to convert them to the revolutionary cause. Many such attempts fail because the revolutionary agitators do not, sometimes figuratively, sometimes literally, speak the same language as the peasant masses. The situation can change drastically, though, if the countryside has been subjected to some modernization. Then and only then will the participation crisis assume truly revolutionary proportions. Initial and imperfect modernization does two things: (1) it worsens "the objective conditions of peasant work and welfare"; and (2) it undermines the traditional system of village or clan land ownership.[40] Worsening conditions have recurrently been the lot of the peasant for centuries; sometimes he has risen up in revolt, sometimes he has remained quiescent. Revolt, however, is not revolution. What makes the situation potentially revolutionary is the intrusion of modern communications upon the peasant way of life. Through their action, the peasant "comes to realize not only that he is suffering but that something can be done about this suffering." [41]

Even this new form of discontent may not suffice to forge a revolutionary alliance between the peasantry and the urban intelligentsia. The peasants tend towards concreteness and specificity in their goals: bread, land, peace. It is generally when the existing social order fails to provide them that the peasant inclines towards revolutionary solutions. The intelligentsia on the other hand seeks more abstract and philosophical ends: justice, equality, perpetual peace. For these diverse orientations to converge in revolution requires "some additional common cause produced by an additional catalyst"—the former is provided by nationalism and the latter is "usually a foreign enemy." [42] Nationalism is one of the most efficacious means of social mobilization yet developed, and a common external enemy has been the securest bond of alliance in international as well as domestic politics. In cases of clear foreign invasion, as that of Japan in China after 1937, the revolutionaries can profit politically from their providing the most effective resistance to the enemy. In cases in which the incumbent government invites foreign forces into the country to help to forestall or win a revolutionary civil war, the revolutionaries can depict the foreigners as conquerors and the government as quislings.

To place revolution within the context of modernization as Huntington and others have done creates several difficulties. It would seem that revolution by definition is always somewhat "populistic" (i.e., from below, from the "left"). This bias is necessary if we consider that the crucial issue that revolution is called upon to solve is the institutionalization of broader political participation. However, one can question a concept of revolution that rules out the possibility of revolution from the "right." Furthermore, the very concept of participation implied in Huntington's analysis is a rather weak one. Is the closeness of the Soviet citizen to the apparatus of party and state really participation or regimentation? Or is there no distinction between the two? In any case, study of historical revolutions might show that the importance of the desire for political participation varies considerably from one revolution to another and hence that it by no means exhausts the meaning of revolution.

REVOLUTION AS THE QUEST
FOR FREEDOM

One of the more philosophic attempts to elucidate the meaning of revolution has been made by Hannah Arendt in her study *On Revolu-*

tion, in which she argues that revolution in its most authentic form is to be understood as the quest for freedom. But what Arendt means by freedom involves a host of philosophical issues. Arendt adheres to the notion of "positive" as opposed to "negative" freedom. Negative freedom views freedom as an absence of restraints, a kind of open field in which the individual's needs, desires, and proclivities can receive free expression. Positive freedom involves the self-realization of the individual in terms of his moral autonomy or self-direction. Arendt's version of positive freedom envisages freedom as the ability to participate in the making of political decisions. Accordingly, it is bound up with the republican form of government, for only there is the people master of itself. Freedom, however, must be radically distinguished from *liberation.* The latter operates on a different plane and concerns man's almost biological need to rid himself of the weight of poverty and oppression. Freedom then is the ability to do something, while liberation is the attempt to avoid something. Revolt as distinct from revolution is engendered by the desire for liberation from misery or tyranny, but involves no really "positive" principle. This explains the often anarchic and purely destructive aspect of revolt. As an almost visceral reaction determined by biological necessity, revolt cannot of itself lead to emergence of authentic human freedom. While resembling revolt in its first moments, revolution moves to a second phase which attempts to institutionalize human freedom by the constitution of a new political order.

There is thus in revolution the idea of an absolute beginning, of a completely new set of institutions to structure and facilitate political participation. Pure revolution, therefore, is almost exclusively a political affair, as according to Arendt's philosophy the "political realm" is "the only realm where men can be truly free." [43] Most historical revolutions, however, have failed to establish the free institutions which are their chief moral justification. What has caused this shortcoming is the intervention of the "social question" (i.e., the problem of mass poverty and misery). In many revolutions the people's preoccupation with liberation has put an end to the original attempts of the revolutionaries to erect a republic of freedom. In other words the political essence of revolution has been overwhelmed by socioeconomic factors. This development constitutes the "grand tragedy" of, especially, the French and Russian revolutions, for "although the whole record of past revolutions demonstrates beyond doubt that every attempt to solve the social question with political means leads into terror, and that it is terror which sends revolutions to their doom, it can hardly be denied that to avoid this fatal mistake is almost impossible when a revolution breaks out under conditions of mass poverty." [44] The French case is typical. There the masses who desired liberation from misery and oppression went in aid of those whose prime concern was to create free institutions. Once this happened, liberation became the major objective, and the revolutionaries began to ignore "what they had originally considered to be their most important business, the framing of a constitution." [45]

This rude intrusion of the social question, by deflecting the leaders of the French Revolution from their true vocation, necessarily led them down the road which ended in a new tyranny more burdensome than the old. We must not blame the perversity or the corruption of the revolutionary elite; it is simply that the social question ends as it begins in a victory of necessity over freedom. The genuine need of the people and the equally genuine concern for them of men like Robespierre compels those leaders to take measures that curtail the development of freedom. This need was "violent, and, as it were, prepolitical; it seemed that only violence could be strong and swift enough to help them." [46]

The American Revolution, however, broke out in far more propitious circumstances. While social differences existed in colonial America, the killing edge of poverty was absent to a degree that shocked European observers. This allowed the founding fathers to concern themselves with the establishment of free and lasting institutions. Therefore, following the logic of Arendt's conception of revolution, the American Revolution is more truly revolutionary than either the French or the Russian. As the political realm was never engulfed by the social question and the need for liberation, the American Revolution ultimately led to the durable Constitution of 1789 and to a highly successful federal political structure.

Unfortunately, and even ironically, the French rather than the American Revolution has become the model for the revolutionary tradition. In Arendt's words, "The sad truth of the matter is that the French Revolution, which ended in disaster, has made world history, while the American Revolution, so triumphantly successful, has remained an event of little more than local significance." [47] The problem is compounded because later revolutionaries look not so much at what the early revolutionaries were trying to accomplish but at the subsequent events. This perspective has transformed necessity into a virtue, a tragic failure into a recipe for action. Especially for professional revolutionaries, forced-draft attempts to improve the condition of the people have replaced the quest for freedom at the heart of revolution. Neither of these two groups, however, accounts for the outbreak of the revolution: it is the collapse of the old regime which allows them to reach the foreground of events. The professional revolutionary, negligible at the outset, assumes great influence over the subsequent development of the revolution. "And since he spent his apprenticeship in the school of past revolutions, he will invariably exert his influence not in favor of the new and the unexpected, but in favor of some action which remains in accordance with the past." [48] This helps to explain the double misfortune that the French Revolution is paradigmatic not only for revolutionaries but for historians as well.

Despite their ultimate fate modern revolutions have in the course of their development elaborated spontaneous institutions which, had they survived, could have provided a true arena for public freedom. In Paris during the great Revolution as well as in 1848 and 1871, in Moscow and St. Petersburg (Petrograd) in 1905 and 1917, in Hungary in 1956, and in many other revolutionary situations, truly popular organs of self-government have irrupted on to the political scene in the form of sections, councils, or soviets. These jerry-built organizations are the closest thing to pure, grass-roots, participatory democracy in the history of the West. The revolutionary leaders have begun by courting the popular councils and have ended by crushing them. For Arendt the destruction of such councils, in the last analysis, constitutes the real tragedy of revolution: the annihilation of freedom.

The revolutionary situation itself creates a vacuum of power which two radically different forms of political organization vie to fill. One is the councils; the other is the pre-existent revolutionary formation or party. The revolutionary leaders are confronted with a dilemma between "putting their own pre-revolutionary 'power,' that is, the organization of the party apparatus, into the vacated power center of the defunct government, or simply joining the new revolutionary power centers which had sprung up without their help." [49] In nearly every case, especially in France and Russia, the leaders have taken the former alternative. They have chosen to destroy the councils, or what amounts to the same thing, to "governmentalize" them because professional revolutionists can conceive of no other political form than that of the nation-state. Accordingly, they understand revolution as the seizure of the nation-state's central power, which they identify with "the monopoly of the means of violence." [50] In short, the perspective of the revolutionary elite is limited by the horizons of the *state*. This deficiency added to the increasing obsession with the social question condemns revolutions to miss the opportunity of bequeathing truly free institutions to the generations that follow.

Despite a plenitude of insight, Arendt's concept of revolution is narrow and tendentious because it defines revolution in terms of certain moral values (i.e., freedom understood as political participation). The essence of revolution, according to Arendt, would be the origination of a stable, free, republican constitutional order. Revolutions that do not attain this goal are somehow unworthy of the name. The *reductio ad absurdum* of such a point of view becomes evident when the American Revolution, which is essentially a colonial secession, is characterized as more authentically a revolution than the French and the Russian revolutions. While moral values are certainly relevant to the full appreciation of revolution, in conceptualizing what a revolution is we must consider more what is actually being done, not what revolutionaries ought to have done to please this or that scheme of moral values.

REVOLUTION AS ATTEMPT
TO BUILD UTOPIA [51]

Revolution as attempt to build utopia is the animating idea of the French nineteenth-century historian H. A. Taine in his classic work, *The Ancient Regime,* as well as in his volumes on the French Revolution and the Napoleonic Empire. Here we are not so much concerned with the historical accuracy of Taine's work, which has been the target of leftist historians of the revolution for almost a century. It is rather his delineation of a revolutionary utopian mentality readily applicable to other revolutions than the French that interests us. It is Taine the social psychologist rather than Taine the historian we must consider.

In Taine's interpretation the French Revolution was largely the result of a peculiar sort of mental framework that he calls the "revolutionary spirit." First confined to aristocratic circles, the revolutionary spirit spread through the middle strata of French society and on the eve of the revolution had even penetrated the urban and rural masses. While Taine gives great weight to problems of social structure and economic disarray in provoking the revolution, he lays even greater stress on the ideological factor embodied in the revolutionary spirit. The latter, which grew to maturity in the last half of the eighteenth century, is composed of two elements. First are the truly prodigious scientific discoveries and advances registered in a short period of time, with Frenchmen often responsible for them. The spectacle of solutions, real or apparent, to so many of nature's riddles filled the intellectual classes with an unbounded confidence in the future of mankind. Furthermore, these discoveries seemed to cast ridicule upon many aspects of the established religion and the traditional beliefs of the people. The idea took root that only science and reason were worthy foundations for human society. The edge of criticism grew more acute as one approached the revolution.

The second component of the revolutionary spirit is what Taine called the "classic spirit." Although in reality conflicting with the factual and empirical orientation of scientific method, the classic spirit seemed to the educated elite its natural complement. The classic spirit entails a tendency to abstractions: to neglect or to suppress what makes things particular and unique, and to concentrate instead on the general, the universal, and the common. It is an attitude that simplifies to the point of emasculating reality and thus is "powerless to fully portray or to record the infinite and varied details of experience." [52] It speaks of man, not of men; of abstract liberty and natural rights, not of the political and legal systems of specific societies. Its method has been summarized thus by Taine: "to pursue in every research, with the utmost confidence, without either reserve or precaution, the mathematical method; to derive, limit and isolate a few of the simplest generalized notions; and then, setting experience aside, comparing them, combining them, and, from the artificial compound thus obtained, deducing all the consequences they involve by pure reasoning. . . ." [53] If we add the spirit of criticism and confidence supplied by the rapid development of the natural sciences to the simplistic and overly generalized classic spirit, we get the revolutionary and utopian outlook.

It is utopian because it paints a picture of a simple, perfect, scientifically organized community; it is revolutionary, at least by implication, because it is clear that the existing society falls miserably short of the possible one. "Conformably to the ways of the classic spirit, and to the precepts of the prevailing ideology, a political system is constructed after a mathematical model." [54] The height of this utopian approach is found in Rousseau's *The Social Contract*, where abstraction succeeds abstraction for two hundred pages. The conviction spreads that only a society fashioned after Rousseau's model, or one like it, can be truly just. The utopia of the social contract, since it is demonstrated with geometrical precision, is considered applicable to all times and to all places; whereas the cultural background of a people is considered so much rubbish which must be cleared away. The revolutionary implications of the utopia emerge clearly: what poses "any obstacle thereto is inimical to the human race; whether a government, an aristocracy or a clergy, it must be overthrown. Revolt is simply just defense; in withdrawing ourselves from such hands we only recover what has been wrongfully retained and which legitimately belongs to us." [55]

On the surface of the revolutionary spirit are calls to reason, equity, justice, tolerance, and moderation. But beneath the phraseology operates an entirely different set of motivations. The revolutionary spirit being utterly convinced of the absolute truth of its tenets takes on the aspect of a religious faith—but of a "church militant" rather than a contemplative sect. Puritanism in the seventeenth century and Islam in the seventh seem to Taine to have foreshadowed it. "We see the same outburst of faith, hope and enthusiasm; the same spirit of propagandism and of dominion, the same rigidity and intolerance, the same ambition to recast man and to remodel human life according to a preconceived type. The new doctrine is to have its doctors, its dogmas, its popular catechism, its fanatics, its inquisitors and its martyrs." [56] Consequently, not only is an attempted overthrow of the old order inevitable, but if it succeeds, a terroristic phase must also occur. The attempt to realize the utopia dictated by the revolutionary spirit necessarily leads to terror because the utopia is so hopelessly out of touch with reality. Unable to see this simple truth, the revolutionaries are forced to seek the cause of their troubles in the machinations and plots of counterrevolutionaries and other "enemies of the people." Adding to the intensity of the terror is the absorption of the revolutionary spirit by the masses. Reaching them last of all, it nevertheless produces in them its gravest consequences: "installed in narrow brains, incapable of harboring more than one idea, it is to become a cold or furious monomania, maddened in the destruction of a past it curses, and in the establishment of the millennium it pursues. . . ." [57]

Taine clearly thought that the vicissitudes of the French Revolution had by no means extinguished the ardor of the revolutionary utopia. It would smoulder for a time and flare up again as in 1848 and 1871. We could extend his argument and say that the French Revolution inaugurated a tradition which has lasted to the present day. Accordingly, revolutions since that time would be made in the name and the hope of a perfectly contrived society in which the three scourges of mankind—poverty, ignorance, and injustice—would find no place. The faith in utopia would be a kind of surrogate religion responsible for the periodic explosions we call revolutions.

While Taine's analysis reminds us of the influence of ideas and ideologies in political life, his stress on the formation of the revolutionary spirit risks becoming a single-factor explanation of revolution. Revolutions cannot be reduced to the operation of a single factor because they are produced by the convergence of forces involving interest as well as ideal. It is very doubtful whether all of these can be included under the umbrella of utopia building. While it may be true that revolutionists behave *as if* they were under the spell of a preformed utopia, this by itself proves nothing. If we are to avoid the classic fallacy of *post hoc ergo propter hoc* (i.e., of assuming an unwarranted causal connection between an earlier and later event), we must also show the baselessness of alternative explanations.

CONCLUSION

There are several ways in which one can criticize concepts or definitions of revolution, but they all boil down to whether a given concept is too narrow or too broad. The six concepts just sketched are in one way or another too narrow. Narrowness generally emerges when concepts focus one-sidedly on either the *manifest* or the *latent* aspects of the revolutionary process. This dichotomy derives from the distinction between manifest and latent "functions" in sociology, which according to Robert K. Merton, "was devised to preclude the inadvertent confusion . . . between conscious *motivations* for social behavior and its *objective consequences*." [58] Merton furthermore points out that "the motive and the function vary independently and that the failure to register this fact in an established terminology has contributed to the unwitting tendency among sociologists to confuse the subjective categories of motivation with the objective categories of function." [59]

Applied to the conceptual problems of revolution, this sociological distinction shows us that certain definitions lay almost exclusive stress on the objective or latent functions of the revolutionary process—what is actually accomplished by the revolution regardless of the wishes and the beliefs of its protagonists. We find the most extreme case of this in Pareto, who rigidly separates the subjective side of revolution (ideologies or derivations advocating freedom, justice, equality, etc.) from the objective or latent side (circulation of the elite). He speaks of the former in contemptuous tones as tantamount to lies or delusions. The derivations in his social psychology are clearly manifest, while the residues are latent. These latter are far more significant in determining the social equilibrium and its momentary collapse (i.e., revolution) than the former. Marx with his stress on the economic content of revolution, as distinct from its political and ideological forms, also stresses latent at the expense of manifest functions. The French revolutionaries may have thought that they did battle for liberty, equality, and fraternity; but the real result of the revolution was the final victory of the capitalist mode of production. Similar is the view of those who see strengthening of the state as the "real" work of revolution because they tend to discount the role of ideologies and intentions. A more moderate stress on latent consequences is observed in theories that place revolution in the context of modernization and development. Revolution thus becomes an episode, however dramatic, in the process whereby the political realm "catches up" to the social and economic realms in the race towards a modern society. Revolutionary zeal and ideology are needed to speed up the pace of development, especially in the industrial sector.

Stressing the manifest functions of revolution are theories such as Taine's that emphasize conscious attempts to build utopia. The state of mind of the revolutionaries is so crucial in this approach that the entire course of the revolution can almost be deduced from it. In the same category is Arendt's concept of revolution, because of her concern with the explicit goals of the revolutionaries. It is when these are deflected away from the quest for freedom towards solution of the social question that revolutions are wont to run aground.

A narrow concept of revolution, therefore, is one that fails to give a proper balance between the manifest and latent aspects of the revolutionary process. Preoccupation with the manifest side of revolution leads to excessively intellectual explanations, in which the protagonists cease to be men of flesh and blood and become instead the incarnation of philosophical abstractions. On the other hand, the spurious realism of concentrating only on the latent functions (i.e., on the results obtained) usually produces an excessively deterministic scheme which robs revolution of its human and dramatic qualities. While there is no fully satisfying solution to this dilemma, the better concepts of revolution strive to accord some importance both to what men think they do and to what they actually accomplish.

Broad definitions of revolution, on the other hand, sin by being too inclusive. That is, they rather indiscriminately apply the term "revolution" to the various forms of political change and violence discussed in Chapter I. Representative of this approach is the redefinition of revolution attempted by the historian Peter Amann. Wishing to cut the Gordian knot presented by terms such as *coup d'etat, wars of independence, civil wars,* etc., and their relationship to revolution, Amann proposes to define the latter as "a breakdown, momentary or prolonged, of the state's monopoly of power, usually accompanied by a lessening of the habit of obedience." [60] The revolution lasts only so long as the state's monopoly of power is seriously challenged by one or more "power blocs." [61] It ends either with the victory of the incumbent leadership or with that of the insurgent forces. Left out of this definition is all that gives revolution its distinctiveness and its impact upon contemporaries. It lacks the sense of the profundity of the crisis in a society undergoing revolution. Of the stakes of revolution only political power is considered; economic and status stratification seems beneath consideration. There is no inkling of what is to be done with power after the insurrectionaries take it over. Purpose and ideology are accidental to this conception of revolution, which is concerned only with the transfer of power.

But do we really want to dub countless coups, revolts, and secessions with the title of "revolution" just because their relationship to revolution is complex and sometimes imprecise? Classifications always have something stiffly formalistic about them, but they nevertheless remain the precondition for more ambitious programs of explanation and theory formation. Without anatomy there can be no physiology.

Finally, we must note the ideological nature of many concepts of revolution. Many theorists have a syndrome of political values which influences the selection of those aspects of revolution that are incorporated into a basic definition. Marx, for example, made a valuational choice that what is really important in life is the way in which men operate upon and transform material nature. From this ideological perspective the economic side of life appears the most important and the true significance of revolution must also lie in that realm. The next step in the argument is the assumption that since the economic results are the chief effects of revolution, its causes must also be mainly economic. In Pareto's case we find the cynicism of the disillusioned democrat and liberal. The early promise of democracy has not been fulfilled: instead of the cure for all social and political ills, pseudodemocracy has brought along with it corruption, demagogy, and the Leviathan state. Alas, it could have been no different, for history is the province of elites. Revolution accordingly appears as no more than one form of competition between these elites. To classic liberals, we have seen, the main problem of politics is keeping the state within certain prescribed limits. This ideological preoccupation quite visibly informs the concept of revolution of people in the liberal tradition, such as Tocqueville and Jouvenal.

Viewing revolution as a crisis of modernization is less dependent upon ideological preconceptions than the previous three outlooks. But even here the residues of nineteenth-century liberal evolutionism emerge in the background.[62] Arendt's highly personal characterization of revolution also reflects the moral and ideological concerns of a social philosopher. If freedom construed as political participation is the *summum bonum* of social existence, then the drama of revolution derives its pathos from the success or failure of institutionalizing this freedom. For Taine and the conservative tradition, revolutions are evil because they disrupt the orderly process of traditional growth. Only those hopelessly deluded by visionary ideas could run against the basic laws of social development. Thus, revolutions must be the work of ideological mountebanks and their victims, the irrational masses.

Hopefully, our elaboration of the notion of revolution in the next chapter is freer of ideological intonations than some traditional views. Our goal is an understanding of revolution that people of varying ideological standpoints will, albeit grudgingly, accept.

NOTES

[1] Crane Brinton, *The Anatomy of Revolution* (Englewood Cliffs, N.J.: Prentice-Hall, 1952), p. 5.

[2] Carl Leiden and Karl M. Schmitt, *The Politics of Violence: Revolution in the Modern World* (Englewood Cliffs, N.J.: Prentice-Hall, 1968), p. 9.

[3] The following discussion of the Marxist concept of revolution emphasizes theoretical notions more than Marx's studies of actual revolutions, such as those of 1848 or the Paris Commune of 1871. This results in a stiffer, more abstract scheme than would emerge if our main interest were simply to expound Marx. Rather our concern is with those ideas which have influenced Marxist-oriented theorists and historians of revolution.

[4] See Chapter VI, "The Marxist Concept of Ideology," for a discussion of attempts by Friedrich Engels and George Plekhanov to qualify the economic determinism of early Marxism.

[5] Karl Marx and Friedrich Engels, *The German Ideology* (New York: International Publishers, 1960), p. 39.

[6] In Marxist parlance an "epoch" is a period of history characterized by a given mode of production (e.g., slavery, feudalism, capitalism, etc.).

[7] Karl Marx, "Preface to *A Contribution to the Critique of Political Economy*," in *Selected Works*, Vol. I (Moscow: Foreign Languages Publishing House, 1958), p. 363.

[8] Friedrich Engels, "On Authority," in *Selected Works*, Vol. I, p. 639.

[9] Friedrich Engels, "Introduction to Marx's *The Class Struggles in France*," in *Selected Works*, Vol. I, p. 123.

[10] Friedrich Engels, *Socialism: Utopian and Scientific*, in *Selected Works*, Vol. II, p. 120.

[11] Karl Marx, "The Bourgeoisie and the Counter-revolution," in *Selected Works*, Vol. I, pp. 67–68.

[12] Friedrich Engels, *Ludwig Feuerbach and the End of Classical German Philosophy*, in *Selected Works*, Vol. II, p. 394.

[13] Karl Marx and Friedrich Engels, *The Holy Family* (Moscow: Foreign Languages Publishing House, 1956), p. 52.

[14] Perez Zagorin, "Critique of the Trevor-Roper Thesis," in *Social Change and Revolution in England 1540–1640*, ed. Lawrence Stone (London: Longman's, 1965), p. 51.

[15] Vilfredo Pareto, *Manuale di economia politica* (Rome: Edizioni Bizzarri, 1965), p. 84.

[16] *Ibid.*, p. 249.

[17] Vilfredo Pareto, *The Mind and Society: A Treatise on General Sociology*, II (New York: Dover Books, 1963), par. 2191.

[18] Pareto points out, however, that "it is necessary not to confuse violence with force. Violence frequently accompanies weakness. We see individuals and classes who have lost the force to maintain themselves in power always make themselves more odious because of the random violence with which they strike. The strong do not strike, save when it is absolutely necessary, but then nothing stops them. Trajan was strong, not vio-

lent; Caligula was violent, not strong." *I sistemi socialisti* (Turin: U.T.E.T., 1963), pp. 26–27.

[19] Vilfredo Pareto, *Corso di economia politica* (Turin: Paolo Boringhieri, 1961), par. 669.

[20] Pareto, *Manuale,* p. 86.

[21] Pareto, *Treatise,* par. 2179.

[22] Alexis de Tocqueville, *L'ancien régime et la révolution* (Paris: Gallimard, 1967), p. 79.

[23] *Ibid.,* p. 129.

[24] *Ibid.,* p. 131.

[25] *Ibid.,* p. 145.

[26] *Ibid.,* p. 319.

[27] Bertrand de Jouvenal, *On Power* (Boston: Beacon Press, 1962), p. 215.

[28] *Ibid.,* p. 216.

[29] Ellul, *Autopsie,* p. 191.

[30] *Ibid.,* p. 190.

[31] *Ibid.,* p. 188.

[32] Modernization has been defined as "changes in all institutional spheres of a society resulting from man's expanding knowledge of and control over his environment. . . ." Its major "transformative process" includes "secularization; commercialization; industrialization; accelerated social mobility; restratification; increased material standards of living; diffusion of literacy, education, and mass media; national unification; and the expansion of popular involvement and participation. . . ." James S. Coleman, "Modernization: Political Aspects," in *The International Encyclopedia of the Social Sciences,* X, p. 395.

[33] Samuel P. Huntington, *Political Order in Changing Societies* (New Haven: Yale University Press, 1970), p. 266.

[34] *Ibid.,* p. 265.

[35] *Ibid.,* p. 308.

[36] *Ibid.,* p. 276.

[37] *Ibid.,* p. 266.

[38] *Ibid.,* p. 290.

[39] *Ibid.,* p. 292.

[40] *Ibid.,* p. 296.

[41] *Ibid.,* p. 298.

[42] *Ibid.,* p. 304.

[43] Hannah Arendt, *On Revolution* (New York: Viking Press, 1963), p. 110.

[44] *Ibid.,* p. 108.

[45] *Ibid.,* p. 129.

[46] *Ibid.,* p. 86.

[47] *Ibid.,* p. 49.

[48] *Ibid.,* p. 264.

[49] *Ibid.,* p. 260.

[50] *Ibid.,* p. 253.

[51] For the purposes of this study a "utopia" is the notion of a future or possible society whose social organization is so perfected that injustice, social conflict, misery, superstition, criminality, and oppression have been forever eliminated.

[52] H. A. Taine, *The Ancient Regime* (Gloucester, Mass.: Peter Smith, 1962), p. 191.

[53] *Ibid.,* p. 201.

[54] *Ibid.,* p. 233.

[55] *Ibid.,* p. 234–35.

[56] *Ibid.,* p. 204–05.

[57] *Ibid.*, p. 251.

[58] Robert K. Merton, *Social Theory and Social Structure* (New York: The Free Press, 1964), p. 60.

[59] *Ibid.*, p. 61.

[60] Peter Amann, "Revolution: A Redefinition," *Political Science Quarterly,* LXXVII (March, 1962), p. 38.

[61] Amann defines a power bloc as a "group too strong to be suppressed by ordinary police action, which has usurped administrative or judicial power traditionally held by the state." *Ibid.*, p. 42.

[62] See Raymond Aron, *The Industrial Society* (New York: Praeger, 1967), Chap. II.

III

THE MEANING OF REVOLUTION

STRATIFICATION AND SOCIAL CONFLICT

THIS chapter will attempt to defend and elaborate the definition of revolution introduced at the beginning of Chapter I. Although the aim here is more to understand *what* is happening in a revolutionary situation than *why*, there is obviously some overlap between this goal and investigation of the "causes" of revolution, which is the main concern of the next chapter. We already have seen that how the revolutionary phenomenon is defined affects the search for its generating causes. Thus, the present chapter cannot avoid some trespass on the province of later ones. Nevertheless, what follows should not be taken as anything more than an explication of *some* of the ingredients of revolutionary situations. It will assume some processes that themselves require explanation, and will stress in the first sections some conflict situations deriving from social structure that either can occur without revolutionary outcomes or that have played a minor role in particular revolutions. Since the emphasis in the chapter is in the main on social structure, there is a conscious playing down of factors of cultural, ideological, and economic *change* which must be taken into account to get a complete picture of the causal nexus of historic revolutions.

The roots of the stratification theory of revolution that guides this study go back as far as the ancient Greeks and, most especially, Aristotle. In fact, the three great classics of Hellenic political thought— Thucydides' *History of the Peloponnesian War,* Plato's *Republic,* and Aristotle's *Politics*—are vitally concerned with the problem of political disorder and, in varying degrees of optimism, with remedies for it. The term they used to denote this disorder was *stasis.*[1] Alternative translations of *stasis,* such as "revolution" or "sedition," reflect a certain vagueness about precisely which political phenomenon is involved. Aristotle, for example, employs *stasis* to describe three rather distinct political processes: (1) an illegal, violent change in the personnel at the helm of the state—what we could call a simple coup d'etat; (2) a significant, but only partial, change in the state's institutional setup or constitution "to make it more pronounced or more moderate"; [2] and (3) basic change in the form of government itself. Only this third kind of *stasis* approximates the sense of revolution whose explication is the task of this chapter.

There are two possible explanations for this excessively loose notion of *stasis* advanced by one whose ability to make relevant distinctions is legendary. In the first place, Aristotle evinced such suspicion of political change *per se* that any form of it appeared similarly threatening. Though not denying the propriety of certain timely reforms, he suggests that "change is a matter which needs great caution." The improvement a projected reform is supposed to bring must be balanced off against the risk of unsettling men's habits of obedience. Understandably, he concludes that "there are some defects, both in legislation and in government, which had better be left untouched." [3] The various forms of *stasis* differ only in degree, because change itself is disturbing, even explosive. A second reason for Aristotle's confusion might stem from his preoccupation with the relatively puny Greek polis. According to Gaetano Mosca, "the upheavals of small states in which bureaucratic organization does not exist or is utterly embryonic" have only the most superficial resemblance to upheavals such as "modern revolutions," which occur in more expansive political organisms.[4] The *stasis* of the Greek city-states as well as the intestine struggles of the medieval and renaissance Italian communes failed to "contribute materially to the maturation of any true social change." The ruling cliques were changed, but social organization usually emerged unscathed in these contests. Thus, "the great historical factors . . . were developed independent from the bloody conflicts which disturbed Greece and Italy." [5]

While Aristotle's antipathy to radical change and his limited range of experience detract somewhat from his analysis of civil strife, he nevertheless succeeded in formulating the rudiments of a stratification theory of revolution. What he considered the ultimate spring of revolution is seen in two maxims of considerable importance to the social psychology of revolution: (1) "it is a defect of human nature never to be satisfied"; and (2) "there is no limit to wants and most people spend their lives trying to satisfy their wants." [6] The generalization that "human nature" is an inexhaustible source of discontent Aristotle linked to an awareness of the conflict potential of social and political equality and inequality (i.e., of social stratification). Accordingly, he finds that "the cause of sedition [*stasis*] is always to be found in inequality," or in terms of motivation, "it is the passion for equality which is thus at the root of sedition." [7] Following Greek usage, "equality" here connotes either an absolute equality in all political and legal capacities, or a proportional equality which guarantees each his "fair share" according to dessert, in other words unequal distribution. Aristotle sees *stasis* emerging out of a dispute over which notion of equality should prevail in society: "Some take the line that if men are equal in one respect, they may consider themselves equal in all: others take the line that if they are superior in one respect, they may claim superiority all round." [8]

To Aristotle the stakes of revolution are the possession of political power and the fruits thereof: a possible redistribution of wealth, the prestige and perquisites of office, or the capability of taking revenge upon old enemies. However, the protagonists of revolution are social classes (i.e., economic strata). Thus, in revolutionary situations where a change of the constitution is at stake, Aristotle usually finds a confrontation between the rich (oligarchs) and the poor (democrats). In an oligarchic regime the poor majority [9] are perpetually discontented because their free birth does not entail a voice in public affairs. These "second-class citizens" believe that equality should be "cumulative" [10] or across-the-board. Their frustration may lead them to act to overthrow the constitution. However, Aristotle diverges sharply from some modern theories of revolution by maintaining that revolution can also be the work of the upper classes. In a democratic constitution, for example, the oligarchs may desire that inequality become cumulative by adding the lion's share of political power to their riches. They may act to overturn the democratic regime and replace it with one of their own. Thus, what many moderns would call a counterrevolution is for Aristotle merely another type of revolution.

However fruitful these suggestions may be, they suffer as do the Marxist and Paretian concepts of revolution from slurring over some complicating features and distinctions of social stratification. Clarification of these issues alone can lead to a proper assessment of the contribution of Aristotle, Marx, Pareto, and others. In Chapter I we spoke of three types or "dimensions" of social stratification. Since the time of Max Weber the distinction between class, status, and power as forms of social inequality has often been made; but it may be only a slight exaggeration to complain that there is "no major writer who has explicated, formulated and consistently retained the tripartite distinction." [11] One of the reasons for this confusion lies in the very concept of social stratification. The latter should be considered a form of social *differentia-*

tion. Nonstratified or mere differentiation simply acknowledges that people look differently, comport themselves differently, do different things, have different tastes and proclivities, etc. So long as these different aspects of human behavior are not *ranked* as somehow superior or inferior, there is no possibility of stratification. Nor does the existence of groups with different characteristics involve stratification in the strict sense. In terms of mere differentiation all groups coexist upon the same social plane. Regarding the division of labor in a modern factory, the sociologist Ralf Dahrendorf points out that from the functional viewpoint of industrial sociology all participants from management down through unskilled labor perform tasks "equally indispensable for the attainment of the goal in question." [12] If, in reality, these functions do involve distinctions of rank, it is done "as an additional act of evaluation, one that is neither caused nor explained by the division of labor; indeed, the same activities may be evaluated quite differently in different societies." [13] Similarly in pluralistic societies, ethnic or religious groups may be differentiated from each other without developing clear distinctions of rank.

Stratification, therefore, implies that a zero-sum or I-win-you-lose relationship exists between higher and lower social strata. The latter can improve their relative position only so far without impinging upon higher-placed groups. If the powerless gain too much power, the distinction between them and the powerful breaks down. If the standard of living of the poor rises dramatically without a compensating movement for the rich, then the existing class hierarchy is in danger. When large and increasing numbers attain high status positions, the status system itself is called into question. Not every gain by the lower strata, nor every loss by the higher spells the imminent collapse of a stratification system. Rather, there is an ideal limit beyond which flattening out of differences produces a crisis in the system. With characteristic exaggeration Rousseau wrote two centuries ago that "if we see a handful of the powerful and the rich at the height of grandeur and fortune, while the crowd grovels in obscurity and misery, it is because the former only appreciate the things they enjoy in so far as the others are deprived of them, and because they would cease being happy if the people ceased being miserable." [14]

A perennial issue in discussions of stratification concerns not so much the fact of sharp inequalities in human societies, but rather the degree of solidarity and group consciousness found in the various types of social strata. Many writers protest that since the term "stratification" implies the existence of clear and distinct *layers* whose boundary lines are "visible" to all, modern societies with their fluid social classes violate the basic meaning of the terms involved. Social classes, therefore, are rather the logical and statistical constructs of social scientists than "objective" self-conscious organizations.[15] They lack the cohesion that gives rise to formal institutions of self-government and policy formation characteristic of caste or estate societies. In modern societies individuals are strung out almost one-by-one on a continuum that leads without marked transitions from the humble to the great. While it is difficult to deny completely the weight of this argument, it seems more profitable to rest content with a somewhat "looser" understanding of stratification that signifies a modicum of cohesiveness in terms of the common "class situation" of a given group of individuals.[16]

A final difficulty in the way of maintaining the tripartite distinction of class, status, and power in the foreground of analysis is presented by social reality itself. The determinants of these three modes of social inequality simply refuse to remain in separate watertight compartments. Though attempts have been made to fasten upon one of the three as mother to the rest, this goal has remained fruitless because "in the long run each can attract the other two, save in a caste society and in certain rigidly structured societies of orders. Rank attracts power and money. Power is the generator of prestige and fortune. Riches give power and rank. . . ."[17] In terms of ideal types we can conceive of two poles or extremes lying at either end of a continuum: in one society the three "pyramids" of class, status, and power are composed of the same individuals occupying the same relative position at all levels; in another the three pyramids are arranged each in an independent manner so that most individuals are high in one pyramid, middling in another, and low in a third. Needless to say, one would be hard pressed to find perfect examples of either society. More realistically we would expect that some historical societies fall towards the first pole or extreme and others towards the second. In any case, the mental experiment of imagining all the possible gradations between the polar extremes should bring home once for all the complexity and historical diversity of social stratification patterns and all this can mean for the study of social conflict and its most acute form, revolution. Though it might be excessive to claim that because "inequality implies the gain of one group at the expense of others, . . . every system of social stratification . . . bears the seeds of its own suppression"[18] in the face of the longevity of certain social systems, the Aristotelian emphasis on the conflict potential of structured social inequality seems the point of departure towards an understanding of revolution.

Accordingly, the first task is to examine each mode of social stratification in turn and to ascertain which forms of social conflict derive from them and whether these play a role in the revolutionary process. Admittedly such a separate treatment is somewhat artificial, but it is essential in order to show how conflict and cleavage "soften up" a society and make a revolutionary outcome likely. A closer look, then, at classes and class struggle, status groups and status resentment, elites and the struggle for power, and stratification inconsistency will help us considerably.[19]

Classes and Class Struggle

In surveying the Marxist concept of revolution in the last chapter we were confronted with a theory that placed class struggle at the very heart of the phenomenon of revolution. But two weaknesses afflict the Marxist explanation of revolution: (1) Marx's failure to discuss explicitly, systematically, and exhaustively what he means by class; and (2) an underestimate of how far status and power can diverge from economic considerations. To point this out, however, is not to deny all importance to economics and to class in revolutions, nor even to rule out *a priori* that a *specific* revolutionary situation is best understood in these terms. Dogmatism is not necessarily best met by counterdogmatism.

One of the most durable conceptions of class as an economic entity was formulated by Max Weber. Weber considered "class" the appropriate term when three conditions were satisfied: "(1) a number of people have in common a specific causal component of their life chances, in so far as (2) this component is represented exclusively by economic interests in the possession of goods and opportunities for income, and (3) is represented under the conditions of the commodity or labor markets. This is 'class situation.' " [20] Classes in the Weberian sense clearly emerge out of market relationships. Whenever we find a significant development of a market economy, we can expect to encounter at least a sketch of class stratification which may come to challenge the older modes of status and political inequality. Although there is nothing particularly modern about markets, especially in commodities, the growth of market relationships to the point of overshadowing all others has been a characteristic of modern Western society. The ensuing socioeconomic system which we call capitalism has become deeply entrenched and has spread its effects throughout the world. In doing so it has challenged the other modes of stratification, transformed, and sometimes destroyed them. Earlier enclaves of the market economy existed in the midst of various social systems, but before the early modern period in the West they failed to erupt out of their isolation and reshape whole societies in their image. Why this is so does not concern us here.[21] Instead we wish to consider whether and how class struggle developing out of a conflict of economic interests figures in the scheme of revolutions.

For some theorists any overt disharmony of interest between rich and poor, labor and management, owners and nonowners exemplifies the underlying dynamic of the class struggle. Such a comprehensive view, however, virtually empties the concept of any significance in the study of revolution. To avoid just this trivialization, T. H. Marshall has marked out three different levels of "antagonism" found in economic relationships. Competition pits individuals and groups against each other because of identical services offered or similar demands made. But as this symmetry can also lead to eventual merger, it is safe to assume that competition is normally a fairly mild sort of conflict.[22] A second type of antagonism develops from the division of labor and involves "the terms on which cooperation is to take place." As in many wage disputes it constitutes "a secondary product of a unity of interest based on difference." [23] Here the level of antagonism has inherent limits determined by the tacit commitment of both sides to maintain a system apparently congenial to them both. Finally, there is conflict concerning "the system itself upon which the allocation of functions and the distribution of benefits are based. . . ." [24] Understandably, then, class relationships, like most others, manifest both harmony and antagonism; and only when the balance has shifted to the latter side does class struggle in the strict sense emerge. In that case we find that "the common interest shared by the rivals dwindles to vanishing point." [25]

That revolutionary class conflict is rather less than an automatic consequence of mere economic stratification has been recognized by many social theorists. Marx, for example, in his early work *The Poverty of Philosophy*, contrasts the proletariat as a "class *in itself*" and the proletariat as a "class *for itself*." Although objective economic change has bifurcated modern society into two truly important classes, the bourgeoisie and the proletariat, it is only when the individual members of the latter coalesce and develop a common consciousness that they constitute a class in the fullest sense of the term (i.e., a class for itself). This historical transition occurs under the impetus of common interests born through common struggle against a common enemy. More precisely, this involves *politicization* of the proletariat, because "the struggle of class against class is a political struggle." [26] Previously the bourgeoisie itself in the "feudal" epoch traversed the two phases, first through economic differentiation and then through political onslaught against the old regime.

Even with these qualifications there is cause to question the explanatory power of class struggle theories with respect to modern revolutions. In the first place, for such theories to apply, class stratification would quite logically have to be the predominant, if not the exclusive, mode of social stratification in a society on the verge of revolution.

•

However, there is the greatest doubt that such a condition anteceded the English Revolution in the seventeenth century or even the French Revolution of 1789. Ironically, the societies in which capitalism appeared to go furthest in developing class stratification in the nineteenth century, the United States and Great Britain, did not experience revolutions. Economic factors are important in all revolutions, but they are not always neatly translated into terms of class struggle. Where this is feasible, it should be done, as in part it has been for Russia in the first two decades of the twentieth century.

For revolutions before the middle of the nineteenth century, the search for class struggle can lead to grave confusions. The most blatant of these is that of simple anachronism: to read back nineteenth-century categories into seventeenth- and eighteenth-century realities. Surveying the historiography of the French Revolution of 1789, Alfred Cobban, for example, has complained that "the bourgeois of the theory are a class of capitalists, industrial entrepreneurs and financiers of big business; those of the French Revolution were landowners, *rentiers,* and officials. . . ." [27] Even more damaging to the generic class-struggle explanations of revolutions, which hold that "revolutions are always movement of the lower class against the upper class," [28] is the lack of symmetry between the dominant system of stratification, and the split between friends and enemies of the revolution. What emerges from the study of the history of certain revolutions is the multiclass (or multistrata) composition of the revolutionary coalition and even of the counterrevolutionary coalition. This is not to say that the different strata are represented in precisely equal proportions on either side of the divide—far from it. It is rather that the peculiar mix on both sides is too heterogeneous to be written off as individual "exceptions to the rule." These exceptions are often the very stuff of the revolution. A recent study of the English Revolution, for example, concludes that the "fundamental cleavage" in the years before outbreak of hostilities took place "within the dominant class" and between supporters and opponents of the Crown.[29] "Around this widening split, all the various conflicts in the kingdom gradually became polarized. The antagonism was thus not a lateral one between the orders of society; it was vertical, by degrees dividing the peerage, the gentry and the merchant oligarchies of the towns. At last it drew in also the unprivileged and normally inarticulate mass of men." [30]

Even in more recent revolutions, in which classes are more pronounced and class struggle is more easily identified, certain obstacles face class-struggle interpretations. Marx, we saw, maintained that the development of revolutionary class consciousness was only a matter of time—a kind of spontaneous combustion that would bring down the old order and allow the new one to develop according to its own logic. Lenin, however, came two generations later when such expectations seemed unrealistic. In a passage of great significance for both students and practitioners of revolution, he frankly acknowledged the impotence of a wholly spontaneous class struggle: "The history of all countries shows that the working class, exclusively by its own effort, is able to develop only trade union consciousness, that is, the conviction that it is necessary to combine in unions, fight the employers, and strive to compel the government to pass necessary labor legislation, etc." [31] In other words, Lenin doubted that the transition from merely economic class action to political class action would occur in the semiautomatic sense of Marx. Lenin's solution to this problem held that "class political consciousness can be brought to the workers *only from without*, that is, only from outside the economic struggle, from outside the sphere of relations between workers and employers." [32] To perform this task of outside help Lenin envisioned the party as the "vanguard" of the proletariat (i.e., as a highly trained elite corps of professional revolutionaries whose job would include political attack on the government, training the proletariat for revolution, supervision of its political and economic activities, etc.) [33] By agitation and propaganda the vanguard party would provide the leadership necessary to push the proletariat towards class consciousness and revolution.

By so heavily stressing the leadership of elements outside the purportedly revolutionary class Lenin raised the issue of how far the revolutionary movement is really the movement of the proletariat. However, even before Lenin wrote, an alternative interpretation of the problem of the workers and their nonproletarian mentors was voiced by a fascinating Polish anarchist by the name of Waclaw Machajski. Machajski by 1898 had concluded that socialism, for all its talk about the proletariat, was the ideology of the rising middle-class intelligentsia (intellectuals, managers, professional and white-collar workers).[34] It was not the ideology of the manual workers (i.e., the proletariat) themselves. Instead of a truly "classless" society, the ultimate goal of these self-proclaimed saviors of the masses was, in effect, "a hierarchical system under which all industries were owned by the government, the private capitalists having yielded place to office-holders, managers and engineers, whose salaries would be much higher than the wages paid for manual labor. . . ." [35] These ostensibly revolutionary cadres would provide the nucleus for a new ruling class which would absorb "the former capitalists and the self-taught ex-workers." [36] Certainly the experience of the Russian Revolution has vindicated Machajski as much or more than Marx or Lenin.

These and other considerations in later chapters cast serious doubts upon the claims of certain class-struggle theories of revolution. For the present several conclusions seem evident: (1) the term "class" is often misapplied to cases in which the system of stratification is something else; (2) segments of the same class are often found on both sides of the revolutionary barricades; (3) the role and nature of "outside" leadership calls into question not only the "spontaneity," but also the very nature of ostensibly class-based revolutionary movements.

Status Groups and Status Resentment

Stratification according to *status groups* is a second basic mode of social stratification. The generic term "status group" includes the three more familiar varieties of *estate, caste,* and *race.* "Status stratification" refers to a hierarchical arrangement of distinct strata in terms of socially acknowledged rank. The marks of rank include distinctions of prestige, honor, and esteem, as well as sets of legal, customary, or even religious privileges or disabilities. In addition, "status honor is normally expressed by the fact that above all else a specific *style of life* is expected from all those who wish to belong to the circle." [37] Endogamy or marriage within the group, though found in class systems too, is more pronounced among status groups, reaching its extreme perhaps in the caste system, in which most forms of intermarriage or exogamy violate religious taboos.

Status stratification differs from class stratification in several salient respects. In some societies wealthy groups and individuals are prohibited from reaching the higher rungs of the status hierarchy because the differentiating principle is honor rather than mere property. In fact, if wealth has been gained in "ignoble" ways (i.e., through vulgar occupations) it is incompatible with status honor. This can close the doors to the parvenu who wishes entry into a higher status group or conversely can spell temporary or even permanent demotion in rank to one highly placed if he sullies his hands in "unworthy," however remunerative, economic pursuits. As Weber points out, "The status order would be threatened at its very root if mere economic acquisition and naked economic power still bearing the stigma of its extrastatus origin could bestow upon anyone who has won them the same or even greater honor as the vested interests claim for themselves." [38] As suggested above, the exact relationship between status and wealth is sometimes obscured by the possibility of ennoblement, perhaps through the outright purchase of status credentials that benefit either the buyer or his descendants. A different complication stems from the survival or reappearance of certain features of status stratification in essentially class relationships. This apparent anomaly can be explained either by the "cultural lag" hypothesis or by the "functional" theory of social stratification.[39] Of greater interest now is to clear up some of the ambiguities surrounding the three major forms of status group: estates, castes, and races.

Definitions of the term *estate* stress its legal and cultural basis. T. H. Marshall argues that an estate is a social group that has "the same status, in the sense in which that word is used by lawyers. . . ." Status here connotes a "position to which is attached a bundle of rights and duties, privileges and obligations, legal capacities or incapacities, which are publicly recognized and which can be defined and enforced by public authority. . . ."[40] Roland Mousnier shifts the emphasis a bit by considering "orders" or estates as groups which are "hierarchically arranged, not according to the fortune of their members and their capacity to consume, not according to their role in the production of material goods, but according to the esteem, honor, and dignity attached by the society to social functions. . . ."[41] It would seem that these legal-political and cultural aspects are both essential to the status position of an estate. Furthermore, there is implied a base value or set of values according to which the several estates of the realm could be hierarchically ranked. Often this base value originates in military prowess, but scholarship as in traditional China or the capacity to hold public office have sometimes been at the core of status rank. Around this core is elaborated a complex network of privileges, prerogatives, and perquisites of rank. The high estates, for example, may enjoy exemptions from taxes and various services; may monopolize (or nearly so) high offices in church, state, and army; may receive special treatment in courts of law; and may benefit from a myriad of ceremonial and honorific signs and tokens of respect and deference. All of this, of course, may come to grate heavily upon the self-esteem of the lower orders.

Estates may be relatively open to recruits from below or may so punctiliously practice endogamy and exclusiveness that some have remarked a definite caste tendency.[42] Understandably an estate society must take steps to restrict upward mobility somewhat. In many cases the potential newcomer must adopt a style of life—to live "nobly" as in France or like a "gentleman" as in England—and maintain this style for some time before he or his heirs will be accorded full recognition of high rank.

Though *caste* has been considered simply as an extreme form of estate, differences between the two status groups seem more significant than this formulation allows. Likewise there is an unfortunate confusion between the notions of race and caste as types of status group. To avoid this problem it is best to stipulate that outside of the Indian context the term "caste" is misapplied or is used to designate a tendency towards crystallization of the status system. According to one specialist, caste connotes "a small and named group of persons characterized by endogamy, hereditary membership, and a specific style of life which sometimes includes the pursuit by tradition of a particular occupation and is usually associated with a more or less distinct ritual status in a hierarchical system." [43] The caste system is thus the super-complex hierarchy which contains the hundreds of castes (or, more accurately, subcastes). Although certain fundamental status demarcations have remained clear through the centuries, the vast number of castes and the regional variations of the system have introduced some indeterminateness in caste ranking. Accordingly, controversy between two or more castes has erupted over their precise rank order.

What really differentiates the Indian caste system from estate systems are the religious concepts of purity and pollution. In the Hindu religion the doctrines of karma [44] and reincarnation [45] establish a series of levels of purity leading down from the highest castes of Brahmans through the low-caste Sudras to those with no caste at all (i.e., outcastes). This religious foundation enjoins some drastic limitations on social mobility,[46] which mark the caste system off from even rigid estate systems. In an estate society an individual or family can be raised from common to noble status; it is impossible for an individual to rise from a lower to a higher caste. Mobility in traditional India occurs for an entire caste, when other castes, especially the Brahmans as religious guardians of the system, acknowledge their claims to a higher status position. Endogamy is also more rigorous in the caste system, which helps to explain the greater preservation of racial differences which existed at the formative period of the system itself. These and other factors explain also the greater significance of formal organization in the caste as opposed to an estate system. In the latter it is usually only the higher estates which are well organized; as one proceeds down the scale organization tends to disappear. In the caste system, however, even the lower castes have developed local institutions to administer their own affairs. Such differences underscore the contrast between the caste system and the estate societies of the medieval and early modern West. Outside of the Christian idea of the equality of men in the sight of God, two major factors have worked against the development of a true caste system in Europe: first, the acquirability of high status; second, the fact that the clergy as the first estate of the realm and for a long time the preservers of higher culture were celibate and could not perpetuate themselves in the manner of a caste.[47]

Racial stratification has been confused with the caste system for two reasons: racial differences played an undetermined role in the origin of the caste system; societies characterized by racial dominance resemble the caste system through their rigid endogomy, the vast "social distance" between groups, and considerable occupational segregation. Whatever the origins of the caste system, later developments have considerably modified or, as some argue, have totally destroyed its racial basis. Regarding the similarities between racial and caste stratification, closer inspection reveals that the differences outweigh the similarities—all forms of status stratification have common elements. Differences include (1) the religious rationale for inequality may be lacking in a racial situation; (2) reforms can raise the status of the dominated race in ways incompatible with the notion of caste; (3) individuals from a subject race may be treated as peers by the rulers without denying the basic structure of inequality; and (4) caste stratification ramifies into kinship, occupational, economic, territorial differences, whereas the overwhelming criterion of racial status is the much simpler physical difference. Pitirim Sorokin has dramatically pointed out the historical basis for considering racial stratification as a unique type of status inequality by showing that it has "assumed the sharpest, most rigidly organized legal and factual forms, with the 'inferior' race turned into slaves and serfs and with the 'superior' race becoming an autocratic master; with the 'inferior' race dispossessed of practically all political, civil, economic, or other rights. . . ." [48] It is hard to deny his conclusion that "human history is full of such racial stratifications." [49]

The prevalent mode of social conflict involving these three kinds of status group is *status resentment*. [50] Status resentment refers to the feelings of envy, injured pride, and frustrated self-esteem that individuals or groups at one level in the status hierarchy feel towards individuals and groups at another level. Especially contentious are the various signs, perquisites, and privileges of unequal status. Although it might seem that status resentment occurs only in the lower strata looking to their betters, it works as easily in the opposite direction. In the first case we find an inferior estate, caste, or race nursing serious psychological wounds inflicted by the arrogance, arbitrariness, or conspicuous consumption of the high and the mighty. And yet, higher status groups have betrayed a sincere disgust at the "rise" of groups formerly far beneath them. In certain situations there rises a double or mutual status resentment when the upward climb and the pretentiousness of a lower group is resented by a higher one, but is ironically considered "too little, too late," by members of the rising stratum. The vicious-circle effect of this type of antagonism has an obvious potential for raising the intensity of social conflict and for lowering allegiance to existing political and social institutions.

A superficial view would have it that the intensity of status resentment varies directly with the "social distance" between the groups involved. However, the opposite hypothesis that narrow or narrowing status differences are productive of status resentment is probably closer to the truth. Following the first view we would expect the enormous status difference between high Brahmans and untouchables to generate status resentment as a matter of course. Yet it has many times been pointed out that the established caste system has often produced a "situation of mutual expectation and willing, almost happy, yielding of definite privileges and deference." [51] Such situations were common in traditional India because all groups adhered to a religious view of the world that made caste ranking and its implications a virtual divine command. Status resentment more often emerged when two contiguous castes disputed relative primacy, but such animosities rarely called the overall system into question. On the other hand, though there occurred a certain rapprochement in the style of life of the old nobility and the wealthier segments of the Third Estate in late eighteenth-century France, status resentment increased rather than decreased in the years before the revolution.

Contrary to what might be expected, therefore, heightened status mobility can have a destabilizing effect on society. First of all, the higher groups will become fearful concerning their own position. Secondly, the lower orders might find the doors open wider than in the past, but not so wide as they would like. In a typical situation of "relative deprivation," the objective improvement of conditions is outstripped by subjective feelings of malaise and increased status resentment. Thus, a system that comes to virtually auction off titles of nobility will breed contempt not only among the old families but also among the erstwhile beneficiaries of the lowered barriers. What can nobility mean if almost anyone with enough money can purchase it? How good is a society where venality takes the place of true merit? Strangely enough, these questions can be asked by high and low alike. Status resentment therefore can be a potent force of disaffection and discontent, which may assume revolutionary proportions. This justifies our elaborate distinction between various sorts of status groups and of the societies characterized by them. Without due acknowledgment of such factors as racial domination, one gets a distorted, simplistic, class-struggle interpretation of certain modern revolutions. In many ethnically complex societies it is instead the racial basis of stratification that provides the major dynamics of revolution and counterrevolution.[52] In the Rwandese and Zanzibari revolutions in the early 1960's, racial-cultural stratification and status resentment were powerful agents of revolutionary change. In the former case the dominated Hutu majority overthrew the dominant Tutsi aristocracy, while in the latter the African (mainlander and Shirazi islander) majority or its champions ousted the Arab oligarchy from political control. While independent socio-economic forces played some role in either case, neither upheaval can be understood without giving paramount importance to racial considerations.

Although it is difficult to disentangle the economic motivations of class struggle completely from racially based status resentment, traditional preconceptions of classes and revolution can produce serious distortion or wholesale confusion not only in African revolutions, but also in places such as Mexico, Bolivia, and Cuba, where revolutionary conflict has a racial dimension irreducible to socioeconomic factors. The "Indians" in the Mexican and Bolivian revolutions and the blacks in the Cuban Revolution were ostensible beneficiaries of revolutionary assaults on the traditional modes of stratification. Economic and political power were closely correlated with Spanish language and/or light complexion in the Latin American revolutions. Thus, in many Third World countries "status politics are a powerful instrument for mobilization to racial revolutionary struggle, and may overshadow economic grievances." [53]

Elites and the Struggle for Power

Perhaps the most elusive stratification system (especially in modern industrial societies) is the hierarchy of political power. Without denying the historically intimate links between political power and the other two systems (class and status group), the autonomy of the political realm has both logical and empirical substance. It is a variable that complicates things both in revolutionary and quiescent periods. Power, however, in its simplest manifestation is a relationship between two or more actors whether or not a political element is involved. A power relation exists when for any reason A can compel B to do something he otherwise is unlikely to do. Power differs from mere influence in that the influencer may be unaware of the exact effect of his wishes upon the influenced. In addition, influence lacks the quality of inflicting automatic sanctions against the target group or individual for noncompliance.[54] For example, there is little doubt that Adolph Hitler had great power over any randomly selected citizen of the Third Reich. Nevertheless, the masses of the German people and especially certain groups within it were not without a real kind of influence over the Nazi leader insofar as he refrained from such measures as immediate and full-scale mobilization for war because he "anticipated unfavorable reactions" from the populace.

Power also is not to be confused with authority or "legitimated power." Power in the raw is unconcerned with the reasons why B executes the command of A; it merely registers the fact that he does. Authority comes into play when B associates his compliance with a sense of the rectitude of A's command. A's "right" to issue command X (i.e., his authority) can be disputed on both general and specific grounds: first, his right to issue commands at all may be questioned; and second, his right to issue a particular type of command—his "jurisdiction"—may be questioned. Authority in its purest and most extreme form has been analyzed by Hannah Arendt: "The authoritarian relation between the one who commands and the one who obeys rests neither on common reason nor on the power of the one who commands; what they have in common is the hierarchy itself, whose rightness and legitimacy both recognize and where both have their predetermined stable place." [55]

Power, influence, and authority then pervade all social relationships; and in this sense to speak of "family politics," or "church politics," or "academic politics," is more than metaphorical. Nevertheless, *political power* has a special reference to the political system or "polity" of a society.[56] To begin to understand the uniqueness of political power and the polity, we must bear in mind that all known societies have suffered from the relative scarcity of certain valued objects. Food, sexual gratification, luxury items, cattle, and, later, social prestige—these and innumerable other things have been the objects of contention. One (and perhaps the main) function of the political system is to prevent the social order from disintegrating under the stress of unrestricted, violent competition for valued things. This viewpoint is not incompatible with the view of those who through the ages have held that the political regime "functions" to preserve an unequal distribution of scarce values, or when this is institutionalized, to preserve the existing pattern of social stratification. It is the perceived relationship between these two "functions" of the polity which constitutes an important variable in social conflict and revolution.

Whether viewed as an order-maintaining or a privilege-maintaining device, the polity is best understood as determining the "authoritative allocation of values for a society." [57] Politics and political power concern the way decisions or policies are made regarding this allocation—or in simple language "who gets what, when, and how." [58] Although nearly every human grouping or institution reaches decisions on allocating values, the political system becomes involved only at a certain level of generality that differs considerably from society to society. This range of variability should not blind us to the ubiquity of political systems: "the greater the size and complexity of a society, the narrower does the scope of private negotiation become; and conversely, even in the smallest and simplest society someone must intervene in the name of society, with its authority behind him, to decide how differences over valued things are to be resolved." [59] This holds true even if the scope of decision is small and only a few are directly affected. Though what kinds of problems reach the polity is an historical variable, we can rest assured that those which involve the bases of social stratification will eventually come up for decision or "nondecision." [60]

The "classic elitists"—Gaetano Mosca, Vilfredo Pareto, and Roberto Michels—have provided perhaps the best known and most successful theories of political power which stress its relative independence from economic and status considerations.[61] Our goal here is to synthesize the conclusions of these and other theorists with respect to social or political conflict and revolution. The central assumption of the elitists is that democracy in the strict sense of rule by a majority is impossible. There is always a more or less organized minority in charge of making authoritative decisions for the global society. Mosca called this minority the "ruling class" (*classe dirigente*) or the "political class" (*classe politica*) or even the "governing class" (*class governante*). Pareto, as we have seen, first used the term "aristocracy" and then "elite" or "governing elite." Michels is associated with the term "oligarchy" because of his alleged "iron law of oligarchy." All three, however, failed to distinguish the political from other modes of social stratification as clearly as their German contemporary, Max Weber.

Two later writers, Guido Dorso and C. Wright Mills, were more sensitive to these issues. Concerned with the distribution of power in American society, Mills postulated a relatively coherent group at the summit of the power structure, which had the basic and final say on the major national decisions.[62] Interestingly, he declined to label this group the "ruling class" because this term confused different things. Marx has erred, Mills argued, by combining the notions of *ruling*, which has political connotations, and of *class*, which has economic connotations. While Marx's emphasis was economic when he used the expression "ruling class," Mosca, who used the identical expression, was preoccupied with political power. In short, Mosca ran into the same confusion as Marx, but for the opposite reason. Accordingly, Mills himself designated his tripartite interlocking directorate of top military brass, big business leaders, and Washington bureaucrats as "the power elite." Most members of Congress, state and local politicians, and leaders of the less powerful interest groups such as organized labor he relegated to the somewhat murky "middle levels of power." Everyone else, and they constitute the immense majority of Americans, were lumped in the amorphous and virtually powerless stratum of the "mass society." Extrapolating from the American context, we might apply the threefold stratification of Mills—power elite, middle levels of power, and mass society, or perhaps simply masses—to the "power structure" of any society, with the proviso that the relation between this hierarchy and those based on class and status must be uncovered by historical investigation.

Dorso attempted a synthesis of Pareto, Mosca, and Marx. This gave rise to a primary distinction between the *ruling* and the *ruled* classes. The former group makes up "the organized power that has the political, intellectual, and material leadership of society . . . ," [63] though no clear line of demarcation separates it from the ruled majority. Two significant relationships characterize the two groups. First, as with Pareto's "circulation of elites," the ruled class is the spawning ground of those individuals and groups that find their way into the ruling class. Second, an essentially moral relationship justifies the hegemony of the ruling class so long and insofar as it rules (i.e., directs society's vital functions) for the benefit of the entire community. When a ruling class becomes a closed corporation devoted to selfish, narrow interests, revolution or social decay is in the offing. However, it is a division within the ruling class itself that can determine the same results. The *political class* is that segment of the ruling class which has direct charge of governing a country on a day-to-day basis. It constitutes a "kind of directive committee" of the ruling class as a whole. In fact, Dorso speaks of it as the "technical instrument of the ruling class." It is the job of the ruling class to oversee the performance of the political class and to supply it with replacements if needed. More significantly, "when a political class begins to harm the collectivity, it is the proper task of the ruling class to intervene promptly to change the first. If it does not do this or fails in its attempt, it is a sign that the ruling class as a whole has entered into crisis and must be changed." [64]

It is however in terms of a division within the political class that Dorso provides further insight for the student of revolution. The political class is bifurcated into the *governing* political class and the *opposition* political class. The best guarantee of political stability is the smooth "exchange" of these two formations in political office. In modern times political parties are the organizational foci of the two factions of the political class. Parties also reach through the ruling class to the ruled classes, thus giving the latter a sense of participation and channeling up their feelings to the centers of political decision. When the exchange process functions properly in all its variants, we find (1) exchange of roles between government and opposition contingents of the political class; (2) exchange of personnel between the ruling and the political class; and (3) exchange of groups between the ruling and the ruled classes.

Figure 1. Dorso's Scheme of Political Stratification

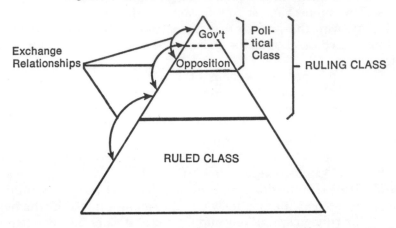

Sometimes, however, the governing political class entrenches itself in power, pursues selfish interests, and takes repressive measures against the opposition political class. It becomes in Dorso's terms a "camarilla." In these circumstances, the opposition political class, disillusioned with the "legal political struggle" [65] which has become a mere sham, appeals to the ruled classes for assistance. It is thus that "revolutionary oppositions are born," [66] especially as the ruling class proves unwilling or unable to resolve the conflict in the interest of the whole community. In this potentially revolutionary situation two possible outcomes emerge if the ruled class still contains elite elements. In the first case, these elements enter the ruling class, revitalize it, reshuffle the various groups involved, and most importantly of all, "eliminate the camarilla which prevents the proper functioning of the political class." [67] Dorso calls this *political revolution. Social revolution* occurs when these same elements remain outside and against the ruling class and call upon the "strength of the ruled class to destroy the mechanism of the political struggle through the destruction of the traditional composition of the ruling class." [68] While Dorso's theory removes certain ambiguities of both the classic elitist and Marxist doctrines, it too underestimates the degree of autonomy of the political class or elite. The "technical instrument" label may be accurate for many historical societies, but not for all.[69] There is a tendency in Dorso to reduce the political process to an emanation of socioeconomic factors.

Therefore, it seems advisable, as Mills suggests, to drop the term "class" when political stratification is concerned. Terms like *political elite, counterelite, middle elite,* and *nonelite* seem most likely to maintain the distinction between the three modes of stratification. This becomes more pressing when we remember that political power is *both* an end and a means in social life. Political power (i.e., control over the polity as maker of authoritative decisions) is useful for partisans of the status quo when existing institutions are being challenged; it is essential to the challengers. Contrived, rapid change of a status or a class system is almost unthinkable without recourse to the coercive and authoritative instrumentalities of the state.[70] However, political power, like other forms of power, is an end in itself. To assert this is not necessarily to subscribe to extreme theories such as Nietzsche's ubiquitous and prepotent "will-to-power." We merely acknowledge that the struggle for power often assumes the aspect of a game played for its own stakes. That no revolution is completely explicable in these terms is the substance of the distinction between simple coup d'etat and revolution, but to exclude them *a priori* would be to impoverish our understanding of the revolutionary phenomenon.

Stratification Inconsistency

Stratification inconsistency occurs when an individual or a group occupies a disparate rank in at least two of the three stratification systems.[71] Accordingly, a "first estate" that was extremely wealthy and dominated the polity (and correctly perceived its situation) could not logically experience stratification inconsistency. It could, of course, harbor a keen sense of status resentment against an upstart group of challengers to its preeminence. On the other hand, an impoverished nobleman, a nouveau riche social climber, a dictator from the wrong side of the tracks, a wealthy member of a subject race, etc., are all theoretically vulnerable to the effects of stratification inconsistency.

To deduce simple behavioral consequences from the fact of "objective" stratification inconsistency would be wrong. In a stable society in which a feudal ethos pervaded all strata, a wealthy commoner might find it utterly undisturbing to kowtow to a nobleman with a fraction of his wealth. His high position on the economic scale would not seem anomalous vis-à-vis his modest status position. In alternate settings, however, widespread and acute stratification inconsistency can produce stress in individuals, groups, and ultimately the global society. Conclusions drawn from American society which find that stratification inconsistency produces "a particular type of marginal man" subject to unique pressures can be readily extended to other societies.[72] Societies most productive of this phenomenon have generally leveled out some traditional social differences, and most forms of social change serve to aggravate it: "Economic prosperity and depression, far-reaching technological and scientific change, political revolutions, and 'social reforms' are factors likely to produce an increase in stratification inconsistency." [73]

Those undergoing stress and strain brought on by stratification inconsistency can be expected to resort to "deviant behavior" (as defined by the society) or to fall prey to extremist appeals, perhaps in the form of a revolutionary ideology. That only a minority of the troubled group adopts a rigid antisystem posture does not deprive stratification inconsistency of considerable explanatory force in the historiography of revolutions. Controversy has been touched off, for example, about the role of the gentry in the English Revolution. According to R. H. Tawney, the gentry, interpreted as a kind of enterprising rural bourgeoisie, had made great gains in the agricultural sector in the decades before the revolution. Their meteoric rise largely at the expense of the old-fashioned, semifeudal aristocracy was attributable to "advanced" economic techniques of estate management, which were essentially capitalistic. In this view the English Revolution turns out to be an attempt both to further economic progress and to resolve the inconsistency between the strong collective economic position of the gentry and their social and political subordination to the titled nobility.[74] Quite different is the thesis propounded by Hugh Trevor-Roper, which focuses on the relationship between one segment of the gentry, the declining or "mere" gentry, and revolutionary politics. The mere gentry was a kind of out-group which failed to benefit from whatever economic expansion did occur, or from the largess and political plums regaled by the Crown. They thus became alienated from many aspects of Stuart society and began to seriously question its moral legitimacy. Some expressed their revulsion through adherence (usually clandestine) to persecuted Roman Catholicism. "Others withdrew less absolutely, into an opposite ideology, the ideology of puritanism, and organized their opposition more hopefully in other country houses." [75] Out of this opposition developed the religious and political beliefs of the radical independents, "whose spectacular actions have given a revolutionary quality to a whole century. . . ." [76]

Who is right (if either party) in this controversy is presently of less interest than the fact that both sides resort to stratification inconsistency to explain the motivation of the leading revolutionary cadres. Whether the key segments of the gentry were rising or declining economically, stratification inconsistency *was* increasing among them and led to first critical, then revolutionary, sentiments and ideologies. The study of other revolutions shows similar trends, though as always we must guard against taking a part of the multifaceted causal nexus as the whole explanation. Without some recognition of the radicalizing potential of serious stratification inconsistency (which in recent times can benefit the radical right as well as the radical left), the well-known phenomenon of "traitors to their class" could only be explained in terms of psychoanalytical categories or personal idiosyncrasies. The study of revolution gives partial confirmation to the hypothesis that "radicals from the upper class are individuals who do not receive the social prestige or recognition which is commensurate with their economic position." [77]

CLEAVAGES, VIOLENCE, AND REVOLUTION

The previous section has isolated some major sources of conflict and cleavage in human society. Each alone theoretically could bring about a revolutionary situation, but it has become a near axiom of mod ern social science that single factor explanations are almost unfailingly simplistic. We would thus expect that a specific revolution would involve more than one of these sources of conflict and cleavage. Nevertheless, even admitting the complexity of horizontal cleavages stemming from the horizontal differences and asymmetries of class, status, and power, we might still end up with an incomplete account of all the variables contributing to the revolutionary situation and outbreak. That revolution is about stratification does not imply that a simple dichotomy between higher and lower strata constitutes the sole or main motive force of revolution. Vertical [78] conflicts and cleavages also can and do play a role in various stages of the revolutionary process. In Chapter I we saw that vertical cleavages between regional, ethnic, or religious groups were productive of mere secession so long as other truly revolutionary elements were lacking. Now we see more clearly what those missing horizontal cleavages are. With this in mind we can conclude that vertical cleavages can readily play the role of the straw that broke the camel's back in hastening the outbreak of revolution. In a troubled society, for example, the rulers might otherwise have succeeded in containing horizontal conflicts below a revolutionary threshold, had not the discontent of vertical groupings—a dissident minority, for example—so sapped the legitimacy and repressive force of the regime. Though they may not desire full-scale revolution, the opposition or secessionism of vertical groups can furnish a healthy push towards such an outcome. Later they may have cause to regret their role, but history is the seat of greater ironies than this.

The importance of vertical cleavages in exacerbating the revolutionary situation is underestimated in theories that link revolution more or less exclusively to the crystallization of rigid social strata (or "classes"). The theory that emphasizes the importance of vertical cleavage maintains conversely that social stability and integration result from strong vertical or "functional" organizations such as the state, army, church, industry, commerce, etc.[79] A highly stratified society then is more prone to revolution than one in which the interdependence and multiclass composition of vertical groups involves a shared pattern of cultural values and peaceful resolution of disputes.[80] While there is little doubt that vertical functional organizations are often favorable to the integration of the global society, their role under other conditions can be quite different. Institutional conflicts between ecclesiastic, military, bureaucratic, and other vertical formations have proven destabilizing and debilitating factors in pre-revolutionary societies. Thus, the theory that holds that "a society marks a tendency to the revolutionary process to the degree that its social stratification is found more strongly integrated horizontally rather than vertically" [81] is not so much wrong as misleading. If taken too literally it leads to the conclusion that on the one hand the caste system is the most vulnerable to revolution of hierarchical systems, and on the other that modern pluralist democracies are virtually immune to it. The first assertion seems clearly false, and the second somewhat less secure than it used to be.

Ideal and Interest

A stratification theory of revolution must furthermore avoid the danger of interpreting the social cleavages associated with inequality solely in terms of conflicts of interest. If one sticks merely to the economic interests of various classes; the status interests of estates, castes, and races; or the power interests of contending elites, he will have purchased "realism" at the price of full understanding. To reduce all moral or ideological statements to rationalizations of these hard interests is to lose sight of an important aspect of the revolutionary process.[82] To see in Cromwell's puritan zeal merely a reflex of the rise or decline of the gentry, or in Robespierre's "incorruptibility" only the vicissitudes of the French middle bourgeoisie, or in Lenin's fanatical leadership the revenge of a bereaved brother is somehow to misread the importance of ideals and idealism in human affairs. There are too many "traitors to their class," too many of the "socially unattached intelligentsia," [83] too many radicals who should be conservatives and conservatives who should be radicals to discount entirely the independent appeal of principles to some men. Revolutionary periods are precisely those which involve the greatest questioning of traditional beliefs about the sanctity of existing institutions. Since, as we have seen, it is wrong to assume that the latent conflict produced by the various modes of social stratification will automatically reach revolutionary proportions, important variables will include "the ways in which an existing cognitive and value system may change, so that conditions perceived as tolerable at one point are perceived as intolerable at another. . . ." [84] Later chapters will have to investigate the sources and influence of what George Pettee has called "ideological cramp," wherein conflicting and contradictory "myths" erode the minimal consensus necessary to keep society a going concern.[85] Here we can only point out that awareness of the complexities of social stratification and conflict helps to explain the force of certain ideologies, not to explain those ideologies away.

Absolute War and Absolute Revolution

Given our contention that revolution differs from other forms of collective violence because the stakes of revolution can involve reconstruction or complete abolition of one or more of the three stratification systems, we can develop a scheme to grasp more vividly the basic differences between historical revolutions. This scheme includes a graphic representation of the different logical possibilities of revolutionary change from the mildest to the highest intensity conceivable. The "quantitative" aspect is intended to be suggestive, perhaps impressionistic, rather than rigorously operational. While all revolutions have common traits, the nature and relationship of the three systems of stratification can produce striking variations in the genesis and development of revolution in distinct historical settings. A revolution in a society where the attributes of class, status, and power are largely fused together will tend to differ substantially from one in a society where the three hierarchies are rather discrete. A revolution in the first case has a greater likelihood to "go all the way" (i.e., to effect more fundamental changes). This follows simply because of the difficulty of isolating the main area of grievance (e.g., status resentment) from political and economic institutions. Where the three hierarchies are more separable, a revolution whose main focus is *one* stratification system might entail only marginal consequences for the other two.[86]

According to the scheme in Figure 2, revolutions could run from those involving moderate change in only one stratification system (score = 1) to a revolution that succeeded in abolishing all three (score = 9). These logical extremes will probably never be encountered in surveying the actual work of historic revolutions, although the likelihood that historians would rank the English Revolution towards the low end of the scale and the Russian or Chinese revolutions towards the upper end is evidence that something meaningful is conveyed by this scale. The 9-score revolution with abolition of all social stratification is, therefore, the upper limiting case of the concept of revolution.

Figure 2. A Scale for Measuring the Intensity of Revolution

	Negligible Change	Moderate Change	Radical Change	Total Abolition
CLASS SYSTEM				
STATUS SYSTEM				
POWER SYSTEM				

Negligible Change = 0   Radical Change = 2
Moderate Change = 1   Total Abolition = 3

For many reasons it is likely to remain a mere logical possibility, which conclusion has striking analogies with the contrast made between "absolute war" and actual wars by the Prussian military theorist, Karl von Clausewitz. In absolute war, Clausewitz maintains, the aim of subjugating the enemy overwhelms all other considerations. But historical wars have generally fallen short of the fanaticism of effort implied by the absolute, because of the "great number of interests, forces, and circumstances in the existence of the state which are affected by the war." [87] The belligerents fall prey to the claims of everyday life, which produces a kind of mutual restraint causing the war to become a "half-hearted affair, without inner cohesion—something quite different from what, according to the conception of it, it should be." [88]

Absolute revolution then, by analogy, would be a tendency to abolish all forms of social stratification at a tempo similar to what Leon Trotsky called "permanent" or "continuous" revolution. No historical revolution has up to now attained the absolute, yet one manifestation of a movement towards it is seen in the various "left oppositions" that emerge during the course of most protracted revolutions. Hyperradical sects such as the Diggers and Fifth Monarchy Men in Cromwell's England, the Conspiracy of the Equals led by Babeuf in the late period of the French Revolution, or various "workers" and anarchistic oppositionists in Lenin's Russia, have caused revolutionary regimes no end of embarrassment. That these fringe elements do not register greater success or that revolutions do not score higher on our scale than they do is attributable to a kind of "law of revolutionary entropy" which deprives revolutions of the energy to accomplish one great leap forward after the other. But our purpose here is merely to conceptualize what historians in particular sense: revolutions differ in some fundamental ways—our scale is meant only as a step in the direction of clarification.

SOME TYPOLOGIES OF REVOLUTION

Typologies of revolution can be formed by selecting one or more traits as the basis of discrimination. An obvious typology with considerable utility would fasten on the purported ideological aims of the revolutionists. Liberal, communist, nationalist, fascist, democratic, even "conservative" revolutions, etc., would be natural claimants for a place in this typology.[89] One drawback in this typology is the notorious lack of consensus on the meanings of the basic terms employed. Were this problem resolved we would still be somewhat in the dark as to the social and political cleavages that resulted in such revolutions.

A somewhat more complex typology set forth by Chalmers Johnson aims to distinguish six "phyla" or types of revolution on the basis of four criteria: (1) targets of revolutionary activity the "stakes" of revolution in our terms; (2) identity of the revolutionists (masses; elites—leading masses)—our "protagonists" of revolution; (3) revolutionary goals or ideology; and (4) spontaneity or calculation in the revolution.[90] The resultant typology unfortunately includes some nonrevolutionary manifestations of collective violence: (1) the jacquerie; (2) millenarianism; (3) anarchistic (nostalgic) rebellion; (4) the Jacobin communist or nation-forming revolution; (5) conspiratorial coup d'etat; and (6) the militarized mass insurrection.

If the distinctions of Chapter I between simple coups, revolts, and true revolutions are well founded, it is clear that only Johnson's types (4) and (6) are authentically revolutionary. The confusion derives mainly from weaknesses in criterion (1) the targets of revolutionary activity, and in criterion (3) revolutionary goals or ideology. As targets of revolution Johnson distinguishes between the *government*, the *regime*, and the *community*. Government is defined as "the political and administrative institutions that make and execute decisions for the community."[91] Regime connotes the fundamental political organization which determines whether a polity is a democracy, dictatorship, monarchy, and the like. (Evidently there is considerable room for change in the first before the second is fundamentally altered.) The community is the underlying sense of mutual commitment which integrates the members of a social system and demarcates them from other such units, as in national identification or in a shared "way of life." By using the term "government" narrowly, this typology is forced to call revolutions those insurrections such as coups and jacqueries which move within the restricted orbit of formal governmental institutions and their personnel. This lowers the stakes of revolution below a meaningful level. Thus it is better to reserve the term "revolution" for those conflicts that modify the regime and/or the community.[92]

The second source of confusion in this typology is a loose concept of ideology that stresses a "summary analysis of goals" based upon "implicit intent" rather than the "formal, explicit doctrine that may be espoused by the revolutionaries. . . ." [93] Such a watering down of the term "ideology" destroys *a priori* the test of a relatively coherent, articulated revolutionary ideology to determine whether a movement is a revolution or some other form of collective violence. With a vague concept of ideology it is easy to fall into the trap of considering jacqueries, anarchist-nostalgic uprisings, and millenarian movements as true revolutions.[94] The whole problem of ideology and revolution deserves a separate and extensive treatment (Chapter VI), which will aid in avoiding trivialization of the term "ideology" so that it becomes indistinguishable from "belief system."

Abortive, Moderate, and Radical Revolutions

A simple though serviceable typology of revolution was developed by Lyford P. Edwards in his *The Natural History of Revolution*.[95] Edwards sets out from the broad premise that once a revolution breaks out three more or less distinct factions emerge: the moderates, the radicals, and the conservatives. The first have a minimal revolutionary program which leaves intact important aspects of the old regime. The radicals wish to go much further, much faster, which makes them infuriated with their supposed partners, the moderates, who seem to drag their feet. The conservatives are counterrevolutionaries wishing to restore or preserve as much of the old order as possible. Now as the moderates find themselves thrust into power at the onset of the revolution, their relationship to the other two factions will determine the ultimate character of the whole process. Often, the moderates beat off the threat from the right and the left, retain power, and keep the revolution on a steady middle course. Thus we have, following Edwards, a *moderate revolution*. Another outcome sees the conservatives, sometimes backed by outside help, overturn the revolutionary coalition, thus killing any hopes for revolution at that time. This gives us an *abortive revolution*, the most frequent type of all. Rarest is the *radical revolution* in which the radicals overthrow the moderates, decimate the conservatives, and institute far-reaching social and political changes—many of which are retained despite subsequently proclaimed "restorations" of the old regime.

The applicability of Edwards' typology seems feasible enough at first glance. Abortive revolutions occurred in Hungary and throughout Germany in 1848, in Hungary in 1919, in Bavaria in 1923, and perhaps most impressively of all, in Spain in the 1930's. Nevertheless, we would wish to distinguish between failures caused by a real counter-revolutionary movement and those in which the ineptitude, inexperience, or quarrels of the would-be revolutionaries led to collapse. Moderate revolutions (scoring from 1 to 3 on our scale) would include the English Revolution, the French Revolution of 1848, and perhaps the Chinese Revolution of 1911. The Great French Revolution, the Bolshevik Revolution, the Red Chinese Revolution, and the Cuban Revolution seem to fall in the category of radical revolutions. The only shortcoming in Edwards' scheme is the obvious need to go beyond the fact that conservatives or moderates or radicals won the day in particular revolutions. Conservative cunning, moderate wavering, and radical ruthlessness may be factors in their own right, but they fail to provide a full explanation of the divergent outcomes of revolutions and themselves require explanation. We want to know if there are particular structural and cultural influences that predispose to failure, to moderation, or to extremism in revolutions. To get answers to these questions we must investigate how horizontal and even vertical cleavage patterns interact with various types and tempos of cultural change in particular situations. Only thus can we be in a position to explain or even to predict why some revolutions go further than others.

Eastern vs. Western Revolutions

Samuel P. Huntington has advanced a twofold typology of "Eastern" and "Western" revolutions, whose geographical labels do not reflect the real basis of distinction.[96] That the Chinese Revolution took place in the Orient and the English, French, and Russian revolutions in the West is less significant than certain dichotomous features they present. Taking seriously the insight that pre-revolutionary social structure and culture deeply influence the course of revolution, Huntington argues (perhaps too neatly) that Western revolutions have broken out in traditionalistic regimes ruled by "absolute" monarchs and dominated socially by landed aristocrats. Financial woes, disaffection of the urban intelligentsia and elites, crisis of self-confidence of traditional ruling groups, and other factors bring about the collapse of the political system of the old regime. Eastern-style revolutions occur in societies in which some modernization, however equivocal, has taken place. The governments of these societies do not disintegrate at the first wave of adversity and must be overthrown in the literal sense. From this basic difference between the two kinds of revolution come forth several major and minor contrasts of high interest.

Perhaps the most significant of these contrasts is the lack of symmetry in the phases of the two revolutionary processes. The paradigm of the Western-style revolution involves three steps: (1) the sudden collapse of the traditional political system; (2) the mobilization of new political groups; and (3) the creation of new political institutions.[97] In the Eastern model the collapse of the old government (and the social order it represents) occurs at the *end* of a protracted struggle in which political mobilization and institution building are roughly simultaneous. In the Western revolution the fall of the old regime creates a vacuum of power, which radicals and moderates fight to fill. If the moderates lose out, the revolution follows the Edwards-Brinton pattern of the rise of the radicals, then the reign of "terror and virtue," and finally the Thermidor or "return to normality." [98] The "main event" of the Western revolution is the fight between moderate and radical revolutionaries. In the Eastern revolution the old government possesses considerable strength when the revolutionary struggle begins, which necessitates a strategic withdrawal of the revolutionaries to rural and remote areas. There they work to build up a power base which can ultimately hope to challenge the conservative forces. At the beginning of revolutionary activity the balance of power is clearly in favor of the legal government. Employing the carrot and the stick (i.e., social reforms and terrorism), the ex-urbanite revolutionaries win both grudging and enthusiastic support from the peasants in the hinterlands. This brings on the phase of "dual power," during which the insurgents control and administer an expanding geographic base while the government retains control in the cities and less remote backwashes. In this more or less lengthy contest of two systems, the revolutionary "state within the state" escalates operations from particular acts of terrorism to guerrilla warfare [99] and in the end to conventional pitched battles with government forces.

This last point is connected to the different place of the cities and the countryside in the two types of revolution. Take-over of the capital city marks the start of the revolutionary struggle for power in the Western revolution, whereas it signifies the final victory in the Eastern revolution. But this contrast is really the consequence of a more profound difference: the capital city and perhaps other urban centers are the epicenters of the Western revolution—the base from which it expands into the countryside to bring the whole country under its sway; the Eastern revolution instead expands and consolidates its rural base before encircling the cities and finally entering them victoriously. Securing London, Paris, and Moscow-Petrograd was utterly essential to the success of the three great Western revolutions. Take-over of Peking and Havana was a more or less ceremonial *coup de grace* in the Chinese and Cuban revolutions.

Similarly out of phase is the place of terror and emigration in the two models of revolution. In the Western model, terror comes relatively late as it coincides with the radicals' victory over the moderates for control of the revolutionary government. In the Eastern model, terror is employed most frequently in the early days when the revolutionaries are still building up the political infrastructure in the hinterlands. When they become the government of the whole country, Eastern revolutionaries can dispense more readily with organized terror, having already accomplished some of its goals in the long years of preparation and struggle. Similarly emigration follows two distinct patterns: in the Western revolution, monarchist or aristocratic conservatives sense the mounting danger from the Western revolutionaries' imminent (or recent) seizure of power and flee across the borders, perhaps to regroup for countermeasures. In the Eastern revolution, emigration occurs only years after the first outbreak of hostilities, when victory of the revolution appears guaranteed.

An extremely helpful contrast, the Eastern-Western typology of revolution risks overdrawing the dichotomy by assuming that the Edwards-Brinton paradigm of the phases of revolution completely "fits" Western revolutions other than the Great French Revolution. Analysis of the Eastern revolution belies the universality of such a paradigm, but begs the more serious issue of the phases of Western revolutions. Postponing to Chapter V full treatment of this problem, we can conclude that it is, first, the rural versus the urban base of revolutionary operations; and, second, the late versus the early collapse of the old regime which lend such cogency to the fully developed contrast between Eastern and Western revolutions.

Social vs. Political Revolutions

In discussing Marx in Chapter II and Dorso in the present one we have run into a frequently made distinction between *social* and *political* revolutions. Marx's main thrust was to question the ground of this distinction, for he considered that an authentic social revolution had to be political as well. Dorso on the other hand defends the distinction by viewing political revolution as entry into the ruling class of new recruits who expel a corrupt and restrictive political class, and social revolution as the wholesale replacement of the ruling class. It immediately becomes evident that any contrast between social and political revolutions must avoid confusing the latter category with coups d'etat that involve a modicum of political change. As with most borderline phenomena there is no completely foolproof way to do this.

One rule, however, is not to overdraw the distinction between social and political revolutions in the first place. Marx's stipulation that social revolutions are *ipso facto* political revolutions helps to clarify the problem from one side. We can furthermore point out that a revolution which is primarily political will have great difficulty in refraining from intervention in the economic and status systems (i.e., in the areas usually termed "social"). This is not difficult to appreciate, for though we have somewhat sharply separated the three systems of stratification, no great knowledge of history is needed to envisage the considerable overlap they present in most societies. For this reason even if the basic goals of the revolutionaries are political, any great change in the polity is likely to reverberate throughout the economic and the status systems. Also, since political power is often a mark and perquisite of status or wealth, a political revolution will most likely have to interfere in "social" affairs to effect the desired political reconstruction. "Moderates," who are called so partly because they see the revolution primarily in political terms, are often drawn into "radical" measures because of the practical difficulties in the way of isolating the political from other sectors of social life.

Given these reservations, the contrast between social and political revolutions can be a useful one. A *political revolution* would be a revolution in which political cleavages, changes, and goals remained paramount throughout the duration of the revolution. A *social revolution* would be one in which cleavages, changes, and goals regarding the class and status systems are most prominent. As more is at stake in a social revolution, it is likely (though not logically necessary) that it will score higher than most political revolutions on our scale of revolutionary intensity. As to the problem of distinguishing between political revolutions and reformist coups d'etat, the former would structure more serious and lasting changes in the polity—especially in the mode of recruitment of the political elite. Secondly, the "spillover" effect of the political revolution on the class and status systems would be more discernible than in the case of a mere coup. Nevertheless the contrast between social and political revolutions should be handled with caution and should not obscure for us the essentially mixed character of "great" revolutions.

REVOLUTION AS AN INTERNATIONAL EVENT

To speak of revolution as an international event conceals two distinct though interrelated issues. The first involves whether or how much great revolutions such as the English, French, Russian, Cuban, and Chinese are mere national events or are parts of a revolutionary wave sweeping over a much broader cultural area. The other issue involves the impact of revolutionary regimes and civil wars upon the existing international system. Each of these issues deserves separate treatment.

Revolution as Transnational Movement

Debate has been vigorous over the transnational or parochial quality of the English and French revolutions. Though no attempt will be made here to resolve all the issues concerned, a survey of some of them will help us to reach some provisional conclusions. A vigorous controversy, for example, has developed over the pan-European character of the uprisings that plagued the West towards the middle of the seventeenth century. Aside from the English Revolution itself, we find the Fronde in France; secessionist movements in the Spanish kingdom (Portugal and Catalonia, 1640); revolts in that same kingdom (Naples and Palermo, 1647); political crisis in Sweden in 1650; and troubles in the Ukraine, Switzerland, and the Netherlands in these same years. Impressed by the chronology of these events, historians have spoken of the "general crisis" of the seventeenth century.

For Hugh Trevor-Roper and others the middle of the seventeenth century was a period of revolutions in Europe. Despite local variations, the common traits of these "revolutions" make them appear almost as a "general revolution." [100] Following the maxim that similar effects have similar causes, Trevor-Roper deemphasizes contagion and imitation in favor of common structural weaknesses to explain the near collapse of so many "absolute" monarchies. The fundamental factor was "a crisis in the relations between society and the state." [101] More specifically, in each of the troubled countries there had developed the overinflated and elaborate structure of the renaissance state, which included "all the offices, metropolitan and local, which formed the bureaucratic machine of government, including offices in the law and the State-Church. . . ." [102] These offices were disbursed not only because of the centralizing proclivities of the renaissance kings, but also because of the government's often desperate need for the revenue produced by sale (venality) of offices. Likewise important was the use of offices as simple patronage and reward.

With the early growth of the renaissance state, "society" could absorb the costs of such luxuriant growth, as it occurred in a period of widespread economic growth. However, by the middle decades of the seventeenth century Europe was in the throes of a depression destined to last most of the century. At some point then, the upkeep of this largely parasitical system outstripped the capacity of the rest of society to foot the bill. It is here that the full acuteness of the general crisis became manifest: European societies, especially at the top in the "political nation," were bifurcated into two factions to which the English labels "Court" and "Country" can be attached. The Court included not only courtiers but all whose livelihood derived in whole or part from offices, monopolies, and other favors. In a clientelistic age, retainers, dependents, and hangers-on were also supported at the largess of office-holding patrons. The Country consisted of those unwilling or unable to benefit from this setup. Often they were provincials righteously indignant at the moral and material wastefulness and corruption it involved.

As the seventeenth century moved into its middle decades, a crescendo of criticism was not placated by sincere though inadequate reforms. The result was a truly "revolutionary situation," according to Trevor-Roper. However, as a revolutionary situation requires a "whole series of political events and political errors" [103] in order to erupt into full revolution, the varying character of political troubles in Europe is explained by the variation in governmental response. The common element in all uprisings was the cleavage between Court and Country, although the radicalism and intensity of the uprisings were first-order variables. The core issues at stake were political and concerned the structure, limits, and uses of political power. In the Trevor-Roper interpretation, economic issues were secondary and religious quarrels (as in England) were reflective of the basic political conflict.

What is most damaging to this "general crisis" thesis is the loose use in it of the term "revolution." Of all the various insurrections only the English was truly revolutionary. The Fronde was, as we termed it, a "complex revolt"—with perhaps a few revolutionary undertones. The Catalan and Portuguese uprisings were part revolts and part regional secessions, while the Neopolitan and Palermitan disturbances were largely the work of the traditional urban mob.[104] Elsewhere in Europe there is grave doubt about anything like an authentic revolutionary situation at this time. The confusions of the general crisis approach thus derive from employing a concept of revolution that is "relatively recent in origin." [105] This leads to an anachronistic attention to "certain problems which accord with our own preoccupations, at the expense of others which have been played down or overlooked." [106] For this reason it seems a mistake to consider the English Revolution merely as one facet of a transnational movement. The continental troubles were too closely associated with the disastrous social and economic consequences of the Thirty Years War from 1618 to 1648. England was not a major protagonist in that conflict, though its restraint was a major bone of contention between the Crown and some of its critics. Even though there were some general features that England shared with other European states, the particular convergence of political, social, economic, and most especially religious issues and conflicts places that country's troubles in a wholly different category.

Equally, if not more, instructive on the transnational character of the great revolutions is the dispute over whether the French Revolution was *sui generis* part of a broader Western or "Atlantic" democratic revolution. According to R. R. Palmer, the French Revolution was part of a much wider process originating about 1760 and binding together the American and French revolutions with movements in the Low Countries, Switzerland, and parts of the Holy Roman Empire, Germany, and Italy.[107] While the direct impact of the French Revolution is not to be ignored in the many flare-ups after 1789, the roots of these often antedated the events in France. In fact, certain upheavals, such as those in Switzerland and Belgium, actually come before the French cataclysm. The common and overall element in all is the contest between what Palmer terms *aristocratic* forces, values, groups, and institutions and *democratic* forces, values, groups, and institutions. Rejecting the common thesis that European conservatism arose as merely the "reaction to the French Revolution," he finds that *both* aristocratic and democratic forces were on the rise after 1760 and that revolutionary politics of the era stemmed from the clash of these two movements. More narrowly, the conflict pivoted around the attempts of what Palmer calls "constituted bodies" (i.e., councils, estates, diets, etc.—generally controlled by the aristocracy) to "defend their corporate liberties and their independence, against either superior authorities on the one hand or against popular pressures on the other." [108] The democratic revolution came upon the scene when excluded elements from below either tried to broaden the representative base of the constituted bodies or, more radically, to cut the Gordian knot with a "wholly new constitution of the state itself." [109]

In this perspective the French Revolution figures as the most dramatic, most violent, most consequential instance of the general age of democratic revolution. It is a kind of first among equals of the numerous revolutionary clashes between supporters of democracy and supporters of aristocracy.

One of the most trenchant criticisms of this view is that of George Rudé. Rudé's doubts come from his conviction of the categorical differences separating the French Revolution from conflicts that preceded it or came in its wake, as well as from his judgment that the so-called native revolutionary movements throughout Western Europe in the 1790's were too weak to succeed or survive without French military and political support. Rudé moreover questions the "democratic" character of the clashes outside of France and prefers the rather different term "liberal." (In some cases "nationalist" seems even more descriptive of events than the other two terms.) At any rate, it is somewhat questionable to call political movements "democratic" when they largely consisted of notables whose political vision generally did not extend as far as the peasants and the lower strata of the cities. In the light of this it is hard to deny Rudé's contention that the French Revolution was "more violent, more radical, more democratic and more protracted" and "posed problems and aroused classes that other European revolutions (and the American, for that matter) left largely untouched." [110]

As to the ostensibly revolutionary or Jacobin movements and regimes that flourished from 1790 to 1814 in Western Europe, Rudé is rightly skeptical about their solidity and their autonomy. Though receptivity to revolutionary ideas varied from place to place, truly indigenous (and rather mild) revolutionary movements were found mainly in Liege, Brussels, and Geneva.[111] Elsewhere, of course, there were "patriot" elements willing to follow the French lead and to cooperate with invading French armies in toppling the old regime and setting up a new one often patterned on the French model. However, even in the most favorable instances "no revolutionary government survived once French military protection had been withdrawn." [112] Of the various factors involved Rudé singles out lack of wide popular involvement and support as the most important weakness explaining this state of affairs. In central and southern Italy, for example, the Jacobin elements most desirous of revolution were mainly "lawyers and intellectuals, merchants and noblemen, cut off from the masses to whom they had little to offer; and, even under French protection, they were constantly exposed to the hostility of the people." [113]

While the contrast between the French Revolution and the struggles before and after it is not so sharply drawn as that between the English Revolution and events on the continent, the burden of evidence in either case seems to favor the essentially idiosyncratic nature of these two revolutions. While students of revolution should not close their eyes to whatever common features unite seemingly disparate events, the violence in England and France was for rather different purposes and was due to rather different causes from those active elsewhere in Europe. If they were in any way "world revolutions" it is that they served as a model and inspiration to the revolutionary tradition. The European regimes surrounding the two revolutionary centers were simply not ripe for revolution in the same way. The greater success of the French vis-à-vis the English in "exporting" their revolution is partly due to the greater force of nascent nationalism throughout Europe in the late eighteenth century.

Concerning the events of 1848 it is difficult to deny their wavelike and transnational character. The epicenter of revolution was Paris in February of 1848, but by the summer much of central and parts of eastern Europe were in the midst of revolutionary turmoil. Unless we postulate the machinations of one and the same conspiratorial grouping, the rapidity and apparent spontaneity of the various uprisings suggests that here similar conditions, similar forces were at work throughout Europe. Furthermore by 1848 we have in Europe (1) modern nationalism as a well-developed and fairly widespread movement; (2) the development of a revolutionary tradition and of cliques of "professional revolutionaries"; and (3) vastly improved communications compared to 1789 and earlier. All of these tended to cut down somewhat the salience of local peculiarities and thus to facilitate the impact of pan-European trends. That so much of the activity of 1848 amounted to little in revolutionary terms is perhaps a further indication that for once similar causes did result in similar effects. To Lewis Namier the common trait explaining both the successes and failures of 1848 was that "1848 was primarily the revolution of the intellectuals—*la révolution des clercs.*" [114] Thus, "the common denominator was ideological, and even literary, and there was a basic unity and cohesion in the intellectual world of the European continent, such as usually asserts itself in the peak periods of its spiritual development." [115] Ironically, it may be that this very universality is the reverse side of the meager results of the risings of that year. No one ranks 1848 as high as 1789 or even 1917 in world-historical importance.

After the Bolshevik Revolution in November of 1917 there were a number of Soviet-style abortive revolutionary drives in Berlin in 1919, Munich in 1923, and Italy in 1919–20. With the exception of Bela Kun's Hungarian Soviet Republic in the spring and summer of 1919, all such attempts seem to have been superficial and futile. World War I certainly had made the chances of radical revolution greater than before the war, but not so great as to be a serious possibility. Though revolutionary socialists were quick to see analogies between what was happening in their countries and what was happening in Russia, these were of the nature of a mirage. Whether it was the dependability of the armed forces, peasant quiescence, worker moderation, lack of a revolutionary tradition, predominance of nationalist feelings over desire for social revolution—conditions in east-central, central, to say nothing of Western Europe, were strikingly different from those in Russia. It would have required a westward sweep of the Red Army analogous to the eastward sweep of the armies of the French Revolution and Napoleon to shore up whatever Soviet dictatorships might have gained a foothold in these countries. For these reasons radical revolutionary activity failed sooner or later in all instances, and the "revolutions" that set up republics out of the debris of the Habsburg and Hohenzollern empires were more moderate and political revolutions than radical or social ones. After World War II the Soviet Army was at the very least a necessary condition for the communist take-overs in Poland, East Germany, Hungary, Romania, Bulgaria, and Czechoslovakia. From 1918 to 1920 the Red Army was embroiled in a civil war on its own soil; after World War II it was not so preoccupied. "The Eastern European revolution then was imposed from outside and from above. It cannot justly be compared with the revolutions of 1688, 1789, and 1917. But because it was imposed it was not less a revolution." [116]

It seems then that revolutions are more responses to indigenous patterns of social conflict than manifestations of a transnational wave. The evidence to the contrary usually proves to be either superficial imitations of the great events of the revolutionary country or thinly veiled attempts to "export" the revolution. In either of these cases the social base of the purported revolutions is too constricted to allow the resultant regimes to stand without outside help. Bela Kun's regime survived as long as it did mainly because it seemed to cater to broad nationalist sentiments, not so much because of its "proletarian" character; when it lost this broad support, it quickly collapsed. [117]

Revolution and the International System

The relationship of revolution to the international system is a two-sided one, involving how revolution impinges upon the international system and how in turn the international system impinges upon revolution. The term "international system" implies that ordinarily there is some sort of structure and process that operates in international politics. The system can be largely informal, depending exclusively on the patterned decisions of the actors in the system for the resulting order, or it can be more formalized, operating through supranational institutions such as the Holy Alliance. The difference though is one of degree. Recent theorists have distinguished several general types of international system, each with its peculiar rules and structure (e.g., the traditional balance of power system, various bipolar systems in which two superpowers compete, the multipolar system, and others). [118] Whatever stability these systems betray is due to the judgment of the major members that they have more to gain than to lose by following the rules of the system in force. Thus, the interest of the chief beneficiaries of the international status quo, in short, the status quo powers, is what imparts a measure of solidity to the reigning system. However, any international system is threatened from within by states which hope to gain by overturning it, and from without by states which do not share its blessings or oppose it according to principle. Especially threatening to any system, but especially to the balance of power system, are rigid ideological differences.

A good example of how revolution affects the international system and is affected by it is the impact of the French Revolution on the classic balance of power system that operated in Europe roughly from the Treaty of Westphalia in 1648 to the revolution, with pronounced effectiveness after the demise of Louis XIV in 1714. In this period religious allegiances declined perceptibly as a source of international discord and the ideological conflicts of later times had not fully emerged. The balance of power system of that era has even become a kind of ideal for both statesmen and scholars, and various of the former have tried to resuscitate it at different points in the last two centuries. Most treatments of the classic balance of power include the following traits: (1) low ideological motivation because of similarity of political and social systems in the member states; (2) limited and specific stakes of conflict: colonies, territory, dynastic settlement, commercial advantages, etc.; (3) no preponderant state but perhaps a "holder" of the balance which throws its weight to either side if some state threatens to upset the system; and (4) periodic readjustments of the system, perhaps through limited war for limited stakes. The strength of this system depends on the minimum benefits that leading actors derive from it as well as on a diffuse conviction that this system is "natural" and hence legitimate.

The epoch of the French Revolution and Napoleon (1789–1814) did irreparable damage to the classic balance of power system. Why and how this was accomplished and whether it was inevitable are thorny historical questions. According to one view, the French Revolution at its outset did not automatically pose a lethal threat to the balance of power system championed by status quo powers such as Austria, Prussia, Russia, and Great Britain.[119] The confrontation between the conservative coalition and the revolutionary regime was exacerbated by a series of misperceptions and miscalculations on both sides. The coalition thought that a show of strength punctuated by sabre-rattling would cow the upstart revolutionary government; the revolutionaries in turn probably overestimated the seriousness of the measures that the coalition was initially able to take against them. The conservative statesmen were furthermore precluded by their very nature as conservatives from appreciating the true significance of the revolution for international affairs. Hence they were prevented either from curbing the revolutionary regime forthwith by an interventionist crusade, or from using the lull before 1792 to come to terms. The conservatives thought that they could cope with the new regime by following the rules derived from the classical balance of power system described above. They considered this system the natural, normal way of international politics. In short, the myopia of the conservative powers was caused by ideological beliefs about the way states are supposed to behave in international politics. Similarly, the revolutionaries allowed their ideological proclivities to depict international politics as a Manichaean conflict between total good and total evil.

Even so, ideological factors alone do not provide a full explanation of why France was at war with much of Europe for a good part of twenty-five years. The actual train of events must also be brought into the picture: "As the war itself was a product of a revolutionary situation in France, the latter was to be influenced in turn by its own product. The war was revolutionized as a result of what is called the 'Second Revolution' in France, an event which was in itself a product of the war. A vicious cycle of war and revolution could not have a more telling illustration than in the case of the French Revolution." [120] As the ideological intensity of the revolution was stepped up, France's foreign policy objectives were correspondingly altered until they were totally incompatible with the survival of the traditional balance of power system.

Ideology furthermore contributed to the destruction of the balance by "sharply increasing the probability of distortion in perception," [121] and by enjoining the mass mobilization of the French people—the nation-in-arms—to counter the threat of foreign invasion. Thus the revolution stimulated the forces of modern nationalism: first in France itself, then in areas sympathetic to it, and finally in areas restive against French hegemony itself. As time went on the conservative powers had to imitate certain of the innovations brought about in revolutionary France for the sake of self-preservation. This development by itself would have ruled out any attempts to restore the classic balance without any changes: "the limited warfare of the eighteenth century was destroyed by a new militarism; the limited diplomacy of the old regime was replaced with a diplomacy of interventionism. While the benign balance of power mechanism of the previous century had not sanctioned crusading intervention, the new system assumed that states could not be protected without it." [122]

Looking at the French and other revolutions, some provisional conclusions about revolution and international systems can be drawn. There is little doubt, for example, that the ideological asymmetry between the revolutionary regime and the status quo powers is a profound source of destabilization. This is especially true when the revolutionary ideology is so universalistic and extreme as to repudiate the existing international system root and branch. Revolutions thus tend to constitute potential threats to the international system especially during radical periods. However, ideology must be measured against objective geopolitical and military considerations to assess the real extent of the revolutionary challenge. Revolutionary France could disturb the international system far more seriously than Leninist Russia because French national power was far stronger in relation to the status quo powers of the 1790's than was Soviet power in relation to those of the 1920's. Had Trotsky won out over Stalin in the power struggle after Lenin's death, we might have seen direct confirmation of this. Although Cromwellian England was extremely formidable in military terms and some preached the necessity of an anti-Catholic crusade, the relative moderation of both Cromwell and the English Revolution itself overcame adventurist temptations to spread the revolution by force of arms. The wars fought by the Commonwealth against the Dutch and the Spanish were fought for unrevolutionary reasons and could have thus been fought as easily by the Stuarts.

Thus we must consider both the ideological distance between the revolutionary regime and the status quo powers, and the power and geopolitical relations involved. Since these things vary considerably, as do decision makers' perceptions of them, no blanket generalization can cover all possibilities. Sometimes it is imperative from the standpoint of the status quo powers to intervene quickly and decisively to nip the revolutionary menace in the bud; sometimes mere containment in the hopes of an ultimate normalization of relations is the least costly policy. The suggestion that the status quo powers automatically open their arms to the revolutionary regime ignores what makes each of the parties what they are: while it takes at least two parties to conflict, it also takes two to compose differences. Nor is the Gordian knot sundered by claiming that *all* states pursue their national interests, sometimes using revolutionary rhetoric as a cover-up for power politics "as usual." While geopolitical realities and traditional goals of foreign policy provide even revolutionary regimes with a basic frame of reference to be forgotten at the peril of the revolution itself, the interpretation of the national interest can vary considerably and is strongly subject to ideological influences. While the ideological stance of revolutionary regimes may tend to moderate over time, such eventual mellowing does not necessarily mean that a new revolutionary regime can be dealt with according to the rules of traditional diplomacy. Thus, the status quo powers have cause to fear both contagion of the revolution and a direct challenge to what they take to be the rules of the game of international politics.

CONCLUSION

This chapter has elaborated upon the concept of revolution presented in Chapter I and has explored some of the consequences of looking at revolution from the tripartite standpoint of social stratification. Though revolution is always "about" alteration of one or more of the stratification systems and though forms of social conflict deriving from those systems are important in causing revolutions, we have tried to avoid making revolution a simple resultant of structural stresses and strains. What has emerged is the striking diversity of historical revolutions. One major consequence of this finding is the inadequacy of theories that focus on one form of cleavage such as class struggle or pure struggles for power to embrace all the manifold antagonisms that underlie revolution. The complex and variable patterns of social stratification suggest that we should consider problems of status resentment and stratification inconsistency also as predisposing groups and individuals to question the legitimacy of the existing order and to look for alternatives. In the next chapter the stress will fall less on the formalistic analysis of social structure and more on the various sorts of social change that exacerbate and bring to light the latent cleavages that seem endemic to human societies.

To capture and conceptualize somewhat this sense of the diversity of historical revolutions we have developed a scale for measuring the intensity of revolution (Fig. 2). This implies not only that revolutions differ in intensity along a scale of 1 to 9, but also that two revolutions that "score" the same may earn that score rather differently. For example, revolution A and revolution B may both have a composite score of 4, but revolution A "earned" its score by summing up 1 in the class system, 2 in the status system, and 1 in the political system; while revolution B got its 4 by summing up 2 in the class system, 1 in the status system, and 1 in the political system. While such rankings ought not to be pushed too far, they at least clarify the different nuances and permutations that are the very groundwork for the comparative study of revolutions.

Alternative ways of pointing out differences between revolutions are suggested by the variety of typologies of revolution surveyed in the middle of this chapter. The most promising of all is Huntington's simple dichotomy between Eastern and Western revolutions, because it calls into question some of the conventional wisdom about the stages of revolution. Most troublesome of all, despite the efforts of Marx and Dorso, is the contrast between social and political revolutions, though the difficulty is empirical more than conceptual. Useful, though by now somewhat ordinary, is Edwards' threefold discrimination between abortive, moderate, and radical revolutions. Also useful are typologies based upon the professed ideology of the leading revolutionary groups (or perhaps upon the significance of their actions as understood from a later ideological standpoint), though such typologies run the risk of distortion and anachronism.

Finally, the diversity of revolutions has implications for considering revolution as an international event. In the first place, we have found that most of the great revolutions are more indigenous growths than parts of widespread revolutionary waves or movements. Though it is futile to deny the almost universal character of those causes we will term *long-term causes of revolution* and whose conglomeration approaches what is often called "modernization," it is when we look to the *middle-term causes of revolution* that conditions in England, France, Russia, and Spain begin to differ more and more from many of their neighbors. Similarly, the threat posed by a victorious revolution or even a growing revolutionary movement to the international system varies according to the intensity of the revolution, its ideology, and its geopolitical setting. Here the differences between revolutions are enormous.

NOTES

[1] This is the inspiration for Jean Baechler's suggestion for a separate subdiscipline to study collective political violence, especially revolution—to be called *stasiology*. *Les Phénomènes Révolutionnaires* (Paris: Presses Universitaires de France, 1970), p. 6.

[2] Aristotle, *The Politics*, Barker trans. (New York: Oxford University Press, 1950), sec. 1301b.

[3] *Ibid.*, sec. 1269a.

[4] Gaetano Mosca, *Elementi di scienza politica*, Vol. I (Bari: Laterza, 1953), p. 292.

[5] *Ibid.*, p. 295.

[6] Aristotle, *The Politics*, Sinclair trans. (Baltimore: Penguin Books, 1962), p. 76.

[7] Aristotle, *The Politics*, Barker trans., sec. 1301b.

[8] *Ibid.*

[9] To Aristotle the distinguishing characteristic of a regime is the spirit that animates it: oligarchy by wealth, democracy by poverty, etc. Numbers are less essential, so that in theory a regime in which the majority of citizens were wealthy would be an oligarchy and one dominated by a poor minority would be a democracy. However, Aristotle admitted that these logical possibilities were exceedingly rare in the real world.

[10] See Robert Dahl, *Who Governs?* (New Haven: Yale University Press, 1964), pp. 85–86.

[11] W. G. Runciman, *Relative Deprivation and Social Justice* (Berkeley: University of California Press, 1966), p. 37.

[12] Ralf Dahrendorf, *Essays in the Theory of Society* (Stanford: Stanford University Press, 1968), p. 162.

[13] *Ibid.*, pp. 162–63.

[14] Jean-Jacques Rousseau, *Discours sur l'origine de l'inégalité parmi les hommes*, in *Du Contrat Social* (Paris: Garnier, 1962), p. 89.

[15] See Oliver C. Cox, *Caste, Class and Race* (New York: Modern Reader Paperbacks, 1970), p. 306.

[16] See below, "Classes and Class Struggle."

[17] Roland Mousnier, "Introduction: Problèmes de Stratification Sociale," in *Deux Cahiers de la Noblesse (1649–1651)*, ed. R. Mousnier *et al.* (Paris: Presses Universitaires de France, 1965), p. 47.

[18] Dahrendorf, *Essays*, p. 177.

[19] The basic argument of the rest of this chapter roughly follows the suggestion of Lewis A. Coser that "the sources and incidence of conflicting behavior in each particular system vary according to the type of structure, the patterns of social mobility, of ascribing and achieving status and of allocating scarce power and wealth, as well as the degree to which a specific form of distribution of power, resources, and status is accepted by the component actors within the different subsystems." *Continuities in the Study of Social Conflict* (New York: The Free Press, 1967), p. 26.

[20] Max Weber, *Economy and Society*, Vol. II (New York: Bedminster Press, 1969), p. 927.

[21] See Max Weber, *The Protestant Ethic and the Spirit of Capitalism* (New York: Charles Scribner's Sons, 1958); R. H. Tawney, *Religion and the Rise of Capitalism* (New York: Mentor Books, 1954); and Robert K. Merton, *Science, Technology and Society in Seventeenth-Century England* (New York: Harper Torchbooks, 1970).

[22] T. H. Marshall, *Class, Citizenship and Social Development* (Garden City, N.Y.: Doubleday, 1964), p. 165.

[23] *Ibid.*

[24] *Ibid.*, pp. 165–66.

[25] *Ibid.*, p. 167.

[26] Karl Marx, *The Poverty of Philosophy* (Moscow: Foreign Languages Publishing House, n.d.), p. 166.

[27] Alfred Cobban, *The Social Interpretation of the French Revolution* (Cambridge: Cambridge University Press, 1968), pp. 172–73.

[28] Alfred Meusal, "Revolution and Counter-revolution," in *The Encyclopedia of the Social Sciences*, XIII, p. 371.

[29] Perez Zagorin, *The Court and the Country* (New York: Atheneum, 1970), p. 32.

[30] *Ibid.*

[31] V. I. Lenin, *What is to be Done?*, in *On Politics and Revolution*, ed. J. E. Connor (New York: Pegasus Books, 1968), p. 40. Also significant are the two sentences which follow: "The theory of socialism, however, grew out of the philosophic, historical and economic theories elaborated by educated representatives of the propertied classes, by intellectuals. By their social status the founders of modern scientific socialism, Marx and Engels, themselves belonged to the bourgeois intelligentsia."

[32] *Ibid.*, p. 53.

[33] *Ibid.*

[34] It seems that little of Machajski's work is available in English. This account is based on Max Nomad, *Aspects of Revolt* (New York: Bookmen Associates, 1959), Chap. 5.

[35] *Ibid.*, p. 100.

[36] *Ibid.*

[37] Weber, *Economy and Society*, Vol. II, p. 932.

[38] *Ibid.*, p. 936.

[39] On the problem of "cultural lag," see Chapter IV, "Monistic vs. Multiple Causation." According to the functional theory of social stratification, "every society, no matter how simple or complex, must differentiate persons in terms of prestige and esteem, and must therefore possess a certain amount of institutionalized inequality." Kingsley Davis

and Wilbert E. Moore, "Some Principles of Social Stratification," in *Class, Status, and Power,* ed. R. Bendix and S. M. Lipset (New York: The Free Press, 1966) p. 48.

[40] Marshall, *Class, Citizenship,* p. 176.

[41] Mousnier, "Introduction," p. 15.

[42] *Ibid.,* p. 17.

[43] André Beteille, *Caste, Class, and Power* (Berkeley: University of California Press, 1971), p. 46.

[44] "The doctrine of karma maintains that every action of an individual has a moral significance; that all bad behavior is laid to his account; that after death his behavior account is balanced and judgment pronounced." Cox, *Caste, Class, and Race,* p. 40.

[45] The notion of reincarnation or "metempsychosis" completes the doctrine of karma by stressing that the "individual reaps his reward either in spiritual well-being or ill-being, in favorable or unfavorable rebirth. . . . The highest spiritual achievement of man is that of reaching the abode of the gods, thus ending the cycle of rebirths. . . ." *Ibid.*

[46] This follows Pitirim Sorokin, *Society, Culture, and Personality* (New York: Harper & Row, 1947).

[47] Cox, *Caste, Class, and Race,* p. 141.

[48] Sorokin, *Society, Culture, and Personality,* p. 279.

[49] *Ibid.*

[50] Status resentment is to be clearly distinguished from "stratification inconsistency" discussed below.

[51] Cox, *Caste, Class and Race,* p. 15.

[52] Status resentment seems to be most socially explosive in a status system based on race. A recent study of two racial revolutions concludes that "racial divisions are the propelling force in the revolutions, the predisposing factors are those that affect racial status in any of its many social dimensions, and the dialectic of conflict is essentially racial." Leo Kuper, "Theories of Revolution and Race," *Comparative Studies in Society and History,* XII (January, 1971), pp. 105–06. See Rene Lemarchand, "Revolutionary Phenomena in Stratified Societies," in *Revolution and Political Change,* ed. C. E. Welch and M. B. Taintor (No. Scituate, Mass.: Duxbury Press, 1972), pp. 282–99; Michael F. Lofche, *Zanzibar: Background to Revolution* (Princeton: Princeton University Press, 1965); and Cynthia Enloe, *Ethnic Conflict and Political Development* (Boston: Little, Brown, 1973), Chap. IX.

[53] Leo Kuper, "Race, Class, and Power: Some Comments on Revolutionary Change," *Comparative Studies in Society and History,* XIV (September, 1972), p. 418.

[54] "Power is a special case of the exercise of influence: it is the process of affecting the policies of others with the help of (actual or threatened) severe deprivations for nonconformity with the policies intended." Harold D. Lasswell and Abraham Kaplan, *Power and Society* (New Haven: Yale University Press, 1963), p. 76.

[55] Hannah Arendt, *Between Past and Future* (New York: Meridian Books, 1961), p. 93.

[56] As we shall see in Chapter IV there are difficulties in applying the term "state" to all political systems. For example, when social scientists sometimes use the term "stateless societies," they do not mean that there is no political system whatsoever, no system of power and authority relations at all.

[57] David Easton, *The Political System* (New York: Alfred A. Knopf, 1963), p. 93.

[58] Harold D. Lasswell, *Politics: Who Gets What, When, How* (New York: Meridian Books, 1965).

[59] Easton, *The Political System,* p. 136.

[60] See Peter Bachrach and Morton S. Baratz, "Decisions and Nondecisions: An An-

alytical Framework," in *Political Power: A Reader in Theory and Research,* ed. R. Bell, D. V. Edwards, and R. H. Wagner (New York: The Free Press, 1969), pp. 100–09.

[61] For an overview, see Geraint Parry, *Political Elites* (New York: Praeger, 1969).

[62] C. Wright Mills, *The Power Elite* (New York: Oxford Univ. Press, 1956).

[63] Guido Dorso, *Dittatura, classe politica, classe dirigente* (Turin: Einaudi, 1955), p. 127.

[64] *Ibid.,* p. 135.

[65] *Ibid.,* p. 166.

[66] *Ibid.*

[67] *Ibid.,* p. 167.

[68] *Ibid.*

[69] However, it does seem applicable to the English Revolution, as we shall see in several contexts below.

[70] See Chapter IV, "Long-Term Causes of Revolution" (below), for a discussion of Max Weber's concept of the state.

[71] This point derives from Robert H. Bohlke, "Social Mobility, Stratification Inconsistency, and Middle-Class Delinquency," in *Middle-Class Juvenile Delinquency,* ed. E. W. Vaz (New York: Harper & Row, 1967), pp. 224, 277.

[72] Gerhard E. Lenski, "Status Crystallization: A Non-Vertical Dimension of Social Status," *The American Sociological Review,* XIX (August, 1954), p. 412.

[73] Robert H. Bohlke, "Social Differentiation and Social Stratification" (unpublished paper: American International College, n.d.), p. 27.

[74] R. H. Tawney, "The Rise of the Gentry 1558–1640," in *Essays in Economic History,* Vol. I., ed. E. M. Carus-Wilson (London: Edward Arnold, 1963).

[75] Hugh Trevor-Roper, *The Gentry 1540–1640* (Cambridge: Cambridge University Press, n.d.), p. 31.

[76] *Ibid.,* p. 34.

[77] Seymour M. Lipset and Reinhard Bendix, "Social Status and Social Structure: A Re-examination of Data and Interpretations: II," *The British Journal of Sociology,* II (June, 1951), p. 243.

[78] Vertical differentiation in terms of religious or ethnic communities can cut through the horizontal planes of class, status, and power stratification.

[79] Henri Janne, "Un modèle théorique du phénomène révolutionnaire?" *Annales: economies, societes, civilizations,* XV (November–December, 1960), p. 1147.

[80] *Ibid.,* p. 1144.

[81] *Ibid.,* p. 1149.

[82] See Chapter VI.

[83] See Chapter IV, "Middle-Term Causes of Revolution."

[84] Harry Eckstein, "On the Etiology of Internal Wars," in *Why Revolution?,* ed. C. T. Paynton and R. Blackey (Cambridge, Mass.: Schenkman, 1971), p. 136.

[85] George Pettee, *The Process of Revolution* (New York: Harper & Row, 1938), pp. 41–48.

[86] We must stipulate, however, that even the mildest revolution dominated by one sort of cleavage will have reverberations, even if faint, on all three stratification systems.

[87] Karl von Clausewitz, *War, Politics, and Power* (Chicago: Henry Regnery Co., 1962), p. 201.

[88] *Ibid.*

[89] Baechler, *Les Phénomènes Révolutionnaires,* pp. 131–43.

[90] Chalmers Johnson, *Revolution and the Social System* (Stanford: Hoover Institute, 1964), pp. 27–28.

[91] *Ibid.,* p. 29.

[92] This problem was resolved by Johnson in his *Revolutionary Change* (Boston: Little, Brown, 1966); see p. 140.

[93] Johnson, *Revolution and the Social System*, p. 29.

[94] See Johnson, *Revolutionary Change*, Chap. 7.

[95] Lyford P. Edwards, *The Natural History of Revolution* (Chicago: University of Chicago Press, 1970), Chap. VII.

[96] Samuel P. Huntington, *Political Order in Changing Societies* (New Haven: Yale University Press, 1970), Chap. 5.

[97] See Chapter II, "Revolution as Crisis of Political Modernization."

[98] See Chapter V concerning the phases of revolution.

[99] The guerrilla warfare so important in the strategy and ideology of Eastern revolution is, somewhat ironically, more associated with counterrevolutionary elements in the three great Western revolutions.

[100] Hugh Trevor-Roper, "The General Crisis of the Seventeenth Century," in *Crisis in Europe*, ed. Trevor Aston (Garden City, N. Y.: Anchor Books, 1967), p. 63.

[101] *Ibid.*, p. 72.

[102] Hugh Trevor Roper, "Trevor Roper's General Crisis: Symposium, III," in *Crisis in Europe*, p. 117.

[103] Trevor-Roper, "The General Crisis," p. 89.

[104] J. H. Elliott, "Revolts in the Spanish Monarchy," in *Preconditions of Revolution in Early Modern Europe*, ed. R. Forster and J. P. Greene (Baltimore: Johns Hopkins Press, 1970), pp. 109–30.

[105] J. H. Elliott, "Revolution and Continuity in Early Modern Europe," *Past and Present*, No. 42 (February, 1969), p. 41.

[106] *Ibid.*

[107] R. R. Palmer, *The Age of Democratic Revolution*, Vol. I (Princeton: Princeton University Press, 1969).

[108] *Ibid.*, p. 23.

[109] *Ibid.*

[110] George Rudé, *Revolutionary Europe 1783–1815* (New York: Harper Torchbooks, 1966), p. 221.

[111] *Ibid.*

[112] *Ibid.*, p. 184.

[113] *Ibid.*, p. 220.

[114] Lewis Namier, *1848: The Revolution of the Intellectuals* (Garden City, N.Y.: Doubleday Anchor Books, 1964), p. 2.

[115] *Ibid.*

[116] Hugh Seton-Watson, *The East European Revolution* (New York: Praeger, 1961), p. xi.

[117] Franz Borkenau, *World Communism* (Ann Arbor: University of Michigan Press, 1962), Chap. VI.

[118] Morton A. Kaplan, *System and Process in International Politics* (New York: John Wiley, 1957).

[119] Kyung-Won Kim, *Revolution and International System* (New York: New York University Press, 1970).

[120] *Ibid.*, p. 36.

[121] *Ibid.*, p. 122.

[122] Richard Rosecrance, *Action and Reaction in World Politics* (Boston: Little, Brown, 1967), pp. 44–45.

IV

THE CAUSES OF REVOLUTION

THE apparently innocuous phrase "the causes of revolution" in reality evokes some of the most difficult problems of explanation in history and the social sciences. A brief survey of certain of these problems is a necessary prelude to understanding what a valid explanation of revolution could be and which among the many competing theories of revolution comes closest to this.[1] For a generation or more, debate has raged over the scientific status of explanations in history and the social sciences. Some of this debate, perhaps, could have been avoided if all parties had not forgotten what they all implicitly recognize: *there are various kinds of explanation, and their methods and objectives are determined by the context of inquiry.* The previous chapter, for example, was concerned basically with "explaining what" revolution is, while the present one deals rather differently with "explaining why" revolutions in fact occur.[2] Answering the second type of question involves investigation of the causes of revolution.

CAUSAL EXPLANATION AND REVOLUTION

Historical Explanation

For one school of thought there is no rigid logical distinction between causal explanations in the natural sciences on the one hand, and in history and the social sciences on the other. In this outlook "scientific explanation" is virtually synonomous with "causal explanation." According to one leading exponent of this view, Carl G. Hempel, an event E. is not explained scientifically unless we have the enumeration of some crucial "initial conditions," plus one or more relevant "general laws" or "covering laws," as ingredients of a *deductive* argument whose conclusion is the occurrence of E.[3] Furthermore, explanation and prediction are logically symmetrical as the form of the argument remains the same, although prediction may be more difficult in practice because of the insufficiency of relevant information. Understandably, the so-called general laws (or universal hypotheses, etc.) have raised doubts both as to whether there are any "laws" in history and human behavior and as to whether such laws are needed to make the explanations of historians and social scientists respectable. Hume sensed the difficulty of these issues more than two centuries ago when he pointed out that even the closest observation of events cannot warrant any assertion of a causal relationship without reference to further general principles. One cannot see a "law of nature"; he can only infer its existence after observing persistent recurrence of a typical sequence of events. However, it is only by implicit or explicit reference to such laws, say many philosophers of science, that true causal explanation is to be distinguished from an accidental, merely chronological, listing of various particular facts.

While the stipulation of *universal* laws or, simply, laws may be too demanding,[4] recognition of "empirical generalizations" or "warranted uniformities" or "truisms" [5] seems unavoidable if a causal explanation is to be more than a dogmatic assertion. However, it is a sheer waste of time to run through the whole logical argument each time a causal argument is proffered, even if this were possible more often than it is. In some instances a "singular explanatory statement" does the job, provided that there are also present "good inductive reasons for thinking that such an argument exists." [6] Unfortunately, there is no simple law of revolution under which we can subsume particular instances with their set of appropriate initial conditions, and accordingly explain part or predict future revolutions. Such complex or macro-events as revolution must be explained in terms of the particularized grouping of lower-level features whose total makes up *this* revolution: "To appeal to a gross covering law would be, in effect, to short-circuit the real work the explanation is intended to do." [7] A revolution is explained or predicted when we have enumerated adequate sets of antecedent conditions with their respective empirical generalizations. The resulting explanation or prognosis is bound to be highly complex, but those seeking simplicity should study something other than the causes of revolution.

In addition, there is good reason to doubt the "completeness" that any explanation of revolution could possibly attain. In a general way explanation of revolution or of complex historical events is not categorically worse off than explanation in the natural sciences. For if a complete explanation of a concrete event requires that every conceivable aspect of it be explained, then no event could ever be completely explained.[8] What we have here is the specter of an "infinite regress" of explanation not backwards in time, but horizontally spread out before us as we survey the event from all the infinite angles and perspectives theoretically possible. Completeness of explanation, then, is relative to and determined by the purposes of the inquirer. Accordingly, political scientists, sociologists, economists, social psychologists, and clinicians might explain the Russian Revolution in rather different terms; and hopefully these explanations are complementary rather than alternative. But even a grandiose synthesis of them all would remain scandalously incomplete from other possible points of view. The problem of infinite regress of explanations back through time is also less troublesome than we might suppose. If a valid explanation entailed every cause in its turn as an effect of a previous cause and so on, explanatory accounts of all revolutions would have to begin in the Garden of Eden. But this threat is easily parried if we assume that "if something can be explained, there is something else which does not require explanation. But the reason it does not require explanation is not necessarily that we know its explanation already." [9] As Ernest Nagel further points out, "Is violence being done to the truth by stopping at some arbitrary point in the regressive series? Is B not a cause of A, merely because C is a cause of B?" [10]

However, there is another kind of incompleteness of explanation in social science that stems from employing "imperfect knowledge" and "imperfect laws." Only in certain branches of physics do we encounter "perfect knowledge," in the sense that we can predict (or "postdict") the state of the system from our knowledge of the laws involved plus the value of the variables at any given moment of time. In the biological and social sciences, however, our theories are not complete, "nor do we fully know the conditions for closure" of the systems studied.[11] Simply stated, *social scientists and historians generally have greater difficulty knowing when to invoke which "laws" in their explanations than do natural scientists.* The main reason for this is that "there are prescribed tests in most sciences whereby it can be decided whether or not a particular event satisfies a precisely formulated law. . . . Historical situations present a multitude of interrelated factors whose relevance or irrelevance to the events we wish to explain is difficult to determine. . . . Furthermore, it is usually the case that not one, but many, generalizations . . . must be used. . . ." [12] This bewildering complexity inherent in historical and social science explanations places heavy demands on the *judgment* of the student of revolution.

"Imperfect knowledge" often forces the social scientist to resort to statistical or probabilistic generalizations that preclude strict explanation or prediction of discrete events. The final step in statistical explanation asserts the likelihood of the event's occurrence, not its occurrence pure and simple. In the final analysis it may be that revolutions are too complex to lend themselves to anything stronger than probabilistic explanations. For this reason we may have to be satisfied with what Carl G. Hempel calls "explanation sketches," rather than with fully developed explanations of revolutions. An explanation sketch "consists of a more or less vague indication of the laws and initial conditions considered as relevant, and it needs 'filling out' in order to turn into a full-fledged explanation." [13] This filling out may prove unfeasible.

In the light of all this, what constitutes a causal explanation of revolution? Should we agree with one student of revolution that the causes of revolution are those antecedents which are logically interrelated with the result and are "sufficient to bring about the result"? [14] In that case our search would be ended when we identify that cause or set of causes sufficient to account for revolution. If class struggle were the "locomotive" of revolution, then an analysis of the class struggle before the French Revolution would suffice to explain that uprising. Or if multiple factors operate in such grandiose happenings, we could ferret them out, arrange them from the least to the most important, and offer the finished product as a truly sufficient account. However, because of "imperfect knowledge" and the peculiar perspective of the inquirer, it seems unlikely that one could advance a cause or set of causes of revolution that would meet the strict and exhaustive logical demands of a truly sufficient explanation. The study of revolution, like the study of many other historical and natural phenomena, must therefore content itself by mentioning "only some of the *indispensable* (or, as it is commonly also said, *necessary*) conditions for these occurrences." [15] Such a modest goal is forced on us because, if we start to elaborate all the jointly sufficient conditions for an occurrence, "every factor we add calls for the addition of further co-operating factors," [16] thus raising again the specter of infinite regress.

More confidently, we can aim for or expect an explanatory account that identifies the more important necessary conditions of revolution with express or tacit reference to the appropriate empirical generalizations. Such an "adequate explanation" might amount to more than Hempel's explanation sketch, but would fall more or less short of full sufficiency. The value of such an explanation is determined as much by the verdict of others in the field as by foolproof logical tests.

By stressing that adequate explanations need not be sufficient explanations, the preceding considerations have suggested that explaining revolutions is not a task doomed to frustration by *a priori* logical tangles. However, much more than this is needed if we are to hack out some causal path through the thicket of events and processes that antecede the historical revolutions. Of considerable help in this undertaking is a doctrine that has been called by some "abnormalism." One exponent of this outlook has suggested some reasons why it is wholly proper to select one cause (or set of causes) from among all those that precede a given historical event such as revolution: "We do not raise the question why so long as things pursue what we regard as their normal or typical course. It is the exception, the deviation, the interference, the abnormality, that stimulates our curiosity and seems to call for explanation. And we often attribute to some one 'cause' all the happenings that characterize the new or unanticipated or altered situation." [17]

Now, revolution as we understand it is perhaps the most striking, dramatic, extraordinary—and in this sense "abnormal"—of political phenomena. Thus the search for its cause or causes is imbued with the clear conviction that something out of the ordinary has developed. Despite the dangers of the term, this sort of "abnormality" must be translated by the social scientist as the breakdown of a previous equilibrium. For R. M. MacIver, the concept of equilibrium simply registers the fact that "a system is operating in a manner congenial to its self-perpetuation, until something intervenes; that a system is relatively closed, until something breaks it open." [18] Of the many complex theories, models, and concepts of equilibrium developed by modern social science, most have been criticized as being unable to explain significant social change or even as being a weapon in the ideological armory of partisans of the status quo.

Therefore, to avoid unnecessary misunderstanding, it must be pointed out that the concept of equilibrium employed here is a somewhat "weak" one (i.e., equilibrium in society is understood more as a tendency than as an accomplished, perfected condition). Furthermore, it is always confronted by forces that tend to overwhelm or disrupt it, though these challenges vary from society to society. For the student of revolution the concept of equilibrium should mean little more than a kind of balance sheet registering the relative ascendency of those forces working against revolution over those working for it.[19] However, without some notion of equilibrium it would be extremely difficult to know how far back to look for the origins of the causal nexus whose result is revolution. It is such a conviction that prompts a recent student of revolution to argue that "the sociology of functional societies comes logically before the sociology of revolution." [20] This outlook, which has been criticized as ideological, is in reality epistemological (i.e., we cannot fully appreciate what the breakdown of the social order is unless we know beforehand what order itself is). Two characteristics distinguish a society in relative equilibrium: (1) the conflicts and cleavages between and within the three basic stratification systems remain below a certain threshold of antagonism; and (2) social change in the technological, cultural, and social realms proceeds in relative harmony.[21] A society in relative disequilibrium lacks these features. George Pettee has translated the "balance sheet" of social equilibrium into personal evaluations: "The loyalty or disloyalty of men to a system will rest on the balance for each of them of the forces of their own purposes, the force of habit and cramp."[22] On the "systemic" level, Harry Eckstein has suggested that the potential for "internal war" is a "ratio between positive forces" working for it and negative forces working against it.[23]

As we move closer to revolution the balance between the stabilizing forces and the destabilizing forces tips towards the latter. The search for the causes of revolution, therefore, need go back no further in time than to the point where the "abnormal" destabilizing forces begin to operate.

Before we can begin to identify the causes of revolution, we must distinguish between *events* and *processes* as causal factors and also decide which of the two revolution itself is. According to R. M. MacIver, an event is "a single manifestation, representing a unique historical moment, dated in time and space. An event thus offers an obvious antithesis to a process, since the latter is continuous through time and need not manifest itself in any event or series of events. The process works its way 'underneath,' the event 'breaks out.'"[24] The collapse of the Stock Market on Black Thursday of October, 1929, was an event; but American economic life, which was so altered by the onset of the Depression, comprised one or several processes. When MacIver goes on to describe an event as a "revelation of hidden forces, possibly a culmination, turning-point, or overt beginning of some movement of human affairs," which often "comes to disturb or disrupt some equilibrium within which it occurs,"[25] he seems to be talking the very language of revolution. However, to construe revolutions as simple events is not so feasible as it seems. For example, precise dating of the outbreak of a revolution is highly problematic with some revolutions: the English, French, Spanish, and other revolutions are almost intractable on this issue. Nor is it correct to adopt the other extreme and understand the revolutionary process as a wholly continuous seamless web of development. Such an interpretation would wholly miss the abruptness and intensity of change associated with revolution.

Since neither simple event nor continuous process fits the complex reality of revolution, which partakes somewhat of both, let us use the term "macro-event" to designate the mixed quality of revolution. Such terminology underscores the fact that revolutions have a trajectory whose beginnings and endings may be quite difficult to mark clearly and whose "phases" imply both process and event.[26]

To register the complexity of revolution by employing the term "macro-event" still does not clear up the problem of which sorts of social phenomena constitute causes of revolution. Events certainly will be important, but so will other things such as "states" (or "dispositions") and processes; and we must resist the temptation to think of the causal nexus of revolution as composed exclusively or mainly of events. Events seem to possess that dynamic quality which Aristotle called "efficient causation" and which gets things done. But philosophers rightly insist that the conditions in lists of necessary or initial conditions include much more than events. One of them deems it an "error" to consider only events or processes as historically efficacious causes: what is to be included depends on the context of inquiry. Furthermore, "a dispositional characteristic is a type of 'standing condition'; and standing conditions, as well as precipitating ones, can be causes." [27] For example, many writers hold that the French aristocracy was "decadent" on the eve of the French Revolution and that this decadence was largely responsible for the overthrow of the old regime. Now such decadence is a state or dispositional characteristic attributable to a specific group; it is neither an event nor a process, properly speaking. However, events may be manifestations of an underlying state, as when aristocrats make some blunder indicative of their sorry condition. Likewise, the decadence itself may be the culmination of a process of decline running back a century or more. Later we will examine "the social psychology of revolution" as an attempt to elaborate the conditions that dispose a people towards revolutionary violence. Here too event, process, and state play a role.

Monistic vs. Multiple Causation

As a complex macro-event, revolution would seem to suggest a multiple rather than a monistic approach to the question of its causes. In fact, extreme single-factor explanations of revolution are relatively rare, because what is usually meant by the expression "the cause of the X Revolution" is that there is a "decisive" cause so paramount that all others pale into insignificance before it. Controversy is always engendered over the allegedly decisive cause, because "it is sometimes selected from a point of view which another investigator may not share, and . . . we cannot always establish on absolute grounds that one of these points of view is superior to others." [28] This is why certain economic interpretations of revolution or even Pareto's preoccupation with circulation of elites invariably incur the charge of gross over-simplification. Monistic theories would have greater plausibility if revolutions themselves were one simple thing, a *bloc* as Clemenceau termed the French Revolution. In fact, historians of the French Revolution have explained it in terms of one crucial feature: popular explosion, masonic conspiracy, birth-pang of bourgeois society, divine chastisement have all been offered as serious accounts of why the revolution occurred. However, recent scholarship seems to show that the revolution "has ceased to be a revolution and become a series of revolutions—the last Fronde of the nobles and the *parlements,* the revolution of the *tiers etat,* the peasant rising, the republican insurrection, the revolt of the *sans-culottes,* the *neuf* thermidor and the various coups d'etat under the Directory ending in that of 18 brumaire." [29]

What is true for the French Revolution also holds for other revolutions; upon close inspection their "bloc" character breaks up into a number of more or less distinct movements. The obvious inference is that the causal sequence that produces the temporary convergence of oppositionist elements in revolutions cannot be reduced to the operation of one paramount factor. The various protagonist groups are moved by distinct goals and impulsions. "Some are urged by cold and hunger, others by envy, cupidity, vindictiveness; others again by compassion and a desire to improve conditions in general." [30] As such a panorama of desires can be gratified in different ways and at different times, therefore, various elements tend to secede from the revolutionary coalition as they receive whatever payoff they longed for. Peasants are particularly prone to jump off the revolutionary bandwagon when they receive their share of a redistribution of land. Such considerations even suggest that "there are enough possible factors to cause revolutions on entirely different sets of causes." [31] This very diversity has caused certain historians to discount nearly all generalizations to be gathered from the comparative study of revolutions. They maintain that the causal pattern of each historical revolution is so idiosyncratic that generalization is either impossible or not worth the trouble. But such a counsel of despair is in its own way as excessive as the cock-sureness of monistic theories of revolution.

However, there is a middle path to the understanding of the kinds of factors to be considered in tracing the causes of revolution that will avoid the pitfalls of both monistic theories and pure skepticism. This middle path is to conceive of revolutions as *a particular sort of social change produced in its turn by different sorts of social change.* Social change operates to push men towards revolution by activating certain human responses ("the social psychology of revolution").

Our previous discussion of social conflict suggests that human society is never perfectly integrated—it never exhibits perfect organic cohesiveness. Naturally, the degree of integration varies enormously, and failure to fully acknowledge this has caused social theorists to advance one-sided conceptions of society that stress harmony at the expense of conflict or vice versa. A balanced appraisal suggests that while there is some overall unity in society, its various aspects or subsystems may sometimes be seriously out of phase with each other. R. M. MacIver has distinguished between three "orders" or subsystems encountered in all human societies. (1) The *social* subsystem includes what we have called the three basic stratification systems of society, plus the kinship system and primary and secondary group affiliations. The social subsystem is a kind of map revealing the various modes of human relationships and associations, including political ones. (2) The *cultural* subsystem embraces "patterns, interadjustments, and trends of operative valuations and goals, as revealed in the mores, the folkways, the traditions, the faiths, the fine arts, the philosophies, the play-activities, and generally the modes of of living of social groups." [32] All this is roughly what Marx had in mind with his notion of "ideology" as part of society's superstructure. (3) The *technological* subsystem refers to the ways in which men collaborate to extract their needs and wants from nature. Thus it involves the various tools, processes, and techniques through which nature's bounty is converted into useful and exchangeable goods. In addition, the division of labor considered in abstraction from social hierarchy belongs to the technological subsystem, as do many activities considered from a purely functional point of view.

Though their interdependence is evident and any attempt to separate them categorically is doomed to failure, the relative autonomy of the three subsystems is observable especially in "modern" or "transitional" societies. In primitive or traditional societies, on the other hand, the greater simplicity of social structure is reflected in the greater integration of the three subsystems at more or less the same pace (i.e., change is *synchronous*). As societies become more complex and subject to outside influences, there is a tendency for the three subsystems to change at various rhythms and tempos (i.e., change is *dissynchronous*). What shows the relative autonomy of the three subsystems is the fact that societies with similar technologies have divergent cultural and social orders, and societies with different technologies betray remarkable cultural or social affinities. "Cultural lag" theories that maintain that technological innovation always leads while the cultural and social subsystems lag behind are given the lie by the diverse modes of historical change: "sometimes the change in technology leads, sometimes the change in religion, knowledge, art, ethics, mores leads. Sometimes technique changes while the rest of the culture does not; sometimes the noneconomic and nontechnical part changes while the techno-economic parts do not change." [33]

Whether and how change in one subsystem affects the others cannot be determined *a priori*. Technological, value-cultural, or social-structural determinisms—all encounter too many exceptions to serve as a general orientation towards social change. What conclusions, then, can one draw from the possibility of dissynchronous changes in the three subsystems? In the first place, revolution is unlikely where change in them occurs smoothly and more or less in tandem. Conversely, a considerable amount of dissynchronous social change, especially if rapid, enhances the chances of revolution in two fundamental ways: (1) by exacerbating one or more of the four types of social conflict discussed in Chapter III; and (2) by promoting a generalized sense of discontent. Figure 3 represents both the autonomy and interaction of the three subsystems and how they impinge upon the mental responses of a collectivity.

Refusal to decide the lead-lag issue *a priori* on the lines of a one-sided deterministic philosophy does not imply considering the three sorts of social change of equal importance in all revolutionary situations. Such a dogmatic view would be just as unhistorical as a simplistic cultural lag theory. The very notion of dissynchronous change lays open the possibility that one subsystem may lead in a given historical context. Or two may forge ahead, leaving one behind. There are many variations on these themes. For example, in one case technology may lead and cause a change in cultural values, while social structure is not immediately affected. However, the new values associated with the burgeoning technology might form the basis of a radical critique of the

Figure 3. Revolution and Social Change

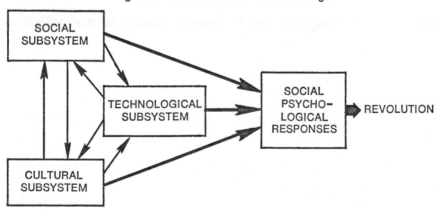

distribution of wealth, status, or power. On the other hand, certain changes in cultural values or social structure may be the prerequisite of technological advance. In addition, perfect synchronicity of change may be lacking *within* each of the three subsystems. The frequent quarrel between science and religious beliefs, for example, occurs within the cultural subsystem: the clash may be precipitated by unusually rapid scientific advance or by the meteoric rise of a revivalist religious movement. In sum, the almost boundless possibilities of dissynchronicity and disintegration between and within the social, cultural, and technological subsystems seem to suggest multiple causation of revolutions on purely theoretical grounds.

Highly dissynchronous social change encourages a general sense of malaise through the breakdown of certain values and beliefs—once again, Durkheim's *anomie*.[34] It is not necessarily change *per se* that is so disorienting, but the hodgepodge of old and new that undermines old guidelines and verities, and perhaps intimates the possibility of something new and better. A study of the Puritan revolutionaries in the English Revolution documents their emergence out of an apparently disintegrating social milieu. This revolutionary elite sought "a new order and an impersonal, ideological discipline," and were distinguished "from their fellows by an extraordinary self-assurance and daring. The saints not only repudiate[d] the routine procedures and customary beliefs of the old order, but they also cut themselves off from the various kinds of 'freedom' (individual mobility, personal extravagance, self-realization, despair, nervousness, vacillation) experienced amidst the decay of tradition."[35] More generally, dissynchronous social change predisposes a society to be more receptive to revolutionists and their message. It is the job of students of each historical revolution to determine precise sources of change and which, if any, of the three subsystems is the focus of infection of the disorientation that contributes to revolution. As is likely, if there is change in more than one subsystem, the impact of change will strike different social groups in different ways. This helps to explain further the heterogeneity of the original revolutionary coalition.

Cyclical and Linear Change

The social, cultural, and technological subsystems are subject to two main types of change, both of which deserve consideration in the study of revolution. We have already spoken of the contrast between cyclical and linear (or evolutionary) processes of change in the context of millenarian movements. Cyclical processes recur regularly or intermittently. Some cyclical processes are predictable and stereotyped, though variations in detail exist—for example, the succession of the seasons. Others such as famines, epidemics, recessions, climatic disturbances, and natural disasters are more difficult to forecast with certainty—though our conviction that they will recur soon grows the longer the interval between now and the last instance of the phenomenon in question. Many cultural patterns seem to obey a cyclical rhythm: romanticism challenges classicism and seems to have won the day only to find itself eventually confronted with a neoclassicist revival. Libertinism is often succeeded by a recrudescence of puritanism, and so on.

Grand theories of history have been propounded which purport to chart the life course of whole civilizations according to the cyclic paradigm of "rise, decline, and fall." Such philosophies of history espy a grandiose rhythm that sweeps the whole cultural organism to its preordained fate.[36] But in so doing they perhaps overestimate the integration and cohesion of the entities they call civilizations and fail to see the myriad of lesser cyclical processes which are often dissynchronous.

Linear processes of change on the contrary are essentially unidirectional, cumulative, and irreversible. That is, they move more or less steadily in novel, unprecedented directions; each later stage in the process builds upon the earlier ones; what is gained in earlier stages is preserved, thus preventing any permanent backsliding. In short, what is done is done, and cannot be undone! The linear, like the cyclical, pattern has its grandiose version in theories of evolutionary progress which envisage mankind, if not the entire cosmos, moving towards some far-off, distant goal. Nevertheless, it seems legitimate to employ either or both concepts of social change without necessarily subscribing to a speculative philosophy of history. Both of them, however, have been challenged from the opposite point of view. Critics of the concept of cyclical processes of change point out that "since history never repeats itself" what appears to be a re-edition of a familiar cycle or a simple recurrence is itself so peculiar and unprecedented that essentially it is something entirely new. But when pushed too far this thesis imperils the very basis of social science by denying the degree of commonness necessary to both comparison and subsequent generalization. Recurrences of a cyclical nature are the social scientist's surrogate for the natural scientist's laboratory experiment. Similarly, some argue that the concept of linear processes of change is an illusion. A recent writer maintains that "in the realm of social behavior in historical time there appear to be no changes or processes of change which could properly answer to the requirements of the concept of irreversibility." [37]

It seems difficult, however, to deny that scientific and technological change in the past several centuries is both cumulative and irreversible, as by extension would be changes wrought by science and technology in men's view of the world and in their daily life. As we shall see below other changes such as secularization and "democratization" may also be considered as basically linear. At any rate, *both linear and cyclical processes of change play a role in the causal nexus of revolution, and the relative importance of each varies from revolution to revolution.* One further suspects that the later revolutions are more characterized by the greater weight of linear as opposed to cyclical change than are the earlier ones. A somewhat different version of this hypothesis suggests that one of the reasons why revolution appears more likely in "transitional" than in more traditionalist polities is that linear factors are more considerable in the former polities. If this is the case, a suggestion of George Pettee deserves the most serious consideration. He points out that "cyclical factors may to some extent be eliminated, secular [i.e., linear] factors cannot . . .," [38] and thus the rulers could conceivably "find means adequate to circumvent the sources of cyclical cramp." [39] Adroit leadership might thus avoid revolt or even revolution if the discontent threatening them derives in the main from cyclical factors. But linear processes are too profound and their ramifications too complex and new to allow of facile manipulation, even by a competent ruling elite. Accordingly, the more modernized a society becomes (and thus more subject to linear factors), the less crucial is the "quality" of the old ruling classes as a cause of revolution. "Decadent" or not, they may be trucking with forces beyond their, or anyone else's, control.

Economic interpretations of revolutions can invoke either or both cyclical and linear change. For example, the Marxist interpretation of both the English and French revolutions maintains that the overriding or decisive cause of the two revolutions is the final victory of the capitalist economic system over an obsolete "feudal" one. The leitmotiv of revolution is linear technological and economic change. A different interpretation of the English Revolution, we have already seen, holds the general downturn of the business cycle as crucially significant. Both of these interpretations are economic, but stress linear or cyclical factors respectively.

The discussion of long-term, middle-term, and precipitant causes of revolution will include linear factors, cyclical factors, and "incidents, neither progressive nor recurring." [40] Included within this third "random" category are nearly all precipitants of revolution, as well as a factor of extreme importance in the middle-term—war.[41]

LEVELS OF CAUSATION

We must now relate cyclical and linear processes of change in the social, cultural, and technological subsystems to the sequence of long-term and middle-term developments that produces the conjuncture of forces which in the end is precipitated into open revolution. However, study of the causes of revolution has been somewhat confused by the medical analogies frequently encountered in the classic comparative studies of Lyford Edwards, Crane Brinton, and George Pettee. Edwards speaks of the "preliminary symptoms" of unrest; Brinton, of a "revolutionary prodrome" composed of not fully developed symptoms; and Pettee, of the various sorts of "cramp" characteristic of societies moving towards revolution. Using Edwards as a case in point, we find certain of his preliminary "symptoms" have a causal potential, others do not. In the latter category falls his stress on such factors as greater geographical mobility and increased social deviancy at a considerable distance before the outbreak of revolution. However, he fails to show how these factors directly contribute to the coming of revolution. In fact, he denies that "a mere increase of travel by itself portends revolution" and contents himself with simply asserting that "an increase of travel does characterize any society in which a revolutionary movement is coming into being." [42] Simple correlation, however, is a far cry from a true causal relationship. For this reason lists of symptoms— which are, after all, mere *effects* of the disease or disturbance to the system in question—are useful in the main as indicators of the authentic causal process at work. Those interested in the *causes* of revolution have to go one step further and probe beneath the surface for the really determinant forces. For example, one could argue that the increased travel Edwards correlates to revolution was due to a breakdown of those traditions that keep people in their natal area and was thus part of the larger collapse of the moral and cultural foundations of the old regime. Or the increased travel might be due to a "demographic revolution" that by increasing population makes the land insufficient to support peasants, thus causing large-scale internal emigration, especially towards urban centers. Thus it is massive and rapid population growth which produces the unemployment, misery, and discontent that are truly part of the causal pattern of revolution. Greater travel is indeed just one effect or symptom of the total disturbance. In a word, identification of the symptoms of revolution may be useful as a premonitory indication of the coming of revolution; they do not necessarily explain why revolutions occur.

Long-Term Causes of Revolution

The first consideration in identifying the long-term causes of revolution is the "how far back?" quandary. The hint of "abnormalism"—to take as point of departure for causal analysis the beginning point of the breakdown of the relative equilibrium—is formally correct but too general to be very useful. One of the few concrete suggestions on this problem—that of Lyford Edwards—is more ingenious than convincing, because he probably gave the wrong reasons for a rather good intuition.[43] While allowing for a range to reflect the historical uniqueness of revolutions, in general the figure of 100 years that has characterized so many studies probing the long-term causes of major revolutions seems a justifiable one. Going back much further we lose the specific focus we need and face the infinite regress dilemma once again. Limiting ourselves to a decade or two before the outbreak of revolution, we risk missing the impact of long-term developments whose effects are developed over a lengthy time-span. Nevertheless, there seems to be no way of eliminating all arbitrariness on this issue, and it may well be that the faster pace of historical change in the last century or so makes for a period now of considerably less than a century in the gestation of revolution.

Less troublesome is the association of long-term causes of revolution with linear processes of change. As the latter are by definition long-range developments, our expectation is that they would prevail over properly cyclical factors the farther back we cast our glance. Some cyclical factors are long-range, but for the most part they operate at a distance of a couple of decades or even less before the outbreak of revolution. Thus a survey of essentially linear trends is where to begin an analysis of the causes of revolution.

1. *Economic Growth,* especially rapid economic growth, has often been selected as a chief long-term cause of revolution. Although economic growth is subject to often drastic cyclic fluctuations, it is hard to deny that for several centuries or more economic growth has blessed and cursed many countries within the orbit of Western civilization. An enormously influential theory of the linearity of economic growth is the five "stages of economic growth" of W. W. Rostow.[44] Rostow begins with (1) the traditional society, in which economic stagnancy is in harmony of sorts with a static view of the world and minimal technological innovation. (2) The preconditions for take-off arrive when both the reality and social attractiveness of economic progress begin to strain at the cultural values and vested interests associated with the traditional economic order. (3) The take-off comes when modern economic considerations dominate the society. Technological innovation, increased capital investment, and the emergence of economic and political leaders committed to growth are essential to this stage. Both agriculture and industry are radically affected in what amounts to "revolutionary changes," and "in a decade or two both the basic structure of

the economy and the social and political structure of the society are transformed in such a way that a steady rate of growth can be, thereafter, regularly sustained." [45] In (4) the drive to maturity, growth—though fluctuating—completes the modernization of the economy and allows the rate of investment to outstrip population growth and thus to dispel the fears of Thomas Malthus. Rostow estimates that take-off requires two decades and the drive to maturity around four. The key indicator that maturity has been reached is the ability of the economy to diversify and seek new areas for development. The next stage, (5) the age of high mass-consumption, finds that wealth previously needed for capital investment trickles down more generously to the generality of men. Consumer goods production expands prodigiously as does the so-called tertiary sector of the service industries.

By Rostow's own reckoning the great revolutions have mostly occurred during the "preconditions for take-off." [46] However, the English Revolution preceded this stage and the Russian Revolution followed upon it. In the light of these exceptions, it would seem hazardous to interpret revolution as a kind of nodal point separating distinct phases of economic growth. (Revolutions are generally near-disasters in terms of short-term economic growth and somewhat so even for long-term growth. It is very difficult to show that later prodigies of growth would not have occurred but for the revolution.) Moreover, even if it were proven that a revolution produced a regime whose economic growth rates were higher than anything possible for a traditionalist or reformist regime, this still does not necessarily mean that the need or desire for rapid economic growth was a significant determinant to revolution. In other words, the effects of revolution must not be transposed backward onto its causes. Here too issues must be decided on the basis of historical evidence. A model of circumspection on just this sort of relationship is the conclusion of an historian of the economic growth of England in the century preceding the English Revolution and civil war. John Nef sees multiple factors at work in the genesis of the revolution and finds that though separating different sorts of causes is difficult, "economic causes were perhaps of less importance than religious or political causes." [47] In fact, the civil war might still have occurred without the disputes between the Crown and the "wealthy classes" on economic issues. On the other hand, "if it had not been for the increased tension resulting from the early industrial revolution, a settlement might possibly have been reached on these other matters without a clash of arms." [48] Nef's analysis illustrates that even though it is usually wrong to consider economic growth as the "decisive" cause of revolution, it almost always must be enumerated among the "necessary conditions" for it.

In fact, the contribution of rapid economic growth to the emergence of a revolutionary situation occurs in ways so subtle that they elude the usual "rise of new social classes" or "rising expectations" theories that link economic growth to revolution. Since these problems will be discussed below, here it is sufficient to conclude that economic growth is one of the most potent sources of dissynchronous social change and hence of revolution. However, the fact that impressive economic growth has characterized both societies that experienced subsequent revolutions and those that did not should be warning enough against any simplistic causal relationship.

2. *Technological Innovation* might seem artificially separated from economic growth here, but in fact the two are distinct. Although we tend to assume their intimate association in Western history, their precise relationship remains somewhat enigmatic: does technological innovation stimulate economic growth or does economic growth provide surplus capital to finance the development of new techniques? Or do we again have a classic case of mutual interdependence or a symbiotic relationship in which each side is essential to the development in a sort of "virtuous circle"? At any rate, economic growth for the student of revolution is not the only—though it may be the chief—ramification of technological innovation. Technological innovation can spell good or hard times for various sectors of the population: groups able to adapt to or champion changes in technique may be numbered among the rising groups so frequently found in accounts of revolution. On the other hand, groups and strata whose livelihood and way of life are menaced by technological innovation may hold the regime responsible for their troubles. We nowadays consider such groups as susceptible to right-wing appeals, but it is by no means clear that contemporary political labels make much sense when transposed to the seventeenth, eighteenth, or early nineteenth century. In this vein, Alfred Cobban's daring suggestion that in part "the revolution in the French countryside was not against feudalism but against a growing commercialization" [49] shows that opposition to technological or economic change may propel some into the ranks of revolutionaries.

A very different consequence of technological innovation occurs when progressive-minded people are convinced by it that drastic social engineering of revolutionary proportions should be effected on the model of technology. There may be more than a grain of truth in Taine's dissection of the "revolutionary spirit" that sees society as an improvable machine to be run by a band of intrepid social engineers. Here we see how change in one subsystem (the technological) impinges upon another (the cultural): technological innovation is so impressive as to modify the ideas of some people and suggest the need to overturn a social system that prevents technology from realizing its potential for social amelioration or utopia. This is, after all, part of the reason why Karl Marx became a revolutionary.

3. *The Growth of Science* can affect the development of revolution by its impact on technology (and hence economy) and on what Friedrich Nietzsche's called "the transvaluation of values." However, the intimate relationship between science and technology that prevails in modern industrial societies is not universal. In earlier days the cross-fertilization of science and technology was slight and the two activities often proceeded wholly oblivious to each other. "In the late eighteenth century the effective liaison between science and technology begins; but until this time the internal problems, the internal development, of each are far more significant than any occasional interaction between them." [50] For this reason the development of "pure" science first and foremost affected those strata of the population with sufficient leisure to follow it at whatever distance. It was an affair of intellectual elites, but intellectual elites are influential well beyond their raw numbers, especially in preparing the ground for revolutions.

We can speak of both "positive" and "negative" ramifications of scientific advance in the pre-revolutionary setting. Negatively, it contributes to the erosion of the system of beliefs that legitimizes or even sanctifies the existing order. According to Gaetano Mosca, though all societies are ruled by a more or less organized minority called the ruling class, force alone seems insufficient to maintain this class in its position for very long. Consequently, there develops a "political formula" which constitutes a "justification of its power in an abstract principle. . . . To say that all functionaries derive their authority from the sovereign, who in turn receives his from God, is to employ a political formula. The alternative belief that all powers are based on the popular will is another political formula." [51] While Mosca considered the social and psychological traits of the ruling class more important than ideas alone, he refused to dismiss the political formula as a "pure and simple mystification." For Mosca changes in the political formula were a kind of barometer for changes in the *de facto* composition of the ruling class. With a force perhaps greater than Mosca would allow, the growth of science can help to undermine the credibility of certain political formulas, in particular those with a strong theological coloration. How can we accept the divine right of kings if there is no divinity, or if the divinity is unconcerned with human affairs? It is not so much what science actually says on these issues, but how intellectual elites interpret the results of inquiry that is important: "the destructive function is essential to revolution, and the destruction of the forces of purpose and consent which maintain state and social system is largely an intellectual task." [52]

Thomas Kuhn's interpretation of the process of scientific growth is highly suggestive with respect to its potentially corrosive effect on established beliefs and political formulas. Stipulating the cultural and technological ramifications which are beyond Kuhn's concern, we can adopt with profit his analysis of the revolutionary quality of scientific growth. Kuhn's main thesis is that science develops through a largely *discontinuous* sequence; scientific advance is not a gradual, evolutionary, simply cumulative process. A "scientific revolution" is instead a clear break with the past and not a logical culmination of previous research trends. Science develops in terms of a succession of "paradigms," which determine the nature, goals, and methods of scientific research for an extended period. The science practiced under the aegis of such an established paradigm and circumscribed by its limits is called "normal science." It consists for the most part of solving the puzzles and mopping up whatever areas of obscurity still remain through application of the basic assumptions of the reigning paradigm. However, the paradigm and its normal science periodically run into apparently intractable problems—intractable, that is, from the standpoint of normal science—and a period of crisis follows. The old paradigm loses its hold as various independent attempts try to illuminate obscure areas. Out of this crisis emerges a significantly novel outlook, which in its turn develops into a paradigm around which will develop a new normal science.

Several immediate applications of Kuhn's interpretation of the growth of science suggest themselves to the student of revolution. For example, his contention that changes in the dominant paradigm "cause scientists to see the world of their research-engagement differently" and thus that "after a revolution scientists are responding to a different world" [53] is of considerable significance. Scientists are, after all, opinion makers and their views ultimately affect the general state of beliefs in society. This "different world" that emerges after a scientific revolution will modify the view of the world of many of the intelligentsia. And it is quite likely that the new world harbors many aspects that are not in keeping with the view of the world associated with the traditional society. That the filtering down of new scientific notions from the scientific community to laymen takes considerable time is only a further reason to place scientific advance amongst the long-term causes of revolution. Kuhn's employment of the term "revolution" to express the unsettling impact of each crisis in the realm of science suggests likewise how this process can have a similar impact, however delayed and distorted, in the overall culture.

4. *Democratization* is one of the more ambiguous processes deserving consideration as long-term and ostensibly linear causes of revolution. Here we understand democratization more as a matter of social relationships than of political institutions. It is in this sense that Tocqueville wrote in the 1830's that throughout Christendom from the eleventh century on "a twofold revolution has taken place in the state of society. The noble has gone down the social ladder, and the commoner has gone up; the one descends as the other rises." [54] In the face of this retrospect and prospect, Tocqueville felt a "kind of religious awe" in contemplating "that irresistible revolution which has advanced for centuries in spite of every obstacle and which is still advancing in the midst of the ruins it has caused." [55] True to his religious convictions he even deemed it a sort of blasphemy to "attempt to check democracy." [56] Tocqueville's interpretation of democratization is close to Sir Henry Sumner Maine's view of modern history as the transition from a society in which human relations depend on *status,* to one in which they depend upon *contract.* According to Maine "the movement of the progressive societies" has been "distinguished by the gradual dissolution of family dependency and the growth of individual obligation in its place. The Individual is steadily substituted for the Family, as the unit of which civil laws take account." [57] Contractualism connotes the voluntary agreement of free individuals, in contrast to the prescriptive relationships dictated by the status derived from birth. Sociologists have something very like this in mind when they envisage the process of modernization as including the diminution of "ascriptive" criteria and the growth of "achievement" criteria in determining the individual's social position and style of life. Factors such as talent, merit, and ambition begin to affect a person's life chances more than family background.

Though one cannot deny that social differences based on simple status have become gradually leveled out over centuries, the persistence of political and economic inequality and the continuing preoccupation of sociologists with a somewhat diffuse notion of social status seem to confirm Mosca's conclusion that the "aristocratic principle" has survived so many attacks and has been reinstituted so often by its erstwhile attackers that one can ask the question of "whether it too has its *raison d'etre* in the nature of things." [58] However, the overall trend seems to be democratization in the sense of decline of many of the status groups discussed in Chapter III. Revolutions thus appear as periods of accelerated democratization, perhaps caused by the resistance of traditionalists and higher social strata. This interpretation is given further substance if we recall once again the emergence in revolutions of "left oppositions" wishing to move farther faster with social and political leveling than seems desirable or feasible to the revolutionary government.

As Tocqueville and others suggest, democratization can occur "in installments" with the rise of successive social strata to greater prominence. Yet we have already had difficulty in explaining any particular revolution exclusively in terms of the rise of one particular social category. An historian, J. H. Hexter, has humorously highlighted the difficulty in "rise of the middle class" theories of social change, and by implication, of revolution:

> One of the odder performances in contemporary historiography takes place when the social historians of *each* European century from the twelfth to the eighteenth with an air of mystery, seize the curtain cord and unveil the great secret. "Behold," they say, "in *my* century the middle-class nobodies rising into the aristocracy." After an indefinite series of repetitions of this performance one is impelled to murmur, "But this is where I came in," or even, "What of it?" And then one begins to wonder why each highly competent specialist thinks that his particular sector of the oft-repeated process is so remarkable as to be worthy of the name of social revolution.[59]

Two possible explanations may be given of this situation: (1) the social historians are anachronistic in interpreting the developments of "their" century in terms of nineteenth-century categories; or (2) a cyclical process akin to Pareto's circulation of elites is always at work, rather than a long-term linear rise of one and the same middle class. In any case, the notions of democratization and the "rise" of this or that social stratum must be used with caution in explaining revolutions lest we lose sight of the complexity of each and the differences between all revolutions.

5. *Secularization*[60] seems to be a linear process of change occurring in the last several centuries, and writers of conservative political views and orthodox religious affiliations have made a direct link between it and the great modern revolutions. In an extreme version of this standpoint Joseph De Maistre characterized the French Revolution as a divine chastisement for the growth of disbelief during the Enlightenment. According to De Maistre France had exercised "a true magistracy over Europe"; and "it was above all at the head of the religious system. . . . Now, since it has made use of its influence to contradict its vocation and to demoralize Europe, it should cause no surprise that it has been brought back to it by terrible means."[61] Less theological and

more sociological is the interpretation of a Roman Catholic historian who sees in the "revolutionary attitude," which is "perhaps the characteristic religious attitude of modern Europe," a further "symptom of the divorce between religion and social life." [62] Pushed to the extreme this disguised religious impulse may turn "against social life altogether, or at least against the whole system of civilization that has been built up in the last two centuries." [63] The undermining of the Christian tradition was the work of secular-minded philosophers, and "it only needed the coming of a dynamic emotional impulse which appealed to the masses for the revolution to become a social and political reality." [64] What provided that impulse was the "democratic ideology of the *rights of man* and the *national will*. . . ." [65]

We do not have to accept either the more extreme or the more moderate of these arguments to see some relationship between the long run of secularization and the revolutionary attitude. We have already alluded to the theological elements of the political formulas in traditional regimes. Charles I, Louis XVI, and Nicholas II ruled according to divine right; and even the last Manchu rulers of China were traditionally supposed to have enjoyed "the mandate of heaven." While secularization was not far advanced by the 1640's,[66] it had certainly made grand strides by the time of the French, Russian, and Chinese Republican (1911) revolutions. Since secularization by definition erodes the divine basis of authority, it seems just to consider it an estimable factor in the genesis of modern revolutions. And furthermore, if there is some validity in speaking of modern radical ideologies of the left or the right as "secular religions," modern revolutionary movements owe much to the general process of secularization. Finally, as we shall see again, there is a dimension of religious conflict in revolutions that cannot simply be explained by the close association of throne and altar in pre-revolutionary society. There is more at stake than just striking down another buttress of the old order: different views of the world seem engaged in a life or death struggle.

6. *Growth of the Modern State.* While the thesis examined in Chapter II that strengthening of the state is the true meaning of revolution was found to be one-sided, a broader association of revolution with the long-term growth process of the modern state is eminently feasible. Especially the earlier revolutions in France and England and those in underdeveloped societies such as China in 1911 and perhaps Japan in 1868 seem to mark distinct movements towards the modern state. However, in assessing the role of this overall process in the century or less before the actual outbreak of revolution, we cannot afford to neglect the circumstance that opposition is formed precisely to protest

those measures that retrospectively we consider harbingers of modernization. Nowadays most authorities believe that the French Revolution was facilitated by the aristocratic revolt or "pre-revolution" in 1787–88, which was a protest led by the *parlements* against the royal government's attempt to reform the structure of public administration. Certain measures taken by Charles I and by the last imperial rulers of Russia and China appear to be modernizing, though they appeared capricious and tyrannical to oppositionists.

But before assessing the role of the growth of the modern state in the causal nexus of revolution, we have to have a much clearer idea of the various types of political organization involved in early modern and modern history.

The political sociology of Max Weber provides us with a scheme that represents "stages" in the development of the modern state. Weber's work is devoted to distinguishing between (1) *feudalism,* (2) *patrimonialism,* and (3) the *modern state.* Only the latter is a "state" in the fullest sense of the term for Weber; the term "polity" can be employed instead, especially when feudalism is involved. The keynote of feudalism is radical decentralization; thus the central unity of the feudal polity is precarious and intermittent. The political hierarchy consists of a series of levels of vassalage leading down from the monarch to the dependents and retainers of a minor local lord. These levels are linked by a "contractually fixed fealty on the basis of knightly militarism." [67] In other words, a religiously sanctioned oath unites superior and inferior in a reciprocal relationship of duty and privilege. However, this does not mean that the vassal is the chattel of his overlord, to be ordered about or exploited. The delimitation of the latter's rights is scrupulously maintained and becomes part of immemorial custom. Thus feudal relationships generally entail enormous discretionary powers on the part of vassals at all levels of the hierarchy.

In this system central government scarcely exists, and persuasion more than compulsion is used to obtain conformity from those ostensibly under the suzerainty of the monarch. The feudal polity therefore is a loose confederation of quasi-independent units. Only in cases of military crisis is the essentially go-it-alone policy of the local units transformed into something like a chain of command. In fact, feudal polities originate from the network of fiefs or land grants parceled out on the basis of past or future military service by the beneficiary. Ostensibly the king "owns" all the land of the realm which he dispenses to his loyal comrades-in-arms. Revocation of these grants is a possibility that time usually transforms into a fiction. Thus, the bonds holding the feudal polity together are somewhat ethereal, and what determines the behavior of the vassal is "the appeal not only to his obligations of fealty, but to his sense of high status which derives from an exalted conception of honor." [68] Fully developed feudalism as "the most extreme type of systematically, decentralized domination" is beset by one constitutional weakness: "the lord is powerful vis-à-vis the individual vassal, but powerless with regard to the interests of all vassals; he must be sure of the support or at least the toleration of the other vassals before he can safely proceed against any one of them." [69] Add to this his frequent lack of control over his vassal's vassals and the diffusion of power in the feudal polity becomes patent. In order to bring some cohesion to this centrifugal situation and to institutionalize the advisory function of the nobility there developed a "polity of estates" which was the immediate backdrop for the resurgence of patrimonialism, the next stage in the development of the modern state.

The patrimonial polity finds the ruler extending his power through the growth of an "officialdom" (not yet a true bureaucracy) responsible more or less to himself. In so doing he curtails the power of the feudal lords and the estates system which represents that power. Whereas the feudal relationship depends upon personal fealty, the patrimonial regime rests upon the status of various offices in the administrative network. There is furthermore an inherent conflict between the vestiges of properly feudal relationships and the ruler's elevation of "new men" to fill the offices that this embryonic state requires. As Weber points out, it was not only the patrimonial monarch's will to power that caused the decline of the estates and the rise of the officialdom: the estates themselves were often a filter for demands for new services, which were "the result of the general economic and cultural development and thus due to objective developmental factors." [70] Consequently, the longer patrimonialism persisted, the closer it approached to modern bureaucracy. This process is what is usually meant when historians trace the development of "absolute monarchy" in early modern Europe.

The patrimonial polity therefore represents a considerable increase in the powers of the central authority. An administrative network is cast over the country which is both cause and effect of the greater proportion of the social wealth finding its way into royal coffers. However, the patrimonial setup is still a far cry from the modern bureaucratic system. Many offices are purchasable and transmissible from father to son as other inheritable property. While the social status of the patrimonial official is originally much beneath that of the traditional landed nobility, such persons are likely to be notables whose families are in some phase of ascent to full aristocratic status. Their place in society, and their pride and tenure of office, may cause them to be something less than passive agents of monarchical centralization. For example, the early phases of the Fronde (1648–53), which was the most serious upheaval in France from the Wars of Religion to the revolution, was dominated by the Parlement of Paris—the epitome of patrimonial officialdom.[71]

It is out of the semibureaucratized patrimonial regime that the modern state developed. In the Weberian scheme the modern state has the following traits:

> *an administrative and legal order subject to change by legislation,* to which the organized activities of the administrative staff . . . are oriented. This system of order claims *binding authority,* not only over the members of the state . . . but also to a very large extent over all action taking place in the area of its jurisdiction. It is thus a compulsory organization with a *territorial basis.* Furthermore, today the use of force is regarded as legitimate only so far as it is permitted by the state or prescribed by it.[72] (Italics mine.)

The modern state has thus broken the "cake of custom" and makes law rather than discovering or applying the prescriptions of immemorial tradition. It is clearly sovereign within a given area and tends to monopolize the means of legitimate force therein. Clearly the feudal polity lacks these attributes and patrimonialism possesses them only in embryonic form. It is perhaps the emergence of bureaucratic organization that Weber considered most characteristic of the modern state. Modern bureaucracy exhibits six essential features in the Weberian scheme: (1) continuity of official business; (2) delimitation of authority through explicit rules; (3) a definite administrative hierarchy with higher organs supervising lower ones; (4) state funding of administration with public accountability of officials; (5) no venality, property, or heritability of office; and (6) written documentation of official business.[73]

With the distinction between the three types of polity in mind, we can readily understand why the common assertion that such and such a revolution "overthrew feudalism" is hopelessly misleading. In a full-fledged feudal system, revolution in the modern sense would be impossible, because *the near absence of a centralized political machine would deprive the revolutionaries of both a target to strike at and a base from which to transform the social order.* Revolution therefore requires as a minimum that a fairly developed patrimonialism is involved. What all the business about overthrowing feudalism amounts to is that revolution has overthrown a patrimonial regime with considerable survivals from an earlier feudal epoch.[74] On the other hand, revolution would seem more likely to succeed in a patrimonial than in a modern political system because of the latter's "monopoly of the means of legitimate force." Perhaps the

likelihood of revolution is greatest in the transition period between patrimonialism and the full modern state, for then the centralizing reforms of the royal government alienate traditionalists while disappoint-
ing radical reformers. The historical evidence would seem to indicate
that without the ravages of war or acute vertical cleavages (race, region,
etc.), the modern state is highly resistant to revolution "from below."

7. *The Growth of Modern Nationalism.* As nation and state are two
radically distinct notions, it is clearly not redundant to treat the growth
processes of the modern state and of modern nationalism separately in
discussing the causes of revolution. That the development of the state
sometimes parallels the growth of nationalism is beyond doubt, but that
the term "nation-state" in most cases grossly simplifies the actual complexity of the population of most states is just as certain. The most blatant consequence of this latter confusion is that what many modern
social scientists call "nation building" is rather "state building," which
often turns out to be "nation destroying" instead.[75] The strengthening
of the state under the guise of "nation building" occurs at the expense
of groups whose claim to nationhood is quite valid. The attempt to
merge already existing nations or near-nations into a novel state-spon-
sored supernation is patently artificial. Terror is the usual means used
to prevent such weak structures from tottering to the ground.

The growth of true nationalism then is the growth of that sentiment of belonging together and differentiation from others which is
such a salient feature of the modern world. Not surprisingly, whether
or not the potentially explosive elements of nationalism will reach revolutionary dimensions is determined by the historical context. However,
one general conclusion is warranted: *nationalism in some manifestation is
always involved in modern revolutions.* To see this more clearly and more
systematically, some sense of the chronology of modern nationalism is
essential.

E. H. Carr distinguishes three stages in the development of nationalism. The first stage is not one of nationalism proper, but rather of
the breakup of the medieval unity of church and state. With the development of the patrimonial state with its self-centered mercantilist economic policy and its attribution to itself of the power to control its
subjects' religion, the territorial framework within which Western
European nationalism, especially in France and England, would mature
takes form. But in this early stage the "nation" is restricted, politically
speaking, to the king, aristocracy, and bourgeois notables. Even so, the
fact that the patrimonial regime developed most impressively in France
and England is not accidentally related to the precocious development
of nationalism in those two countries. Here we have an instance of how

patrimonial centralization paved the way for the development of nationalism by shifting the focus of political and cultural identification away from the region and towards the kingdom as a whole.

The second of Carr's stages of nationalism runs from the Napoleonic wars to the outbreak of World War I. It involved the "democratization of nationalism," which to Carr means the close association of nationalism and the middle classes. Especially significant to the student of revolution is Carr's selection of Rousseau as "the founder of modern nationalism" because he in "rejecting the embodiment of the nation in the personal sovereign or the ruling class, boldly identified 'nation' and 'people'; and this identification became a fundamental principle both of the French and of the American revolutions." [76] Nineteenth-century middle-class nationalism could develop in relative tranquillity because of the international economic order, whose central clearinghouse was in London. Two "salutary illusions" allowed this system to work: (1) that economic life was governed by inexorable "laws of nature" beyond human control, and (2) that politics and economics were utterly separate realms. The first disguised the control function of the British, and the second prevented economic issues from exacerbating political conflict.

This house of cards collapsed with World War I, which ushered in the third of Carr's stages: the "socialization of the nation," with its "natural corollary" of the "nationalization of socialism." [77] Three main causes have provoked the new turn of nationalism in the twentieth century: "the bringing of new social strata within effective membership in the nation, the visible reunion of economic with political power, and the increase in the number of nations." [78] Since the masses have a voice in the political system, their economic needs loom larger in the determination of public policy, foreign and domestic. Out of this develops a species of economic nationalism compounded of welfare measures and protectionist trade policies. Hence the increasingly socialistic flavor of nationalism as in "integral nationalism" and fascism, and the nationalistic orientation of socialism as manifested by the "patriotic" behavior of most European social democratic parties at the outbreak of World War I. Finally, European imperialism has spread the seeds of nationalism on a global scale.

Besides the usual reservations about the "stages" of anything so complex and effervescent as nationalism, several of Carr's insights require clarification before we can apply them to revolution. While the twofold characterization of Rousseau as founder of modern nationalism and as chief philosopher of the French Revolution suggests the intimate relationship of nationalism and revolution in 1789, it would be wrong to neglect the strong nationalist overtones of the English Revolution a century and a half previous. Christopher Hill has traced the idea of the "Norman Yoke" during, before, and after the revolution. This multiform notion chastises the English monarchy, aristocracy, and all that goes along with them (sometimes Romanizing clergy, sometimes the common law itself) as tainted by the Norman conquest and usurpation of 1066. More specifically it charges that "the ruling class is alien to the interests of the majority of the population. Even if they no longer speak French, whether or not they are of Norman descent, the upper classes are isolated from the life of the working population. . . . The people could conduct its own affairs better without its Norman rulers, whose wealth and privileges are an obstacle to equality. *The nation is the people.*" [79] (Italics mine.) English nationalism at this time becomes associated with recovery of Anglo-Saxon virtues, values, and institutions.

Likewise the staunch Protestantism of the King's opponents is virtually inseparable from nationalistic feelings: Protestantism is English, Catholicism is alien. According to Hans Kohn, with the revolution "the tendencies of a nascent nationalism which had germinated under the Tudors now broke through in a volcanic eruption." [80] Kohn further gives priority to the religious dimension of the revolution, whose Calvinistic orientation caused English nationalism to be expressed "in an identification of the English people with the Israel of the Old Testament." [81] But Kohn's assessment of the new role of the people in the revolution is of even greater help in understanding how nationalism can operate in revolution: "They were no longer the common people, the object of history, but the nation, the subject of history, chosen to do great things in which every one, equally and individually, was called to participate. Here we find the first example of modern nationalism, religious, political, and social at the same time. . . ." [82]

The French Revolution was similarly accompanied by attempts to define the nation by excluding aristocracy, clergy, and even monarchy. An argument originally advanced by aristocrats that their privileges derived from Frankish conquest and subjection of the Gallo-Roman forebears of the Third Estate was turned on its head to show the archaic and illegitimate nature of these same privileges of rank.[83] Clearly nationalistic was the condemnation of the aristocracy at the hands of the Abbé Sieyès in his *What Is the Third Estate?* of 1788. Part of his onslaught can be summed up as follows: "Now the Third Estate . . . comprised the crushing numerical majority of the nation, all those who had no pretensions to privilege or status different from that implied in common citizenship, all those, moreover, who by their skill and effort maintained the social fabric. *They were therefore the nation.* The privileged orders were aliens, an encumbrance, an idle limb." [84] (Italics mine.) In these two early revolutions the latent egalitarianism of nationalism emerges into clear light. We also perceive a self-differentiating "we versus they" phenomenon, whose revolutionary implications were carried further in France than in England.

The nationalist character of the uprisings in central Europe in 1848 is clear. In the Russian Revolution of 1917 (which was just as much a non-Russian revolution), Ukrainian, Polish, Jewish, Armenian, Georgian, and other nationalist movements were in collusion with leftist revolutionary movements for some time. George Kennan points out that the Tsarist regime had pursued Russification and Great Russian supremacy, policies virtually calculated "to make sure that if there were anyone among the minority elements who was not already alienated from the autocracy by its general social and political policies, he would sooner or later be brought into opposition by the offense to his national feelings." [85] In China before the Japanese invasion of 1937, Chalmers Johnson sees nationalism as "primarily an ideological phenomenon restricted to educated elites." [86] The Japanese attack, however, led to the mobilization of the peasant masses and the increasing identification of the Chinese communists with Chinese nationalism. The communists acquired legitimacy as defender of the nation's cause against the foreign invader—a legitimacy that even revolutionary changes unforeseen by the peasant have not succeeded in dissipating. The Japanese therefore acted as a catalyst speeding up the transformation of Chinese nationalism from Carr's stage two of democratization to his stage three of socialization.[87]

Revolution can thus occur either during the transition from Carr's stage one to stage two, or from stage two to stage three. The likelihood of revolutionary movements being also nationalist is even higher than the likelihood of nationalist movements becoming truly revolutionary. The nationalist movements we saw in Chapter I tend to be more revolutionary as the task of "nation building" or sometimes "nation destroying" is the more prolonged and difficult. Finally it seems that egalitarianism, which is common both to nationalism and to many revolutionary ideologies, provides a vital linkage between nationalism and revolution. Thus the growth of nationalism is amongst the most important long-term causes of revolution.

Middle-Term Causes of Revolution

Understandably there can be no hard and fast distinction between middle-term and long-term causes of revolution. Chronologically, middle-term causes emerge into full prominence during the last decade or two before the outbreak of the revolution. They are in part ramifications of long-term factors or are cyclical or "random" factors that weaken the existing order.

1. *Economic Depression* (i.e., a downward swing in the business cycle marked often by high prices, unemployment, inflation, and poverty in some combination) has often been singled out as a radicalizing force in the years immediately preceding revolutions. The noted formulation of James C. Davies combines the long-term linearity of economic growth with the cyclic fluctuations of the business cycle: "Revolutions are most likely to occur when a prolonged period of objective economic development and social development is followed by a sharp reversal." [88] This is the case because such a sequence produces first "an expectation of continued ability to satisfy needs—which continue to rise" and then "a mental state of anxiety and frustration when manifest reality breaks away from anticipated reality." [89] Constant misery is no more or less conducive to revolutionary behavior than is constant improvement of conditions. It is rather the sudden gap between expectations and reality produced by cyclic downturn that dissipates confidence in the existing regime. Davies calls his theory "the J-curve hypothesis" for reasons apparent in Figure 4.

Davies thus envisages a point where the anxiety and fear produced by sudden reversal of the improving trend becomes intolerable and the ensuing frustration makes the government a scapegoat.

Figure 4. Davies' J-Curve of Revolution

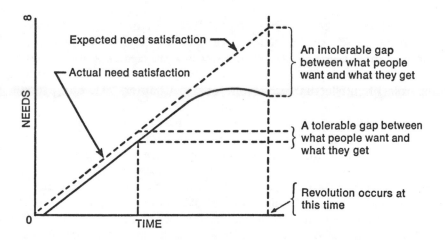

Whether it is in fact responsible for society's recent woes is not particularly important; what is important is that it is considered so responsible.

Politicization of discontent becomes truly revolutionary when a number of rather distinct groups with different interests, ideals, and attitudes becomes momentarily united in angry opposition to the government. "Marx to the contrary, revolutions are made not only by economically depressed classes and their leaders but by the joint effort of large numbers of those people in all social groups who are experiencing frustration of different basic needs." [90] His stress on objective development causes Davies to debunk any conspiratorial design to revolution, at least until very late in the day when "people begin to share their discontents and to work together." [91]

Though originally offered as a general hypothesis, Davies' later work acknowledges the inadequacy of the J-curve as a universal and comprehensive explanation of revolution. Treating of pre-revolutionary France, for example, he concedes that "more or less independently of frustrated rising expectations in the eighteenth century, French society was already deeply fragmented." [92] We can extend this proviso to nearly all revolutionary situations, and thus the J-curve assumes its proper place as a middle-term factor that can be of enormous significance in the complex causal network of revolutions. A rapid economic decline measurably accelerates revolutionary discontent (it, of course, does not create it *ex nihilo*), and provides the stimulus for food riots and other forms of economic protest that may serve as precipitants of revolution. As a part, and not the whole, the J-curve can be used profitably by students of revolution.

2. *Alienation of the Intellectuals.* What Lyford Edwards called "the transfer of the allegiance of the intellectuals" and Crane Brinton "the desertion of the intellectuals" is clearly a middle-term cause of revolution. Deferring fuller examination of the actual leadership role of intellectuals in revolutions to Chapter VII, our present concern is more with the critical function of intellectuals in undermining the legitimacy of societies moving towards revolution. Karl Mannheim has written of the socially unattached intelligentsia, whose emergence he considers "one of the most impressive facts of modern life." [93] Previous groups who concerned themselves with intellectual matters, such as priestly orders, were locked into the social structure in very definite positions. Modern intellectuals, however, do not constitute a class and are recruited from nearly all strata of society. It is not that intellectuals are wholly removed from conflict and cleavage between social strata; rather they incorporate all forms of social conflict. Nevertheless, the detached and composite quality of the intelligentsia allows

the possibility that it alone can "rise above" the partiality and interest-bound mentality of classes and parties. The intelligentsia thus has two historic roles: it can align itself with one or the other of "the various contending classes"; or it can attempt to fulfill its "mission as the predestined advocate of the intellectual interests of the whole." [94] By taking the first option the intellectuals provide the intellectual defenses of the interests of either rising classes (utopias) or declining classes (ideologies)—sometimes to the point of outright mendacity. By taking the second option they attempt to apply the insights of science to welfare of the whole community. While some of Mannheim's further formulations are misleading, his stress on the socially detached aspect of the intelligentsia should be kept in mind during the discussion that follows.

According to Lyford Edwards, the usual role of the intellectuals or "publicists" is to justify the position of the ruling class or "repressors" in the eyes of the immense majority of the "repressed." [95] That is, they articulate Mannheim's "ideologies" or Mosca's "political formulas." However, on occasion the publicist-intellectuals rebel against their customary role and unleash a crescendo of criticism making the existing regime appear both ridiculous and morally bankrupt. In a more positive vein they advance and propagate "a new body of knowledge and a new code of morals, including new standards of wisdom and foolishness" [96]—Mannheim's "utopia." This shift from defense to critique of the status quo constitutes an "advanced symptom" of revolution. While suggestive, Edwards' analysis is excessively simplified. An obvious correction is that the intellectuals' transfer of allegiance is never complete: some intellectuals will to the end side with the old regime. More serious is his mistake concerning what is the *normal* role of the intellectuals.

While it is correct to stress the need of societies and their rulers for a moral, religious, or philosophic foundation, it is wrong to ignore or underestimate the inherent ambivalence towards the surrounding society involved in intellectual activity as such. "In all societies," writes Edward Shils, "even those in which the intellectuals are notable for their conservatism, the diverse paths of creativity, as well as an inevitable tendency towards negativism, impel a partial rejection of the prevailing system of cultural values." [97] Their concern with ideas, perhaps as ends in themselves, predisposes intellectuals to develop ideas in directions not wholly congenial to the ideational buttresses of the existing social order. This latently critical activity can become blatantly critical and thus cross the threshold into properly revolutionary ideas. Thus Shils even argues that "furnishing the doctrine of revolutionary movements" is to be numbered among the "most important accomplishments" of modern intellectuals.[98] In this connection we must recall that the latter are in many ways the descendants of the priests and prophets of old insofar as all are preoccupied with the "ultimate" questions.[99] Herein perhaps lies the source of a distinctive trait of intellectuals that often appears as arrogance and self-righteousness to other members of society, not least to those at the peak of the social hierarchy. The intellectuals' concern with the "ultimate questions" seems inseparable from the "implied attitude of derogation to those who act in more mundane or routine capacities." [100]

It is thus a kind of occupational disease for intellectuals to consider themselves as the conscience of society and thereby to run afoul of the established authorities in church and state. If they do not produce revolutionary movements like rabbits out of a hat, their critical action hastens the evaporation of the regime's authority and helps to give focus to the manifest discontents of pre-revolutionary society. Before the English Revolution, according to Michael Walzer, the Puritan ministers constitute, perhaps, "the first example of 'advanced' intellectuals in a traditional society. Their exile had taught them the style of free men; its first manifestation was the evasion of traditional authority and routine." [101] Being outside the traditional church establishment, they acquired a "self-reliance" destined to judge the existing political and religious institutions as rotten to the core. Walzer states: "Years before English merchants and gentlemen were ready for an independent venture in politics and religion, the ministers had arrived in the political world and were already active, energetic, creative." [102] A similar missionary zeal animated the *philosophes* before the French Revolution, and they are more clearly the prototype of modern intellectuals than the radical Puritan clergy. They were "not professional philosophers sitting in cool ivory towers for contemplative purposes only, but crusaders whose mission it was to recover the holy places of the religion of humanity from Christian philosophy and the infamous things that supported it." [103]

In the nineteenth century, the modern intellectual emerges as a distinct social type, perhaps nowhere so distinctively as in Russia. There we see the alienation of the intellectuals assume its starkest oppositionist form because of the peculiar conditions of Russian society. Nowhere else is the intelligentsia so relentlessly critical; nowhere else is their rejection of the existing order so complete; nowhere do extremist ideologies find a heartier welcome. In the early part of the twentieth century the Chinese intelligentsia looked to Western values to fill the void left by the disintegration of the Confucian basis of their civilization.[104] Further evidence would only confirm the close correlation of alienated intellectuals and the onset of the revolutionary situation.

Now we must turn to the ways in which intellectuals prepare the coming of revolution. Two themes pervade the critical work of intellectuals before a revolution: (1) the immorality of all or part of existing social or political institutions, and (2) the ridiculousness of these institutions. Moral disapproval implies a rigid ethical standard by which to gauge the shortcomings of the old regime. The relativism or nihilism of certain intellectuals is largely a pose assumed to shock the unwary. Behind it there is usually a rigid ethical doctrine whose principles indict the traditional order. Alienated intellectuals are exponents of what Max Weber called an "ethic of ultimate ends" as opposed to an "ethic of responsibility." The former ethical style assumes a moral perfectionism which demands that conduct always follow the narrow road of moral purity. Devotees of an ethic of ultimate ends feel " 'responsible' only for seeing to it that the flame of pure intentions is not quelched: for example, the flame of protesting against the injustice of the social order." [105] Even when the formal ethical philosophy of alienated intellectuals is pragmatic or utilitarian, it is applied to society with all the verve of divinely inspired commandments.

The ethical critique of intellectuals seems to run through two distinct phases. In the first, criticism is diffuse and apolitical: it condemns the luxuriousness, arrogance, moral and sexual laxity of the high and the mighty and exposes the misery and ignorance of the lowest strata. Social manners and mores are subjected to a ruthless dissection. Most of this type of criticism has little direct political or revolutionary impact. However, eventually there comes a second phase in which distinctively political targets are marked out for acid criticism. With politicization of criticism—implicitly, and occasionally explicitly—revolutionary themes begin to be aired. The political system increasingly comes under attack: first, because it supports morally tainted social institutions and represses the more daring dissenters; second, because it stands in the way of the "transvaluation of values" which the intellectuals consider necessary for the rejuvenation of society.

Strangely enough, moral outrage may not be the most serious solvent of the legitimacy of existing social institutions. To proclaim that an individual, group, institution, or entire social system is radically evil may be countered by simple denial of the facts alleged or by appeal to different values. Accordingly it is often more damaging to portray the target—whatever it is—as ridiculous, silly, and laughable. Satire and caricature can become more potent weapons of dissenters than edifying discourses. When skillfully done, this not-so-harmless funmaking may even bring a smile to the lips of those under scrutiny. But the business may be far graver than anyone realizes, for as Lyford Edwards points out: "A ruling class can survive even though it knows itself to be tyrannical. It cannot survive if it is made to appear foolish in its own sight." [106] *A fortiori*, it is difficult for people to feel respect for those who are made to look perpetually silly. While satire is always with us, there seems to be an extraordinary growth of it before the great Western revolutions. Perhaps this partially explains why whose whom we would expect to be most active in opposing revolution greet it initially with favor or at least benevolent neutrality. It is hard to take up the cudgels in defense of something you think is essentially ridiculous.

It is hard to overestimate the importance of the critical function of intellectuals in altering the climate of opinion in a society so as to make various segments of society more receptive to the idea, and eventually the reality, of revolution. Talcott Parsons has suggested that the emergence of the modern intelligentsia betokens the greater autonomy of the cultural vis-à-vis the social subsystem than is seen in other times.[107] Thus intellectuals would be prime agents of cultural change, which is perhaps the chief source of dissynchronous social change and therefore of revolution.

3. *Division and Ineptitude in the "Ruling Class"* constitute two logically distinct problems prominent in lists of the necessary conditions of revolution. They deserve somewhat separate discussion. Plato in the *Republic* points out: "Is it not a simple fact that in any form of government revolution always starts from the outbreak of internal dissension in the ruling class? The constitution cannot be upset so long as that class is of one mind, however small it may be." [108] Though the notion of the ruling class was less troublesome in Plato's day than in ours, his thesis has found echoes among modern students of revolution. Edwards denies the possibility of success against a ruling class "so long as they have confidence in themselves and faith in what they stand for. . . ." [109] Brinton, exercising his customary caution, restricts himself to merely pointing out that in three at least of the revolutions he studied "we find the ruling classes . . . markedly divided, markedly unsuited to fulfill the functions of a ruling class." [110] Louis Gottschalk broadens the emphasis a bit by asserting that "the necessary immediate cause of revolution" is in "the weakness of the conservative forces," [111] which variable does not necessarily imply the existence of a potent revolutionary movement.[112] This last point suggests that a strong revolutionary movement may fail if it challenges a strong and monolithic ruling elite, whereas a weak one may succeed if confronted by a ruling elite riven with dissension and half sympathetic to the revolutionary cause. It also lends credence to "collapse" as opposed to "overthrow" theories of revolution.

The "traitors to their class" phenomenon which sees so many members of the upper social strata in the front ranks of the revolution is simply the most visible symptom of the political fragmentation of pre-revolutionary ruling classes. Their defection not only strengthens the revolutionists; it *ipso facto* weakens the defenders of the old regime. Thus, each individual defection is a "double loss." The historical evidence offers tremendous support for the conclusion that division of the ruling classes is a necessary condition for a successful revolution. Even Leon Trotsky finds that "the ruling classes, as a result of their practically manifested incapacity to get the country out of its blind alley, lose faith in themselves; the old parties fall to pieces; a bitter struggle of groups and cliques prevails; hopes are placed in miracles and miracle workers." [113] This situation for Trotsky makes up "one of the political premises of a revolution, a very important although a passive one." [114] Trotsky, of course, emphasizes the passive or dispositional role of elite fragmentation because he wishes to reserve the active and dynamic role in revolution to the revolutionary class and its leaders. We do not have to follow him in this. Thus, we might operationally call the group composed of the top 1–4 percent in the three stratification systems a "ruling class" and then agree that revolution is highly unlikely if that group retains unity in the face of a threat from below. On the other hand, we have found that it is precisely tension between the three systems that not only gives the term "ruling class" its nebulous quality but also prompts some people to join the opposition.

However, some students have maintained that all the advantages of elite unity would come to nought if they did not include a preponderance of control over the means of physical coercion. A relatively united elite is both willing and able to use military, police, and other formations to repress threats to the social order, whereas a fragmented elite is not. Had Charles I in 1640, Louis XVI in 1789, Nicholas II in 1917, or others had strong and reliable security forces which they were willing to use to repress dissidents, who can say with certainty that revolution would have broken out at that time, if at all? [115] A revolutionary situation is not the same thing as a successful revolution. Understandably, control over the military was a major bone of contention between Charles and Louis and their respective legislative oppositions in the early days of the English and French revolutions. On the other hand, a chief cause of the abortiveness of the Russian Revolution of 1905 was that, despite scattered mutinies, the bulk of the security forces remained loyal to the Tsarist government. Three years of World War I were enough to change this by 1917. Such considerations have led one student of this general problem to conclude that "whatever government or party has the full allegiance of a country's armed forces is to all intents and purposes politically impregnable." [116] One of the reasons why governments lose control over the military is, of course, mutiny of the lower ranks, who come from the lower social strata. Thus, division within the elite is not the only source of military unreliability, though it may be in a given situation.

Studies of revolution have often made mention of the uncommon ineptitude or even of the decadence of ruling classes before revolutions. Many of these studies further suggest the intriguing hypothesis that had better leadership been available to the regime, the revolution could have been avoided through a judicious mixture of firmness and reform—the exact blend varies from author to author. Before tackling these issues we should point out that three levels of leadership exist to which one can apply the labels "inept" or "decadent": (1) the ensemble of groups called the "ruling class"; (2) Dorso's "political class" (i.e., those in informal and formal positions of political power); and (3) the small clique of advisers, favorites, and notables surrounding the head of state.

Wholesale judgments about the incompetence or decay of such broad formations as the ruling class must be made with caution. They are judgments often passed after a considerable lapse of time. Herbert Butterfield has exposed the hollowness and anachronistic quality of many attempts to show how the "losers" in a particular conflict were morally reprehensible while the "winners" were paragons of virtue.[117] And even if such assertions are more than mere tautologies, Pettee made a necessary qualification by stressing that a "ruling class which is in a state of decay is not all and equally and uniformly decadent however. Different factions of it are more and less devoted to the old myth, more and less receptive to innovation, more and less dissolute." [118]

The historiography of revolution has fastened on three main factors of decadence and incompetence of broad ruling strata: *isolation, obsolescence,* and *irresponsibility.* Isolation means, first, that the rulers have become so cut off from the rest of society that they cannot divine the old and new grievances that percolate in the lower strata. Indeed, the way of life of the upper strata is so remote from their compatriots that "two nations", in Disraeli's phrase, seem to inhabit the same land. There is a breakdown not in communications, but in the preconditions for communications. A different aspect of isolation has been stressed by Mosca: a ruling class isolated from the masses finds that "frivolousness and a wholly abstract and conventional culture takes the place of a sense of reality and of an accurate knowledge of human qualities." This entails the growth of "sentimental and exaggerated humanitarian theories on the innate goodness of the human species," [119] which debilitate the ruling class by preventing it from taking harsh measures of self-defence. By curtailing the circulation of elites, isolation removes the possibility of the regeneration of the ruling class, because it is uniquely amongst the lower strata that "necessities of life, the continual and harsh struggle for bread, the lack of literary culture keep awake the ancestral instincts for struggle and the inexhaustible toughness of human nature." [120] Such an isolated ruling class is easy prey for any halfway formidable enemy from within or without. However, this notion of ruling class isolation is based on French history and fits less neatly the history of other revolutions.

Explanations that point to the obsolescence or effeteness of pre-revolutionary ruling strata often are weakened by a naive progressivist bias: ruling classes are overthrown, it is held, because they are "backward," averse to "social progress" or "modernization." Close study, however, often reveals that the groups in question were rather less than complete reactionaries and, ironically, that some of the insurgents held "backward" ideas hardly in keeping either with the later course of history or with "progressive" ideas. Despite such reservations, it is still safe to conclude that when high status groups lose touch with those political, military, and other social functions originally associated with them without taking on new ones, they tend to lose confidence in themselves and squander society's faith in them. One does not have to accept Sieyès' caricature of the French aristocracy as wholly parasitical to appreciate that function and status, performance and privilege had become radically severed in eighteenth-century France. We can even go further and say that obsolescence of the ruling class in this sense plays at least some role in all revolutions. However, it must not be given exclusive importance for the simple reason that one can find examples of ruling classes which were "obsolete" on nearly all grounds, but which avoided or withstood the revolutionary test. Pareto's maxim that the fact of their overthrow is "proof" of the complete decay of a ruling class is either false or tautologous.

Irresponsibility is a charge often leveled by contemporaries and historians at ruling classes struck by revolution. What is usually alleged is that the upper strata have been seduced and debauched by a life of idleness, luxury, and frivolity. The allurements of *la dolce vita* turn aristocrats and notables away from any productive or protective function which custom dictates is the *quid pro quo* for special privilege. It is hard to deny that dissoluteness of elite groupings was on the upswing before the three great Western revolutions. The court life of the early Stuarts, Louis XV and Louis XVI, and the last Romanovs was positively repugnant to important sectors of society. Even if we discount the opposition's polemical exaggerations of the social costs of this carefree existence, it seems clear that what Veblen called "conspicuous consumption" and "conspicuous waste" saw a flurry of growth before the outbreak of revolution, despite some genuine reform efforts. Marie

Antoinette's apocryphal "Let them eat cake" is symptomatic of a kind of social irresponsibility that sometimes overtakes aristocratic formations. Arrogance is almost always a characteristic of high status groups; but sometimes it is combined with an authentic ethic of social paternalism and sometimes it is not. And yet, in this connection too one must guard against a view of history that seems to embody the biblical "The wages of sin is death." Before one can truly assess the precise importance of decadence and incompetence of ruling strata in the causal nexus of revolutions, comparative studies would have to explain why revolutions have often failed to develop in cases in which all or nearly all the symptoms of decadence were present.

Somewhat more concrete is the charge of ineptitude concerning a smaller group, the political elite or what Dorso called the "political class." The government political class or the Court was on the whole less competent than the men who, first as the Country "party" and later as the Parliamentarians, constituted the opposition political class. The same seems to hold if we compare the servants of the King in France before and just after 1789 with the leaders of the Third Estate, the patriot "party." As for Russia before and after 1905, the split was between government and a somewhat vague group spearheaded by the intelligentsia and called somewhat ambitiously "Society." " 'Society' thought of itself as an idealistic fellowship of dedicated men and women struggling for truth and justice, and of the government as an organized group of bureaucrats who kept the country shackled by tradition and whose administration preserved unchanged the conditions of an outlived past." [121] While the Tsarist bureaucracy produced several authentic statesmen in its closing years, the various oppositionist groupings probably included the greater political talents. Nor is one impressed by the bureaucratic elites at the fall of the Ch'ing dynasty in 1911 or of the Spanish monarchy in 1931. It would seem that Dorso's "exchange" between government and opposition political classes approaches zero before revolution and that capable people who might normally find their way into government service are led into intransigent opposition. Here too the regime's loss is a gain for the revolutionary movement.

Finally, we must consider the quality of the heads of state and their immediate entourages as a possibly important, even crucial, variable in the final crisis-ridden years and months before the revolution displays its full force. Nearly all accounts of pre-revolutionary heads of state absolve them of outlandish cruelty or moral turpitude. Charles I on strictly moral grounds was a cut or two above his father James I, to say nothing of Henry VIII. Louis XVI was more morally pure than his predecessor, and far less the tyrant than the Sun King, Louis XIV.

Nicholas II was less ruthless than his namesake and morally superior to more than one Russian autocrat before or since. Louis Napoleon's ambitions were far less boundless than his uncle's, and so on. "Well-meaning" is the label most frequently attached to these and other rulers displaced by revolutions. And yet historians after exhausting the adjectives *chaste, pious, kind, patriotic, honorable,* etc., tend to conclude that these ill-starred rulers were politically incompetent—while virtuous in the modern sense, they lacked what Machiavelli called *virtú* (i.e., political adroitness). More specifically, they give in when firmness is necessary; they are immovable when flexibility is called for; they fail to perceive the gravity of the political situation; they lack perseverance, choose bad advisers, and sometimes even fall under the sway of their politically obtuse wives.

These negative evaluations clearly pinpoint the question of the preventability of revolution through good leadership. Could an Elizabeth I have averted the clash between the royal government and the parliamentary majority that touched off civil war and revolution? Would a Louis XIV or Henry IV have committed the blunders of the later Louis? Could a Peter the Great or Catherine or even Nicholas I have averted the destruction of the Russian monarchy? And so on for every case of successful revolution. Or do historians looking backward endow the "losers" with qualities appropriate to such a fate and the "winners"—those who have maintained or strengthened their power in the face of adversity—with the earmarks of statesmanship, albeit ruthless statesmanship. The "great man" theory of history would bid us look no further: those of heroic proportions survive and prosper, the mediocrities allow themselves to be swept aside.

No easy answers to any of these questions can be given. While it is usually true that pre-revolutionary heads of state and their governing teams fail to measure up to the standards of political sophistication of certain of their predecessors, the "well-meaning, but inept" hypothesis should not be given more importance than it deserves. If revolution were essentially a matter of personal shortcomings of particular rulers and their confidants, it would be rather superfluous to trace its long-term and most of its mid-term causes. Once more the laborious distinction between simple coups d'etat and revolution would break down. Nevertheless, though Charles, Louis, and Nicholas were not the first rulers of their countries to die of political causes, their deaths had another and revolutionary significance. In the light of this it is best to conclude that consummate political skill or *virtú* can at best postpone the result if the seeds of radical change are sown too deeply and too far afield. Furthermore it is nothing short of anachronistic to think that the political style of Henry VIII would automatically have spared Charles

I, or that of Louis XIV served his descendant, or that of Peter the Great been possible for the last of the Romanovs. A style of leadership that "works" in one epoch fails in another. A change in the political culture has supervened, which closes off certain avenues of political strategy and tactics, though it may open up new ones that tradition-bound rulers are incapable of perceiving or following.[122]

A corollary of the "well-meaning, but inept" hypothesis maintains that since reform is preventative medicine for violent revolution, the main failure of pre-revolutionary leaders is the absence or inadequacy of reform efforts. At first glance this argument seems convincing: peacefully introduce all the reforms desired by oppositionists and they will have no discernible reason to overthrow the regime. But simple answers do not usually cover complex realities. In the first place, demands for reform tend to grow in number and seriousness with the development of the revolutionary crisis. Secondly, the aggregate impact of these reforms would amount to the introduction of a new system, not just a modification of the old one. This is why it becomes nearly impossible for the government to accede to the demands of the more determined oppositionists: it is idle to expect a ruling class as a corporate entity to commit political suicide knowingly.

Although castigated as thoroughly immobilist by critics, pre-revolutionary regimes are to a surprising degree reforming regimes. George Pettee speaks of "the peculiar mixture of sporadic reform and reaction" plus pure immobilism that is "typical before a revolution." [123] He attributes this incoherence to the uneven quality of the declining elite. This, however, is to miss a vital point: *sincere and serious reform efforts can hasten as well as forestall the coming of revolution.* Samuel P. Huntington more than most has sensed that whether reform is a "substitute" for revolution or is a "catalyst" for it depends upon specific historical conditions.[124] Of prime significance are "the nature of the reforms, the composition of the revolutionaries, and the timing of reforms." [125] Certain sorts of reform can help to induce revolution by whetting appetites for further reforms incompatible with the existing regime or by convincing oppositionists that the regime has no backbone. Other sorts of reform can by unclogging the channels of elite circulation actually strengthen the regime, for example, by bringing potential revolutionaries back within the system. In either case, all significant reform alienates somebody whose real or imaginary interests are hurt. Politics is necessarily controversial.

Huntington goes further and analyzes the differential effect of reform on two "crisis strata" [126] of modernizing societies: the urban intelligentsia and the peasantry. Reform programs aimed to satisfy the former group "only increase the strength and radicalism of that class.

They are unlikely to reduce its revolutionary proclivities. For the government interested in the maintenance of political stability, the appropriate response to middle-class radicalism is repression, not reform." [127] When this somewhat ironic feature of reform is added to conservative disgust over any reform at all, one sees readily why measures that in the abstract should gain support for a regime actually serve to weaken it and thereby to facilitate revolution. It is not only the roads of hell that are paved with good intentions, so too is the path to the scaffold. Very different, Huntington suggests, can be the results of peasant-oriented reforms: defusing of a revolutionary situation is a real possibility. Because the demands of the middle-class intelligentsia (and especially of its student vanguard) are ideological and maximalist in the extreme, it is exceedingly difficult for government to placate the attendant discontent through reforms. Peasant demands, however, have historically had a concreteness and specificity that makes them in principle more feasible. In certain cases therefore, "if the government is strong enough to compel some redistribution of land, such action will immunize the peasant against revolution." [128] (Even here, the pro-peasant reform will alienate the landlord classes, and if the new agrarian system is less productive than the old, economic problems can hurt the government in other ways.) Summing up the above conclusions, it seems evident that reform instituted by a somewhat divided, somewhat inept, political leadership is as likely as not to accelerate the drift towards revolution.

Of division and ineptitude amongst the ruling classes (and the political elite), the former seems the more fatal weakness. However, the exact significance of these factors is likely to vary considerably in different revolutions and can thus only be measured by rigorous and unpolemical historical analysis. It is difficult even in long retrospect to avoid casting the "enemy" as a complete villain.

4. *War* has been so often and intimately associated with revolution that one wonders how the old maxim that governments undertake foreign wars to alleviate domestic discontent ever gained currency. No doubt under certain conditions governments have succeeded in pulling the ranks of a divided people together through this stratagem, but it is a dangerous gamble especially when wars come to affect the daily lives of the people. Thus, if we need a maxim about war and political stability, one more in keeping with the historical record might be "War is the midwife of revolution." The relationship is quite direct in the case of the Russian and the Chinese revolutions, the downfall of the German and Austro-Hungarian empires with their moderate and abortive radical revolutions, and wherever communist revolutions after World War

II were something more than Soviet impositions (e.g., Yugoslavia). And similarly with the overthrow of Louis Napoleon's Second Empire during the Franco-Prussian War of 1870–71. War is less immediately involved with the outbreak of the English and Great French revolutions, but as we shall see it is still important in various ways. The lack of a serious war for over a generation in Europe may explain in part the petering out and easy containment of revolutionary activity during the dramatic year of 1848.

First, we must elaborate the distinction between the *deferred* and *immediate* effects of war on the coming of revolution. The former are in the main financial blows to the regime's stability. A series of costly wars, whether victorious or not, can put a mortgage on later generations. For example, the French monarchy never really recovered financially from the expenditures laid out for the glorious wars of Louis XIV (d. 1714). And later, while the French share in the American victory in the War of Independence was a moral compensation for earlier costly defeats at British hands, the expense of this revenge accelerated and aggravated the government's financial crisis. Another deferred influence of war upon revolution is found when a government squanders its moral capital in a series of unpopular or unsuccessful wars.

The immediate effects of war on the coming of revolution are more numerous than the deferred effects. Some serve to discredit and delegitimize the government in the eyes of many; others serve to evoke new conditions detrimental to the survival of the existing political or social order. Of the first sort, simple war-weariness is a potentially corrosive force. People who are sick and tired of a given war may be receptive to a radical message that under peacetime conditions might never reach them. While all parties to World War I naturally experienced war-weariness, Russia seems to have had the earliest and acutest case of all. Moreover, the famine and destruction produced by some wars can redound to the discredit of the government, which seems incapable either of making peace or of feeding and safeguarding its people. As war, especially modern war, generally involves concentration of powers in the government, it will naturally be held accountable for more things. War-weariness and resentment over the human and material costs of war may combine to produce the feeling that not only *this* war conducted by *this* government is wrong, but that the system of government that fights wars this way or gets involved in them at all is all wrong—war breeds revolutionaries.

War, and in particular "total war," is also a prime force in accelerating the decline of old values and beliefs so essential to a regime's legitimacy. Sigmund Neumann has written of World War I, for example, that "War's supreme efforts necessitated swift action and firm integration, disciplined regimentation and tight centralization. Institutions had to be streamlined and individuals turned into robots. In the baptism of fire certain hitherto moral standards were tested anew and well-established social concepts redefined." [129] War may thus produce *anomie*—a breakdown in the traditional value system. But anomie is an uncomfortable situation for most men and is often a preparatory stage for a new ideological dispensation. Revolutionists on both sides of the political spectrum profited immensely from the disorientation (of the young especially) that World War I produced. Whatever else a revolutionary movement may be, it is a phenomenon that gives meaning to the lives of otherwise disillusioned people.

Another source of war-induced discontent is the tendency of governments to make far-reaching promises of reform and reward for the sacrifices associated with a protracted struggle. At its end, however, they often prove unwilling or unable to deliver the land reform, or expanded suffrage, or right to a job or whatever; and the proposed beneficiaries feel betrayed.[130] Of greater moment, perhaps, is the exacerbation of nationalism in war due either to conscious government policy or foreign invasion. Governments that stimulate the forces of nationalism for military purposes may have produced a monster that will turn on and destroy its creators. War can encourage nationalism not only in ethnically homogeneous states, but also in multiethnic empires. In the second instance nationalist revolutionaries can seize upon the government's weakness or imminent defeat to mobilize a full-fledged onslaught against the regime. In either case modern war involves the mobilization of the people, and the aftermath of World War I has illustrated how the nation-in-arms can spell trouble for government. While paramilitary forces made up of demobilized soldiers are probably not enough to make authentic revolution, they can provide necessary assistance.

5. *Government Financial Crisis* has preceded revolution so often that we can regard it as an important middle-term cause of revolution. The governments of France, England, Russia, Spain, and China faced chronic financial difficulties at the general period of their respective revolutions. Nearly all the pre-revolutionary governments made unsuccessful attempts to increase taxes and to reform the tax structure to bring in desperately needed revenue. While the mere fact of financial crisis lends credence to the charge of ineptitude and irresponsibility, the actions the government takes to remedy the situation also alienate vital support. Much of the quarrel between Charles I and Parliament concerned taxes and expenditures. Parliament was willing to grant most of Charles' requests, but at the price of political concessions which

would have drastically redressed the balance of institutional power in its favor. Charles was unwilling to comply. In France, taxes were wholly inadequate because aristocratic privilege usually meant tax exemptions; therefore loans were contracted which resulted in a vicious cycle of government indebtedness. Albert Soboul considers the resulting deficit "a chronic ill of the monarchy and principal of the immediate causes of the Revolution." [131] The apparent intractability of this problem is suggested by the nearly 50 percent of the "budget" of 1788 that was slated to cover interest on the debt.[132] Though the English and the French cases are the most striking, other examples show how the contrast between societies with rapidly expanding economies and their near-bankrupt governments enhances revolutionary possibilities.

However, tax and other financial troubles point to revolution only if certain of the other long-term and middle-term causal factors are operative. Soboul and others may be correct that the royal government's financial deficit is the chief immediate (i.e., middle-term) cause of the French Revolution, but such a conclusion should not be generalized. For it is doubtful that a revolution could succeed in a society where the ruling groups were united and the intellectuals tame, despite a grim governmental financial picture. Taxation can make people angry and dispose them to revolt, but whether this revolt will be transformed into revolution or merely add to the conjuncture of forces working towards that result depends on a number of historical variables.

Precipitants of Revolution

Precipitant causes are the third and final level of causation in revolution. They are by definition discrete events and understanding their role may be eased if we recall the source of analogy of the term "precipitant." In chemistry a precipitant is a substance which introduced in minute quantities causes another substance (the precipitate) which is in solution to leave that state. In other words, it promotes a drastic and immediate reaction amongst preexisting ingredients. Lyford Edwards defines a precipitant of revolution as "some act, insignificant in itself, which precipitates a separation of the repressors and their followers from the repressed and their followers." [133] He mentions the Petrograd Strike in March, 1917; the fall of the Bastille; and Charles I's attempt to arrest five dissident M.P.'s among his examples. However, the inherently complex nature of revolution as a "macro-event" makes it rather more difficult than Edwards thought to fasten on the one among "a series of lawless actions which coincides with the completion of the psychological preparation for revolution." [134] Louis Gottschalk describes the significance of precipitants of revolution as demonstrating "clearly that the conservative forces are no longer able to resist the revolutionary tide." [135]

Building upon this foundation, Chalmers Johnson prefers the term "accelerator" to "precipitant," and stipulates that accelerators "always affect an elite's monopoly of armed force, and they lead either mobilized or potential revolutionaries to believe that they have a chance of success. . . ." [136] ("Preponderance" is perhaps more accurate than "monopoly" of armed force, if we recall that patrimonialism lacks some of the attributes of the "modern state.") According to Johnson there are three types of accelerator. The first type directly affects the regime's armed forces and their effective reliability. The second type is "an ideological belief held by a protesting group that it can . . . succeed in overcoming the elite's armed might." [137] Johnson cites belief in divine intervention on the revolutionary side, or in the masses' rallying to it, or in the revolutionary potential of general strikes, etc., as examples. But in doing so he loses the specific-event quality of precipitants, because an "ideological belief" is not an event in this sense. The third type of accelerator includes attacks on the armed forces, such as revolutionary guerrilla operations.

Leaving out Johnson's second type of accelerator, the distinction between the other two is valid and useful because it underscores the contrast between "accidental" and "planned" precipitating events. *Accidental precipitants* are those whose revolutionary significance and consequences are almost completely unanticipated by the authorities, the revolutionaries, and the perpetrators of the deed.[138] Riots, strikes, mutinies, and other events that get out of hand demonstrate that the security forces are somehow insufficient to quash the revolutionary movement. Understandably, overeager revolutionaries are prone to overestimate any embarrassment of the forces of order as indicative of fatal weakness. Such pseudoprecipitants, of course, enormously outnumber the genuine article. When the latter occur, revolutionists, however reluctant or even surprised some of them may be, are encouraged to press the further steps that may culminate in the definitive overthrow of the existing regime. A precipitant then is a point of no return in the revolutionary process, as people on the fence are forced to take sides, the precipitating event or events may lay bare the polarization between those willing to go the route of revolution and those who are not.

Planned precipitants are those riots, strikes, mutinies, assassinations, attacks, attempted coups, and so forth, which revolutionary activists instigate in the express hope of triggering a broader revolutionary response. This sort of gambit is more characteristic of the last two centuries, after the development of some traditional revolutionary strategies. The revolutionary elite judge the situation volatile enough so that their spark will set off a grand revolutionary conflagration. Needless to say, the timing of such planned precipitants is a fruitful source of controversy, polemic, and recrimination among the activists. These considerations make one think of a third sort of precipitant midway between the wholly fortuitous and the wholly contrived, in which the revolutionaries have not orchestrated the entire operation but move in very quickly to take it over and make it serve their purposes.

Finally, it seems more in keeping with our overall emphasis on the complexity of revolution and the difficulty of marking its outbreak with utter precision that more than one precipitant or accelerator may be necessary to really turn the issue. However, there are definite limits to this if we wish to avoid robbing the notion of precipitant of real significance.

THE SOCIAL PSYCHOLOGY OF REVOLUTION: MISERY AND RISING EXPECTATIONS

Needs, Frustration, and Revolution

To this point our emphasis has been largely, though not exclusively, on social stratification and on the various sorts of social change, without acknowledging much that it is, after all, men and women, common as well as uncommon, who "make" revolutions. We have said little concerning the motivational mechanisms which the three levels of causation just discussed work upon and stimulate into action. This vital area of inquiry can be called "the social psychology of revolution." Despite some controversies, substantial agreement exists on why large numbers of men of different sorts are sometimes moved to revolution. The core hypothesis of most social psychological approaches to revolution is a deceptively simple one: *men have basic needs, wishes, or instincts, which if frustrated give rise to feelings of aggression that sometimes take the form of revolutionary behavior and violence.*

Pitirim Sorokin formulated this line of thinking in the strongest terms: "The immediate cause of revolution is always the growth of 'repression' of the main instincts of the majority of society, and the impossibility of obtaining for those instincts the necessary minimum of satisfaction. The remoter are whatever occasions such a growth of repression." [139] Revolutions then are caused by peculiarly intensive and extensive repression of basic instinctual needs. Realizing that the biological roots of behavior interact somewhat with properly cultural influences, Sorokin was led to relativize his concept of instinct repression considerably. Repression turns out to be a function of comparing what we now enjoy with what we once enjoyed or comparing what we enjoy with what others enjoy. Among the repressed instincts and "reflexes" important in revolution Sorokin includes the desire for food, clothing, shelter, reflexes of individual and collective self-preservation, sexual desire, instincts of ownership and self-expression, impulses of "fighting and rivalry, creative work, of variety of experience and adventure," and so on.[140] Serious and prolonged repression of these instincts "will inevitably force people to look for some way out." [141] This "way out" can involve the breakdown of the usual habits, restraints, and inhibitions of human behavior. Revolution then is not merely a narrow political process but a radical reorientation of nearly all aspects of social life. This includes a " 'biologization' of behavior and a relaxation of the checks which deterred the individual from committing anti-social acts." [142] Once this process has reached the mass of people, revolution in the political sense is mere frosting on the cake.

Sensing perhaps the dead end of specifying instincts for so many forms of human behavior, Lyford Edwards simplifies Sorokin's scheme by adopting the "four elemental types of wishes" formulated by the sociologist W. I. Thomas. These include (1) the wish for new experience, (2) the wish for security, (3) the wish for public recognition, and (4) the wish for response in personal intimacy. On this basis Edwards concludes that "all revolutions may thus be conceived of as due to the repression of one or more of these elemental wishes, and the violence of any revolution is, it is assumed, proportional to the amount of such repression." [143] Revolution then is an escape from excess repression, though Edwards stipulates too that "subjective" feelings of repression can actually increase in times of "objective" betterment for the repressed strata of society. George Pettee develops a similar social psychological framework with his notion of "cramp," whose four types—economic, social, ideological, and political—are the major causes of revolution. "The cramped individual is one who not only finds that his basic impulses are interfered with, or that he is threatened by various ills, but who also feels that his repression is unnecessary and avoidable, and therefore unjustified." [144]

Sorokin, Edwards, and Pettee also agree that revolution occurs when a more or less large majority of society feel severely repressed. As public opinion polls are a recent device, no one can or should speak with utter certainty on this question. However, it seems doubtful whether a "repressed" or "cramped" numerical majority is really a necessary condition for revolution, though it may be for some particular revolutions. Since different groups and strata feel repressed for different reasons, it seems wiser to look for a heterogeneous coalition of "crisis strata," which may or may not comprise a majority. There is considerable doubt, for example, whether the vast mass of Englishmen felt repressed enough in 1640 to contemplate revolution as the only way out of their ills.[145] The "masses" so dear to partisans of this or that revolution are usually the highly visible but numerically modest "revolutionary crowds" of the bigger cities. The enigma of the silent majority is nothing new.

Recently the "need hierarchy" of Abraham Maslow has influenced the social psychology of revolution. Maslow's five need areas constitute a hierarchy in the sense that the more primordial needs must be met before the human organism can move on to the others. They include (1) physical needs (water, food, sex, etc.); (2) safety needs (order, predictability, dependability); (3) need for love, affection, belongingness; (4) need for self-esteem; (5) need for self-actualization.[146] From even this brief sketch we can see possibilities of rapprochement between various approaches to needs, their fulfillment, or repression.[147] What links these theories of motivation to revolution and political violence is some rendition of the "frustration-aggression" hypothesis, for example: "Frustration does not necessarily lead to violence, and violence for some men is motivated by expectations of gain. The anger induced by frustration, however, is a motivating force that disposes men to aggression, irrespective of its instrumentalities. . . ."[148] Here revolution is subsumed under the general category of collective political violence, all of whose manifestations stem from similar motivational sources. Thus, generally speaking, "the primary causal sequence in political violence is first the development of discontent, second the politicization of that discontent, and finally its actualization in violent action against political objects and actors."[149] Revolution is violent aggression undertaken against "political objects and actors" prompted by intensive politicization of frustration and discontent caused by destructive social conditions.

While we have rejected as unviable the idea of "peaceful revolution," the social psychologists of revolution give excessive prominence to the factor of violence in revolution. This leads them to discuss the causes of all forms of collective violence as variations on a single theme. But the core idea of collective political violence is that it strikes *against* something—against repression and its reputed sources. No doubt this is largely the case with revolution, but such a one-sided emphasis is to blur needlessly the distinction between revolution and revolt. Revolutions differ from revolts because they are not only against something, but also *for* something radically new—however vague that something may be in the early phases. Thus, the social psychology of revo-

lution must guard against neglect or underestimation of those processes of change that stem from the social, cultural, and technological
subsystems and their interactions. It is these that endow revolution with
that "abnormality" that distinguishes it from more common forms of
political violence.

Relative Deprivation and Revolution

Admitting that widespread feelings of repression, frustration, and
anger predispose a society to political violence and perhaps revolution,
we must now examine how changing conditions serve to stimulate the
appropriate behavioral responses. Two great historical theories have
offered alternative explanations of why revolution is more likely in certain circumstances than in others. Karl Marx's thesis that increasing
misery of the working class ineluctably drives them to revolution can be
generalized. We have thus the "misery" theory of revolution, which
holds that objective worsening of social conditions, especially of the
standard of living, is the decisive cause of revolution. Running largely
counter to this is the "prosperity" theory of revolution associated with
Alexis de Tocqueville. Tocqueville wrote, "It is not always in going
from bad to worse that one falls into revolution. It happens most often
that a people, which had supported the most crushing laws without
complaint as if it did not sense them, rejects them violently when their
burden is lightened. The regime that a revolution destroys is almost
always better than the one that immediately preceded it. . . ." [150] Most
Western theorists of revolution have sided with Tocqueville, though
Davies' J-curve combines a long-term Tocquevillian improvement followed by a short-term Marxian deterioration. As all of these theories
depend upon or are coherent with some notion of *relative deprivation*
(hereafter termed RD), some explication of that notion is necessary
before we can properly evaluate how far misery, prosperity, or, more
broadly, decline or improvement of social and political conditions influence the coming of revolution.

RD in its most basic sense means the gap between what people get
and what they think they should get. More elaborately, it is "a perceived discrepancy between men's value expectations and their value
capabilities. Value expectations are the goods and conditions of life to
which people believe they are rightfully entitled. Value capabilities are
the goods and conditions they think they are capable of attaining or
maintaining. . . ." [151] Moreover, one can distinguish between the *scope*
of RD (i.e., the number of things considered) and its *intensity* (the degree of resentment felt). [152] Social discontent is thus a function of the

scope and intensity of RD among various strata and groups of the population. Since the components of the revolutionary coalition are motivated by different sets of grievances and ambitions induced by dissynchronous social change, they each are likely to experience different sorts of RD.

Ted R Gurr has elaborated three major types of RD, to which we can add a fourth. His first type, "decremental deprivation," is represented by Figure 5. With decremental deprivation, the group's value expectations remain relatively constant, while its value capabilities deteriorate, sometimes drastically.[153] This widespread situation we have suggested is the usual motivational basis for simple revolt. At first glance, however, it seems misleading to relate a situation in which value expectations are "relatively" constant to the emergence of revolution, which entails some novel ideas and sentiments. Nevertheless decremental deprivation can figure in the revolutionary process in several ways. (1) The deterioration of conditions can become so acute that normal values lose their force entirely; that is one of the reasons why revolutionary overtones often develop in prolonged revolts originally due to decremental deprivation. (2) Revolutionary elites can capitalize on frustration and discontent associated with decremental deprivation and rechannel it toward their own purposes. Peasants are often the source of such a revolutionary displacement of energies. (3) Discontent and, more so, open revolt can weaken the old regime and make it more vulnerable to true revolution. Nonrevolutionary forms of protest induced by decremental deprivation can thus hasten the downfall of the old order. Crisis strata which are economically backward and thus liable to

Figure 5. Gurr's Decremental Deprivation

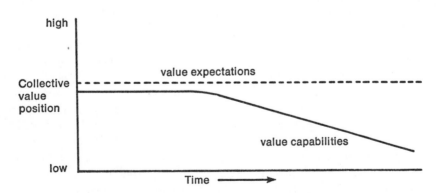

SOURCE: Ted Robert Gurr, *Why Men Rebel* (Princeton: Princeton University Press, 1970), p. 47.

Figure 6. Gurr's Aspirational Deprivation

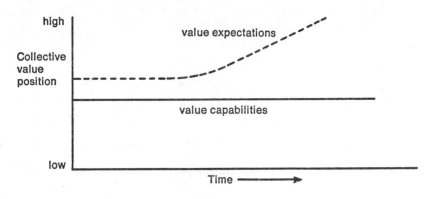

SOURCE: Gurr, *Why Men Rebel,* p. 51.

decremental deprivation do not necessarily embrace traditionalist or conservative ideologies: Trevor-Roper's declining gentry did not in early Stuart England, nor did troubled American farmers in the Populist era.

Figure 6 represents "aspirational deprivation," which occurs when a group's value expectations increase while its value capabilities remain rather constant. A society most conducive to aspirational deprivation would be one undergoing vast economic and cultural change. The economic advances of one group might, for example, have a "demonstration effect" on other groups, who begin to wonder why they do not receive their "fair share" of the increase. The twentieth century has displayed Western ideals and material accomplishments before larger and larger numbers of people in nonindustrialized countries. The contrast between these things and the traditional penury of vast rural and urban masses has been pointed up through vastly improved communications. As these examples show, the changed perspective that gives rise to aspirational deprivation can originate from within the society, from outside it, or from both sources. With all forms of RD there is a point where the gap between value expectations and capabilities endangers political stability. Since aspirational deprivation involves visions of new things, it can result in revolutionary conclusions, especially if an ideology promising to deliver the goods comes on the scene.

The third of Gurr's types of RD is "progressive deprivation," which is an adaptation of Davies' J-curve. Figure 7 represents it. For a time rising expectations are matched by rising capabilities and there is an equilibrium between them. Thus, it takes only a short-term setback to trigger deep and widespread resentment.

Figure 7. Gurr's Progressive Deprivation

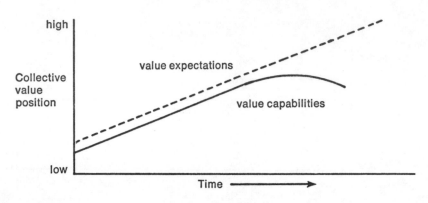

SOURCE: Gurr, *Why Men Rebel,* p. 53.

A fourth form of RD is similar to progressive deprivation but lacks the pronounced downward swing of value capabilities near the close of the period under scrutiny. Both value expectations and capabilities increase at a steady clip, but the former "accelerates" much faster than the latter. Figure 8 represents what we can call "accelerated deprivation." In accelerated deprivation there is a nodal point beyond which the hiatus between expectations and capabilities becomes acute and hence destabilizing. Moreover, with this fourth sort of RD the concept of rising expectations is preserved even for those situations where the Davies' J-curve is not observed. Accelerated deprivation thus best represents the overview of those in the Tocquevillian tradition (e.g.,

Figure 8. Accelerated Deprivation

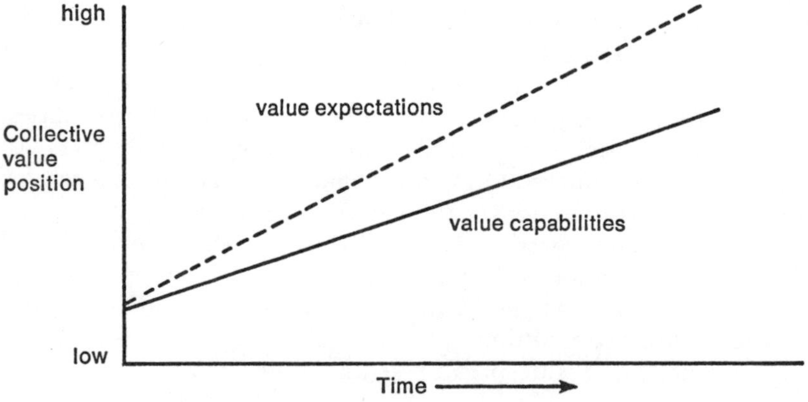

Crane Brinton, who maintained that the "men who made the French Revolution were getting higher and higher real income—so much that they wanted a great deal more. And above all . . . they wanted much that cannot be measured by the economist.") [154]

This last remark of Brinton, however, suggests some limits to RD as the master idea in the study of revolution. Though concerned with more than revolution, Ted Gurr concludes that "generally, economic values are likely to be most salient for most people." [155] And a recent analysis of Davies' work on the J-curve characterizes it as tantamount to simple economic determinism. [156] As economic phenomena lend themselves more readily to statistical treatment than other social processes, there is a natural temptation to look for pregnant correlations between the economic ups and downs of a society and its political vicissitudes. This can be a profitable endeavor if once again the part is not taken for the whole. Nevertheless, the bitter religious conflict so evident in nearly all revolutions is not easily reducible to economic terms. Much more is involved than the simple fact that the established religion comes under attack as a buttress of the established social order. Revolutionary ideologies have a quasi-religious mystique that sometimes is intolerant of possible competitors. People who would otherwise join or sympathize with the revolutionary movement are prevented from doing so because of attachment to the religion of their fathers. Conversely, moderates who are militant anticlericals may side with the revolution if their feelings are strong enough. It is hard to see how the notion of RD could completely explain antagonisms of this sort. Likewise forms of social conflict such as class struggle, status resentment, and the struggle for power can generate forms of political behavior and violence that are not clearly determined by RD.

Misery, Prosperity, and Revolution

A closer inspection of the impact of economic growth—in particular rapid economic growth—upon society may allow us to reach a synthesis of Marx and Tocqueville that is not sequential in Davies' sense, but synchronic. The Tocquevillians maintain that economic growth or overall prosperity portends revolution because it sets off a "revolution of rising expectations" which eventuates in progressive or accelerated RD. People with enough to eat and time to think about their condition more readily become discontented than those whose struggle to survive occupies their every waking hour.

The main weakness in the Tocquevillian standpoint is that all social groupings fail to benefit equally from overall growth or prosperity; in fact, some do not benefit at all and others are virtually pauperized. It is a generally neglected consequence of economic growth that normally certain groups and strata of society "see their positions menaced, their habits disrupted, and their certainties disavowed" [157] by such growth. Rapid economic growth produces newly rich as well as newly poor groupings, neither of which are the staunchest defenders of the status quo.[158] The newly rich are disposed to feel status resentment as their new economic position separates them from their social origins, but these same origins deny them entry into higher status groups. Economic growth also increases stratification inconsistency because of the "(almost Marxian) 'contradiction' between this new distribution of economic power and the older distribution of social prestige and political power." [159] Thus, the "winners" who benefit most from economic growth are likely to be "marginal men" who have often proven susceptible to revolutionary appeals.

More damaging to the Tocquevillian thesis is the conclusion that economic growth "can significantly increase the number of losers." [160] These "losers" can be divided into two basic categories. The first includes those from high status groups, whose economic base is depressed or destroyed by the technological innovation often involved in economic growth. The second category of losers are victims of the ironic fact that it is sometimes likely that "the number getting poorer will increase with rapid economic growth." [161] This fact is often lost among the statistics that report gross national product or per capita income. Neither shows how income is actually distributed amongst the various social categories. Especially vulnerable are the occupational groups made superfluous by economic development; for them "progress is translated by a fall into poverty or misery." [162] We might expect among these little people a growth of the sense of decremental deprivation and perhaps some exacerbation of class struggle.

Other possible consequences of economic growth that might enhance the chances of revolution include disruption of kinship organization and rapid urbanization.[163] As economic growth usually promotes occupational and geographical mobility, the economic role of the clan is disrupted and individuals are set adrift to fend for themselves. The role of deracinated, déclassé individuals has perhaps sometimes been overdrawn in accounts of revolution; however, the revolutionary crowds of big cities do contain numbers of individuals whose ties to kith and kin have been cut by economic and demographic changes. While there seems to be a definite connection between urbanization and the major Western revolutions, there is some cause to doubt the universality of the revolutionary potential of rapid urbanization. It has been suggested that under certain conditions "urban migration is, in some measure, a substitute for rural revolution" and consequently that "the susceptibility of a country to revolution may vary inversely with its rate of urbanization." [164] Thus, whether revolution occurs largely despite or largely because of urbanization can be determined only by historical inquiry.

These considerations should underscore the socially ambivalent nature of economic growth. Even if economic growth occurred in a way that it never has as yet (i.e., by raising the economic position of all groups and strata proportionally and by growing synchronously with other processes of change), rising expectations still might develop faster and more disruptively in some sectors of society than in others. In any case, neither the extreme Marxian position nor the extreme Tocquevillian position is in complete accord with the economic facts of pre-revolutionary societies. Nor, of course, does rapid economic growth have a monopoly of destabilizing tendencies: a rapid economic decline will bring "movements in the *relative* economic positions of people and will therefore set up contradictions between the structure of economic power and the distribution of social and political power." [165] Thus *either* rapid economic growth or rapid decline—in short, economic instability—can be propitious for the growth of discontent, opposition, and sometimes revolution. This conclusion fits in with our emphasis on dissynchronous social change *per se* being charged with revolutionary potential. However, the search for the causes of revolution is an unraveling process, and economic phenomena may or may not constitute the most important stands. Though economic phenomena are never void of significance, grand theories of economic determinism of whatever stripe seem to have an inbuilt tendency to distort and oversimplify the causal nexus of revolution.

SPONTANEITY AND CONSPIRACY

There is perhaps no more vexsome question in the study of revolution than the extent and role of revolutionary organization before the outbreak of revolution. The reaching of firm conclusions about particular revolutions, let alone revolutions in general, is impeded by the ideological overtones of the whole "conspiracy versus spontaneity" debate. Quite naturally, men of action or historians sympathetic to the revolutionary cause tend to see revolution as a spontaneous grass-roots movement welling up from the vast masses of oppressed humanity. This tendency is reinforced by the strong legitimating force of the democratic idea: action done by the "people" must be right. Accordingly, it seems an ideological imperative for the supporters of particular revolutions or admirers of revolutions in general to deny or to play down the importance of organized leadership in revolutionary upheavals.

On the other hand, opponents of particular revolutions, as well as conservatives in general, tend to see revolutions as the fruit of the machinations of an insidious clique of plotters. Strangely agreeing that the people "normally" can do no wrong, men of the right are wont to picture them as misled by unscrupulous revolutionary demagogues out for their own aggrandizement. This clique is the "unmoved mover" which manipulates the masses at its own discretion. Thus, many histories of revolution penned by conservatives give us a configuration of revolution diametrically opposed to that presented by historians of the left. All of this necessitates delving more deeply into the "explosion hypothesis" congenial to friends of revolution and into the "simplistic conspiracy theories" associated with its enemies in the hopes of reaching a synthesis with a "catalytic theory of revolutionary leadership." Our guiding assumption is not so much that splitting the difference between contrasting views is a sure route to the truth, as that reality is usually more complex than ideologists of whatever persuasion are able or willing to admit.

The Explosion Hypothesis

According to the explosion hypothesis, revolutions are the result of a sort of spontaneous combustion in which all the major and minor conflicts which have been smouldering for decades or more suddenly burst into flame. Whether the decisive factor is misery, prosperity, or some combination of these, the actual outbreak of revolution *surprises* most people—including most revolutionaries or would-be revolutionaries who happen to be in the right place at the right time.[166] Thus, strictly speaking, revolutions are not *made*, they *happen*. The old regime "collapses" rather than being "overthrown." Spontaneity may be replaced by organization afterwards, as revolutionary factions consolidate and compete for the mantle of power. But in the times just before and after the outbreak of revolution professional revolutionaries have been described as more like spectators than *dramatis personae:* "They watched and analysed the progressive disintegration in state and society; they hardly did, or were in a position to do, much to advance and direct it." [167] Therefore, it is not "conspiracy that causes revolution, and secret societies—though they may succeed in committing a few spectacular crimes usually with the help of the secret police—are as a rule much too secret to be able to make their voices heard in public." [168]

Certainly the equivocation, confusion, attempts at compromise and reconciliation seen in the last days of the old order and in the first days of the new one might seem to indicate that no one fully knows what is taking place, let alone is pulling the strings from a strategic background. For some, revolution is one of the all too rare historical moments when the masses really make history. Soon the popular élan dissipates or is dissipated by the revolutionary government, and the domination of political life by organized minorities returns. Lending strength to the explosion hypothesis is the emergence of popular "councils" in so many revolutions and near-revolutions. Words similar to the following have been written about other revolutionary settings than central Europe in 1919: "These councils had not been planned nor were they organized by any political party or group, although workers' councils came into being in both Germany and Austria during the great strikes of January 1918 and the idea of councils was clearly borrowed from Russia. Almost simultaneously they sprang up everywhere, in every state and every town. . . ." [169] No doubt it would be wrong to discount this sort of evidence even if proffered by observers or historians whose sentiments are deeply involved in the phenomena they describe.

One of the dangers of looking at revolution from below is that for some enthusiasts the "popular movement" is construed as a self-sufficient whole equivalent to the "real" or "true" revolution. In this way the revolutionary elite or government are envisaged as betrayers of the true spontaneous revolution, rather than as essential or even preponderant actors in it. Yet it is a strange concept of revolution indeed that characterizes the Cromwells, the Robespierres, the Lenins, and even the Maos and their cadres as excrescences upon the revolutionary organism. That popular spontaneity has almost always come to some sort of grief should be evidence enough that some organization, planning, and leadership from above is utterly necessary if revolutions are to institute coherent and lasting changes. This is not at all to deny spontaneity and a measure of genuinely popular initiative in even the earliest phases of revolution; but it is to place certain limits on the accuracy of revolutionary histories written exclusively from the vantage point of the masses.

Simplistic Conspiracy Theories

What simplistic conspiracy theories allege is that the broadly diversified, nationwide, and chronologically distinct events that culminate in revolution are the work of a single conspiratorial group. This group knows what it wants and how to get it. They begin with undermining confidence in the existing regime and increase in boldness as the hour of revolution approaches. Propaganda, agitation, terrorism, corruption, assassination—no means, legal or illegal, are alien to these cynical plotters. To the criticism that evidence of such plots is scanty, if not nonexistent, conspiracy theorists reply (with a certain cogency) that as secret undertakings conspiracies are not likely to leave many traces for the authorities to follow up.

Simplistic conspiracy theories see revolution as a "whole" extending from a more or less remote time before the outbreak through the seizure of power and up to the consolidation or overthrow of the revolutionary regime. One formation has masterminded the whole scenario, though factional disputes may punctuate the actual process of making the revolution. To support this claim, conspiracy theorists make use of what might be called "the method of pregnant correlations"; for example, from the clear facts that large numbers of Jacobins and other revolutionists had been Masons before the French Revolution or that the Bolsheviks and other revolutionary groupings contained "disproportionate" numbers of Jews, they infer that the French Revolution was a "Masonic plot" and the Russian, a Jewish one. Now, one does not have to deny all efficacy to Masonic intrigues in the French and other revolutions nor dismiss as anti-Semitic bigotry all reference to the important role played by Jews in 1917 to see that in these instances "the method of pregnant correlations" is beset by a host of logical and empirical difficulties. The most obvious is the age-old logical fallacy of *post hoc ergo propter hoc*, which assumes that an earlier event is the cause of a later one simply because it preceded it. Another is the one we have all along encountered: mistaking a partial explanation for a sufficient or adequate one.

However, rejection of simplistic conspiracy theories for these and other fatal weaknesses should not mean a dogmatic refusal to admit the possibility that some looser notion of organization can help us to grasp the causes of revolution better. Here it is well to recall that those who most vociferously reject the label "conspiracy" for movements they approve of, are often the first to shout "plot" when it is a question of ideological enemies. The point now is to raise the question of how far rhetorical exaggerations are pure fiction. There may be a rational kernel in some conspiracy theories of revolution that the student would do well to investigate—the last word has not been said on the Masons and the February Revolution in Russia in 1917, for example.

A Catalytic Theory of Revolutionary Leadership

A catalytic theory of revolutionary leadership rejects the extremes of pure mass spontaneity and pure conspiracy. It acknowledges that both spontaneity and organization play a role that varies from revolution to revolution. A catalyst is something that, added in small quantities to a mixture of ingredients, promotes a rapid and decisive reaction. The catalyst analogy is applied to revolutionary leadership to emphasize that utter mass spontaneity has not produced nor could it produce the revolutions history records. Most spontaneous collective behavior falls into subrevolutionary categories (e.g., revolt). Spontaneity in revolution can destroy things and even produce makeshift localized institutions, but it requires leadership to organize the apparatus of the state to further the aims of the revolution. Both dimensions are intimately associated in revolution.

The best refutation of simplistic conspiracy theories is to recall our analysis of the long-term and middle-term causes of revolution. No conspiracy produces economic growth, modern nationalism, secularization, the modern state, technological innovation, scientific advance, or democratization. Even with the middle term factors such as economic fluctuations, war, government financial woes, poor leadership at various levels, it seems unthinkable that any of them have been staged by an opposition bent on revolution. The "desertion of the intellectuals" does of course provide an important contingent of conscious revolutionaries; but it has not been shown that this is the decisive, let alone the sole, cause of revolutions, as simplistic conspiracy theories would have it. However, planned precipitants of revolution are by definition conspiratorial.

The basic starting point of a catalytic theory of revolutionary leadership is that without leadership (often of a clandestine nature) a revolutionary situation produced by a conjuncture of long-term and middle-term causes may remain an unrealized potential. Leadership then is necessary to give some coordination to the forces at play so that revolution will indeed "break out" and, when it does, will not fizzle out into mere disorder. Otherwise the hodgepodge of groups and strata, conflicts and cleavages might work against each other rather than against the old regime. The disintegration of the original revolutionary coalition is inevitable, but leadership keeps it together long enough to accomplish the definitive overthrow of the old regime. Thus a catalytic theory of revolutionary leadership resembles conspiracy theories in the common conclusion that organization is behind much that at first sight appears as purely spontaneous behavior—the difference residing in the number of actions so considered and the actual amount of direction involved.

Most students of revolution agree that leadership becomes increasingly prevalent after the outbreak of revolution and the setting up of a provisional revolutionary government. From this point on spontaneous mass action is as often as not an embarrassment to the revolutionary government, which is often compelled to use stringent methods to quell recurrent outbursts of revolutionary enthusiasm or frustration. Sometimes, of course, these "spontaneous" interventions are manipulated by one or another faction of the revolutionary elite. However, since we are here concerned with the causes of revolution rather than with its later course or "phases," the question now turns on the existence and effectiveness of a revolutionary party or "protoparty" in the time before the revolution is an accomplished fact. It is this group which catalyzes the ingredients of the revolutionary situation by developing a strategy and tactics, and by channeling the spontaneous initiatives of the masses into a clearly revolutionary direction. A brief look at the English and French revolutions, which occurred before the development of the professional revolutionary, might give us some insights that would hold with greater force for most subsequent revolutions.

It is clear that before 1640 or 1789, tightly organized political formations adhering to a fully revolutionary ideology did *not* exist in England or France: there was nothing in existence like Lenin's Bolsheviks. However, in a somewhat looser sense of "party" there was in either historical context a coordinated opposition, many aspects of which were potentially revolutionary. In pre-revolutionary England there was the Country "party," which we have seen was a "loose collaboration or alliance of men in the governing class . . . alienated for a variety of reasons from the Court." [170] As a protoparty, the Country lacked "the formal mechanisms of leadership, organization, and propaganda" that distinguished full-scale parties.[171] However, it did incorporate a modicum of organization, an ideology of sorts, and methods of recruitment. While the Country as a whole was too unwieldy, amorphous, and parochial to amount to a modern "antisystem" opposition party, the level of organization at its core was far from unimpressive. In it we find "a group united by conviction, linked through family and friendship, *meeting to concert the tactics of opposition.*" [172] (Italics mine.) This leadership formation spearheaded and directed the growing opposition to Charles I; they engaged in electioneering and in what, save for its somewhat anachronistic ring, must be called agitation and propaganda. The Country's persistence coupled with Charles' intransigence brought England to the brink of revolution, at which point the more cautious members of the group switched to the Royalist camp, while the revolutionary impetus evoked new and unforeseen responses from groups further down the social scale. Had there been nothing like the Country party, it is doubtful that the English Revolution would have occurred at the time and in the way it did, if at all.

In France a century and a half later, the "Patriot" party played a somewhat similar role to that of the Country. This was a socially diverse grouping made up of men from all three estates (clergy, nobility, commoners) in the reign of Louis XVI. It too was not a modern political party, but it did have some central direction at its core in a Committee of Thirty, about which we know far less than we would like. The Committee of Thirty should not be considered a *deus ex machina* invoked to explain the myriad events before the revolution: "the point is not that everything done everywhere was done on the basis of orders from the Committee of Thirty. It is rather that . . . what control the state of communications permitted *was* provided by this group." [173] Though understandably a clandestine group such as this was anxious to cover up its traces, too many of them lead back to it. The top echelon of the Patriot party, like that of the Country party, was a "loose political coalition based on informal groupings of like-minded notables." [174] Nevertheless, the record of oppositional activities is impressive: one historian attributes to the inner circle of the Patriot party essential responsibility for the protest in 1788, the election campaign in 1789, the emergence of the National Assembly out of the Estates General, elaboration of the Declaration of the Rights of Man, and the abolition of aristocratic privileges in August, 1789.[175] All in all they "provided the basis for whatever unity or continuity may be perceived in the early phases of the French Revolution." [176] Later the Patriot party fell victim to the stresses and strains of the increasing radicalization of the Revolution.

The Spanish Revolution provides more modern and somewhat different confirmation of the crucial importance of leadership and organization to the success of revolution. One cause of the ultimate failure of the Spanish Revolution may be that leadership and mass spontaneity never properly coalesced because of deep-seated political differences. The Anarchosyndicalist federation, the CNT (*Confederacion Nacional de Trabajo*) was "Spain's mass movement of revolutionary spontaneity." [177] but it dissipated its "strength in multiple uncoordinated ventures. . . ." [178] Of the other members of the Republican coalition of political groups and parties, the Communist Party was the only "united and effective political organization." [179] While the communists were perhaps the only hope for coherent overall leadership in the Spanish Revolution, their ideology and sectarianism simply clashed against the ideology and sectarianism of too many other groups. In the later stages of the civil war, violence among the various sorts of revolutionaries was almost as ruthless and bitter as between Loyalist and Francoist forces. The communists imposed some coherence through terrorism, but the costs of this terrorism decimated the ranks of the most rabid revolutionaries. Had the roots of Spanish communism been deeper, it might have avoided measures that purchased one sort of strength at the price of losing another.

While the history of these and other revolutions illustrates the pivotal importance of leadership, planning, and organization, without eventual popular response a movement would remain too restrictive to become the advance guard of a genuine revolutionary breakthrough. Though a recent study of revolution concludes that revolution is "always the work of the elite," because it is in its ranks that "the decision is made and from it that the new order arises," this study also cautions us not to neglect the role of the people.[180] The reason for this is that "victory will finally go to the fraction of the elite which will have convinced or given the illusion to the people that it alone is capable of satisfying their demands." [181] After all, revolutionists of one sort or another were no scarce commodity in Russia for nearly a century preceding 1917, but their persistent problem was their inability to establish much of a foothold among the masses. With rapid industrialization around the turn of the century, and the traumas of 1905 and the First World War, there emerged a situation similar to what William Kornhauser calls a "mass society"—that is, "a social system in which elites are readily accessible to influence by non-elites and non-elites are readily available for mobilization by elites." [182] Both of these conditions must be met before we can speak of a fully revolutionary situation: the catalyst and the catalyzed are both essential if the revolutionary process is to run its full course. Though speaking narrowly of the Leninist-style party in "proletarian revolutions," George Lukacs has frankly articulated the consequences of a catalytic theory of revolutionary leadership: "precisely because it [the party] strives to reach the maximum possibilities on the terrain of revolution—and the momentary will of the masses is often the most important element or symptom in this respect—it is sometimes forced to take a position against the masses themselves, to show them the right way, denying their present will." [183]

CONCLUSION

Explaining the why of revolutions is a more complex undertaking than the clichés of some ideology would indicate. As a macro-event, revolution is produced by a multiplicity of interdependent causes. A sufficient account of all causes is probably out of the question; we can at best uncover those factors that are necessary conditions and then fashion an adequate explanation out of them. While each revolution is unique, certain causal features are common enough to merit special comparative emphasis. To avoid infinite regress in explanation, we have employed a loose notion of social equilibrium that considers revolution an *abnormal* historical occurrence. Thus, our causal inquiry is concerned mainly with those factors that, beginning in the not too distant past, have produced certain effects and have been seconded by other later factors so as to produce a revolutionary situation. This outlook tends to rule out a monistic explanation and even to greet with skepticism claims that this or that feature is the "decisive" cause of all or some revolutions.

MacIver's analysis of the global society into social, technological, and cultural subsystems provides a conceptual scheme that meshes well with our predispositions towards multiple causation. Since abruptness together with intensity of change is the most salient characteristic of revolution, it is no surprise that revolutionary change is the resultant of a myriad of changes in social organization, technology, and cultural values. Giving change in the three subsystems a theoretical equivalence obviously does not imply that they are of equal weight in each specific historical context. Dissynchronous change both between and within the three subsystems is at the heart of the destabilizing process that culminates in revolution. By linking such change to social psychological responses, we hope to give full justice to the human element in what otherwise might prove an overly abstract systemic analysis. Furthermore, we distinguish between cyclical modes of change that perhaps can be contained or reversed by governmental action and linear developments that can be slowed down but not permanently arrested. Both sorts of change operate in our three subsystems, though some factors such as war seem random rather than clearly cyclical or linear.

We found no difficulty in relating multiple causation and dissynchronous change to the well-established formula of long-term, middle-term, and precipitant causes of revolution. Long-range developments such as (1) economic growth, (2) technological innovation, (3) scientific advance, (4) democratization, (5) secularization, (6) the modern state, and (7) the growth of nationalism ramify and intersect in the causal nexus of most revolutions. We can see how these developments impinge upon one or more of our subsystems, sometimes spilling over from one area to another. While there is some sense in subsuming all of these things under the rubric of the "modernization of societies," such a generic treatment tends to obscure the didssynchronous quality of pre-revolutionary change. The lead-lag problem and the considerable autonomy of discrete processes of change (e.g., in science and technology) cry out against any simplistic formula.

That societies have modernized or have undergone our seven long-term modes of change without producing revolutions suggests that a middle-term level of change must also operate. These middle-term factors may be produced partly by long-term factors and partly by more narrow cyclic (or random) fluctuations. (1) Economic depression, (2) alienation of intellectuals, (3) division and ineptness of rulers, (4) war, (5) government insolvency often come into the picture to exacerbate and give focus to the social and political malaise stemming from deeper and older processes of change. The intervention of some or all of these middle-term factors increases the probability of a revolutionary outcome. If an appropriate combination of long-term and middle-term factors reaches a certain conjuncture, a revolutionary situation exists. It then requires precipitating factors, planned or unplanned as the case may be, to cause the revolution to break out in the fullest sense of the term. All activist revolutionary strategies, whether putschist or guerrilla in nature, must assume that the conditions are "ripe" (i.e., that a revolutionary situation exists) before the revolutionaries can supply the *coup de grace* to the old regime.

It is, of course, the operation of these causes upon men that allows a usually trivial event to serve as a precipitant of revolution. Thus, the social psychology of revolution is a most important, though elusive, side of the study of revolution. Theories of repressed needs and wishes, or of frustration-induced aggression, help to explain the anger and recourse to violence so manifest in revolution. But sometimes the explanations are so generic that riot, secession, or revolt could just as easily have been the result of the causes invoked: in short, the distinction between revolution and other forms of collective violence is blurred. Some of this confusion may be dispelled by the notion of relative deprivation, not all forms of which would equally lead to revolutionary violence. "Decremental deprivation," for example, would seem to produce revolt rather than revolution.

We have chosen not to decide between the misery and the prosperity theories of revolution on the ground contested by the rival theories. Consideration of Davies' thesis of prosperity (or well-being) followed by misery (or discontent), as well as a closer look at the actual impact of rapid economic growth, warns against such easy answers. Prosperity is not evenly distributed in societies with rapid economic growth. On the other hand, the most miserable are sometimes the last to join the revolutionary movement. We must thus distinguish linear from cyclic economic factors and relate their impact not only to RD, narrowly speaking, but also to the modes of social conflict discussed in Chapter III.

Finally, we tackled the problem of spontaneity and conspiracy in the revolutionary process. While noting that friends of revolution tend to invoke spontaneity and enemies to cry conspiracy, we have sought a middle position. The explosion hypothesis is convincing for the very beginning of those revolutions in which the collapse of the old regime momentarily stuns all factions. But even here leadership moves into the vacuum and inclines politics in directions that pure spontaneity cannot account for. Furthermore, the extreme stress on revolutionary spontaneity seems to make all discussion of strategy beside the point.[184] The historic revolutions have not all followed the pattern of urban mass insurrection. The revolutionary coup d'etat and the guerrilla war must also be considered; and these revolutionary strategies involve considerable planning and conspiratorial activity. On the other hand, simplistic conspiracy theories invariably have particular ideological axes to grind. They ignore many of the long-term, and some of the middle-term, causes of revolution. Or they strain to explain complex and grandiose trends as results of a sinister and supremely patient plot. The catalytic theory of leadership, finally, acknowledges the variable mix of spontaneity and contrivance, elite action and mass action in revolutions. Its animus, however, is to emphasize the role of leadership in the crucially important areas of revolutionary ideology and organization.

NOTES

[1] All or parts of the following works are relevant to the first part of this chapter: May Brodbeck, ed., *Readings in the Philosophy of the Social Sciences* (New York: Macmillan, 1968); May Brodbeck and H. Feigl, eds., *Readings in the Philosophy of Science* (New York: Appleton-Century-Crofts, 1953); Ernest Nagel, *The Structure of Science* (New York: Harcourt, Brace & World, 1961); Israel Scheffler, *The Anatomy of Inquiry* (New York: Bobbs-Merrill, 1963); Carl G. Hempel, *Aspects of Scientific Explanation* (New York: The Free Press, 1965); Patrick Gardiner, ed., *Theories of History* (New York: The Free Press, 1959); Patrick Gardiner, *The Nature of Historical Explanation* (New York: Oxford University Press, 1961); William Dray, *Laws and Explanation in History* (London: Oxford University Press, 1957); W. H. Walsh, *The Philosophy of History* (New York: Harper Torchbooks, 1967); Morton White, *Foundations of Historical Knowledge* (New York: Harper Torchbooks, 1965); George Homans, *The Nature of Social Science* (New York: Harbinger Books, 1967); Abraham Kaplan, *The Conduct of Inquiry* (Scranton: Chandler, 1964); Arthur C. Danto, *Analytical Philosophy of History* (Cambridge: Cambridge University Press, 1968).

[2] William Dray, "Explaining What," in *Theories of History*, ed. P. Gardiner, p. 405.

[3] Hempel, *Aspects*, p. 231 ff.

[4] White, *Foundations*, p. 51.

[5] Michael Scriven, "Truisms as the Grounds for Historical Explanation," in *Theories of History*, ed. P. Gardiner, p. 458.

[6] White, *Foundations*, p. 5.

[7] Dray, *Laws and Explanation*, p. 70.

[8] Hempel, *Aspects*, p. 421.

[9] Dray, *Laws and Explanation*, p. 72.

[10] Nagel, *Structure*, p. 578.

[11] May Brodbeck, "Explanation, Prediction, and 'Imperfect Knowledge'," in *Philosophy of the Social Sciences*, ed. M. Brodbeck, p. 375.

[12] Gardiner, *Historical Explanation*, p. 98.

[13] Hempel, *Aspects*, p. 238.

[14] Louis Gottschalk, "Causes of Revolution," *The American Journal of Sociology*, L (July, 1944), p. 1.

[15] Nagel, *Structure*, p. 559.

[16] Walsh, *Philosophy*, p. 191.

[17] R. M. MacIver, *Social Causation* (New York: Harper Torchbooks, 1964), p. 172.

[18] *Ibid.*, p. 173.

[19] It must be recalled that some forms of collective violence actually have a stabilizing function if they prompt the rulers to make certain concessions.

[20] Chalmers Johnson, *Revolutionary Change* (Boston: Little, Brown, 1966), p. 3.

[21] See "Monistic vs. Multiple Causation" below.

[22] George Pettee, *The Process of Revolution* (New York: Harper & Row, 1938), p. 64.

[23] Harry Eckstein, "On the Etiology of Internal Wars," in *Why Revolution?*, ed. C. T. Paynton and R. Blackey (Cambridge, Mass.: Schenkman, 1971), pp. 99–109.

[24] MacIver, *Social Causation*, p. 125.

[25] *Ibid.*, p. 126.

[26] Cf. Peter Calvert, *A Study of Revolution* (New York: Oxford University Press, 1970), Chap. I.

[27] Dray, *Laws and Explanation*, p. 152.

[28] White, *Foundations*, p. 107.

[29] Alfred Cobban, *Aspects of the French Revolution* (New York: W. W. Norton, 1970), p. 93.

[30] Pitirim Sorokin, *The Sociology of Revolution* (New York: Howard Fertig, 1967), p. 395.

[31] Pettee, *Process*, p. 30.

[32] MacIver, *Social Causation*, p. 273.

[33] Pitirim Sorokin, *Social and Cultural Dynamics*, Vol. IV (New York: Bedminster Press, 1962), p. 313.

[34] Emile Durkheim, *Suicide* (New York: The Free Press, 1951), Chap. 5.

[35] Michael Walzer, *The Revolution of the Saints* (Cambridge, Mass.: Harvard University Press, 1965), p. 317.

[36] E.g., Oswald Spengler, *The Decline of the West*, 2 vols. (New York: Alfred A. Knopf, 1928).

[37] Robert A. Nisbet, *Social Change and History* (New York: Oxford University Press, 1969), p. 296.

[38] Pettee, *Process*, p. 41.

[39] *Ibid.*, p. 51.

[40] *Ibid.*, p. 41.

[41] No one has yet succeeded in showing that wars obey a definite cyclical pattern. See Quincy Wright, *A Study of War*, abridged ed. (Chicago: University of Chicago Press, 1965), pp. 343–45.

[42] Lyford P. Edwards, *The Natural History of Revolution* (Chicago: University of Chicago Press, 1970), p. 27.

[43] Edwards argues that the "great" revolutions take from three to perhaps five

generations to develop. The first generation, which experiences the preliminary symptoms of unrest, has also lived in the time before society began to deteriorate. The second generation is raised with their fathers' recollection of the "good old days." Thus these two generations are either eyewitnesses or hearsay witnesses to the fact that society can work satisfactorily and they hope that a return to better times is "just around the corner." This serves as a deterrent to the development of revolutionary sentiments. By the time of the third generation and, *a fortiori,* the fourth and the fifth, almost no one is alive with the conviction that *this* system once worked well. The road is therefore open for radical ideas to present themselves as the only ones with a cure for present evils.

[44] W. W. Rostow, *The Stages of Economic Growth* (New York: Cambridge University Press, 1964).

[45] *Ibid.,* pp. 8–9.

[46] Chart opposite p. 1 in *Stages;* and W. W. Rostow, *Politics and the Stages of Growth* (New York: Cambridge University Press, 1971), p. 55.

[47] John U. Nef, *Industry and Government in France and England, 1540–1640* (Ithaca: Cornell University Press, 1969), p. 151.

[48] *Ibid.*

[49] Alfred Cobban, *The Social Interpretation of the French Revolution* (Cambridge: Cambridge University Press, 1968), p. 52.

[50] A. Rupert Hall, "Scientific Method and the Progress of Techniques," in *The Cambridge Economic History of Europe,* IV, p. 98.

[51] Gaetano Mosca, *Teorica dei governi e governo parlamentare,* ed. G. Ambrosini *et. al.* (Milan: Dott. A. Giuffré, 1958), pp. 52–53.

[52] Pettee, *Process,* p. 75.

[53] Thomas Kuhn, *The Structure of Scientific Revolutions* (Chicago: University of Chicago Press, 1966), p. 110.

[54] Alexis de Tocqueville, *Democracy in America,* Vol. I (New York: Vintage Books, 1961), p. 6.

[55] *Ibid.,* p. 7.

[56] *Ibid.*

[57] Sir Henry Sumner Maine, *Ancient Law* (Gloucester, Mass.: Peter Smith, 1970), p. 163.

[58] Gaetano Mosca, "Il principio aristocratico e il democratico," in *Partiti e sindacati nella crisi de regime parlamentare* (Bari: Laterza, 1949), p. 23.

[59] J. H. Hexter, *Reappraisals in History* (New York: Harper Torchbooks, 1961), pp. 80–81.

[60] Secularization is understood here as the decline of theological considerations in people's view of the world, as well as the decrease in the social, political, economic, and moral influence of organized religion.

[61] Joseph de Maistre, *Textes Choises* (Monaco: Éditions du Rocher, 1957), p. 185.

[62] Christopher Dawson, *The Dynamics of World History* (New York: Mentor Omega Books, 1962), p. 129.

[63] *Ibid.,* p. 130.

[64] Christopher Dawson, *The Movement of World Revolution* (New York: Sheed & Ward, 1959), p. 62.

[65] *Ibid.*

[66] However, Christopher Hill has spoken of a "tradition of plebeian anticlericalism and irreligion" in England before the revolution. *The World Turned Upside Down* (London: Temple Smith, 1972), p. 21.

[67] Reinhard Bendix, *Max Weber: An Intellectual Portrait* (Garden City, N.Y.: Anchor Books, 1962), p. 360.

[68] Max Weber, *Economy and Society*, Vol. III (New York: Bedminster Press, 1969), p. 1078.

[69] *Ibid.*, p. 1079.

[70] *Ibid.*, p. 1087.

[71] A. L. Moote, *The Revolt of the Judges* (Princeton: Princeton University Press, 1971), p. 98.

[72] Weber, *Economy and Society*, Vol. I, p. 56.

[73] Bendix, *Max Weber*, p. 424.

[74] Significant is Weber's remark that patrimonialism "remained dominant in Continental Europe up to the French Revolution. . . ." *Economy and Society*, Vol. III, p. 1087.

[75] See Walker Connor, "Nation-Building or Nation-Destroying," *World Politics*, XXIV (April, 1972), pp. 319–55.

[76] E. H. Carr, *Nationalism and After* (London: Macmillan, 1945), p. 7.

[77] *Ibid.*, p. 19.

[78] *Ibid.*, p. 18.

[79] Christopher Hill, *Puritanism and Revolution* (New York: Schocken Books, 1970), pp. 57–58.

[80] Hans Kohn, *The Idea of Nationalism* (New York: Macmillan, 1961), p. 165.

[81] *Ibid.*, p. 166.

[82] *Ibid.*

[83] Franklin L. Ford, *Sword and Robe* (New York: Harper Torchbooks, 1965).

[84] J. L. Talmon, *The Origins of Totalitarian Democracy* (New York: Praeger, 1960), pp. 74–75.

[85] George Kennan, "The Breakdown of the Tsarist Autocracy," in *Revolutionary Russia: A Symposium*, ed. Richard Pipes (Garden City, N.Y.: Anchor Books, 1969), p. 13. For a documented study of the role of nationalism amongst non-Russian peoples in the Russian Revolution, see Richard Pipes, *The Formation of the Soviet Union*, rev. ed. (New York: Atheneum, 1968).

[86] Chalmers Johnson, *Peasant Nationalism and Communist Power* (Stanford: Stanford University Press, 1962), p. 25.

[87] *Ibid.*, p. 20.

[88] James C. Davies, "Toward a Theory of Revolution," in *When Men Revolt and Why*, ed. J. C. Davies (New York: The Free Press, 1971), p. 136; first published in the *American Sociological Review*, XXVII (February, 1962).

[89] *Ibid.*

[90] James C. Davies, "The J-Curve of Rising and Declining Satisfactions as a Cause of Some Great Revolutions and a Contained Rebellion," in *Violence in America: Historical and Comparative Perspectives*, ed. Hugh D. Graham and Ted R. Gurr (New York: Bantam Books, 1969), p. 694.

[91] *Ibid.*

[92] *Ibid.*, p. 700.

[93] Karl Mannheim, *Ideology and Utopia* (New York: Harcourt, Brace, & Co., n.d.), p. 156.

[94] *Ibid.*, p. 158.

[95] Edwards, *Natural History*, Chap. IV.

[96] *Ibid.*, p. 63.

[97] Edward Shils, "The Intellectuals and the Powers: Some Perspectives for Comparative Analysis," in *On Intellectuals*, ed. Philip Rieff (Garden City, N.Y.: Anchor Books, 1970), p. 32.

[98] *Ibid.*, p. 35.

[99] *Ibid.*, p. 44.

[100] *Ibid.*, p. 45.

[101] Walzer, *Revolution of the Saints*, p. 121.

[102] *Ibid.*, p. 125.

[103] Carl Becker, *The Heavenly City of the Eighteenth-Century Philosophers* (New Haven: Yale University Press, 1960), p. 122.

[104] Benjamin Schwartz, "The Intellectuals in Communist China: A Tentative Comparison," in *The Russian Intelligentsia*, ed. Richard Pipes (New York: Columbia University Press, 1970).

[105] Max Weber, *From Max Weber: Essays in Sociology* (New York: Oxford University Press, 1960), p. 121.

[106] Edwards, *Natural History*, p. 64.

[107] Talcott Parsons, " 'The Intellectual': A Social Role Category," in *On Intellectuals*, ed. by P. Rieff, pp. 3–26.

[108] Plato, *The Republic*, Cornford trans. (New York: Oxford University Press, 1960), sec. 546.

[109] Edwards, *Natural History*, p. 63.

[110] Crane Brinton, *The Anatomy of Revolution* (Englewood Cliffs, N.J.: Prentice-Hall, 1952), p. 60.

[111] Gottschalk, "Causes of Revolution," p. 7.

[112] *Ibid.*, p. 8.

[113] Leon Trotsky, *The Russian Revolution* (Garden City, N.Y.: Anchor Books, 1959), p. 311.

[114] *Ibid.*

[115] Firm and effective measures of repression might thus constitute what R. M. MacIver aptly calls "antiprecipitants." An antiprecipitant is some action or event "which thwarts or balks the operation of the intrusive fact. . . ." *Social Causation*, p. 179.

[116] Katharine Chorley, *Armies and the Art of Revolution* (London: Faber & Faber, 1943), p. 16. See Johnson, *Revolutionary Change*, Chap. 5 on these points.

[117] Herbert Butterfield, *The Whig Interpretation of History* (New York: W. W. Norton, 1965).

[118] Pettee, *Process*, p. 58.

[119] Gaetano Mosca, *Elementi di scienza politica*, Vol. I (Bari: Laterza, 1953), p. 154.

[120] *Ibid.*, p. 155.

[121] Sidney Harcave, *The Russian Revolution of 1905* (New York: Collier Books, 1970), pp. 27–28.

[122] See Machiavelli, *The Prince*, in *The Prince and the Discourses*, ed. Max Lerner (New York: Modern Library, 1950), Chap. XXV.

[123] Pettee, *Process*, p. 58.

[124] Samuel P. Huntington, *Political Order in Changing Societies* (New Haven: Yale University Press, 1970), Chap. 6.

[125] *Ibid.*, p. 367.

[126] This useful term was used somewhat more narrowly by Sigmund Neumann, who had in mind the "new middle class, a restless unemployed, and a militia of irregulars" of interwar Europe, which provided the "social basis" of fascism. *Permanent Revolution* (New York: Praeger, 1965), p. 106.

[127] Huntington, *Political Order*, p. 373.

[128] Ibid., p. 376.

[129] Neumann, *Permanent Revolution*, p. 232.

[130] Jean Baechler, *Les Phénomènes Révolutionnaires* (Paris: Presses Universitaires de France, 1970) p. 160.

[131] Albert Soboul, *Histoire de la Révolution Française*, Vol. I (Paris: Gallimard, 1962), p. 108.

[132] *Ibid.*, p. 109.

[133] Edwards, *Natural History*, p. 98.

[134] *Ibid.*, pp. 98–99.

[135] Gottschalk, "Causes of Revolution," p. 8.

[136] Johnson, *Revolutionary Change*, p. 99.

[137] *Ibid.*

[138] Perhaps the limiting case of the accidental precipitant is seen when the initiative comes from the other side. Stanley Payne points out "the paradox that the [Spanish] revolution was precipitated in the final instance not by the revolutionaries but by the counterrevolutionaries." *The Spanish Revolution* (New York: W. W. Norton, 1970), p. 371.

[139] Sorokin, *Sociology of Revolution*, p. 367.

[140] *Ibid.*, pp. 367–68.

[141] *Ibid.*, p. 371.

[142] *Ibid.*, p. 372.

[143] Edwards, *Natural History*, pp. 3–4.

[144] Pettee, *Process*, p. 33.

[145] Freud's contention that human society *inevitably* produces rebelliousness because of the necessity to repress certain instincts should be measured against all assertions that the violence of particular uprisings was solely due to peculiarly repressive social conditions. *Civilization and its Discontents* (Garden City, N.Y.: Anchor Books, n.d.), p. 41.

[146] James C. Davies, *Human Nature in Politics* (New York: John Wiley, 1963), p. 9.

[147] Ted R. Gurr, *Why Men Rebel* (Princeton: Princeton University Press, 1971), p. 17.

[148] *Ibid.*, p. 36.

[149] *Ibid.*, p. 12.

[150] Alexis de Toqueville, *L'ancien régime et la révolution* (Paris: Gallimard, 1967), p. 277.

[151] Gurr, *Why Men Rebel*, p. 13.

[152] *Ibid.*, pp. 29–30.

[153] Professor Gurr suggests here that value capabilities are "perceived to decline," but such caution seems misplaced because without change in value expectations it is hard to see how people would succumb to the optical illusion that their value capabilities are declining unless they really are. Thus decremental deprivation, strictly speaking, turns out to be not relative deprivation, but "absolute deprivation."

[154] Brinton, *Anatomy*, p. 32; cf. Edwards, *Natural History*, p. 36.; and Pettee, *Process*, p. 32.

[155] Gurr, *Why Men Rebel*, p. 66.

[156] Isaac Kramnick, "Reflections on Revolution: Definition and Explanation in Recent Scholarship," *History and Theory*, XI, No. 1 (1972), p. 42. Professor Davies contends, however, that the J-Curve must not be given a too narrowly economic sense.

[157] Baechler, *Les Phénomènes Révolutionnaires*, p. 186.

[158] Mancur Olsen, "Rapid Growth as a Destabilizing Force," in *When Men Revolt and Why*, ed. J. C. Davies, pp. 215–27.

[159] *Ibid.*, p. 217.

[160] *Ibid.*, p. 219.

[161] *Ibid.*

[162] Baechler, *Les Phénomènes Révolutionnaires*, p. 186.

[163] Olsen, "Rapid Growth," p. 217.

[164] Huntington, *Political Order*, p. 299.

[165] Olsen, "Rapid Growth," p. 223.

[166] Hannah Arendt, *On Revolution* (New York: Viking Press, 1963), p. 263.

[167] *Ibid.*

[168] *Ibid.*, pp. 263–64.

[169] F. L. Carsten, *Revolution in Central Europe 1918–1919* (London: Temple Smith, 1972), p. 323.

[170] Perez Zagorin, *The Court and the Country* (New York: Atheneum, 1970), p. 75.

[171] *Ibid.*

[172] *Ibid.*, p. 99.

[173] Elizabeth L. Eisenstein, "Who Intervened in 1788? A Commentary on *The Coming of the French Revolution*," *The American Historical Review*, LXXI (October, 1965), p. 82.

[174] *Ibid.*, p. 102.

[175] *Ibid.*, p. 100.

[176] *Ibid.*

[177] Payne, *Spanish Revolution*, p. 371.

[178] *Ibid.*, p. 231.

[179] *Ibid.*

[180] Baechler, *Les Phénomènes Révolutionnaires*, pp. 149–50.

[181] *Ibid.*, p. 150.

[182] William Kornhauser, *The Politics of Mass Society* (New York: The Free Press, 1963), p. 39.

[183] György Lukács, *Storia e coscienza di classe* (Milan: Sugar Editore, 1967), p. 405.

[184] See Mostafa Rejai, *The Strategy of Political Revolution* (Garden City, N.Y.: Anchor Books, 1973) for an analysis of different revolutionary strategies.

V

THE PHASES OF REVOLUTION

THOUGH any discussion of the phases or stages of revolution is logically dependent upon a time for the outbreak of revolution, after which the first phase can be said to begin, we have concluded in our discussion of the precipitants of revolution in the last chapter that finding a precise date for the French and English revolutions to "break out" is difficult. For other revolutions, such as the Russian Revolution of 1917 or the French Revolution of 1848, this problem is less severe, and the time for the commencement of the initial phase of the revolution is rather clearly demarcated. Whatever the ultimate resolution of the dating problem in each specific case, we have already seen that revolutions emerge out of situations characterized by one or more aggravating circumstances: serious and, especially, unsuccessful wars; taxpayers' revolts; and prolonged and acute institutional conflict. With these factors in mind we can undertake a critical analysis of the Edwards-Brinton model of the phases or stages of revolution. This model, as its very terminology reveals, attempts to develop a paradigm for all great revolutions by generalizing the historical course of the Great French Revolution. While subsequent discussion will cast serious doubt on the neatness and universality of this three-stage trajectory of the revolutionary process, a critical exegesis of it will elucidate certain features of revolution and provide elements of a more adequate theory of "stages."

THE CLASSIC MODEL: THE FRENCH REVOLUTION AS PARADIGM

The Moderate Interregnum

Phase I of revolutions according to the Edwards-Brinton model is the *rule of the moderates*. The moderation of the moderates is, of course, underscored when we contrast them with their erstwhile allies and eventual antagonists, the radicals or extremists. We have already suggested that moderation involves a vision of revolutionary goals that falls toward the lower end of the scale of revolutionary intensity. The moderates want to change fewer things (and these less profoundly and more slowly) than radicals do; and thus their disposition is to declare the revolution over rather early in the day. The moderates furthermore tend to rest content with alterations in the country's political system, such as a shift from absolute to constitutional monarchy or from monarchy to republic. Since these changes usually involve a modification of the status system, the moderates will tolerate some changes there as well. The moderates are not usually interested in profound economic reorganization, though they are willing to reform specific economic abuses. The moderates' preoccupation with political and sometimes religious change can stop short of considering democracy as a desirable form of government. The English Presbyterians and even the more radical Cromwellian Independents, the French Feuilliants and Girondists, wished to reserve political participation to the financially independent segments of the population. More recent moderate revolutionaries have naturally been more effusively democratic, as the idea of democracy has gained respectability across wide expanses of the political spectrum.

Given the frequent connection between political attitudes and ideologies and social position, we might expect certain correlations between moderation and high rank in the old regime's stratification systems. According to Crane Brinton, the moderates constitute "the richer, better known, and higher placed of the old opposition. . . ." [1] They are prominent *notables* in the Weberian sense,[2] men who in less crisis-ridden times might find themselves leaders of the government rather than of an increasingly intransigent opposition. Swept up perhaps more by events than by pre-formed revolutionary ideology, the moderates never entirely lose hope of some last-ditch grasp at reconciliation to avert or cut short civil war. These sentiments, however, are joined with others that go far to explain the vacillation, indecision, and division of moderates in many revolutions. The moderates are, after all, revolutionaries, even if reluctantly so or imperfectly so. Consequently, they "distrust the conservatives, against whom they have so recently risen" and find it difficult to believe that "the extremists, with whom they so recently stood united, can actually be their enemies. All the force of the ideas and sentiments with which the moderates entered the revolution give them a sort of twist toward the Left." [3] Thus the moderates often have little defense against being crushed between the millstones of the counterrevolutionary right and the radical left.

While for these and other reasons moderates met a sorry fate in the French, Spanish, and Russian revolutions—the "great" revolutions so naturally impressive to theorists of revolution—the outcomes of some not-so-great or "moderate" revolutions show that events can take a different course. Unless we deny that upheavals in France in 1848 and in 1871, in Germany after World War I, and in China in 1911 constitute even mild revolutions, we are forced to admit that moderates can sometimes act with the ruthless abandon usually associated with radicals and so foreign to the stereotype of moderates as inherently stricken by political paralysis. The June Days of Paris in 1848 and the suppression of the Paris Commune in May, 1871, show how moderates can be capable of the most strenuous and bloody exertions to defend their "political" revolution against those who claim that without "social" revolution an insurrection produces a mere change of masters. Nevertheless, the state of mind of the moderates is just one of the variables determining the moderate-radical confrontation: the dispositions and fighting strength of the periphery surrounding the revolutionary center must also be taken into account. Rural and provincial France in 1848 and 1871 were simply not in the proper mood to follow the lead of radical Paris. Things were different in the days of the Great Revolution.

In the Edwards-Brinton scheme, the moderates of the great revolutions are beset by a fatal incapacity in military affairs and organization. Edwards suggests that the moderates "always try to govern the army by political instead of military methods. The results are uniformly and universally disastrous. The army is demoralized and defeated. The revolution is put in jeopardy. The government of the moderate reformers loses popularity and prestige. . . ." [4] A case in point is the famous Order Number I issued by the Petrograd Soviet in March, 1917, and which nearly destroyed military discipline by turning the Russian Army into a debating club. As Adam Ulam points out, the framers of Order Number I "did not intend such consequences; they were simply ignorant of military affairs. And there was not a single Bolshevik among them." [5] The moderates are clearly in a dilemma: on the one hand, they may mistrust the existing forces as creatures of the old regime; and yet they fear to create a brand new military force whose political complexion is unpredictable. For example, the Presbyterian moderates in the English Revolution fought a kind of political cold war with the New Model Army developed by Cromwell and the Independents. Their fears were well-grounded, as a military coup known as Pride's Purge was the prelude to a somewhat more radical period after 1648. Events in France after 1789 or in Spain after 1931 seem to confirm Edwards' indictment of the moderates' bungling of military affairs. But once again, the French experiences of 1848 and 1871 and the German experience of 1919 tell a different story of the moderates' utilization of military (or paramilitary) units to annihilate the radical challenge.

Further reflecting the weakness of moderates in the great revolutions is the phenomenon of "dual sovereignty" or "dual power," [6] which George Pettee qualifies as "anarchy thinly covered by legal continuity." [7] All of these formulations imply that a solid, coherent state organization does not immediately succeed upon the collapse of the old order. In fact, stressing "collapse" rather than "overthrow" suggests that no strong monolithic organization exists which could immediately pick up the pieces and assemble an effective revolutionary regime. Especially is this so in the French and English revolutions, where the Jacobin Clubs and the New Model Army needed some time to develop into bodies that presaged modern party organization. Later revolutions generally present organized revolutionary parties; but they are often highly competitive (Russia and Spain) and the one which in the end outdistances the rest is relatively weak in numbers at the time of "outbreak" or "collapse." Some months at least are necessary for the mushroom growth that assures the party leadership that they are indeed riding the wave of the future. Here too we must set Eastern-style revolutions aside, for in that setting the revolutionary party has some years in the periphery to develop into a kind of party-state, which eventually will culminate its growth in the final, rapid, and ignominious collapse of the official government.

Thus, in certain revolutions—the ones Edwards, Brinton, and Pettee have in mind—the moderate ascendency forms an *interregnum*, in the sense of an interlude between two regimes possessed of full sovereign authority. More specifically, the dual power situation finds the moderates in control of what remains of the apparatus of the old regime (at least in the capital city) and the more radical formations in control of a shadow government that increasingly becomes a countergovernment, a new *imperium in imperio*. As Brinton points out, this countergovernment is "better organized, better staffed, better obeyed" than that of the moderates [8]; but his contention that it is also "illegal" needs some qualification. The New Model Army, for example, was created at the behest of Parliament, though it later turned upon its masters, who themselves trod upon a shaky legal basis. As the denouement of Pride's Purge approached, the Army undertook ostensibly "illegal" acts, but as a whole it was not, strictly speaking, illegal. Nor were the Jacobin Clubs, the Parisian sections, and the revolutionary

Commune of Paris straightforwardly illegal, though their actions from 1791 onwards increasingly became such. A similar equivocal legal situation holds for the Soviets in Moscow and Petrograd during the middle months of 1917. In this case the Provisional Government, despite certain contrary appearances, represents a breach in the legal continuity of Russian political history. Thus, it is better to speak of these countergovernments as *extralegal* than as clearly illegal because of the unsettled legal situation implied by the very notion of revolution. Had the moderate governments acted more vigorously and legally proscribed once and for all the New Model Army, the Jacobin Clubs, the Bolshevik Party, or Spanish anarcho-syndicalist fighting squads, and not just individual members of these groups, we could speak more confidently of the precise legal status of countergovernments in the dual power situation.

Whatever the legal niceties, the period of dual power evolves from fairly extensive cooperation—which Brinton has christened the "revolutionary honeymoon"—through heightened tension and competition to its termination in a radical coup. Pride's Purge on December 6, 1648; the Parisian insurrection or *journées* begun on May 31, 1793; the Bolshevik coup in November, 1917—all signal the end of the unstable balance of a dual power situation. What dual power means in everyday terms is that large numbers of people ranging from military and government officials, local leaders, to ordinary citizens are confronted with two sometimes contradictory sets of policies, decrees, or instructions to decide between. This only serves to worsen the crisis of legitimacy that has already brought down the basic foundations of the old regime. Should one follow the decrees of the National Assembly or the Commune (i.e., city administration) of Paris? Does the Provisional Government or the Soviets speak for the "people"?

Several causes operate to shift the balance of both power and authority away from the official government of the moderates toward the countergovernment of the radicals. Brinton cautiously points out that the "legal government is unpopular with many for the very reason that it is an obvious and responsible government and therefore has to shoulder some of the unpopularity of the government of the old regime." [9] Its adversary is less encumbered by the burden of unpleasant memories and decisions. Edwards, more emphatic, observes that the government of "moderate men ends in wreck. If the total ruin of the revolution is to be avoided a change must be made. The revolution must go onward, and go onward rapidly." [10] Pettee elaborates this same point: "Either the left must win and eliminate all the cyclical accumulated cramps through liquidation, and the secular cramp through revolutionary changes, or a right reaction must move in, securing itself through liquidation in order to preserve what it can of the old privileges. Neither policy can be attempted in practice until a new state is created although much is accomplished in this period through uncontrolled processes." [11] Emergence out of the limbo of dual power is induced by the moderates' difficulties in resolving the grievances of a variety of social groups and strata. The radicals choose among these, and thus are in a better position to deliver the action they promise: the moderates want conciliation of as many groups as possible, the radicals are more willing to play favorites openly.

Before we concentrate attention on the radicals, we should examine the claim often made either by the radicals themselves or by later sympathizers, that a substantial majority of the "people" favors both the ouster of the moderates and the formation (and continuance) of a radical regime. Edwards, for example, asserts that the radicals "could not hold power for a week without the tacit consent of the revolutionary majority." [12] Yet given the newness of opinion polls and the understandable reluctance of radicals to hold free elections or abide by their results, it is somewhat presumptuous to talk with utter conviction about the political dispositions of the mass of ordinary people. This can only be done if "tacit consent" is tendentiously defined as reluctance to openly proclaim one's hostility to the radical revolutionary regime. Moreover, the evidence, however impressionistic, supports Pettee's conclusion that "in a revolutionary situation there is no majority." [13] The conscious counterrevolutionaries and revolutionaries both constitute "tiny nuclei of men who literally will stop at nothing, each surrounded by a half integrated penumbra of men shading off to those who will stop at anything. Between the two groups is the 'plain,' the great mass whose consent will go unquestioningly to the victor." [14]

Brinton goes one step further by stressing the growth of political apathy and nonparticipation after a certain high point of involvement has been reached. Even before the disenchantment associated with the "Thermidorean reaction" sets in, there is good reason to doubt whether the growing mass of revolutionary dropouts is enamored of the radicals. Instead the bulk of them appear to be "cowed conservatives or moderates," who are "quite incapable of the mental and moral [and] physical strain of being devoted extremists in the crisis of a revolution." [15] For this reason, all talk of the "people" or the "masses" or the "majority" as supportive of the radical factions—or even of the general course of the revolution—must be taken with extreme caution. If anything, the growing hostility or indifference of the majority seems to be the fate of most revolutions, though hard data on this whole question would appear to be lost forever in the mists of history.

The Radicals and the Terror

The seizure of power by radicals or extremists is generally associated in the minds of historians and theorists with the launching of a revolutionary dictatorship whose most salient feature is a Reign of Terror—or as Brinton correctly puts it, a Reign of Terror *and Virtue*. For the conservative critics of revolution, radicalism, dictatorship, and the Terror are three ways of saying the same thing. For others, like George Pettee, the revolutionary dictatorship must be distinguished from the Terror, for though the former "does resort to terrorism," which is "simply a special means of dealing with opposition to the state," such terrorism outlives the Reign of Terror, whose purposes are rather different.[16] Simple terrorism is thus an exaggerated form of the self-defense practiced by all government, whereas the "dictatorship contributes to the terror without making it." [17] The Terror is made instead by "all the good and bad elements in society itself, impatient and without any conventional guides or coherent direction, rising to a higher and higher pitch of nervous tension and violence. . . ." [18] In short, the radical dictatorship may employ terrorism both before and after the drama of the Terror is played out. From this perspective, which will receive a closer analysis below, the Reign of Terror occurs when both elite and masses are swept by currents beyond their control; while terrorism is a strategy employed for limited objectives and against specific targets.

This valid distinction must be coupled to another one between the Reign of Terror and instances of mob violence such as the September (1792) Massacres in France or the atrocities committed by either side during revolutionary civil wars as in Russia and Spain. There has been no lack of violence, atrocities, and terrorism in a number of moderate or even abortive revolutions; but moderate or counterrevolutionary elements have succeeded in nipping radical movements in the bud and thus have deprived us of further examples of the relationship between radicals and Reigns of Terror and Virtue. Therefore we have to examine more closely the logical and empirical connections between revolutionary radicalism, the Terror, and the radical dictatorship.

Who then are the radicals whose deeds loom so large in the history of the great revolutions? A sort of operational understanding of them would suggest that they are men whose views of the goals or stakes of the revolution lie higher on our scale of revolutionary intensity than those of the moderates. In simple terms, they wish to go further faster than do the moderates—at least on the average. This last stipulation raises the possibility of a bone of contention between radicals and moderates other than the abstract and ultimate *goals* of the revolution. The *means* employed to defend or to promote the revolution are also a kind of litmus test to discriminate between the two factions. For Edwards, the question of methods illustrates best the unfailing superiority of radicals over moderates: "In plain English, the revolution is on the point of being wiped out in blood and the radicals save it by wiping out its opponents in blood." [19] Whether or not the threat to the revolution is always so ominous as Edwards believes, there is no question that the radicals are less constrained by constitutionalism and legalism than the moderates are. Robespierre at the beginning of the Reign of Terror conveys this point with clarity:

> The aim of constitutional government is to preserve the Republic. The aim of revolutionary government is to found it.
> The revolution is the war of liberty against its enemies. The Constitution is the rule of liberty when victorious and peaceable. . . .
> Constitutional government is chiefly concerned with civil liberty, revolutionary government with public liberty. Under constitutional rule it is almost enough to protect individuals against the abuses of public power; under revolutionary rule the public power is obliged to defend itself against all the factions that attack it. [20]

For Robespierre or for Cromwell, constitutionalism is a value whose full realization must sometimes be deferred. For some later radical revolutionaries, since the revolution is to eventuate in a new society in which traditional notions of constitutionalism make no sense, there need be little trouble about it in the course of the revolution itself. Thus, if we look at the three major components of revolutionary ideology, a radical as opposed to a moderate ideology tends to be (1) more hostile to more aspects of the old regime, (2) more expansive or "utopian" regarding the shape of the new society to come, and (3) more willing to invoke and follow the maxim that the end justifies the means when the welfare and furtherance of the revolution is at stake.

It is possible, however, to go beyond these operational contrasts between moderates and radicals by employing some modest sociological and social psychological criteria, especially by restricting ourselves to the top leaders and most reliable militants. [21] First and most obvious among these further contrasts is that the radicals as a group tend to be men placed lower than the moderates in the social hierarchies of the old regime. The extent of the difference varies from revolution to revolution, though it should never be exaggerated. The radical leadership embraces old regime notables; people of middling social circumstances; but surprisingly few ex-peasants, ex-workers, and ex-artisans. The balance of non-notable elements is stronger among the radicals than among the moderates, however. (The difference, we shall see below, is in part related to an intensification of the class struggle characteristic of protracted revolutions.) A recent study of Pride's Purge, for example, shows that those members of the Long Parliament who supported the Purge and the step-up of the revolution that followed (abolition of the monarchy and the House of Lords, etc.) were as a group of lower social standing than the moderate victims or opponents of the Purge. The radical minority derived "in marked degree from families which were insecure ('declining gentry,' in a famous phrase), or from outside the traditional political establishment (*nouveaux riches,* lesser gentry, families of obscure and usually urban origins.)" [22] Once the revolution began the erratic descent that resulted in the Restoration of the monarchy in 1660, whatever flare-ups of revolutionary radicalism that occurred were centered in "the Army, in London and a few other towns, and in the congregations of the gathered churches"; and these involved "only a handful of the old governing class." [23]

Though some such social asymmetry distinguished moderates and radicals in other revolutions, the contrast between these groups is sometimes overdrawn. Such overemphasis often emerges in discussions of the differences between the relatively moderate Girondists and the more radical Montagnards or Jacobins in the early days of the French Revolution. After the *journées* at the end of May, 1793, the National Convention underwent its own version of Pride's Purge with the expulsion of some two dozen moderate deputies. The circle of later expellees and resigners widened to include about 150 members, who have henceforth been called "the Gironde" or even "the Girondist party." Modern research, however, has questioned the very existence of anything like modern party organization, not only for the Girondists, but even for the Montagnards within the Convention and for the wider Jacobin movement outside. Strangely enough, both the Girondist and Montagnard parliamentary contingents included members and ex-members of the Jacobin Club, though most of those deputies termed "Girondists" by tradition had been expelled or had ceased to be active members by the time of the purge.

Whether we wish to term these groups "parties," "factions," or something looser still, much of the literature suggests that the political differences between Girondists and Montagnards (or more broadly, Jacobins) stem mainly from social and economic causes. In short, the Girondists are held to represent the *grand bourgeoisie*—"represent" here referring both to social background and defense of interests; while Jacobins are held to represent the middle and petite bourgeoisie. However, closer analysis reveals that similarities in social background between Girondin and Montagnard are perhaps more substantial than the differences: "The Convention was a remarkably homogeneous body and no difference of social origin distinguishes the 200 so-called Girondins either from the Mountain or from the rest of their colleagues. The 749 deputies in the assembly were almost all of the middle-class, the great majority of them being professional men." [24] Outside the Convention the views of the Girondist deputies did tend to reflect those of the upper social strata, while the Jacobins were oriented more towards the middle and lower strata; but this is insufficient warrant for a simple "class" explanation of political and ideological differences.

In sum, the differences between the Girondists and Montagnards are not those between two coherent political parties, each reflecting and representing clearly different social classes. As in the case of the contrast between Presbyterians and Independents, we must look not only to social background, but also to individual personality traits, personal followings, and divergent views on the political and military issues of the day. One study concludes that if there is any bond which held the Girondists together, it was a regionalist "hostility to Robespierre and to the delegation and city of Paris," [25] which led some Girondists to espouse various ideas that were later proscribed as "federalism" during the Reign of Terror.

Since the time of the French Revolution, classes have become more important and more clearly differentiated as a type of social stratification; and political parties—especially those devoted to revolution—have become better organized, better disciplined, and better led. Modern political parties often cater to the interests and opinions of distinct classes and status groups, while their leaders in many cases originate in the strata championed by the party. Though one is struck by the key positions held by middle-class intelligentsia in parties all across the political spectrum, in modern revolutions moderates and radicals tend to congregate in distinct political parties appealing to socially distinctive clienteles. The problem of clearly delineating and contrasting the sociological sources of support of Kadet *moderates* and Bolshevik *radicals* in Russia, or of the *moderate* Radical Party and the *radical* Socialist Party in Spain, is considerably easier than with the political formations of the English and French revolutions. Even so, it is a Marxist, Karl Kautsky, who reminds us that "parties and classes are . . . not necessarily coterminous. A class can split up into various parties, and a party may consist of members of various classes. A class may still remain the rulers, while changes occur in the governing party. . . ." [26] The very range of possible party-class relationships suggests that factors such as leadership and shifting currents of opinion, as well as social background, affect the degree of moderation or radicalism of revolutionary political parties.

It is by looking to all of these factors that Crane Brinton is able to discern peculiar behavioral traits of radical revolutionaries in the great revolutions. For instance, he finds that they all "displayed a willingness to work hard, to sacrifice their peace and security, to submit to discipline, to submerge their personalities in the group." [27] Only a comparison with a deep-seated and fanatical religiosity serves Brinton to convey the prodigies of revolutionary zeal displayed by radicals in the different revolutions. The Jacobins, for example, acted more like Wagnerian heroes than prosaic bourgeois gentlemen in 1793–94, because "they had many interests other than economic interests," and these other interests indeed "modified their economic interests." [28] Accordingly, the Reign of Terror, the high-water mark of radical rule, was not in the main "a phase of the class-struggle, but even more a civil war, a religious war." [29] Though the militancy of the radical revolutionists is not a function of class consciousness, Brinton (and many others) are reluctant to explain it in terms of the personality theories of individual psychology (e.g., Freudian psychoanalysis). Instead they appeal to the social psychology of social movements,[30] which study shows how men are taken up in a broader wave which causes them to behave in ways wholly foreign to their normal behavior. ("Normal" in the present context would connote their pre-revolutionary and, if they survive, their post-revolutionary life style.)

Brinton for one concerns himself with the topmost levels of the radical movement and concludes that "once the crisis period is over, they will, save for the few born martyrs, cease to be crusaders, fanatics, ascetics." [31] A similar conclusion is reached in a study that studies the lower-level radical militants in the French Revolution: "The revolutionary . . . is only a provisional being, who does not resist time, wear and tear, lassitude—a creature of exceptional circumstances. . . . Our men of 1793 were not . . . ideologues or professors in revolutionary theory. Just when they donned their slippers, this was the end of their career as political activists. With the passage of the great hopes and the great dangers, there was thus a return to the banality of everyday life." [32]

At this point our interest is not in why this retreat occurs, but rather in how it intimates that psychological idiosyncrasies alone do not explain why various sorts of people become radical revolutionaries. Behavior so correlated with the ups and downs of revolutions, it is suggested, must be explained essentially as a social psychological reflex of extraordinary trends, events, and circumstances. Thus, the deradicalization of ex-radicals is cited as further proof that their initial outlook and behavior is due more to external pressures than to peculiar innate dispositions. Though all of these points are well taken, and (as we shall see in Chapter VII) theories of the "revolutionary personality" leave considerable to be desired, it would be wrong also to deny all force to psychological variables in explaining why certain individuals push their way to the front of radical movements, where as top leaders and militants they play for a time a decisive role.

In the Edwards-Brinton paradigm of revolution, the Reign of Terror (and Virtue) punctuates the phase of radical hegemony. Wholesale controversy, however, rages over why the Terror occurs, either in specific revolutions or in great revolutions. Closely related is the controversy over the moral implications of the Terror. In the historiography of the French Revolution, for example, there are two main competing theories of the Terror: the conspiracy thesis (*thèse du complot*) and the thesis of circumstances (*thèse des circonstances*).[33] Though the connection is less than strictly logical, the first thesis is usually championed by those hostile to the revolution, while the second is dear to its defenders. However, to achieve a wider historical application and clearer logical contrast, a dichotomy between *irrationalist* and *instrumental* theories of the Terror in revolutions is more useful.

Irrationalist theories of the Terror maintain that since revolutions are both causes and effects of the breakdown of traditional moral and religious codes, they open the Pandora's box of human passion and aggressiveness. Man is thrown back to dependence on normally repressed drives and instincts. The Reign of Terror is accordingly an expression of the baser and uncontrolled urges of man's animal nature. It thus epitomizes the "anarchy and disorder" that many conservatives feel is the essence of revolution. The violence of the Terror overwhelms both the leaders and the rank and file of the radicals; and, as poetic justice might have it, it even turns round to destroy the original Terrorists—giving rise to the old maxim that revolutions, like the Greek god Kronos, devour their own children.

One of the most eloquent statements of this sort of thinking is also one of the earliest. Thucydides in his *History of the Peloponnesian War* asserts a theory of human nature that sees civilization erected precariously over the dormant volcano of the passions of *fear, honor, and interest*. It is only the fragile "cake of custom" that allows some sort of order to reign in human society. But certain circumstances—such as war, revolution (*stasis*), plague, or famine—erode the fabric of moral restraints. In addition, these four scourges tend to go along together, though any one of them can bring the others in its wake. Alone or in some combination, these factors present mankind with stresses and strains that cause dramatic changes in human behavior. Thucydides' picture of the process whereby *stasis,* fomented in part by Spartan and Athenian power rivalries, spread to nearly all the Greek city-states merits lengthy quotation:

> When troubles had once begun in the cities, those who followed carried the revolutionary spirit further and further, and determined to outdo the report of all who had preceded them by the ingenuity of their enterprises and the atrocity of their revenges. The meaning of words had no longer the same relation to things, but was changed by them as they thought proper. Reckless daring had to be loyal courage; prudent delay was the excuse of a coward; moderation was the disguise of unmanly weakness; to know everything was to do nothing. Frantic energy was the true quality of a man. A conspirator who wanted to be safe was a recreant in disguise. The lover of violence was always trusted, and his opponent always suspected. He who succeeded in a plot was deemed knowing, but a still greater master in craft was he who detected one. . . . The tie of party was stronger than the tie of blood, because a partisan was more ready to dare without asking why.[34]

Thucydides' account has been echoed by both philosophic critics of revolution and antirevolutionary historians of the various upheavals. For Edmund Burke, the "father of modern conservatism," a Terror follows quite naturally when men "venture upon pulling down an edifice which has answered in any tolerable degree for ages the common purposes of society, or on building it up again without having models and patterns of approved utility before their eyes." [35] Hegel, who in his youth was enraptured by the French Revolution, after making the same point as Burke about the futility of first sweeping the slate of society clear and then trying to build a new society from scratch, condemns the quixotic drive to "Absolute Freedom": "The will of its re-founders was to give it what they alleged was a purely rational basis, but it was only abstractions that were being used; the Idea was lacking; and *the experiment ended in the maximum of frightfulness and terror.*" [36] (Italics mine.) Thus, the "irrationalist" theory of the Reign of Terror maintains two basic principles: (1) the collapse of traditional values unleashes hatred, aggressiveness, and the unbridled will-to-power; and (2) since the attempt to create a radically new society according to the dictates of an abstract ideology must fail, the radical leaders find scapegoats to explain the frustration of their designs. The Terror stems from these two causes.

The instrumental theory, on the other hand, conceives of the Terror as essentially a rational ends-means calculation to deal with circumstances that threaten the very survival of the revolution. Lyford Edwards reflects this standpoint with his statement that a "terror is a scheme for scaring people." [37] The Terror becomes the order of the day because the internal and external enemies of the revolution seem poised to strike it a deathblow. To parry this blow the radicals institute the Reign of Terror (i.e., "an organized, governmental regime set up with a calculated purpose of social control").[38] Death and destruction are really incidental to the radicals' ultimate goal of governmental consolidation. A revolution can divide society to the point of political paralysis, and the Reign of Terror is a means of restoring effective power to the new leadership. The victims of the Terror are for the most part overt or covert counterrevolutionaries; and we can console our feelings at the destruction of innocents, say Edwards and others, once we realize that the likely alternative to the Terror is a bloody, prolonged civil war.

Perhaps, Edwards argues, the main function of the Terror is not the ostensible one of striking down proven counterrevolutionaries or even the "prophylactic" one [39] of preventing new oppositionists. As the Terror occurs at the high point in the trajectory of a revolution, we can assume that an enormous strain has been mounting on the nervous systems of leaders and followers alike. Indefinite accumulation of pressures inherent to the revolutionary crisis could end in the nervous collapse of vast numbers of people. Here the Terror is instituted "to serve as a safety-valve for the discharge of wrought-up emotions." [40] Though the Terror looks to the novice like a "wild orgy of unrestrained passion," in reality it is "an elaborately planned and carefully worked-out stage show for purposes of emotional catharsis. . . ." [41] Edwards' instrumental theory of the Terror furthermore causes him to challenge some common ideas on how and why the Terror is brought to a close. Certain historians of the French Revolution, for example, consider the fall of Robespierre on 9 Thermidor (July 27, 1794) as indicative of a wholesale shift in the composition of the political elite that would rule France until Napoleon I. The dissolution of the Robespierrist Committee of Public Safety is even considered a turning point in the class struggle, with the "Red Terror" favored by the lower classes being succeeded by the "White Terror" championed by the old and new rich. According to Edwards, however, "a terror is generally terminated under the same rulers with whom it began." [42] Consequently, the end of the Terror in France and elsewhere does not necessarily signify the ouster of the radicals by more moderate elements, let alone any great shift in class relationships. The fate of the Robespierrists really provides no exception to this rule, because the sovereign National Convention, which both made and broke Robespierre, remained in basic control of the situation throughout.

To buttress his theory that the Terror is an instrument taken up and then discarded by one and the same group of men, Edwards points to the ebbing away of Terroristic laws, institutions, and practices as opposed to their immediate and total liquidation. Although the difficulty that not all revolutions have their Reigns of Terror so clearly demarcated as does the French Revolution prevents an easy solution to the problems of how and why Terrors end, Edwards' insight that the Reign of Terror and the radical ascendency are not wholly coterminous is highly suggestive. Cromwell and his lieutenants weathered whatever stages one finds in the English Revolution rather well. Lenin and his lieutenants initiated and terminated War Communism (1918–21), the earliest Russian version of a Reign of Terror. Though Edwards may have underestimated the significance of the ninth of Thermidor in the French Revolution, Robespierre's immediate successors, the so-called Thermidoreans, were not necessarily less of a thorn in the sides of conservative or counterrevolutionary groups.[43] In any case, Edwards' findings suggest that any explanation of the Terror must leave some role to conscious policy.

However, if the irrationalist theory of the Terror overstates certain points through ideological excess, the instrumental theory has the earmarks of apologetics. While it would be wrong to deny the impact of dire circumstances in the genesis of revolutionary Terrors, these circumstances cannot be divorced from revolution as a process. Regarding the French Terror, R. R. Palmer concludes that though the Terror may have been generated by circumstances, "the chief of these circumstances was the internal chaos which the Revolution had produced. It began as a means of defence against the menace of invasion, but invasion was a menace because of the disunity. . . ." [44] Similar strictures hold for other revolutions as well. Furthermore, the "stage show" analogy of Edwards ignores the variegated social backgrounds of the Terror's victims and, more significantly, the fantastic, almost paranoic, credulity of the Terrorists in plots, conspiracies, and intrigues of all kinds. Executions in France, Russia, and Spain were doubtless undertaken partly for their deterrent impact on oppositionists, but there is a considerable gap between the abundance and ferocity of denunciations of "counterrevolutionary" or "foreign" plots and their actual number and menace. Plots, of course, exist, but the ingenuous credulity of the radicals ill accords with interpretations of the Terror as a measured response to a genuine threat by means of a manipulation of popular fears. In the early days of the Bolshevik regime, for example, "the fear of counter-revolutionary conspiracies had become deeply ingrained in the Soviet leadership," and consequently a " 'White Scare' (comparable to the 'Red Scare' hysteria in the West) gripped the members of the party." [45] Similar "White Scares" are too frequent in too many revolutions to be written off as mere excess or studied insincerity. In other words, the radicals probably believe in some of the allegations that later appear so bizarre; and there is just enough smoke around to keep alive their suspicion that somewhere counterrevolution is about to ignite.

Perhaps an even graver weakness in the instrumental theory of the Terror is its underestimation of the role of ideology; recognition of this latter motivation is why Brinton used the expression "The Reign of Terror *and Virtue*." Virtue here is defined ideologically. If all that were involved was defending the revolution against attack, the instrumental theory would provide an adequate explanation for the Terror. But the Terrorists also wish to promote *revolutionary virtue*—that is, to modify human behavior according to ideological prescriptions. How great is the change envisaged varies according to the nature of each revolutionary ideology, but certain common features stick out. The periods identified as Reigns of Terror by historians of the English, French, and Russian revolutions, for example, show a concerted attack not only on the obviously political targets, but also on forms of behavior which the old regime may repudiate in theory but tolerates in practice. Among the list of "immoral" and hence counterrevolutionary practices that have evoked crackdown campaigns in certain phases of certain revolutions are to be found drunkenness, philandering, gambling, dancing, cursing, prostitution, fancy dress, religious belief or disbelief, idleness, bachelorhood, linguistic usages, art for art's sake, etc. Certain of these behavior patterns and attitudes are incompatible with the notion of the *new man* implicit in most revolutionary ideologies. This often remarked puritanism or asceticism of the radical revolutionaries clashes with the notion that revolutions tolerate boundless social experimentation—there is less of this than sometimes thought and the experimentation is supervised from above. Accordingly, the Terror's victims include social "undesirables" such as pimps, prostitutes, petty thieves, vagabonds, and troublemakers of all sorts, in addition to old regime notables and active oppositionists. There is an earnestness to the radicals that demands a moral as well as a political purgation of society. The spartan personal lives of so many radical revolutionary leaders are too emphatic to be a mere coincidence—to be self-righteous one must first be righteous.

Thus, it is hard to avoid the conclusion that the Terror stems in part from the attempt to realize ideological imperatives by forced-draft methods. The lingering corruption of the old regime must be exorcised before the new regime can be considered complete. However, if the Terror scores impressive successes against political targets such as counterrevolution and foreign intervention, its program of rapid and drastic moral regeneration encounters serious obstacles—the chief of which seems to be the generality of men themselves. Whether indelibly tainted by socialization in an "immoral" pre-revolutionary regime (as the radicals may come to believe) or biogenetically incapable of sustaining the heights of revolutionary virtue (as the conservatives believe), ordinary men and women are perhaps the greatest source of disappointment to the revolutionary elite. But to admit that one's goals are unattainable is not easy: scapegoats may provide an outlet for the bitter realization of failure. As Talcott Parsons points out, "No revolutionary movement can reconstruct society according to the values formulated in its ideology without restriction." [46] This principle would help to explain Brinton's conclusion that to some extent the Terror is "an over-compensation for the inability of the extremists to carry their ordinary brothers along with them." [47]

Though the Reign of Terror is the dramatic high-point of the radical phase in the Edwards-Brinton model of revolution, the *radical dictatorship* can precede and will outlast the Terror, narrowly speaking. We must thus examine some of the more salient features of this novel regime. We have already seen Robespierre's characterization of revolutionary government as waging a ruthless war to secure the blessings of constitutionalism. The implication is that the mark of ultimate success of the dictatorship would also speed its dissolution. Though it is hard to think of anyone exceeding Robespierre's frankness, Lenin is even less preoccupied by reservations when he writes:

> Dictatorship is power, based directly upon force, and unrestricted by any laws.
> The revolutionary dictatorship of the proletariat is power won and maintained by the violence of the proletariat against the bourgeoisie, power that is unrestricted by any laws.[48]

This sort of bluntness is rare amongst earlier revolutionary radicals, less because of conscious hypocrisy than because of the strength of constitutionalist preconceptions. The English and French revolutions, after all, emerged during acute constitutional crises. Though radicals in the English Revolution accepted Pride's Purge, the execution of Charles, Cromwell's dissolution of the Rump of the Long Parliament, and other "illegal" acts, they "still retained vestiges of the constitutional past." [49] This caused them to refrain from pushing forward with a maximalist political program implemented by extreme dictatorial methods. The French Revolutionaries were so preoccupied with constitutions that they wrote three of them in the early years: 1791, 1793, and 1795. The first was the product of the moderates, the second of the radicals, the third of the Thermidoreans; the constitutions were thus rallying points for the various factions.

The differing influence of constitutionalism in the different revolutions reminds us that despite some common traits among radicals of all revolutions, their specific ideologies must be put into historical perspective. On the whole, later radicals stand to the left of their predecessors in the sense that their concept of revolution is more drastic. One consequence of this is the somewhat different shape the radical dictatorship takes in the later revolutions. If we consider constitutionalism as the legally enforced restraint on the scope and procedures of governmental power and, following Lenin, pure dictatorship as rule "unrestricted by any laws," then we can say that the later radical regimes are less constitutional and more dictatorial. Their leaders do not face, or face in milder form, what Carl J. Friedrich calls the "dilemma of Cromwell." The latter "was haunted by a sense that his arbitrary exercise of power needed a sanction. This sanction he sought to obtain from several Parliaments which were elected in rapid succession. Yet, since they endeavored to restrain him as well as to sanction his rule, they were dissolved one after the other." [50] When Cromwell assumed plenary power as Lord Protector in 1653, his supporters produced The Instrument of Government, which comes close to being the only written constitution in British political history.

Differences between radical dictatorships (e.g., regarding the residual influence of constitutionalism) are not solely the product of abstract ideological conceptions. The level of technology, the state of communications, the ambience of political culture serve to differentiate revolutionary as well as nonrevolutionary regimes. Also important is the international system: the severity of the threat of foreign intervention will affect the shape of domestic political arrangements. England's greater security in this regard must be considered a contributing factor in the relative moderation of its revolution. Other revolutionary regimes have been less fortunate, and some of the severity of their radical dictatorships is due to this vulnerability. With these reservations in mind we can survey the characteristics which in addition to the Terror serve to define the radical ascendency. The following interdependent features seem most significant: political centralization, economic control, revolutionary justice, the revolutionary army, intense social conflict, the ultrarevolutionary opposition.

The radical dictatorship achieves a degree of administrative and political centralization without precedent in the country's history. It consolidates this newfound control by sending out newly created agents with enormous powers. Cromwell's Major-Generals, the Representatives on Mission of the Jacobin-dominated Convention, Lenin's Commissars and Cheka are merely the best known of a network of officials who constitute a tight apparatus of administrative-political control in the radical dictatorship. The capital city assumes a political primacy that may have been foreshadowed in the old regime, but required the revolution and the radicals to reach perfection. From this central vantage point the radical dictatorship exercises a surveillance and a control over the lives of citizens that is a bold departure from the past. For some people this is the first time that decisions of the central government affect their daily lives on a regular basis. The flow of information and directives to and from the seat of government increases prodigiously. The modern state appears for the first time, perhaps to retreat as in Restoration England, or to develop further as in Napoleonic France, or even to develop into a "totalitarian" state as in Stalinist Russia. Whether to suppress counterrevolution, to mobilize for a new kind of warfare, to promote revolutionary virtue, or to forestall total economic collapse, the radical dictatorship appears somewhat omnipresent, if not really omnipotent.

The radical dictatorship extends economic control along with political centralization. Though it is wrong to speak of a command or planned economy regarding the English and French revolutions, there was substantial growth of centralized intervention compared to the policies of the old regime. The French Law of the Maximum was a clear-cut attempt to curtail inflation by controlling prices and wages in 1794. The Committee of Public Safety also tried to regulate some areas of production, though this resulted more from wartime needs than from ideology. The array of collectivist measures in Lenin's War Communism derived from military needs, economic devastation, and ideology—ideology was naturally a much stronger influence in the Russian Revolution than the French. In less than a year from November, 1917, to November, 1918, the Soviet regime issued decrees (1) establishing workers' control over industry, (2) nationalizing the banks, (3) nationalizing foreign trade, (4) nationalizing big industry, (5) levying a huge confiscatory tax on the wealthy, and (6) nationalizing internal trade. In the Spanish Revolution the strength of anarcho-syndicalist ideas and the pronounced regionalism of Spanish history impeded the central (Madrid) government's efforts to control economic life. There the revolution from "below" was quite real and seemed to be moving towards a radically decentralized collectivism. However, in the later stages of the civil war the Negrin Government, under the strong influence of the communists, launched a program including "restriction of the scope of agrarian collectives; reduction of worker control to harmless proportions; centralization of state control of all important industry" in order to facilitate effective one-man management of firms.[51]

Understandably, the extent of the radical dictatorship's economic control is different in each revolution. Neither Cromwellian Independents (nor their Leveller critics on the left, for that matter), nor the

Jacobins were modern collectivists (i.e., advocates of some form of public ownership of the basic means of production and exchange). In fact, few of the requisites of modern economic planning such as reliable statistics or large-scale industrial units were available in many countries before the nineteenth or twentieth centuries. Thus, when the Jacobins took steps towards a controlled economy and autarchy, their actions derived not only from the "element of religious faith," or from the pressure of the Parisian *sans-culottes*, but equally as much from the "collapse of private enterprise." [52] Revolution means economic disarray, and revolutionary governments are compelled to do something about it. This selfsame principle explains why the Jacobins took economic measures somewhat to the "left" of their true economic ideas and why the communists in Russia (NEP) and Spain moved provisionally to the "right" of the principles of revolutionary socialism. After the ninth of Thermidor French governments, which continued to be radical in important respects, retreated from the economic policies of the Terror. Likewise, the Soviets after 1929 repudiated the NEP market economy and moved to a purer collectivism. In short, the economic innovations of the radical dictatorship are a peculiar mixture of ideology and *ad hoc* pragmatism.

  Revolutionary justice is inseparable from the economic and political aspects of the radical dictatorship. A "counterrevolutionary" comes to mean not only someone who repudiates the revolution politically but equally someone who by his economic activities—hoarding, profiteering, evasion of restrictions, or merely insufficient cooperation—is considered a foe of the revolution. With this expansion of the category of crime, the radical dictatorship sees the proliferation of extraordinary institutions dispensing summary justice with little obstruction from legal precedents or procedural guarantees. Trials before bodies such as the Revolutionary Tribunal in France or the Cheka in Russia usually come to speedy and foregone conclusions. The distinction between police and judicial functions falls victim to the demands of political conformity. That this sort of system leads to abuses—even if we admit the "right" of the radical dictatorship to destroy its enemies—is acknowledged by the leaders tacitly by measures of restraint or openly by invoking the "tragic necessities" of revolution. The wide scope of crimes against the revolution and the vast opportunities for denunciation before the revolutionary courts provide ample opportunity for settling old scores with little connection to the revolution. It would be wrong to deny a certain efficacy to institutions of revolutionary justice; but sometimes this efficacy involves a "blunderbuss" rather than a "sharpshooter" attack on alleged counterrevolutionaries, which may incite so much discontent as to outweigh the removal of real enemies of the revolution.

A most impressive achievement of the radical dictatorship is its creation of a revolutionary army, which may have been partly responsible for the radical take-over as in the English and Chinese communist revolutions, or which serves to defend the radical regime in civil wars as in France, Russia, and Spain. Let us recall that disintegration of the old regime's military force through demoralization and polarization is crucial to the early victories of the revolution. At that time the radicals' interests lie in neutralizing the armed forces. They play officers off against men, demand a purge of the high command, and do everything possible to destroy military discipline. However, the threat of foreign intervention, the resurgence of counterrevolution, and the growing split between moderates and radicals force the latter to acknowledge the need for a strong and loyal military arm. Though taking over the armed forces of the old regime intact is out of the question, elements of the old military will have to come over to the radicals or their survival will be in serious jeopardy. While whole units do defect to them, perhaps of greater importance (at least temporarily) is the individual defection of professional military men of high rank. Without their help when fighting first starts, the radical dictatorship could be defeated and overthrown. Although these officers may be none too friendly to the radicals (some redefect or are executed as counterrevolutionaries or incompetents—radicals tend to blur the differences in these two latter categories), their initial support, perhaps through patriotism, gives the radical regime time to consolidate its power and make new military arrangements.

Contrary to the dreams of some revolutionaries that armies can dispense with ranks, strict discipline, lengthy service, and professionalism of any type the radical dictatorship creates a military force of the highest quality. Cromwell's work with the New Model Army resulted in a highly disciplined machine, superior man-to-man to anything the Royalists or any European monarch could put into the field against it. While the Committee of Public Safety encountered serious problems of desertion, discipline, and equipment—with its nation-in-arms idea of a revolutionary army, its receptivity to military innovation, its promotion of skilled commanders regardless of age and professional background, and its willingness to resort to harshness to forestall or quell mutiny, it made the French Army preeminent on the European continent. Leon Trotsky's ruthless measures to restore military discipline and fighting edge to the Red Army were so successful that for a time it was contemplated to apply similar methods to the shattered Russian economy. All of this, however, earned Trotsky the mistrust of revolutionary idealists and of those who, recalling the French Revolution, feared a Bonapartist dictatorship.[53] In Spain, where a good part of the military establishment remained loyal to the increasingly revolutionary regime, centrifugal tendencies impeded the efforts of successive governments to integrate all anti-Franco forces into a single chain of command. Ideological heterogeneity on the Loyalist side barred full utilization of anti-Franco officers and defended "spontaneous" people's militia units. While the Spanish communists, perhaps covertly recalling Trotsky's organizational feats, strove to bring greater order and discipline to the People's Republican Army and other units, the Spanish political situation was significantly different from the Russian two decades before.

The military achievements of the radical dictatorship, however, are not attributable to administrative measures alone. The government succeeds somewhat in infusing its sometimes ragamuffin troops with some of its own revolutionary zeal. By also tapping the forces of nationalist feeling, it links defense of the fatherland with defense of the revolution, and these two things with defense of the radical dictatorship. Both politically and militarily innovative, the radical dictatorship raises the morale and fighting level of its new armies by an imaginative use of both the carrot and the stick. Its leaders eliminate certain of the worst abuses of military life under the old regime by shortening enlistment periods; by attacking corruption; and by paying, feeding, and equipping troops better than ever before. These reforms are, of course, costly and the civilians who have to foot the bill often resent it bitterly; but the radicals are willing to trade overall popularity for military effectiveness, which in the short run is more important to them. On the other hand, the radicals punish military unreliability with great severity, as Cromwell's suppression of Leveller-influenced mutineers in November, 1648, or Trotsky's orders in the summer of 1918 to shoot Commissars and regiment commanders if their troops ran away, amply illustrate. Similar instances in the French, Chinese Communist, and Spanish revolutions likewise reveal an astute balance between harshness and reward that goes far to explain military successes enjoyed by the radical regime.

If we look away from activities of the government to what occurs in everyday social life, a somewhat different picture of the radical dictatorship emerges. A cause as well as an effect of the radical regime is the growth of social conflict. Particularly important is the intensification of conflict (1) between classes, (2) between the center and the periphery, (3) between town and country, and (4) between devotees of the old religion and the new one or its ideological surrogate.

The modern communist dictum that the class struggle intensifies rather than diminishes after the seizure of power by the revolutionary class is supported by the history of revolutions, though the reasoning behind this conclusion is more questionable. Though earlier chapters have criticized overemphasis on sharpened class struggle as a *cause* of revolution, these doubts are not incompatible with the conclusion that *sharpened class struggle is a major effect of revolution*. There is nothing very new in this idea: Tocqueville alluded to it in the fragments of a work that was to carry further his study of the French Revolution. He wrote that *"violent and persistent class hatreds are not merely the products of unjust social conditions but of the struggles that upset these."* [54] In more precise terms he suggested that "what inflames, embitters, exasperates people and what makes the hatred of an aristocracy enduring is not only the extent of these abuses but the duration and the sharpness of the struggle over them." [55] This is not simply to argue that mountains grow out of molehills, but that the scope, duration, and intensity of conflict can move beyond the limitations of the original controversy. Blows and counterblows are struck during the contest which serve to prolong and aggravate it, so that one wonders if the combatants in the heat of struggle recall what originally set them at odds—George Santayana once wrote that "fanaticism consists in redoubling your effort when you have forgotten your aim." [56] Old family feuds often run this way, and so too may revolutionary ones.

Another simpler and more material explanation of the sharpening of class struggle during the radical dictatorship complements Tocqueville's. The economic devastation of revolution and civil war (with or without foreign embargoes) is enormous. The statistics, where available, illustrate dramatically the precipitous decline of production, trade, and consumption associated with a prolonged revolutionary crisis. The poor generally suffer the worst hardships, and their ranks are swelled by those whom the revolution has impoverished by policy or accident. The economy during the radical dictatorship is caught in the pincers effect of serious depression and rampant inflation. (As always happens in these situations some people find a way to profit from the distress of others.) The poor get poorer and their frustration increases. Whether the ensuing resentment reflects the traditional antirich feelings of urban "plebeians" or peasants, or the newer egalitarianism of the radical ideology, the poorer strata demand strict measures ranging from outright confiscations to decrees limiting the accumulation of wealth and profits. The wealthier groups feel both their possessions and self-esteem is threatened. Mild measures often appear to them as attacks on the very system of private property. The radical dictatorship often sides with the poor, but for ideological and practical reasons peculiar to each revolution, there are limits to how far they are able or willing to go. Invariably it is too far for the tastes of some, not nearly far enough for others.

The language of class struggle increasingly permeates the rhetoric of the radical phase, although the measures taken may sometimes have more bark than bite. Quite naturally, the place of private property in the radicals' ideology will affect the seriousness of actions against the rich. In the English Revolution, the generally shared belief in the sanctity of private property meant that only Royalists saw their holdings sequestered or (merely) threatened. In France, the Maximum and other national and local measures were "class legislation" insofar as they catered to the poorer groups. Though neither the Jacobins nor their *sans-culotte* supporters were complete social levellers or collectivists, contrasting views on the distribution of national wealth drove something of a wedge between these two radical formations. This division is explained as between advocates of a "conception of limited and controlled property [the *sans-culottes*] and the partisans of the total right of property such as it had been proclaimed in 1789 [the Jacobins]. Still more [does it represent] the opposition of supporters of regulation and taxation and the adepts of economic liberty; [an] opposition of consumers and producers." [57] Understandably, when the revolutionary ideology itself preaches class struggle and collectivism, the rich have a harder time of it. Lenin's War Communism will attest to this last point, though the NEP in turn attests to the harsh impact of reality upon ideology. In the Spanish Revolution the communists did their utmost to tone down the virulent class struggle preached and practiced by some socialists and anarchists, because it interfered with victory in the civil war. In any case, the radical dictatorship cannot control every local manifestation of class conflict, even if it wished to do so. To try might lose the dictatorship needed support.

Conflict between the *center* and the *periphery* (i.e., between the region of the capital city and the outlying districts) may be something of a tradition even before the coming of the revolution. Nevertheless, the rise of the radicals exacerbates this conflict appreciably. Two major causes—one basically political, the other basically economic—explain this. In the first place, the capital city in Western revolutions is the epicenter of the revolution. It is also a stronghold of the radicals. Thus, the radical regime is likely to take special care of its main source of strength, and it will choose many of its important personnel from denizens of the capital. Further, the radical supporters in the city feel aglow with a species of revolutionary pride that their home town is in the forefront of the great revolution. With modifications, the following description of revolutionary Paris could be applied to other Western revolutionary capitals: "the Parisian revolutionary was so imbued with the role he had to play in the Revolution that quite often he succeeded in making himself completely odious to provincial folk with his airs of 'master-in-revolution,' with the mixture of disdain, condescension and mistrust that he affected in regard to the 'provincial brothers.' The Parisian felt himself not just the revolutionary *par excellence*, he was all too much led to think that he had a monopoly on this title." [58]

It is not only the superiority complex of the revolutionaries of the capital that produces conflict between center and periphery. The radical dictatorship must provide for its most avid supporters in material terms. As economic distress spreads, the government is led to a policy of requisitions (often simple confiscations) in order to feed and provision the center. That this is not done for humanitarian reasons is seen when favoritism to the capital leaves other areas depleted and often on the verge of starvation. Humanitarianism would consider provincials no less worthy of survival than inhabitants of the center. Understandably, the dwellers in the periphery sense the politics of the government's economic policies and moral outrage is added to the more material damage of low or no profits. As government policy is often enforced at gunpoint, the periphery nurtures a hatred of the center that needs only the proper spark to burst into flame. In this sort of atmosphere flourish real or alleged counterrevolutionary sentiments, which further widens the gap between capital and periphery. Often a kind of civil war of skirmishes is fought, which has little to do with the overriding issues and ideologies of the revolution: essentially the situation is that two groups of people wishing to eat regularly compete for scarce resources. A vicious cycle thus develops because government policy provokes resistance in the periphery, which provokes harsher policies and so on.

A general conflict between town and country involves some of the same issues dividing center and periphery. In each region the provincial capitals or large towns play a role similar to the national capital. With obvious exceptions in each revolution, the towns are more favorable to the radicals than the surrounding countryside and the problem of feeding urban dwellers at the expense of country folk embitters relationships. The radical dictatorship exacerbates this situation because it favors the town over the country pretty much for the same reasons it prefers the center over the periphery. Nevertheless, one must never lose from sight *the pronounced local variations in the response to the revolution as a whole and to the radical dictatorship.* Though it is often complained that revolutionary history is written too much "from above," (i.e., looking at the various revolutionary elites and their foes) and that it should be studied more "from below" (i.e., looking at the lives of the mass of ordinary people), focusing on the dramatic events in the center and big cities to the detriment of rural and peripheral areas is an equal or greater source of distortion. Brinton has suggested that it is with local history that "you see the Terror as it really was, no steady and efficient rule from above . . . , but a state of suspense and fear, a dissolution of the sober little uniformities of provincial life. . . ." [59]

The prism of localism strongly distorts the radiations from the radical revolutionary center. Pro-radical and antiradical factions develop sometimes entirely on the basis of local issues or personal disputes. Leading notables carrying their old clienteles behind translate ancient antagonisms into the language of moderation, radicalism, or counterrevolution. It must be recalled that the centralization of the radical dictatorship is impressive only relative to what immediately preceded it and perhaps to what immediately followed it. If it takes a revolution to forge a measure of national unity over the claims of local particularism, this only proves the strength of the latter. In many places, in many revolutions, most of the people would prefer neutrality and non involvement to exertions and sacrifices in favor of any of the forces in contention. Cavaliers and Roundheads, Jacobins and Royalists, Reds and Whites, Loyalists and Nationalists, Communists and KMT—all have found local populations who have wished a plague on the two houses. While such localism disturbs the radicals, it sometimes serves them by keeping antiradical uprisings confined to small areas. It is thus no surprise that some localities are a microcosm of the radical center, others a hotbed of moderation or counterrevolution, and others still an isolated backwash trying ostrich-like to escape the conflict by ignoring it. In the end, perhaps, it is the prevalence of localism and pettiness that disillusions many radical revolutionaries.

Just as serious as the prevalence of localism is the conflict created by the radicals' offensive against traditional religious institutions. If what Brinton termed "the element of religious faith" (i.e., ideological enthusiasm) truly distinguishes radicals, we can understand their disposition to declare war on the established church. Radical revolutionary ideology tends to make a monopolistic claim on men's spiritual allegiances. Thus, to trample on existing religious beliefs and their institutional expression, the Church, seems simply to defend evident truth against superstition, whether the "truth" in question is militant Protestantism, rationalistic deism, or atheistic materialism. Furthermore, since the Church is often a pillar of the old regime, an attack on it would follow from the very nature of the radical dictatorship. The Church of England lost its bishops, its privileged position, and liturgical self-determination under Cromwell, although it was not destroyed, nor even fully disestablished—another proof of the moderation of the English Revolution. The Civil Constitution of the Clergy in 1790 was an attempt to break French Catholicism off from the papacy and to transform priests into civil functionaries. Though it split the priesthood, the

Civil Constitution was insufficient for radical purposes, as later measures such as closing Parisian churches and persecution of practicing Catholics after 1793 demonstrate. However, the radicals themselves were deeply divided: some were antireligious zealots who wished to extirpate all trace of religious sentiment overnight; others were merely anticlericals who attacked the church as a source of superstition and counterrevolution. Many of this latter group wished like Robespierre to have some sort of public religious cult. Robespierre even accused the more rabid dechristianizers of being tools of the counterrevolution because they needlessly divided society. Antireligious activity was particularly intense in Leninist Russia, but perhaps the Spanish Revolution represents the extreme of antireligious outrages. In any case, the radical dictatorship brings a confrontation with the church for both philosophical and political reasons, though the exact shape of the struggle depends both on the nature of radical ideology and on the outlook and organization of the churches.

However, religious feelings run deep and are often strengthened by persecution. This may account for some improvement in the Church's position, even while radicals of one stripe or another remain in power. Radical leaders often have to restrain some of their more fanatical followers, since political expediency demands a letup of the attack on religious traditions. In addition, the religious and political spectrums in revolutions are not always identical (i.e., a radical in political affairs may be moderate in religious questions, while a political moderate may be exceedingly militant on religious issues). Religious convictions are not mere reflexes of economic or political position. Thus, certain radicals will feel ambivalence caused by the cross-pressures of political and religious attitudes. Similarly, persons who have supported the radicals for political or religious reasons may wish to desert them when they overstep certain bounds. These considerations hold mostly for the English and French revolutions, for later ones see a closer correlation of political and religious radicalism. Nevertheless, apparent anomalies such as the strongly Catholic Basques fighting on the same side as bourgeois anticlericals, communists, and anarchists in the Spanish Revolution are not uncommon. This illustrates once more that the various components of the revolutionary coalition can have quite different motivations. The point is that their grievances against the old regime (or later, against counterrevolutionary movements) appear more salient to them than the differences among the coalition partners. We can expect that, as happened between the United States and the Soviet Union after World War II, these residual differences will reemerge when the common threat is eliminated. Politics indeed makes strange bedfellows, but so too does religion.

A most interesting feature of the radical dictatorship is the problem of the ultrarevolutionaries, which category includes Levellers, Diggers, and Fifth Monarchists in the English Revolution; Hébertistes and Babouvistes in the French Revolution; Left Socialist Revolutionaries and Anarchists in the Russian Revolution; Anarchists and others in the Spanish Revolution; and similar groups in other revolutions. Operationally defined, the ultrarevolutionaries are simply the most radical of the radicals—so radical in fact that the radical dictatorship feels forced to act against them. The historiography of revolution speaks of them as "the lunatic fringe," the revolutionary "purists," the "idealists" of revolution, or in communist parlance as "infantile leftists." The term *"ultra*revolutionists" was used by Robespierre to designate opponents to his left (the followers of Hébert and other groups); they were so revolutionary that they actually promoted counterrevolution, so Robespierre said.[60] Cromwell had earlier complained of his critics on the left that "they must end at the interest of the Cavalier in the long run." [61] Thus the precedent was set long ago for Lenin, Stalin, and others to brand leftist critics of their policies as deviationists who consciously or not do the bidding of the counterrevolution. Taken literally, these allegations are usually pure nonsense even though some collusion—a sort of negative coalition of counterrevolutionary and ultrarevolutionary oppositionists—may take place. More substantial is the radicals' charge that the ultrarevolutionists merely by their opposition or their extremist behavior "objectively" weaken the radical dictatorship and hence make the game of the counterrevolution easier. This assumes, of course, that the radicals rather than the moderates or ultrarevolutionists are the safe custodians of the revolution. Though ideology tinctures judgments on this issue, there is more than a grain of truth to the radicals' assertion that the ultrarevolutionists exhibit a self-defeating lack of political realism.

To do justice to this last conclusion we have to be beyond a merely "operational" understanding of the ultrarevolutionaries. With the proviso that important ideological differences distinguish ultrarevolutionary sects in the various revolutions, we can say that the ultrarevolutionary syndrome consists of (1) utopianism and revolutionary purism, (2) populism and advocacy of decentralization, and (3) militancy and direct action. Utopianism and revolutionary purism imply that, compared to the radicals, the ultrarevolutionary concept of revolution ranks higher on the scale of revolutionary intensity and/or that the ultrarevolutionaries demand prompt delivery of all the planks in a platform shared with radicals. The ultrarevolutionaries are the impatient optimists of revolution who think that utopia is just around the corner. Accordingly, they consider the moderates as outright counter-revolutionaries and suspect that the radicals are made of the same inferior cloth. The goal of building a wholly new social order must never be sullied by compromises or expediency. One consequence of this revolutionary purism is greater commitment to the international character of the revolution. The ultrarevolutionaries have one eye abroad, for they think that events at home are merely the opening of a worldwide upheaval. Accordingly, they are the most zealous proponents of the export of the revolution by military and other means. Should the revolution hit obstacles at home, their cure for its ills is always more revolution. The ultrarevolutionaries are thus the fundamentalists of revolution, who take its hopes and dogmas literally; and their faith often undergoes the test of persecution and sometimes of martyrdom. However, though certain ultrarevolutionary groups and individuals merit the description "the lunatic fringe," not all such parties, groups, and factions are composed solely of madmen or mountebanks.

The ultrarevolutionary faith in the mass of the people, in a sort of grass-roots democracy sometimes expressed in "spontaneous" institutions or popular insurrections, can be described in terms of *populism* and *advocacy of decentralization.* Belief in the unerring instincts of the masses causes the ultrarevolutionaries to view extreme decentralization of political power as essential to popular rule. From this perspective parliamentary institutions may seem too far removed from the masses. Similarly, the centralized radical regime may appear as the hegemony of a party clique little better than the rule of bourgeois or aristocratic notables. However, populism in theory does not wholly rule out elitism in practice: the ultrarevolutionary minority may feel compelled to lead the people until the latter have awaked sufficiently to recover full sovereign power. There is thus some justification in the epithet "anarchists" hurled at the ultrarevolutionaries by the more discreet radicals. If they are not anarchists in the strict sense of the term—which they sometimes are, as in the Russian and Spanish revolutions—their hostility to the centralized state and their faith in mass spontaneity have affinities with modern anarchist teachings. Little imagination is required to envisage the conflict with the radicals, who begin to desire order as their position becomes more and more consolidated.

Militancy and direct action suggests that the ultrarevolutionaries not only discuss their nostrums but that they also act to realize them. Mutiny, riot, mass insurrection, coup d'etat, assassination, terrorism— these and more peaceful methods of agitation and propaganda are among the forms of political activism most congenial to them. Though the radicals often practice or condone such expedients, the ultrarevolutionaries have even greater faith in their effectiveness and in the end employ them against the radicals. More than Royalists plotted against

Cromwell, and no devotee of Tsarism shot Lenin in 1918. The radicals, naturally resenting the ideological as well as the material barbs launched at them by ultrarevolutionaries, often act against their tormentors. It is particularly galling to be called "betrayers" of the revolution for which they fought so hard. Recalling perhaps their own treatment of the moderates, radicals act to avert the same fate for themselves. But the issue has more pathos than this: the ultrarevolutionaries are in some sense the "conscience of the revolution" [62] and their carping criticism reminds the radicals of the unpleasant truth that reaching the ultimate goals of the revolution has proven more arduous than anticipated. The ultrarevolutionaries are a kind of caricature of the radicals, for like a caricature they bizarrely accentuate recognizable features of the original. It is thus easier to shrug off criticism when it comes from moderates or counterrevolutionaries than when it comes from within the same "spiritual family." Suppressed guilt feelings may go far to explain why the radicals make such efforts to show how their critics to the left are really "counterrevolutionaries."

In the English Revolution, the Levellers and the Fifth Monarchy Men—as well as smaller sects and movements such as the Diggers, the early Quakers, and the Ranters—can be qualified as ultrarevolutionary groupings. The Levellers, whose ideology was rather moderate, are ultrarevolutionaries only because their views did go beyond those of the Cromwellian Independents and their opposition to the latter sometimes took dramatic, and occasionally violent, form. They, along with the much smaller and communistic Diggers, constituted a secular opposition, because their policies met common, everyday problems in fairly rational terms. We must also speak of distinctly *religious or theological* ultrarevolutionary oppositions in the English Revolution because "there were always those who saw a more mystical and visionary significance in the victories with which the Lord had blessed the 'people of God.'" [63] The most important of such millenarian groups were the Fifth Monarchists, who impatiently awaited the return of King Jesus to earth to inaugurate the fifth and final world monarchy. During the latter part of his protectorate Cromwell was plagued by attempted assassinations, plots, and actual insurrections traceable to men of Fifth Monarchist beliefs. The following indictment of Cromwell by a prominent Fifth Monarchist illustrates the depths of disillusioned bitterness that is found amongst ultrarevolutionaries in all revolutions: the Lord Protector

> hath oppressed and forsaken the poor, because he hath violently taken away a house which he builded not. . . . The flying roll of God's curses shall overtake the family of that great thief there; he that robbed us of the benefit of our prayers, of our tears, of our blood. . . . These shed

their blood for the cause of Jesus Christ, and for the interest of his kingdom; but that which they purchased at so dear a rate is taken from us by
violence. We are robbed of it, and the cause of Christ is made the cause
of man.[64]

Cromwell's sincere, but mostly unavailing, efforts to reconcile the
Leveller and Fifth Monarchist leaders illustrates rather well the substantial underlying agreement between radicals and ultrarevolutionaries—family quarrels, however, are often the most violent.

In the French Revolution, the Enragés or the broader circle of
Hébertistes (i.e., the followers of Hébert or those labeled such), and
later the disciples of Gracchus Babeuf, represented the major ultrarevolutionary factions. These groups had the highest hopes of the
revolution, and when human happiness was not immediate and things
became even worse, their alternative to radical dictatorship was to push
ahead and give fuller substance to the trilogy of liberty, equality, and
fraternity. Though the so-called Hébertistes were far from modern socialists, their egalitarian social and economic ideas went beyond what
the Robespierrist Jacobins could tolerate. *Hébertisme* in this sense had
strong support amongst the Parisian *sans-culottes;* but as with so many
ultrarevolutionary movements they were not a strongly organized, disciplined political party. Nevertheless, as a pressure group they exerted
considerable leverage upon the radical dictatorship during the Reign of
Terror, though a falling out was inevitable. The Hébertistes favored a
harsher soak-the-rich economic policy than the government would permanently sanction, and their dechristianizing mania was too much for
orthodox radicals like Robespierre. Above all, their conviction that
popular sovereignty was embodied in the 48 Parisian sections, instead
of in the National Convention and its Committees, threatened to completely fragment the backbone of the radical dictatorship.[65]

Arguing, as the radicals are wont to do, that any opposition is tantamount to counterrevolution, the Robespierrists executed Hébert and
his friends and brought those sections where *Hébertisme* was rife into
line. This "governmentalization" of the Parisian sections anticipates the
similar measures of the Bolsheviks with the trade unions and the soviets. For some historians the suppression of the Hébertistes even signifies a kind of Robespierrist pre-Thermidor in the sense that "if the
Revolution was not over, at least the first step in reaction had been
taken." [66] The radical dictatorship is a *government;* and the tasks of government, even revolutionary government, are not those of an insurrectionary mass movement. What separated Robespierrists from Hébertistes separates radicals from ultrarevolutionaries in other revolutions:
for the former, consolidation of existing gains is utterly essential before

pushing the revolution further; for the latter pushing the revolution further is utterly essential to preserve existing gains.

In Russia ultrarevolutionary movements were manifested both in political parties with some organizational coherence and in spontaneous insurrectional committees and groups. The Left Socialist Revolutionaries figured most prominently among these political parties and, with reservations, the Anarchists and Left Communists.[67] The Kronstadt Rebellion of 1921 is the best example of an ultrarevolutionary outburst in which political parties played a role, albeit a minimal one. Each of these groups experienced the usual ambivalent relationship with the Leninist radicals: there is a change from close alliance to outright war (exception made, of course, for the Left Communists) with considerable wavering in the meantime. The Left SR's seceded from the parent SR Party on the very issue of supporting the Bolsheviks and for a time were partners in Lenin's coalition government. One description of the ethos of this party fits perfectly our typification of ultrarevolutionaries: "inconsistent, romantic, unrealistic, and politically naive to the point of childishness. But they did not sacrifice their principles to power." [68] The non-Marxist Left SR's were drawn to the Bolsheviks because the latter seemed to herald leaping over capitalism straightway into socialism while simultaneously launching international revolution.[69] What soured them on Lenin was his apparent preference for a peace-at-any-price settlement with Imperial Germany instead of a revolutionary war. When Lenin added other "betrayals," they somewhat reluctantly resorted to familiar terrorist methods against both the Germans and the Bolsheviks. Anarchist groups in Russia faced a similar dilemma: as revolutionary collectivists they could only welcome the Bolshevik coup, but as anarchists they could not countenance the Marxist idea that the proletariat would provisionally use the state to destroy the bourgeoisie and lay the foundations for the future communist society. Had not Bakunin warned that "every state, whatever its origin or form, must necessarily lead to despotism"? [70] Though their very mistrust of organization makes anarchists no match in the long run for Leninists, Nestor Makhno's anarchist guerrillas, after initially cooperating with the Bolsheviks, succeeded in keeping Red Army units at bay for some time.

The uprising of the Kronstadt Naval Base against the Bolshevik government in March, 1921, also illustrates ultrarevolutionary disillusionment with a radical dictatorship. While stimulated somewhat by economic grievances, the rising took on a definitely political coloration. The Kronstadters' propaganda against the Bolsheviks runs true to the ultrarevolutionary pattern: "In place of the old regime, a new regime of arbitrariness, insolence, favoritism, theft, and speculation has been established, a terrible regime in which one must hold out one's hand to the authorities for every piece of bread, for every button, a regime in which one does not even belong to oneself, where one cannot dispose of one's labor, a regime of slavery and degradation. . . . Soviet Russia has become an all-Russian concentration camp." [71] Though the Kronstadters were not dominated by any one party or ideology, their melange of ideas is very close to the ultrarevolutionary syndrome.

Somewhat more equivocal is the position of the Left Communists, who as members of the ruling party were opposed to the antiregime activities of all other ultrarevolutionaries. According to Robert Daniels, the Bolshevik Party from the outset (i.e., 1902) had been bifurcated into Leninist and Leftist currents: "the difference between the two tendencies was that of power and principle—of revolutionary pragmatism and revolutionary idealism." [72] Though the lines were blurred sometimes, there persisted "a vital difference of emphasis between those whose eyes were on the ends of the revolution and those whose attention was consumed by the means which its success seemed to require." [73] This latent contrast burst into the foreground immediately following the civil war, when Lenin engineered a partial rollback of the revolutionary measures of War Communism (the NEP—March, 1921) without relaxing political controls. Lenin not only made concessions to agrarian capitalism but also welcomed the influx of "bourgeois specialists" into military and economic institutions. The populistic egalitarianism of *State and Revolution,* ostensibly Lenin's blueprint for life under socialism, was shelved indefinitely. With economic recovery and efficiency the top priority, "workers' control" over industry became even more of a myth. Predictably, the ultrarevolutionary Left current within Bolshevism asserted itself in heartfelt protest against the "degeneration" of the revolution. A Leftist manifesto of the time lamented that "the Communist Party . . . after becoming the ruling party, the party of organizers and leaders of the state apparatus and of the capitalist-based economic life . . . irrevocably lost its tie and community with the proletariat." [74] The potential for open rebellion contained in these sentiments never materialized, because the individual Left Communist either responded to the party's demands for solidarity or withdrew from active political life.

A similar scenario could be described for the Spanish Revolution, with the communists and their allies in the role of the radicals, and the Anarcho-syndicalists, left-wing socialists, and anti-Stalinist communists as ultrarevolutionaries. As usual the radicals became obsessed with practical problems (viz., organizing victory in the civil war), while the ultrarevolutionaries protested the defilement of the revolution that compromise and delay seemed to involve. While similar episodes have marked the history of Chinese communism, one of the most thought-provoking peculiarities of the Chinese Revolution has been the recurrent tendency of Maoist radicals to behave like ultrarevolutionaries. But even in the case of China there seem to be people whose extremism has to be curbed by the authorities. In any case, the encounter between radicals and ultrarevolutionaries tells us almost as much about the general character of a revolution as does the encounter between moderates and radicals.

The Thermidor

In the Edwards-Brinton paradigm, a "Thermidor" or "Thermidorean reaction," which marks the ebbing away of revolutionary energies and a "return to normality" (or normalcy), must inevitably occur. The very terminology once again illustrates the impact of the French Revolution on the study of revolution; for it was on 9 Thermidor, Year III, according to the new revolutionary calendar (i.e., July 27, 1794), that Robespierre, Saint-Just, and their close associates were removed from power, thus supposedly terminating the forward thrust of the revolution as embodied in the Reign of Terror. Historians dispute just how drastic a shift in policy and politics the fall of Robespierre represents. To some it indicates a continuation of a gradual mellowing of the revolution begun by the fallen Terrorists themselves; to others the Thermidor involves a clear-cut reaction against the revolution and a retreat on nearly all its fronts, promoted by the upper classes regrouping after the disorientation of the Terror. What many historians and theorists agree on is that the Thermidor was *inevitable, decisive, irreversible.* That is, the Thermidor *had* to occur; it represents a qualitative change in political life; the trend towards winding the revolution down had to continue until a new normalcy was firmly established.

Like so many other features of the French Revolution, the notion of Thermidor has been generalized into a law valid for all revolutions. Thus, it makes little difference if the Thermidor results in a somewhat artificial attempt to restore root and branch of the old regime: what is important is that once the critical high-point represented by the Terror has been passed, the real work of the revolution has been accomplished and a new social order with some admixture of the old comes to acquire legitimacy. Edwards sees the culmination of this trend as follows: "Finally, the new constitution, or basic law, which largely restores the old, pre-revolutionary organization of government, is forced through, though against the fierce opposition of the revolutionary minority. . . .

The revolutionary government itself, as it gets older, ceases to be revolutionary and presently ceases to think of itself as revolutionary. *The revolution is complete.*" [75] (Italics mine.)

The major symptoms of the Thermidor in this view include (1) attack on the most extreme Terrorists; (2) relaxation of the puritanical standards of revolutionary virtue; (3) concessions to the traditional religions; (4) firmer legal guarantees for ordinary citizens; (5) return of political exiles; (6) growth of careerism, corruption, and self-serving at the expense of revolutionary idealism; (7) repeal of the most radical economic legislation and policies; and (8) crystallization of new patterns of economic, social, and political stratification. Of course, the overall pace of the Thermidor and the emphasis among these eight features vary from revolution to revolution. But one thing is sure: for the great mass of men the Thermidor means a "depoliticization" of everyday life insofar as they turn their backs on high-blown ideological goals and return to the more prosaic pursuits of making a living and enjoying the simpler pleasures of existence. These are the developments that caused Crane Brinton to suggest that "the full flavor of the Thermidorean reaction is reserved for the social historian," because only in social history does "the full extent of the popular abandonment of the Republic of Virtue" become manifest. [76]

As we shall soon see, there are grave difficulties in the notion of Thermidor and its universal application. However, a deeper sounding of opinion on the features and causes of Thermidors will aid us in eventually forming a less rigid interpretation of periodization in revolution. Most explanations of reputed Thermidors in specific revolutions or of the phenomenon in general focus on two sets of interrelated causes: causes relating to social psychology, and causes relating to social structure. The first set of causes emphasizes the biological and psychological exhaustion produced by the revolution in general, its civil and foreign wars, and the Reign of Terror. Thinking as much of the French Revolution as the Russian, Leon Trotsky aptly sums up the problem of revolutionary exhaustion: "A revolution is a mighty devourer of energies, both individual and collective. The nerves give way. Consciousness is shaken and characters are worn out. Events unfold too swiftly for the flow of fresh forces to replace the loss. Hunger, unemployment, the death of the revolutionary cadres, the removal of the masses from the administration, all this led to . . . a physical and moral impoverishment. . . ." [77]

Confronted with this growing exhaustion or fatigue, the radical leaders have a choice between fighting it, and accommodating it while minimizing its antirevolutionary recoil. George Pettee sees the difference between Lenin and Robespierre (and their deaths) in these terms: "Robespierre tried to maintain a terrific tension of moral effort, as well as military action, after it was impossible to do so," while the Bolshevik leader sensed circumstances better and "introduced the relaxing N.E.P at the first signs that exhaustion had itself become the most important single factor in the political situation." [78]

While small elites may seem the chief beneficiaries of the Thermidorean relaxation, it wells up from all groups and strata of the population, save the most militant. Sheer physical and mental wear and tear combines with loss of militants in combat to dissipate the energy and enthusiasm necessary to sustain the previous pace of the revolution. For example, food shortages, which may in the short run activate revolutionary crowds, in the long run can produce apathy and lethargy. The moral exhaustion that makes the Thermidor possible develops because the radicals' high-pressure drive to revolutionary virtue demands too much renunciation of gratification and delivers too little for most men in the way of compensatory satisfactions. The radicals, in effect, have attempted to divert or "sublimate" the various drives and passions of mankind into revolutionary channels, but with diminishing returns. The gaiety and frivolity depicted by historians of the French Thermidor or the libertinism of the English Restoration illustrate the resurgence of the age-old temptation to have fun now and let tomorrow take care of itself—the perfect antithesis to revolutionary idealism.

Causes of a sociological order thought to complement the psychological ones in explaining the Thermidor include such processes as "institutionalization," "routinization," "bureaucratization," and the "iron law of oligarchy" in some variant or other. All of these point to a certain rigidification of society and polity during the Thermidorean phase. If the revolutionary crisis is a destratification and disordering of society, then the Thermidor represents a sort of restratification and reordering of it. Marxist accounts of "bourgeois revolutions," for example, interpret the Thermidor as a time when the big bourgeoisie breaks its previous alliance with "plebeian" elements in order to recast society in its own image and interest. For the classic elitists the Thermidor would represent the process whereby a revolutionary counterelite is transformed into an established elite and its bogus egalitarianism is revealed for what it is—a propaganda trick to get the masses to support an insurgent elite in its struggle against the rulers of the old regime. Theories of institutionalization and bureaucratization simply develop the insight that a movement out of power is not the same thing as a government based upon that movement. Talcott Parsons maintains that "the basic conflict comes to be transferred from the form, the movement vs. the society, to that between the 'principles' of the movement and the temptation of its members to use their control of the society to gratify their repressed need-dispositions, some of which are precisely needs of conformity with the patterns of the *old* society which they have tried to abolish." [79] He goes on to conclude that the "price of success" of revolutionary movements is a dilemma caused by their inability both to "have the cake of the motivational advantages of revolt, and eat it by being the focus of institutionalization of an orthodoxy too." [80]

Gaetano Mosca, in assessing Roberto Michels' initial statement of the "iron law of oligarchy," offers some concrete suggestions why something like the Thermidorean slowdown or rollback of the revolution is bound to occur. In the first place, there is the "psychological transformation that the exercise and above all the stability of power produces in those who lead any great association, even if it is of a pronounced revolutionary character." [81] This may not be corruption in the Actonian sense, but it does represent a tarnishing of original revolutionary ideals. It is not only the topmost rungs of the revolutionary elite who feel tempted to use office for personal and mundane purposes. The transformation of the ordinary militant into the functionary is a good part of the later history of most revolutions. In the French Revolution, many *sans-culotte* militants, "even if they were not moved by ambition alone, considered the procurement of a position as the legitimate payment for their militant activity." [82] If this trend to bureaucracy meant "paralysis of the critical spirit and the activity of the masses" in the French Revolution,[83] Leon Trotsky's description of the Russian Revolution goes even further by asserting that "the ebb of 'plebeian pride' made room for a flood of pusillanimity and careerism. The new commanding caste rose to its place upon this wave." [84] Similar accounts have been presented for all revolutions, though the Spanish Revolution was defeated too quickly for any of these trends to reach fruition. The Chinese Communist Revolution, however, presents so many distinctive traits that it will serve below to help revise our thinking on the stages of revolution.

Another factor frequently invoked in relation to Thermidors is the aging of the revolutionaries, both as a natural process and as a result of the decimation of younger militants in fighting. While not an airtight rule, there is some force to the maxim that aging and age "usually makes men less enthusiastic, more cautious, and reveals the difficulties in the way of realizing the dreams of youth." [85] Furthermore, there is a "natural conservatism" stemming from the "affection that everyone feels for any type of work to whose creation he has after long efforts contributed." Such sentiments produce an unwillingness to risk what has already been won for the sake of possibly illusory goals: *"love for the instrument becomes stronger and more active than for the end that should be reached through the instrument."* [86] (Italics mine.) Thus, "love for the instrument" (a kind of institutional patriotism regardless of whether the institution is a political party, a revolutionary government, or a bureaucratic structure) obscures, if it does not entirely block out, perception of the transcendent goals of the revolution. The power and perquisites of office loom increasingly as ends in themselves. While bureaucracies are not so hostile to innovation as sometimes maintained, bureaucratic mentality and routine are somewhat of an impediment to continuing a revolution without respite. We can add to this the conviction of Mosca, Michels, and Pareto that even if an elite "from below" succeeds in ousting the old elite taken as a bloc, "the new and old oligarchies always end by mixing together, or at least many elements of the old enter the new." [87] While this tendency should not be exaggerated, the aggregate impact of the infiltration of elements of the old elite—especially the middle elite of the old regime—would be to further moderate the course of the revolution.

Thus, the combined effect of biological-psychological and sociological factors has a debilitating effect on the forces making for continued revolutionary radicalism. In France, as we have seen, these factors produced a distinct, but not wholly unequivocal, "stage" called the Thermidor. It now remains to be seen whether the tripartite trajectory of revolution—which comprises the moderate interregnum, the radical dictatorship and the Terror, and the Thermidorean reaction—is a valid paradigm for all revolutions that are neither abortive nor moderate. Our answer will entail a reexamination of certain features of the older revolutions, as well as interpretation of the newer ones.

PITFALLS OF PERIODIZATION

Rigidity and Overgeneralization

In Chapter III it was pointed out that because of differences in political culture, level of urbanization, economic development, political and military strength of the old regime, etc., Eastern-style revolutions diverged in important respects from the pattern of Western revolutions. A major divergence was that the Edwards-Brinton scheme derived from the West was largely inapplicable to Eastern revolutions. Now it is time to examine how closely the Western revolutions live up to the model. A first difficulty concerns dating the beginning and ending of the three major stages. While Pride's Purge (December 6, 1648) seems an authentic turning point from moderate to radical rule in the English Revolution, the Cromwellian Independents were the most moderate of radicals, thus taking some of the sting out of the change-over. Furthermore, the English Reign of Terror and Virtue was not concentrated so much in time and intensity as its French counterpart. It was more erratic and half-hearted, and fell with its full ferocity upon the Catholic Irish rather than Protestant Englishmen. Cromwell's regime took extralegal repressive measures—as one would expect in the radical dictatorship—but his "dilemma" (i.e., the sense that his arbitrary exercise of power needed a sanction) prevented him from launching a full-scale Terror in the French manner. In addition, England was safer than France from foreign intervention, and the numerous plots and risings of the 1650's were rather easily thwarted.

If identifying a Terror as the high-point of the radical dictatorship is difficult, pinpointing the onset of the Thermidorean reaction is more vexatious still. (We can say this without denying that on the whole the middle and late 1650's represent a slackening of revolutionary energies.) Brinton, for example, suggests Cromwell's forced dissolution of the Rump of the Long Parliament [88] on April 20, 1653, as "perhaps the best date for the English Thermidor. . . ." [89] One trouble with this is that the successor to the Rump was the handpicked Little or Barebones Parliament, which produced some fairly radical measures and would have produced more had its not-so-radical majority surrendered its powers to Cromwell as Lord Protector in December, 1653. Another noted historian, however, considers 1653 the "high point of the Revolution" for Cromwell, who was to play the role of the chastened ex-radical only *after* the failure of the Barebones experiment. [90] The point here is not to reveal particular historians' disagreements, but rather to show the difficulties one faces when he looks at the English Revolution through French-colored glasses.

At first glance the Russian Revolution seems to offer better confirmation of the general validity of the Edwards-Brinton paradigm. March to November, 1917, displays the features of moderate misrule and growing paralysis; and the Bolshevik coup ending this period ushers in not only a new stage of the Russian Revolution, but of modern history. War Communism is a good example of the radical dictatorship, and the intensive regime-directed terrorism stands comparison with the Robespierrist precedent. Still more, the economic relaxation of the NEP in 1921, with a partial letup in other areas, seemingly exemplifies the coming of that permanent return to normalcy associated with the notion of Thermidor. Or so it seemed when Lyford Edwards in the mid-1920's wrote that "Russia ceased to be communistic, or even very socialistic." In Edwards' view the issue with the highest priority after the civil war was the stabilization of the new system of property relations set up by the revolution: "State capitalism met these requirements and so Lenin established it." Edwards felt that NEP "state capitalism" would in all likelihood "continue to exist for generations, irrespective of what political faction administers the government." The issue was determined when the bulk of the Soviet citizenry came to accept the NEP as legitimate, and "that occurred some time during the year 1922 and marked the *end of the Revolution.*" [91] (Italics mine.) Edwards' prognosis of orderly, "evolutionary" development in Russia was given the lie shortly after he wrote, when Stalin initiated the monumental agricultural collectivization and industrialization drives with the beginning of the First Five Year Plan in 1929. The social, economic, and political ramifications of this "second revolution" were many, deep, and lasting. Even if the Soviet economy is state capitalist and not "truly socialist," as some socialists argue, its state capitalism after 1929 is categorically different from that of the NEP.

Once again, it is not personal errors of judgment that concern us: it is rather that such a forecast as Edwards' follows quite logically if one considers the Thermidor as the irreversible termination of revolution which follows a period of radicalism, and if one is examining a period of relative relaxation. If revolutions have a three-stage trajectory and we have passed the peak, there is nowhere to go but down. Brinton, who wrote after the Soviet collectivization and who is more cautious than Edwards, was also misled by a dogmatic conception of the Thermidor. This is clear, for example, when he maintains that "Stalin's apparent return to Communism in 1928–29 is really no more significant than Napoleon's apparent repudiation of the corruption and moral looseness of the Directory. . . ." [92] The shades of hundreds of thousands of Soviet citizens who died because of Stalin's policies might have cause to dispute Brinton's analogy here. However, the sensitivity of Brinton the historian seems to contradict the rigidity of Brinton the theorist when he admits that it is difficult "to dismiss the Russian Revolution as really finished, or even as finished as were our other revolutions at a comparable interval of time—35 years—after their beginning." [93] One can only conclude from Edwards' mistake and Brinton's hesitations that mechanical application of the scheme of the French Revolution to the Russian is dangerous.

Hypertrophy and Entropy in the Revolutionary Process

Despite the somewhat negative nature of the discussion just preceding, the work of theorists and historians has not been in vain. The various arguments treated provide the basis for some conclusions, which, if looser than the Edwards-Brinton paradigm, accord somewhat better with the historical experience of revolutions. In the first place, instead of speaking of a universal three-stage process, we can distinguish two contrary tendencies in revolution. One of these can be called the *law of revolutionary hypertrophy* and the other the *law of revolutionary entropy*. "Law," of course, must be understood rather loosely, because the two tendencies are themselves rather complex resultants of other, simpler uniformities of human behavior which perhaps more seriously warrant the term "law."

The law of revolutionary hypertrophy refers to the increasingly radical thrust of revolutions once they become manifest. We have already mentioned how the Parliamentary opposition to Charles I in the early 1640's did not consciously intend a full-scale revolution, and how many of the French Patriots of the late 1780's thought of themselves as reformers rather than revolutionaries. We furthermore have described how the radicals outflank the moderates and find themselves in danger of being outbid by the ultrarevolutionaries. In short, revolutions seem to get out of hand—especially when viewed by the earlier revolutionary leaders. This is so because revolutions unleash forces which, if left unchecked, will push the revolution to higher and higher levels on the scale of revolutionary intensity and towards the ideal limit of the abolition of all forms of social stratification. Indicative of something like a law of revolutionary hypertrophy is the succession of jumpings on and off the revolutionary bandwagon. For every defection of relative moderates there seemingly occurs an addition of radical neophytes. Moreover, what was radical today seems fated to look rather tepid tomorrow. This is not surprising. Revolutions are a time of questioning and luxuriant speculation, and ideas once the province of madmen and eccentrics are given a serious hearing. Thus, a certain momentum is developed, which may carry the revolution in unforeseen directions.

Greater understanding of revolutionary hypertrophy can be achieved by analyzing Leon Trotsky's theory of "permanent revolution." Trotsky developed his theory in order to show that the abortive Russian Revolution of 1905, though initially a bourgeois rather than a socialist one, could be transformed into a proletarian revolution. His main target was those Marxists who argued that a "bourgeois revolution" by definition inaugurates a lengthy period of capitalist rule and that "semifeudal" Russia was too backward to allow for any revolution other than a "bourgeois-democratic" one. The proletariat would thus have to bide its time until material conditions were "ripe" enough to permit its own revolution. Trotsky countered with the idea of a "permanent" or "uninterrupted" revolution: "The Revolution, having begun as a bourgeois revolution as regards its first tasks, will soon call forth powerful class conflicts and will gain final victory only by transferring power to the only class capable of standing at the head of the oppressed masses, namely, to the proletariat. Once in power, the proletariat not only will not want, but will not be able to limit itself to a bourgeois democratic programme." [94]

Rather than depending on reaching a preconceived level of technological development, the proletarian seizure of power depended "upon relations in the class struggle, upon the international situation, and, finally, upon a number of subjective factors: the traditions, the initiative and readiness to fight of the workers." [95] That this raised the (un-Marxist) possibility that the working class might come to power sooner in a backward country than in more advanced ones Trotsky freely admitted. Nor did the problem of skipping over allegedly necessary stages of historical development trouble Trotsky overmuch, for "living historical process always makes leaps over isolated 'stages' which derive from theoretical breakdown into its component parts of the process of development in its entirety." [96] In any case, the *final victory* of the proletarian revolution could only be on an international scale, for which a proletarian revolution in a backward country would act as a spark.

Shorn of its Marxist terminology, Trotsky's theory of the permanent revolution suggests that social conflict can intensify after the outbreak of a revolution and push it well beyond its originally perceived destination.

> For an indefinitely long time and in constant internal struggle, all social relations undergo transformation. Society keeps changing its skin. Each stage of transformation stems directly from the preceding. This process necessarily retains a political character, that is, develops through collisions between various groups. . . . Outbreaks of civil war and foreign wars alternate with periods of "peaceful" reform. Revolutions in economy, technique, science, the family, morals and everyday life develop in complex reciprocal action and do not allow society to achieve equilibrium.[97]

Seen in this light, revolutionary hypertrophy suggests that both the stakes and the protagonists of revolution can become progressively altered. Exacerbation of conflict forces the revolutionary government into ever more drastic measures. This is done both to consolidate previous gains and to avoid outbidding by extremists. Cromwell, Robespierre, Lenin, and Stalin not only repressed ultrarevolutionary oppositions, they also took over part of their program. However, as Trotsky admitted that there was no historical example of a truly "permanent" revolution, we further point out that revolutionary hypertrophy encounters a number of psychological and sociological countervailing factors, whose ensemble we term "the law of revolutionary entropy." No revolution has become "absolute" in the sense described in Chapter III and it is doubtful that one ever could.

The net result of those composite factors which we have called "the law of revolutionary entropy" is to counteract hypertrophy by dissipating the moral and physical energies required to sustain a frenetic pace of political and social change. The farther a revolution goes, the greater become the obstacles to still further transformation. In fact, entropy can become so strong that not only may a revolution stop in its tracks, but there may be strategic as well as nonstrategic retreats on a wide variety of fronts. Since we have already discussed the factors that contribute to revolutionary entropy as reputed causes of the Thermidorean reaction (psychological and moral exhaustion, bureaucratic and oligarchic tendencies, etc.) we do not have to cover that ground again. With the particular conclusions of previous discussions in mind, several general conclusions about the problem of stages of revolution can be offered. (1) The fate of every revolution is determined by the relative strength of hypertrophic and entropic forces—if there is such a thing as a "dialectic" of revolution, surely it is in the contest between the two sets of factors. (2) The prevalence of entropic factors may be so decisive and so well coordinated that a definite terminal stage similar to the French Thermidor occurs, or triumph of entropy may be rather erratic and indefinitely delayed because of successful attempts to reactivate revolutionary energies. (3) Such antientropic attempts can come "from above" (i.e., from the revolutionary government); "from below" (i.e., from spontaneous mass action or from minorities excluded from power); or from joint efforts of two or three of these groupings. (4) Radical revolutionaries, in particular twentieth-century ones, have intuitively sensed these three principles (or have learned the lessons of revolutionary history) and have acted to avoid revolutionary entropy with greater success than commonly assumed. Since this last point raises the greatest theoretical difficulties for the Edwards-Brinton paradigm, it deserves consideration in a separate section.

Revolutionary Entropy and the Lessons of History

This section will examine four antientropic attempts to revitalize and extend revolution. The two earlier ones can be considered as ultimate failures; the two later ones reached a higher level of success. This difference may be partially due to the lessons of history that modern revolutionaries have had longer to learn. Although three of these attempts involve dictators' efforts to consolidate personal power, any crude "power politics" interpretation of them would miss their true distinctiveness and hence their instructiveness. Each episode in its different way will cast doubt on the common ideas of revolutionary Thermidor and vindicate a more flexible view such as that represented in the four conclusions at the close of the previous section.

Following an abortive Royalist insurrection known as Penruddock's Rising, Cromwell decided early in 1655 to divide England into eleven military-political districts, each to be headed by a Major-General with considerable powers. While the charge of these Major-Generals included control over "subversive" activities and normal criminal justice, their true interest lies more in their role as promoters of revolutionary virtue. That is, at a time when the English "Thermidor" *ought* to have settled into a pattern of relative normalcy, Cromwell and his supporters took decisive steps to advance the moral-cultural revolution that supposedly is inseparable from the bypassed radical phase of 1649–53. The Major-Generals were to suppress such gatherings as horse races, cockfights, bearbaitings, etc., on the grounds that they bred Royalist subversion.[98] Further, they were to act to rid their regions of idlers and persons with no visible means of support, since such categories were allegedly susceptible to Royalist enticements. However, one senses a note of ideological zeal in these measures that goes beyond a mere concern for internal security. This is clearer when we note that by "their constant carriage and conversation" the Major-Generals were instructed to "encourage and promote godliness and virtue, and discourage and discountenance all profaneness and ungodliness" and to strive along with local officials to see to it that "the laws against drunkenness, profaneness, blaspheming, and taking the name of God in vain . . . be put into more effectual execution than hitherto. . . ."[99]

The Major-Generals not only spurred local justices of the peace into more zealous activity but were also a direct threat to wrongdoers of various descriptions. Though the regime of the Major-Generals was considerably milder than the French Reign of Terror, it did resort to a kind of "revolutionary justice" over and above ordinary legal rules and procedures. Understandably, this attempt to promote virtue by military means aroused opposition. One source of opposition came from "that widespread class of good fellows who care more for the ease and enjoyment of life than for its stricter duties, who form a vast and inert mass when spiritual action is called for, but who offer stubborn resistance to a Government which calls on them for a forward step towards a purer and nobler life."[100] The other major source of opposition came from the upper strata of notables, who saw the regime of the often upstart Major-Generals as a direct threat to their social and political preeminence. The system was disbanded in 1656. However, that the experiment was tried for more than a year demonstrates that attempts to recover the ideological élan of a revolution were not unthinkable to so moderate a radical as Cromwell, and thus that the "English Thermidor" is less than monolithic.

With the French Revolution there are countless indications that the ninth of Thermidor did not extinguish revolutionary passions. Measures taken by the Thermidorean regime and later by the Directory [101] suggest a recrudescence of radicalism. The entire period from the fall of Robespierre to the rise of Napoleon is punctuated by recurrent campaigns against priests and émigrés. Georges Lefebvre considers the "Second Directory," a government established by a virtual coup in September of 1797, as beginning a new, if somewhat subdued, Reign of Terror.[102] It even partially rehabilitated the Jacobins, who had been proscribed after the fall of Robespierre. Furthermore, "by insistently denouncing the Royalist peril, the Directory had reawakened the revolutionary spirit and at the same time aroused the enthusiasm for universal propaganda and war to the death against tyrants. . . ." [103]

Attempts to avoid entropy can also come "from below." The spring of 1796 saw a bizarre example of this in the Conspiracy of the Equals inspired by Gracchus Babeuf. This abortive insurrection illustrates how despairing radicals can team with ultrarevolutionaries to oppose "betrayal" of the revolution and push it still further. Babeuf's plotted insurrection probably had no real chance of success, and his "communistic" ideas would have forced an eventual split between his disciples and his radical Jacobin allies.[104] Babeuf had originally supported the removal of Robespierre and the dismantling of the Terror, but was disillusioned at the apparent retrogression of the revolution afterwards. He thus concluded that a merely political revolution was insufficient to establish the absolute equality of all producers. His semicollectivism, while a far cry from socialized production, was well outside the mainstream of revolutionary thought; and his plans for revolutionary dictatorship foreshadow later doctrines. The idea of a truly social revolution comes out in a manifesto produced by a follower of Babeuf: "the French Revolution is but the forerunner of another revolution, far more grand, far more solemn, and which will be the last. . . . Never was a more vast design conceived and put into execution." [105] The true meaning of the revolution could only emerge after a violent purgative had expelled the new oppressors who had followed Robespierre. The Babouvist attempt, which was betrayed to the authorities and easily quelled, was thus antientropic in the sense of revamping the revolution so as to reach its "true" destination—the abolition of all social stratification.

Our third example, Stalin's launching of massive collectivization and industrialization in 1929, has aroused vigorous debate among historians. Some see this activity merely as a personal political gambit of Stalin; others, as the crushing of potential opposition to the Soviet regime as a whole; others again, as an effort at forced-draft modernization to transform the Soviet Union into a strong industrial and military power; and still others, as the implementation of the collectivist principles of Marxism-Leninism. In fact, there is some truth in all of these interpretations. For present purposes, however, collectivization and the Great Terror of the purges of the 1930's represent an authentic attempt to revitalize and advance the revolutionary process. There was danger that the relaxed atmosphere of the NEP would allow the solidification of a new social order departing in fundamental ways from the precepts of the revolutionary ideology. "Trotsky was not alone in deeply deploring the crowding into the party of men from the lower middle classes. The lower levels of the Soviet administration were flooded by the peasantry. On the other hand, quite a few stalwart Communists suffered a 'sea change' into entrenched bureaucrats, to whom words like Communism, the International, and the World Revolution were so many clichés devoid of real content." [106] To retain the NEP indefinitely would have jeopardized the long-term ideological goals for which the Bolsheviks had originally taken power. What had been a strategic retreat would have been converted into the best of all possible worlds. It is misleading, therefore, to consider Stalin's policies in the late 1920's and early 1930's as dictated solely by his struggle first with the Left and then with the Right opposition.

Stalin and his supporters launched a Second Socialist Offensive [107] which hearkened back to the "first offensive" of War Communism. The chief difference between the two campaigns was that in 1918–21 the Soviet government had to acquiesce in agricultural capitalism, while in 1929–30 the Stalinists felt strong enough to liquidate this anti-Marxist system. The collectivization of agriculture produced a massive loss of life, resistance and repression, and a chronic weakness of the agricultural sector. Opposition within and without the Communist Party to both the ends and the means of this second socialist offensive helped trigger the Great Purges, whose victims came from nearly all segments of Soviet society. Here too while Stalin's "paranoic suspicion" may explain certain excesses of the period and some particular decisions, "the possibility of a Stalin was a necessary consequence of the effort of a minority group to keep power and to carry out a vast social-economic revolution in a very short time. And *some* elements of Stalinism were, in those circumstances, scarcely avoidable." [108] Ironically, Stalin had to intervene at several junctures to restrain the ferocious enthusiasm of many communists. This "dizziness with success" problem (to use an expression of Stalin's) also plagued Robespierre during the Terror and

Mao Tse-tung during the Cultural Revolution from 1966 to 1969. The revolutionary leaders launch a campaign of revolutionary revitalization, but the grass-roots revolutionaries exceed their somewhat vague instructions and create near-chaos. In any case, the collectivization drive and the Stalinist Terror constituted a concerted effort to ward off revolutionary entropy by taking the offensive. This is the case even if parallel and later developments such as concessions to economic self-interest, growing nationalism, mitigation of the attack on religion, and the rehabilitation of traditional Russian cultural and historical themes while Stalin still lived, constitute a kind of "Great Retreat" from certain ideals of Lenin's time.[109]

The Chinese Communist Revolution is of interest to the student of revolution for a variety of reasons. It is, of course, the premier example of the Eastern-style revolution, in which the lengthy struggle for power leaves a permanent mark on the subsequent course of the revolution. But perhaps its most significant features are not in its drive to victory in 1949. Two events after that time, the Great Leap Forward of 1958–59 and the Great Proletarian Cultural Revolution of 1966–69, dispel once and for all any simplistic idea of inevitable revolutionary Thermidor. Both of these episodes, by no means untarnished successes, illustrate the lengths to which modern revolutionaries may go to avoid entropy and to continue the revolution. While our three previous examples suggest that such attempts are not unique to the Chinese Revolution, the character and intensity of this "shock treatment" approach to revolutionary recovery goes beyond all precedents. We have already pointed out that the Great Leap and the Cultural Revolution and other phenomena can be understood in terms of ultrarevolutionary impulses getting the better of merely radical ones. More basically, the Chinese Revolution and the Chinese Communist Party are bifurcated between radical and ultrarevolutionary strains of thought and action, with moderation or "modern revisionism" running a poor third. There has been an oscillation between the two major tendencies, which thus reveals greater resilience and influence of ultrarevolutionary motifs than in any previous revolution.

In the early 1950's Chinese communism seemed to be embarked on a path of bureaucratic centralization similar to what had developed by that time in the USSR. In terms of a long-standing Chinese communist dichotomy between being "red" and being "expert," [110] the expert tendencies appeared to be outstripping the red ones. At that time, "large numbers of old and new intellectuals were recruited into the Party. Expertise became a prime qualification for Party membership. Untrained rural cadres were dropped from the Party rolls. Managers were coming into their own again. A 'new class' was in the process of coming into being." [111] The onslaught against these entropic and possibly Thermidorean developments began in 1955, but culminated in the Great Leap Forward of 1958. While economic aspects of the Great Leap such as decentralization of industry and the "People's Communes" originally seemed most salient, reappraisal in the light of the Cultural Revolution reveals definite political and ideological factors at work. As an example, "decentralization to the primary level would reduce the influence of the rich peasants and the Party bureaucracy and would mean that Mao's ideological directives could reach the masses without passing through the various levels of the Party hierarchy." [112] This direct top-to-bottom relationship was to be reenacted during the even profounder shock of the Cultural Revolution. The Great Leap, however, ran into serious difficulties: as an attempt at an "economic miracle" it proved almost wholly disastrous, but as an antientropic catharsis it registered greater success. This was obscured in the early 1960's when retreat on nearly all fronts of the Great Leap coincided with a serious downswing in the personal political fortunes of Chairman Mao. In fact, the expression "Liu's NEP" was employed by observers to describe this period, because the moderate economic policies of Liu Shao-chi, Mao's later disgraced "rival," seemed to be moving China back onto a path interrupted by five years of experimentation. [113]

It is out of the question here to recount the facts or to survey the conflicting interpretations of the Cultural Revolution. As usually happens in such cases, there were premonitory signs—more blatant, of course, in retrospect than at the time. The Socialist Education Campaign of the early 1960's involved massive attempts to indoctrinate the peasants with properly revolutionary ideas. In 1965 traditional military ranks were abolished in the People's Liberation Army. And so on. However, in mid-1966 the Cultural Revolution was officially launched. It involved a cataclysmic shake-up of nearly all institutions, with the Chinese Communist Party being hit hardest of all. The most dramatic manifestation was the Red Guard movement, composed of the most militantly Maoist of Chinese youth. In three years of turmoil and near civil war, all levels of the party were purged at a tempo and thoroughness comparable to the Soviet purges of the 1930's. More broadly, teachers, intellectuals, elders, bureaucrats, experts—anyone with claims to status in terms of achievement—were subject to attack and humiliation by the resurgent egalitarianism of the Red Guard and kindred movements. In the end Mao had to rely upon the Army to restore some semblance of order to the rapidly disintegrating polity.

In our terms the Cultural Revolution represents an authentic antientropic effort to revitalize and advance the revolution through an alliance of certain leaders of the revolutionary government (the Maoist faction) and a variety of elements "from below." Since the initiative originally came from above and many of Mao's critics fell victim to the purge, some interpreters have seen the Cultural Revolution exclusively from the angle of a personal and factional power struggle.[114] There is, of course, some truth to such "realist" interpretations, but two major considerations show that power politics does not exhaust the significance of the Cultural Revolution.

The first of these considerations concerns Mao himself and the second, the hypertrophy of the Cultural Revolution. Mao's concept of the Chinese Revolution has moved beyond radicalism to embrace elements of the ultrarevolutionary syndrome. To him and his closest associates any signs of routinization, oligarchy, or stratification are considered inherently counterrevolutionary. These attitudes have given rise to a peculiarly Maoist concept of the class struggle. According to Franz Schurmann the "class struggle" as Western Marxists and others understand that term was terminated successfully in China by the mid-1950's.[115] What class struggle has subsequently meant there reveals a peculiarly "mentalist" emphasis in Chinese communism, which considers altering people's thought patterns by various "rectification campaigns" as important to the revolution as institutional reconstruction.[116] Thus, class struggles in China, up to and including the Cultural Revolution, are attempts to root out ideas and behavior patterns deemed unbecoming to a truly revolutionary society. Anything less than total dedication to the revolution—any tendency to localism, nepotism, corruption, and elitism—is condemned as "bourgeois," or as "taking the capitalist road" when broader policies are involved. The contrary attitudes, actions, and policies are "proletarian." Thus, Mao's concept of class struggle is "inward-directed in two senses: First, it is aimed against those among the Party cadres and the working masses whose special privileges have made them a new class of 'labor aristocracy' and, second, against any remaining influence of bourgeois ideology and undesirable traditions within each individual, regardless of his social background." [117] No balanced interpretation of the Cultural Revolution can afford to underestimate the role of these important ideological precepts of the "thought of Mao Tse-tung."

Even if Mao's motivations in promoting the Cultural Revolution were basically power-oriented, the succession of events went well beyond any such calculations. In plain language, the Cultural Revolution got out of control; in sociological terms, the "latent functions" of the Cultural Revolution soon exceeded manifest power or ideological considerations in importance. Mao's appeal to elements of Chinese society, in particular the youth, over the heads of the bureaucratic party middle-elite succeeded well beyond his original expectations. The activities of the Red Guards were "destratifying" Chinese society through a king of generational revolt. But there was a danger also of doing irreparable damage to economic, political, and educational institutions under the pretext of ridding them of bureaucratic excrescences. While Mao postponed calling off his rabid and youthful devotees as long as possible, the menace of prolonged instability became obvious. The "dizziness with success" problem of Stalin also had its Maoist version, when the Chinese leader complained of certain excesses of ultraleft groupings.[118] It is thus hard to avoid the conclusion that "like a runaway train derailed," the Cultural Revolution for a time, "responded less to the frantic manipulations of its engineer than to the imperatives of the terrain over which it has traveled." [119] Even with a relaxation after 1968, the Cultural Revolution not only reveals something about the nature of the Chinese Revolution; it also illustrates the effectiveness of antientropic campaigns and thus the complexities of periodization in revolution. During the peak period Mao suggested the possibility of further such upheavals,[120] and if the sociological and psychological forces that compose revolutionary entropy remain as relentless as they have proven in the past, indeed more upheavals will be necessary, not only to advance the revolution but also to prevent backsliding.

CONCLUSION

The antientropic attempts to revitalize the English and French revolutions were in the long run unsuccessful. Revolutionary entropy did eventuate in a sort of Thermidor terminating the revolutionary crisis. The experiment of social control by the Major-Generals in England, as well as the Babouvist plot of 1796 or "Directorial terror" in 1797 in France, emerge as temporary, though significant, reversals of an overriding trend. Given such reservations the English and the French revolutions betray a three-stage process of moderation, radicalism, and the emergence of a new nonrevolutionary "equilibrium." This holds, however, only with the proviso that one cannot always be utterly precise as to the watershed date separating one stage from the next and that resurgences of revolutionary energy confute any idea of Thermidor as a smooth linear trend. With respect to other revolutions (e.g., the Russian and the Chinese), we have already established the inapplicability of any three-stage model.

In his study of the Russian Revolution Nicholas Timasheff concluded that "every revolution is a series of dislocations and reconstructions, but the process of dislocation and reconstruction may assume different rhythms." [121] Timasheff merged the Edwards-Brinton moderate and the radical stages into a single phase, because he considered the former as merely the prelude to the latter. After this somewhat questionable procedure he was ready to distinguish revolutions according to the number of distinct phases they traversed. Coups d'etat were "one-phase processes" because dislocation and reconstruction took place simultaneously. . . ." [122] Revolutions following the Edwards-Brinton model were accordingly "two-phase revolutions"—minus the separate moderate phase, because "the primary process of dislocation and reconstruction was superseded by another one, in the opposite direction, partly restoring the old system of values and even personal statuses within it." [123] More interesting still is Timasheff's thesis that "there may be more complex revolutions in the course of which the trend reverses itself more than once, so that they form a three, or a four-phase process." [124]

A "phase" can be (1) a trend towards realization of the stated ideological goals of the revolution, (2) a trend away from them, or (3) a stable trend that neither departs from nor approaches these goals in any marked degree.[125] Any talk of trends here assumes a measure of dissynchronicity, because of heterogeneity between and among the ends and means of revolutions and because governments are forced to set priorities. What is true of the Russian Revolution, therefore, also covers other revolutions: "Not only have the individual processes followed different patterns, but the reversals of the trends have not taken place simultaneously and, in consequence, it is easy to offer many instances of simultaneous movements in opposite directions." [126] We might explain this incoherence by appealing to the discordant action of sets of hypertrophic and entropic influences.

In 1946 Timasheff visualized the Russian Revolution as manifesting a four-phase process which would add no further phases—in other words, the revolution was definitely terminated. He plotted a curve of its course, which we have modified by adding somewhat uneasily a fifth phase representing a return to certain "totalitarian" features of the regime and a sixth representing "destalinization" (which seems a better choice for a terminal stage of the Russian Revolution).

We can similarly graphically represent the wavelike course of the Chinese Communist Revolution from the end of World War II to the early 1970's. The following graph is based upon the periodization of Franz Schurmann as modified by the Cultural Revolution of the late 1960's and other considerations.[127]

Our final conclusions in this chapter would simply reinforce those found at the end of the section above, "Rigidity and Overgeneralization." Periodization of revolutions can prove an exceedingly difficult task, made more difficult by the fact that, contrary to some conven-

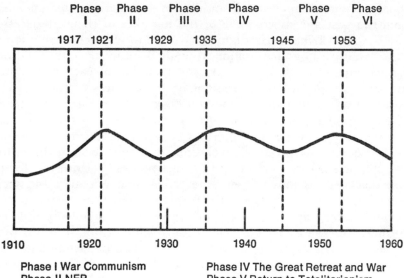

Figure 9. The Course of the Russian Revolution

Phase I War Communism
Phase II NEP
Phase III Collectivization

Phase IV The Great Retreat and War
Phase V Return to Totalitarianism
Phase VI Destalinization

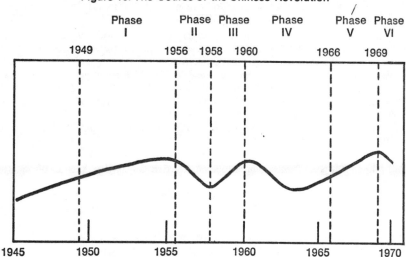

Figure 10. The Course of the Chinese Revolution

Phase I Consolidation and Collectivization
Phase II Relaxation of the Mid-1950's
Phase III The Great Leap Forward
Phase IV Liu's "NEP"
Phase V The Cultural Revolution
Phase VI Aftermath of the Cultural Revolution

tional wisdom, people and ironically revolutionaries sometimes learn from the past and avoid some of the mistakes of their predecessors. The Edwards-Brinton paradigm taken from the French Revolution was a bold venture in generalization, though Brinton more than Edwards was sensitive to its limitations. A reexamination of earlier revolutions and an evaluation of the revolutionary experiences of the past three decades suggest that each revolution gives birth to forces that tend to push it onward (hypertrophic forces) and forces that tend to wind it down (entropic forces). The interplay between these two kinds of forces could theoretically produce revolutions that run through three, four, five, six, or even more clear and distinct phases.[128] However, for reasons that stem as much from general beliefs about man and society (some might say from ideology) as from the comparative study of revolutions, it would appear that entropy in the end will have its way, even in China. But before it does, one or more antientropic adventures may register substantial successes. Human effort and determined *leadership* may not be able to avoid the inevitable, but they can defer it longer than sometimes recognized.

NOTES

[1] Crane Brinton, *The Anatomy of Revolution* (Englewood Cliffs, N.J.: Prentice-Hall, 1952), p. 135.

[2] "Persons who, *first,* are enjoying an income earned without, or with comparatively little, labor, or at least of such a kind that they can afford to assume administrative functions in addition to whatever business activities they may be carrying on; and who, *second,* by virtue of such income, have a mode of life which attributes to them the social 'prestige' of a status honor and thus renders them fit for being called to rule." Max Weber, *Economy and Society,* Vol. III (New York: Bedminster Press, 1969), p. 950.

[3] Brinton, *Anatomy,* p. 135.

[4] Lyford P. Edwards, *The Natural History of Revolution* (Chicago: University of Chicago Press, 1970), p. 146.

[5] Adam B. Ulam, *The Bolsheviks* (New York: Collier Books, 1971), p. 322.

[6] Leon Trotsky, *The Russian Revolution* (Garden City, N.Y.: Anchor Books, 1959), pp. 199–208; and Brinton, *Anatomy,* pp. 139–51.

[7] George Pettee, *The Process of Revolution* (New York: Harper & Row, 1938), p. 106.

[8] Brinton, *Anatomy,* p. 147. Historically, notables have shied away from the semi-bureaucratic, disciplined organization of modern political parties. Parties of notables or "cadre parties" are loose, limited purpose alliances. While radical revolutionaries did not have modern "mass" parties at their disposal in any pre-twentieth century revolution, their organizational achievements go well beyond what moderate notables are willing or able to produce.

[9] Brinton, *Anatomy,* p. 148.

[10] Edwards, *Natural History,* p. 149.

[11] Pettee, *Process,* p. 115.

[12] Edwards, *Natural History,* p. 150.

[13] Pettee, *Process,* p. 132.

[14] *Ibid.*, p. 133.

[15] Brinton, *Anatomy*, p. 168.

[16] Pettee, *Process*, p. 137.

[17] *Ibid.*

[18] *Ibid.*

[19] Edwards, *Natural History*, p. 150. This way of putting things obscures the question of whether the radicals do indeed "save the revolution" or save what according to someone's ideology the revolution "ought to be."

[20] Quoted in R. R. Palmer, *Twelve Who Ruled* (Princeton: Princeton University Press, 1970), p. 264.

[21] Though we have seen that the radicals do not necessarily constitute a modern political party, Maurice Duverger's analysis of levels of participation in parties provides some useful analogies. By *top leaders* we mean the "inner circle" of some dozens of men who steer the radical forces. They are surrounded by another wider circle of *militants*, who as true believers in the radical mission, mere careerists, or something of both, devote the bulk of their free time to promoting the radical cause. Surrounding them in turn is a still wider circle of *supporters*, who give verbal support to the radical leadership and on occasion trouble themselves more directly. Finally, the outer circle is composed of mere *followers* (corresponding to Duverger's voters), who go along with the radicals, sometimes get involved in riots and the like, but whose participation is essentially passive and somewhat unreliable. Maurice Duverger, *Political Parties* (New York: John Wiley, 1963), pp. 90–116.

[22] David Underdown, *Pride's Purge* (Oxford: Oxford University Press, 1971), p. 4.

[23] *Ibid.*, p. 354.

[24] M. J. Sydenham, *The Girondins* (London: The Athlone Press, 1961), p. 182.

[25] *Ibid.*, p. 198.

[26] Karl Kautsky, *The Dictatorship of the Proletariat* (Ann Arbor: University of Michigan Press, 1964), p. 32.

[27] Brinton, *Anatomy*, p. 171.

[28] Crane Brinton, *The Jacobins* (New York: Russell & Russell, 1961), p. 175.

[29] *Ibid.*, p. 72.

[30] See Hadley Cantril, *The Psychology of Social Movements* (New York: John Wiley, 1963); and Eric Hoffer, *The True Believer* (New York: Mentor Books, 1958).

[31] Brinton, *Anatomy*, p. 201.

[32] Richard Cobb, *Terreur et Subsistances 1793–95* (Paris: Librarie Clavreuil, 1965), p. 52.

[33] Brinton, *Jacobins*, p. 232.

[34] Thucydides, *The Peloponnesian War*, in C. A. Robinson, Jr., ed., *Selections from the Greek and Roman Historians* (New York: Rinehart & Co., 1959), pp. 97–98.

[35] Edmund Burke, *Reflections on the Revolution in France* (New York: Liberal Arts Press, 1955), p. 70.

[36] Georg Hegel, *Hegel's Philosophy of Right* (Oxford: The Clarendon Press, 1958), p. 157.

[37] Edwards, *Natural History*, p. 175.

[38] *Ibid.*

[39] This idea was introduced some years ago in the specific context of Stalinist totalitarianism: "Social prophylaxis" refers to a process whereby "the state authorities, anticipating future developments, attempt to eliminate or render harmless all groups of people among whom a social or political conflagration might possibly develop." Jerzy G. Glicksman, "Social Prophylaxis as a Form of Soviet Terror," in *Totalitarianism*, ed. Carl J. Friedrich (Cambridge, Mass.: Harvard University Press, 1954), p. 62.

[40] Edwards, *Natural History,* p. 174.

[41] *Ibid.,* p. 175.

[42] *Ibid.,* p. 189.

[43] Palmer, *Twelve Who Ruled,* p. 12.

[44] *Ibid.,* p. 57.

[45] Paul Avrich, *Kronstadt 1921* (Princeton: Princeton University Press, 1970), p. 131.

[46] Talcott Parsons, *The Social System* (New York: The Free Press, 1964), p. 529.

[47] Brinton, *Anatomy,* p. 209.

[48] V. I. Lenin, *The Proletarian Revolution and Renegade Kautsky* (New York: International Publishers, 1934), p. 19.

[49] Underdown, *Pride's Purge,* p. 5.

[50] Carl J. Friedrich, *Constitutional Government and Democracy* (Waltham, Mass.: Blaisdell, 1968), p. 129.

[51] Stanley Payne, *The Spanish Revolution* (New York: W. W. Norton, 1970), p. 305.

[52] Palmer, *Twelve Who Ruled,* p. 11.

[53] Leonard Schapiro, *The Origins of the Communist Autocracy* (New York: Praeger, 1965), p. 236. Trotsky's military reorganization should be contrasted with the approach of the Provisional Government.

[54] Alexis de Tocqueville, *The European Revolution and Conversations with Gobineau* (Garden City, N.Y.: Anchor Books, 1959), p. 161.

[55] *Ibid.*

[56] George Santayana, *Reason in Common Sense* (New York: Collier Books, 1962), p. 22.

[57] Albert Soboul, *Les sans-culottes parisiens en l'an II* (Paris: Editions du Seuil, 1968), p. 26.

[58] Cobb, *Terreur,* p. 7.

[59] Brinton, *Anatomy,* p. 191. See Chapter VII below for counterrevolutionary responses of peasants and others.

[60] Palmer, *Twelve Who Ruled,* p. 117.

[61] Quoted in Christopher Hill, *God's Englishman* (New York: Harper Torchbooks, 1972), pp. 153–54.

[62] As Robert V. Daniels calls the Left Communists in *The Conscience of the Revolution* (New York: Simon & Schuster, 1969).

[63] Austin Woolrych, "Oliver Cromwell and the Rule of the Saints," in *The English Civil War and After,* ed. R. H. Parry (Berkeley: University of California Press, 1970), p. 61.

[64] John Rogers quoted in Samuel R. Gardiner, *History of the Commonwealth and Protectorate,* Vol. III (New York: AMS Press, 1965), p. 266.

[65] Soboul, *Les sans-culottes,* p. 133.

[66] Palmer, *Twelve Who Ruled,* p. 293.

[67] The reservations are that Anarchists did not consider themselves a political party, which notion they thought was bound to the state, and that the Left Communists were not a party but a faction of a party.

[68] Schapiro, *Origins,* p. 129.

[69] *Ibid.,* p. 128.

[70] Mikhail Bakunin, *Bakunin on Anarchy* (New York: Vintage Books, 1972), p. 219.

[71] Quoted in Avrich, *Kronstadt,* p. 166.

[72] Daniels, *Conscience,* p. 4.

[73] *Ibid.*

[74] Quoted in *ibid.,* p. 161.

[75] Edwards, *Natural History,* p. 200.

[76] Brinton, *Anatomy,* p. 243.

[77] Leon Trotsky, *The Revolution Betrayed* (New York: Merit Publishers, 1965), p. 88.

[78] Pettee, *Process,* p. 143.

[79] Parsons, *Social System,* p. 527.

[80] *Ibid.,* p. 529.

[81] Gaetano Mosca, "Il principio aristocratico e il democratico," in *Partiti e sindacati nella crisi de regime parlamentare* (Bari: Laterza, 1949), p. 29.

[82] Soboul, *Les sans-culottes,* p. 243.

[83] *Ibid.,* p. 244.

[84] Trotsky, *Revolution Betrayed,* p. 89.

[85] Mosca, *Partiti,* p. 30.

[86] *Ibid.,* p. 31.

[87] *Ibid.,* p. 33.

[88] I.e., the House of Commons originally elected in 1640 minus Royalist defectors, the victims of Pride's Purge, and other expellees, plus some replacements.

[89] Brinton, *Anatomy,* p. 227.

[90] Hill, *God's Englishman,* p 143

[91] Edwards, *Natural History,* pp. 201 05.

[92] Brinton, *Anatomy,* p. 247.

[93] *Ibid.,* p. 251.

[94] Leon Trotsky, *Permanent Revolution* (New York: Pioneer Publishers, 1965), p. 162.

[95] *Ibid.,* p. 195.

[96] *Ibid.,* p. 116.

[97] *Ibid.,* p. 8.

[98] Gardiner, *Commonwealth and Protectorate,* Vol. III, p. 318.

[99] *Ibid.,* pp. 318–19.

[100] Gardiner, *Commonwealth and Protectorate,* Vol. IV, p. 40.

[101] The Directory was a five-member executive council that took over some of the duties of the Committee of Public Safety after it was disbanded with the fall of Robespierre.

[102] Georges Lefebvre, *The Directory* (New York: Vintage Books, 1967), p. 106.

[103] *Ibid.,* p. 104.

[104] *Ibid.,* p. 37.

[105] Quoted in J. L. Talmon, *The Origins of Totalitarian Democracy* (New York: Praeger, 1970), p. 187.

[106] Raphael R. Abramovitch, *The Soviet Revolution* (New York: International Universities Press, 1962), p. 317.

[107] Nicholas Timasheff, *The Great Retreat* (New York: E. P. Dutton, 1946).

[108] Alec Nove, "Was Stalin Really Necessary?," in *The Soviet System in Theory and Practice,* ed. Harry G. Shaffer (New York: Appleton-Century-Crofts, 1965), p. 75.

[109] And thus Timasheff entitled his study of 1946. However, from 1946 to Stalin's death in 1953 there was a relapse into extreme rigorism; the real retreat began in 1953 and has proceeded more slowly in certain areas of policy than expected.

[110] The idea of "being red" corresponds closely to the ultrarevolutionary syndrome. It suggests concern with the ultimate ideological goals of the revolution, a "populistic" desire to keep leaders close to the masses, and certain types of decentralization. Being "expert," though ideally harmonious with being red, is associated with the creation of specially trained personnel to fill important positions in a rationalized division of social labor.

[111] Franz Schurmann, *Ideology and Organization in Communist China* (Berkeley: University of California Press, 1971), p. xlviii.

[112] James C. Hsiung, *Ideology and Practice* (New York: Praeger, 1970), p. 188.

[113] *Ibid.*, p. 194.

[114] Charles Neuhauser, "The Chinese Communist Party in the 1960's: Prelude to the Cultural Revolution," in *China in Ferment,* ed. Richard Baum and Louise B. Bennett (Englewood Cliffs, N.J.: Prentice-Hall, 1970), p. 34.

[115] Franz Schurmann, "The Attack of the Cultural Revolution on Ideology and Organization," in *China in Crisis,* Vol I., ed. Ping-ti Ho and Tang Tsou (Chicago: University of Chicago Press, 1968), p. 541.

[116] Robert J. Lifton, *Thought Reform and the Psychology of Totalism* (New York: W. W. Norton, 1963).

[117] Hsiung, *Ideology and Practice,* p. 101.

[118] Phillip Bridgham, "Mao's Cultural Revolution in 1967: The Struggle to Seize Power," in *China in Ferment,* pp. 137–38.

[119] Richard Baum, "China: Year of the Mangoes," in *China in Ferment,* p. 144.

[120] Hsiung, *Ideology and Practice,* p. 299.

[121] Timasheff, *Great Retreat,* p. 330.

[122] *Ibid.*

[123] *Ibid.* As we shall soon see, five or six phases are possibilities, even if for the sake of argument we do not follow the Edwards-Brinton separation of moderate and radical phases.

[124] *Ibid.*

[125] *Ibid.*, pp. 330–31.

[126] *Ibid.*, p. 334.

[127] Schurmann, *Ideology and Organization,* pp. xxvi–xxxiv.

[128] Or the risk that overelaborate analyses of the phases of particular revolutions may end up looking like—to use James C. Davies' expression—"a side view of a windy sea," may deter the cautious from cocksure discussion about phases in general.

VI

IDEOLOGY AND REVOLUTION

IDEOLOGY AS RATIONALIZATION

THE role of ideology in political life is among the most contentious issues in all of social science. Before surveying the problem of ideology and revolution directly, three general conceptions of ideology will orient us to some of the terminological and empirical difficulties involved. The Marxist, the Realist, and the Mannheimian concepts of ideology, however different, share the conviction that ideology is something of a dissimulation which rationalizes a set of "hard" interests that provide the real motive force of politics. Thus, they see the task of social science as the unmasking of these motive interests through a rigorous and relentless critique of ideologies.

The Marxist Concept of Ideology

Having discussed the background of the Marxist concept of ideology in Chapter II, our task now is to elaborate it briefly. Historical materialism teaches that society's economic organization, the mode of production and exchange, is the major determinant of its social and cultural structures and processes. Thus, the "substructure" has a controlling influence over the "superstructure," which is composed of the state and of "ideological" elements such as moral codes, philosophies, art, law, religion, and literature. As Marx and Engels put it in an early work: "We set out from real, active men, and on the basis of their real life-process we demonstrate the development of the ideological reflexes and echoes of this life-process. The phantoms formed in the human brain are also, necessarily, sublimates of their material life process. . . ." [1] What makes this process ideological is that the persons whose minds are so shaped are generally unaware of the true source of their beliefs and modes of thinking. They are beset by "false consciousness," which functions to defend or disguise the predominance of the ruling class.

In fact, a specialized segment of the ruling class superintends the ideological needs of the existing system: "its active, conceptive ideologists, who make the perfecting of the illusion of the class about itself their chief source of livelihood. . . ." [2] The remainder of the ruling class are too busy to bother themselves with ideology-mongering. Since the relationship of ideology to the material base is essentially passive, ideological change or conflict is essentially a barometer of more fundamental movements. "But even if this theory, theology, philosophy, ethics, etc. comes into contradiction with the existing relations, this can only occur as a result of the fact that existing social relations have come into contradiction with existing forces of production. . . ." [3] After the death of Marx (1883) Engels qualified the rather one-sided relation of ideology (i.e., culture) to the economic base. Though insisting that the "material mode of existence" is the primary agent, he conceded that "this does not preclude the ideological spheres from reacting upon it in their turn, though with secondary effect." [4] Even so, this concession does not abandon the basic thrust of the Marxist concept of ideology. Thus, despite its stimulating effect upon both Marxists and non-Marxists (Weber, Pareto, and Mannheim, for example), the originally broad concept of ideology (which Marx and Engels identified with nearly all beliefs that failed to measure up to their standards of "science") is not very useful in political analysis. Later Marxists have been forced to give the concept a more narrowly political connotation so that they often call Marxism itself an "ideology."

An interesting attempt to salvage the Marxist viewpoint was made by George Plekhanov, the "teacher" of Lenin, who objected to the "one-sidedness" and schematism of "vulgar Marxism." Theories that maintained that all ideological phenomena are determined directly, exclusively, and immediately by the economic base, he argued, short-circuit the actual complexity of Marxist analysis. Instead of a simplistic cause and effect relation between material base and ideological superstructure, he posited a five-factor relationship with some feedback between different factors. His scheme was intended to reserve primacy for economic forces but to make their operation more subtle and more indirect. The five factors are

(1) the state of the productive forces;
(2) the economic relations these forces condition;
(3) the sociopolitical system that has been developed on the given economic 'base';

(4) the mentality of men living in society, a mentality which is determined in part directly by the economic conditions obtaining, and in
part by the entire sociopolitical system that has arisen on that foundation;

(5) the various ideologies that reflect the properties of that mentality.[5]

As the mentality or "psychology" of an epoch, which gives rise to different ideologies, is only partly determined by the first two factors, the
role of the third factor, the "sociopolitical system" introduces an element of flexibility in the conceptual scheme. However, the impact of
this revision is lessened when we recall that the sociopolitical system itself derives from the economic base. What we have in effect here is an
attempt to develop an "indirect" rather than a "direct" form of economic determinism: the concessions are geared to preserve that "primacy" of economic forces and relationships, which, after all, is what
makes Marxism distinctive.

Also of interest is Plekhanov's recognition of some "dissonance between ideologists and the class whose aspirations and tastes they express," [6] though Marx and Engels had made a similar point.[7] But here
too Plekhanov is quick to point out that this "dissonance" still is encompassed within the framework of the interests and economic position of
the class in question. It must be clear, then, that according to Marxism
the key to understanding ideology and revolution is class analysis. The
old ruling class and its allies will espouse ideologies that depend on an
obsolete economic system, while the rising class and its allies profess an
ideology that points to the future. Ideological differences within the
broad revolutionary movement are manifestations of divergent class interests. The major weakness of the Marxist concept of ideology is simply its diffuseness; it shares this defect with all loose definitions of
ideology that equate this diffuseness with "belief system." Another
problem is the exclusive linkage of ideology to social class. This grossly
oversimplifies the revolutionary process. Finally, Marxism, in common
with the other approaches in this section, underestimates the "autonomous" role that ideas and ideologies can play in politics and revolution.

The Realist Concept of Ideology

The Realist concept of ideology is nearly as old as human speculation on the ends and means of politics. It is a corollary of theories of
"power politics" found in ancient Indian, Chinese, and Greek civilization. Thucydides puts a doctrine of political realism in the mouths of
the Athenian delegation at the famous dialogue at Melos: "For of the
Gods we believe, and of men we know, that by a law of their nature

wherever they can rule they will. This law was not made by us, and we are not the first who have acted upon it; we did but inherit it, and shall bequeath it to all time; and we know that you and all mankind, if you were as strong as we are, would do as we do." [8] But men are not usually so frank as the Athenians were portrayed in the Melian dialogue: they rationalize their power drives and interests by an appeal to higher moral, religious, or cultural principles—which modern Realists call "ideologies." The Athenians themselves try to unmask the dissimulation and delusions of the Spartan enemy by complaining that "of all men whom we know they are the most notorious for identifying what is pleasant with what is honorable, and what is expedient with what is just." [9]

Thucydides gives us the gist of later and more elaborate versions of the Realist concept of ideology: power is the main stakes of politics and ideology is employed to delude enemies, win over neutrals, and perhaps reassure ourselves and our friends. As Hans Morgenthau, a modern theorist of Realism, puts it, "While all politics is necessarily pursuit of power, ideologists render involvement in that contest for power psychologically and morally acceptable to the actors and their audience." [10] Morgenthau furthermore avoids the trap of "vulgar Realism," which automatically considers all moral, religious, and cultural principles invoked in political struggles as mere cover-ups for sordid power interests. Such principles are "either the ultimate goals of political action . . . those ultimate objectives for the realization of which political power is sought—or they are the pretexts and false fronts, behind which the element of power inherent in all politics is concealed. . . ." [11] In fact, the picture may be still more complex because one and the same principle may be a goal of political action, an ideology, or "both at the same time." [12]

Despite these qualifications, the animus of the Realist is to be skeptical, indeed mistrustful, of claims by revolutionaries and nonrevolutionaries alike that they act in the service of high ideals and altruistic sentiments. Such professions, more often than not, are ranked as ideologies to befuddle the unwary. In Chapter II we saw that Vilfredo Pareto considered revolutionary ideologies—which he called "theories," "dogmas," "derivations," etc.—as essentially fraudulent devices of a new elite which aspires to take power. His Realist concept of ideology distinguishes between the degree of *truth*, the degree of *effectiveness*, and the degree of *social utility* of an ideology.[13] According to Pareto's view, revolutionary ideologies would (1) very often rank low in truth-content as gauged by scientific method, (2) often prove effective in mobilization of people for action by appealing to underlying sentiments, and (3) sometimes prove socially useful by ousting a decadent elite and returning a vigorous new one in the revolution sanctioned by the ideology. For Pareto and modern political Realism in general, "science and ideology belong to two separate fields which have nothing in common: the first to the field of observation and reasoning, the second to the field of sentiment and faith. . . ." [14] Since an ideology's objective truth has little to do with its social utility, what truly disturbs Pareto is "the ideology which claims to pass itself off as science, the surreptitious exchange between a value judgment and a factual judgment." [15] This is why Pareto devoted considerable attention to separating science and ideology in Marx's revolutionary theories.

Though Realists can always marshall evidence for the dominance of power over ideology, they often succumb to a reductionist tendency towards what we have called vulgar Realism. We have already had occasion to question the notion of revolution as a struggle between power-hungry, cynical elites. The reason for this is simple: people, politicians, and revolutionaries are more sincere than is often thought. Such sincerity, of course, can range from the most naive innocence to the most implacable fanaticism. Though the Realist injunction to look behind any ideological facade is no more than sound methodology, this must be done with an open mind. In addition to being a political and economic animal, man is also an ideological animal—this is nowhere clearer than in the revolutionary situation. Realism as a general theory of politics has greater relevance for those nonrevolutionary periods and contexts wherein an unwritten, though imperfect, ideological consensus allows men to play the game of unabashed power politics.

Mannheim's Concept of Ideology

Because of the complexity of Karl Mannheim's ideas, what follows here should be considered a schematic simplification of his thoughts on ideology. Mannheim's theoretical foundation assumes that there is no absolute, fixed standpoint situated outside the historical process by which to measure truth: he calls his doctrine "relationism" rather than relativism. Since truth is related to a specific historical configuration, its content changes when the total historical milieu has been transformed. Instead of speaking of absolute truths and falsehoods, Mannheim proposes to distinguish between "situationally congruous ideas" and "situationally incongruous ideas." [16] The former "fit into" the existing historical situation, while the latter "transcend" it either by looking too far back or by looking too far ahead. "In the same historical epoch and in the same society there may be several distorted types of inner mental structure, some because they have not yet grown up to the present, and others because they are already beyond the present." [17] The atavistic form of thought-distortion Mannheim calls "ideology"; the futuristic form he calls "utopia." Unfortunately, he obscures the initial sharpness of this dichotomy by refinements and reservations added to ensure its universal applicability.

Mannheim sets out by separating the "particular" and the "total" concepts of ideology. The particular concept of ideology is involved whenever we consider the "ideas and representations advanced by our opponent" as "more or less conscious disguises of the real nature of a situation, the true recognition of which would not be in accord with his interests." [18] These obfuscations range from "conscious lies to half-conscious and unwitting disguises." [19] Thus, the particular concept of ideology is little more than a tenet of political Realism. The total concept of ideology, in contrast, concerns the mentality of whole epochs, whole classes, and other groups. Accordingly, the student of revolution is more interested in the total than the particular concept of ideology. For example, classes (or strata) whose social position is threatened from below usually react by declamations of an ideological nature. They or, more commonly, their agents from the intelligentsia try to absolutize the existing social structure with appeals to divine law, the sanctity of tradition, or the "natural order" of things. In short, ideology is inherently defensive and conservative of the status quo. A favorite stratagem of privileged strata is to proclaim the danger and foolhardiness of the ideals of those strata rising to challenge them: "whenever an idea is labelled utopian it is usually by a representative of an epoch that has already passed." [20] Though the conservative impulse normally stands latent, "goaded on by opposing theories, conservative mentality discovers its *idea* only *ex post facto*." [21]

At first glance it would seem that utopia is diametrically opposed to ideology, as it functions to promote rather than retard social change. A utopia takes form because "certain oppressed groups are intellectually so strongly interested in the destruction and transformation of a given condition of society that they unwittingly see only those elements in the situation which tend to negate it." [22] Mannheim's utopia then is a peculiar set of social aspirations rather than a blueprint of an ideal society. In fact, from his perspective, traditional utopias such as that of Sir Thomas More would be closer to ideologies than to utopias. Utopias furthermore are divided into "absolute" utopias, which are beyond realization, and "relative" utopias, which are somewhat in advance of their time. Though both ideology and utopia distort and "transcend" existing reality, Mannheim's personal sympathies dispose him to prefer utopia as by far the lesser of the two evils. Ideologies are anachronistic in the sense of being retrograde and obsolete, while the opposite anachronism of utopias makes them both harbingers of things to come and agents in their coming. Thus utopias have a greater measure of "actuality" or "relevance" than ideologies "in so far as they succeed through counteractivity in transforming the existing historical reality into one more in accord with their own conceptions." [23]

Though things seem simple enough, with ideologies being conservative or reactionary and utopias being radical or revolutionary, Mannheim warns us that to determine "what in a given case is ideological and what utopian is extremely difficult." [24] One source of difficulty is that the utopias of rising classes often are largely "permeated with ideological elements." [25] If this were not troublesome enough, Mannheim points out that threatened conservatives, whose natural defense is pure ideology, sometimes resort to a "counter-utopia which serves as a means of self-orientation and defense." [26] The only way to save the original distinction between ideology and utopia from intolerable confusion is to make a retrospective analysis of how a particular set of ideas did in fact function: "Ideas which later turned out to have been only distorted representations of a past or potential social order were ideological, while those which were adequately realized in the succeeding social order were relative utopias." [27] But for contemporary observers without a crystal ball, Mannheim's near-obsession with the social *function* of ideas restricts, if it does not exclude, any judgment whether a given doctrine is ideological or utopian. Contrary to Marxist as well as common usage, Mannheim's utopia turns out to be an epitome of political Realism.

Though Mannheim's work contains help for the student of revolutions, his inability to maintain the sharpness of his dichotomy without appeal to the unknown future limits the overall usefulness of his conceptual scheme. Mannheim's weaknesses derive from his reluctance to give equal weight to the *structure* as compared to the function of political ideologies. This weakness reflects the reductionist treatment of ideas that he shares with "vulgar" Marxism and "vulgar" Realism. A balanced appraisal would determine whether ideas and ideologies are reactionary, conservative, liberal, reformist, radical, revolutionary, etc., by looking both at what they say and what they do. Confusion and ambiguity are bound to arise if we consider ideologies and utopias as vague "styles of thought" or "mental complexes" rather than as coherent political doctrines that find currency in various groups in society. That a given doctrine wins out (i.e., in Mannheim's terms, proves its utopian pedigree) is not necessarily proof of either its suitability to the times or its superiority over competitors. Mannheim seems to ignore the problem of the self-fulfilling prophecy. It may be the force of the idea alone or even the force of arms, not just the force of circumstances, that causes it to prevail in a given situation.

IDEOLOGY AND MYTH IN THE
REVOLUTIONARY PROJECT

Ideologies and Myths

Like so many others, the term "ideology" has a quality of indeterminateness that itself is a fruitful source of "ideological" contention.[28] Before seeing how this problem weighs on the study of revolution, a brief summary of our general conclusions might make what follows more profitable. First, greater explicitness and coherence of ideology distinguishes revolution from mere revolt. Second, there are three structural aspects of revolutionary ideology: *critique,* which lays bare the shortcomings of the old regime; *affirmation,* which suggests or even spells out in detail that a better society is not only desirable, but possible; and in recent times, *strategic guidance,* which tells the best way to make a revolution. Third, the intellectuals play a dominant role in the formulation of revolutionary ideologies. Fourth, the later revolutions tend to manifest a greater reliance on "preformed" ideology (to be discussed below in the section "Preformed and *Ad Hoc* Ideologies") than do the earlier ones. Finally, the heterogeneity of the original revolutionary coalition, plus the ups and downs of the "phases" of revolution, are both cause and effect of the emergence of several, sometimes competitive, ideologies. These conclusions must now be elaborated and supplemented.

Loose definitions of "ideology" have equated it with at least three different phenomena: belief systems, political theory or philosophy, and myths. Sometimes ideology stands for all three indiscriminately. The loosest usage of all considers as ideologies the political beliefs of any individual or group. In this way ideology can be made to explain everything or nothing at all. To avoid this dead end, we will reserve the term "belief system" as the generic category for political opinions that have any coherence at all—regardless of precise structure, function, and origins. In this way ideology will be a belief system, but one of a very particular sort.

Equally unfortunate is the confusion between ideology and political theory (or philosophy). In one sense this confusion commits the reverse errors of that between belief system and ideology: it narrows things down too much. According to Dante Germino, political theory refers to "that intellectual tradition which affirms the possibility of transcending the sphere of immediate practical concerns and 'viewing' man's societal existence from a critical perspective." [29] Ideology, on the other hand, involves a "set of ideas about the ordering of society claiming the prestige of (phenomenal) science. . . ." Ideology furthermore appeals to a theory of knowledge that reduces all knowledge to sensory data. Since it seems easy enough to know the world around us, the next step of ideology aims "at the transformation of the world through making it conform to abstractions divorced from the realities of human existence in society." [30] Though the genuine political theorist is often involved in the struggles of his time, this does not prevent him from dealing with the *perennial* problems of political life. The ideologist, on the contrary, carries his partisanship to the point of losing all critical detachment. The sole value of ideas is their force as "weapons" in the cause to which he is committed: like the Sophists of old he sometimes takes pride in "making the weaker argument appear the stronger."

Though Germino's contrast may be overdrawn and tendentious, there is good cause to distinguish the "intentions" and structure of authentic political theory from those of ideology. The relationship between the two is analogous to that between "pure science" and technology. While pure science and political theory pursue general disinterested knowledge both technology and ideology seek immediate practical results. Though technology may depend sometimes on scientific discoveries and ideology can claim some filiation from grandiose philosophical systems, they both involve an abridgment or simplification of the results of the research or speculation. This is not to deny that such distortions or vulgarizations may be helpful to society on a somewhat different plane of interest: technology and ideology have their place. Nevertheless, whereas the practical, activist intention of ideology strives to mobilize men's *passions,* true political theory is intended to appeal to their *reason.* This is not to say that the function of ideology is exhausted by its emotive or affective role. Ideologies have some cognitive role in bringing perceptual order to the political world and serve to elaborate and apply value judgments (evaluative function) to political phenomena.[31] However, the specific difference between political theory and ideology is the latter's hortatory emphasis, which is likely to cause some distortion in cognitive and evaluative areas.

Myth is the third concept often confused with ideology. Part of the reason for this confusion lies in the contrast between structural and functional notions of myth itself. Mircea Eliade's structural view of myth finds echoes among many anthropologists and students of comparative religion:

> Myth narrates a sacred history; it relates an event that took place in primordial Time, the fabled time of the 'beginnings.' In other words, myth tells how, through the deeds of Supernatural Beings, a reality came into existence, be it the whole of reality, the Cosmos, or only a fragment of reality—an island, a species of plant, a particular kind of human behavior, an institution. . . . In short, myths describe the various and

sometimes dramatic breakthroughs of the sacred (or the 'supernatural') into the World.[32]

Since myth is what gives meaning to the plenitude of human existence, in certain societies it serves as "the exemplary model for all significant human activities." [33] Ritual is a rehearsal of the sacred model of the myth performed in order to bring about certain desired results. Myth in this structural sense pervades primitive or archaic societies in which "desacralization" or secularization is minimal. Since it functions to keep society whole and to uphold tradition, myth is very different from an ideology, which despite Mannheim may well be radical or revolutionary.[34]

Nevertheless, Eliade is by no means alone when he sees survivals, transformations, and intimations of myth in some modern political ideologies. He suggests, for example, that Karl Marx adopted "one of the great eschatological myths of the Middle Eastern and Mediterranean world, namely: the redemptive part to be played by the Just (the 'elect,' the 'anointed,' the 'innocent,' the 'missioners,' in our own days by the proletariat), whose sufferings are invoked to change the ontological status of the world." [35] The Marxian vision of a classless society is no more than a refurbishment of the myth of the Golden Age, which comes at the end instead of the beginning of history.[36] Parts of other revolutionary ideologies are also considered to be infused with ancient mythical motifs: "The old religious idiom has been replaced by a secular one, and this tends to obscure what otherwise would be obvious. For it is the simple truth that, stripped of their original supernatural sanction, revolutionary millenarianism and mystical anarchism are still with us." [37]

However, modern political ideologies, revolutionary and nonrevolutionary, differ in important ways from the structuralist conception of myth with its close association to archaic and primitive societies. For one thing these ideologies do not narrate or repeat a sacred story, but claim to embody a "scientific" view of history. The connection between the new ideologies and the old myths is an intriguing puzzle that needs further thought and research, and thus any claim that modern ideologies are a recrudescence of ancient myths must be met with due caution. One common element is that certain ancient myths and modern (utopian) ideologies evoke a mode of human existence categorically superior to the present one. The men of "that time" were or will be as far above us as we tower over the beasts.[38] Structural similarities between things, however, can often occur without a genetic relationship between earlier and later phenomena. Modern political ideologies are, after all, a product of conditions that differ considerably from those in earlier or simpler societies.

Very different from structuralism is R. M. MacIver's functional notion of myth: "By *myths* we mean the value-impregnated beliefs and notions that men hold, that they live by or live for. Every society is held together by a myth-system, a complex of dominating thought forms that determines and sustains all its activities." [39] From this perspective it makes precious little difference whether we look at "the most penetrating philosophies of life, the most profound intimations of religion, the most subtle renditions of experience, along with the most grotesque imaginations of the most benighted savage"—all of these things can give meaning to life and sustenance to the social fabric.[40] From the standpoint of social order, the most important myth is the *myth of authority*. Thus a precondition of revolution would be the disintegration of the general myth-complex and, in particular, the myth of authority. Revolution itself suggests the victory of new and different myths, which soon settle into an established position. Though there is a ring of general truth to MacIver's functionalist notion of myth, it simply is too loose to be of much help on the problem of revolution. We are no better off working with "myth" than we are with "belief system"—the two are virtually indistinguishable.

George Sorel's doctrine of myth is more narrowly and more directly related to the revolutionary process. As a kind of revolutionary pragmatist, Sorel believed that the acid test of the worth of ideas comes in the most agonistic forms of human *action* rather than in pure intellection. The significance of myth thus emerges through revolutionary practice. Interesting, especially in the light of Mannheim's theories, is Sorel's contrast between myth and utopia: "myths are not descriptions of things, but expressions of a determination to act. A utopia is, on the contrary, an intellectual product; it is the work of theorists who . . . seek to establish a model to which they can compare existing society in order to estimate the amount of good and evil it contains." [41] Since myth is essentially a stimulus to immediate action, "any attempt to discuss how far it can be taken literally as future history is devoid of sense." [42] A utopia's appeal to reason is a fatal weakness from the standpoint of revolution, because mere rational conviction is unable to propel vast human masses into movement or to evoke heroic sentiments and great deeds. In fact, a utopia is likely to short-circuit revolution, since it diverts attention away from direct revolutionary action. A myth, on the other hand, arouses the subrational level of sentiment and passion: it alone can endow the masses with the bellicosity required for a revolutionary showdown. The value of a myth is not gauged by the calipers of reason and science; the appropriate test is in the laboratory of practical action.

Consequently, Sorel's notion of the myth pays no attention at all to structure: all that matters is the effective function of the myth in inducing class war and revolution. This at least avoids the looseness of MacIver. More complex, however, is the relation of the Sorelian myth to ideology.

> Ideology, according to Sorel, differs from Utopia by its tie to myth. Ideology is a rational structure with its foundations in myth. Sometimes it builds a machine serving the historic creative forces of an era, and then it communicates the power of revolutionary personal experience of them. In other cases it upholds a facade behind which work reactionary forces, and then it builds on dead myths which were once historical experiences and whose memory it keeps alive.[43]

The danger from the Sorelian standpoint is that the myth-sustained ideology will degenerate into a pure utopia or a conservative apologetic. In any case, Sorel implies an explanation of the peculiar strength of certain ideologies: their original myth-impulse continues to arouse passionate commitment, while the ostensibly rational structure of the ideology meets the minimum needs of those who value logic.

This is probably why Lyford Edwards included the Sorelian myth (or a modification of it) among the motive forces of revolution. Extreme discontent compounded by strong economic claims and intensified by acute social criticism are not enough to produce revolution. What is missing is some extra push: "a dynamic of a genuinely spiritual and religious kind." [44] According to Edwards this dynamic is supplied by the "social myth," which represents the "fusion of ideas propounded by the revolutionary intellectuals with the elementary wishes of the repressed class. . . ." [45] Since Sorel rejects the role of intellectuals in the genesis of myth, Edwards' "social myth" is more akin to a myth-sustained ideology than to a pure Sorelian myth. Nevertheless, Edwards concurs fully with Sorel that from a rational standpoint aspects of the myth may well be "mutually inconsistent and contradictory" or "incapable of verification by experience." [46] The important thing is the faith that the myth evokes.

Despite the important insights provided by those who link myth and politics, structuralism is too narrow and functionalism much too broad for us to replace the term "ideology" with the term "myth," or even to identify the two. Elements of myth can be found in revolutionary ideologies; but the precise relationships vary according to the case, with "a myth providing grounds for an ideology, and an ideology often procreating a myth." [47] Before the French Revolution, for example, large numbers of educated people subscribed to the myth of the noble savage, which extolled the virtues of primitive folk untainted by the corruption of civilization. According to Mircea Eliade, this myth "was but a renewal and continuation of the myth of the Golden Age, that is, of the perfection of the beginnings of things. . . . The state of innocence, and the spiritual blessedness of man before the fall, in the paradisiac myth, becomes, in the myth of the good savage, the pure, free and happy state of the exemplary man. . . ." [48] The myth became ideological when Rousseau among others began to identify the noble savage with the poor and lowly of their society. The sufferings and humiliations of these people provided an indictment of the old regime, while their apparent virtues proved that man was basically good and that only social convention and pressure made him behave badly. While not all those enraptured by this myth took the final step, it is easy to see how a revolutionary ideology could be established on this foundation.

A viable notion of ideology must be distinct enough to avoid confusion with the related phenomena of belief systems, abstract political theories, and myth. It must also take account of both structural and functional aspects of ideology. [49] These conditions are largely met by Carl J. Friedrich's definition of ideology presented in Chapter I. [50] Though Friedrich calls his approach a "functional political concept of ideology," his emphasis on the programmatic and strategic aspects of ideology reveals an awareness of structure. Building upon Friedrich, we can now offer the following definition of ideology: *a political ideology is a programmatic and rhetorical application of some grandiose philosophical system* (a Weltanschauung), *that arouses men to political action and may provide strategic guidance for that action.* The ideology thus constitutes an abridgment and politicization of broader philosophical themes. Furthermore it contains rhetorical elements that evoke an emotive response among people who become devotees of the ideology. The ideology is programmatic in the sense of wishing to preserve, reform, or overturn the existing political or social order and may even provide a detailed strategy to accomplish this.

Preformed and *Ad Hoc* Ideology

A preformed ideology has been articulated fairly well in advance of the outbreak of the revolution and heavily influences the political practice of the revolutionary movement and its leadership. An *ad hoc* ideology, in contrast, develops gradually during the course of the revolutionary struggle. We have seen already that some schools of thought consider revolutions to be attempts to implement the prescriptions of a preformed ideology, while others find that ideology is generally brought into play to justify actions determined by other factors. However, several considerations advise against making either of these alternatives a hard and fast rule: (1) both preformed and *ad hoc* elements play a part in most revolutions; (2) several distinct ideologies may be in competition for mastery over the revolution; (3) every revolution presents its own mix of preformed and *ad hoc* ideology. A glance at the ideological configuration of several revolutions may help us to get a sense of the possibilities.

The English Revolution of the 1640's and 1650's occurred too early to call upon an established revolutionary tradition. We have previously noted the reformism and moderation of the Parliamentary leaders in the early days. The original "Country" opposition to the King and the Court was based upon a diffuse set of moral, religious, and political beliefs rather than upon a coherent ideology. However, during the long period of crisis from 1640 to the King's execution in 1649, there was enough time for the emergence of ideologies deserving of the name. Least deserving perhaps was the "ideology" of the Cromwellian Independents, which became reluctantly republican after the execution of the King. This outlook was relatively moderate in terms of political change, still more moderate in regard to social and economic matters, though rather innovative with respect to religious problems. Since this ideology was very often most explicit on what it opposed, we would point out its antidemocratic and antiegalitarian thrust. This came out clearly in the Army's Putney Debates in the fall of 1647, when representatives of the Army's rank and file pressed for a wider suffrage and other reforms. While Cromwell and his associates could swallow some slight modification of the suffrage, they balked at anything that would extend political participation beyond the upper social strata. Democratization seemed in their eyes to lead straightway to anarchy and "communism."

The Leveller movement, which had some Army support, developed a less rudimentary ideology than the Cromwellians. Though the exact shape of Leveller ideology is a matter of some debate, their individualism and civil libertarianism, as well as their reservations about full adult male suffrage, suggest that they belong to "the liberal, rather than the radical democratic tradition of English political thought." [51] High on their agenda were religious toleration, equality before the law, due process of law, equality of opportunity, limited government, etc.— ideas that came to characterize the great liberal tradition. Far to the left of the Levellers and far beneath them in influence are the Diggers, sometimes called the "True Levellers." This minuscule communist seçt could be written off as the true lunatic fringe, were it not that its ideologist, Gerard Winstanley, produced an authentic ideology of utopian communism. Of him Eduard Bernstein wrote: "He represents the most advanced ideas of his time; in his Utopia we find coalesced all the popular aspirations engendered and fertilized by the Revolution." [52]

Though Bernstein's judgment is excessive, it shows how ideology can develop during the course of revolution itself.

The English Revolution thus presents relatively little preformed ideology, though there was a substantial growth of *ad hoc* ideology as people became emboldened in their ideas and half-forgotten religious and social ideas were ventilated. The challenge of the Levellers, and later of the Fifth Monarchists and others, promoted a crystallization of ideological positions. In fact, if we consider the years around 1648 as a unit, we can represent the ideological spectrum of the English Revolution and superimpose the categories of moderate, radical, and ultra-revolutionary upon it:

Figure 11. The Ideological Spectrum of the English Revolution

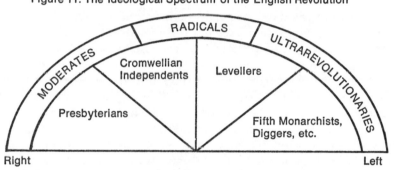

(This spectrum does not indicate proportions of political strength.)

Like most twentieth-century revolutions, the Russian Revolution broke out in a society in which the level of preformed ideology was much higher than in seventeenth-century England. Marxism was a well-established doctrine, though it split into reformist and revolutionary tendencies. Lenin's *What Is to Be Done?* was written fifteen years before the fall of the monarchy and his *State and Revolution* shortly before the collapse. Other parties and factions such as the Kadets, the Mensheviks, the Socialist Revolutionaries, and the Anarchists had ideologies of varying degrees of coherence. We can represent the ideological spectrum of the years 1917–21 as in Figure 12.

Considering only the ideology that won out in the end, Bolshevism, we can say that its preformed nucleus remained relatively unaltered by *ad hoc* accretions and innovations in the Leninist years, 1917–24. What happened rather was that Bolshevik tenets on collectivism, world revolution, populism (*State and Revolution*) were put in a kind of suspended animation due to the weakness of the regime and the harshness of conditions. But strategic and tactical flexibility—one step backward, two steps forward—had been a characteristic of Lenin-

Figure 12. The Ideological Spectrum of the Russian Revolution

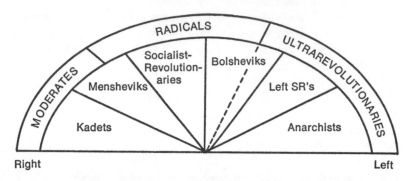

ism from the early days. As Lenin pointed out in 1920: "Everyone will agree that an army which does not train itself to wield all arms, all the means and methods of warfare that the enemy possesses, or may possess, behaves in an unwise or even in a criminal manner. But this applies to politics even more than it does to war. In politics it is harder to forecast what methods of warfare will be applicable and useful to us under certain future conditions."[53] Such complex circumstances caused Lenin to reiterate and strengthen another quintessential element of Bolshevism: the hegemony of the party. "Whoever weakens ever so little the iron discipline of the party of the proletariat (especially during the time of its dictatorship) actually aids the bourgeoisie against the proletariat."[54]

Thus, the impact of revolutionary practice during Lenin's time did not cause a deemphasis of preformed ideology in favor of *ad hoc* ideology, but set the stage for precisely such a development. Ideological changes of greater import began to be registered after Stalin had enunciated his doctrine of "socialism in one country." This led in the end to a virtual repudiation of the Marxist idea of the "withering away of the state" and a serious downgrading of "proletarian internationalism" to the advantage of "Soviet Patriotism." These and other modifications justify the awkward, but accurate, term "Marxism-Leninism-Stalinism" as a description of the growing importance of *ad hoc* ideology in Soviet communism after Lenin's death.

In the Chinese Communist Revolution the distinction between preformed and *ad hoc* ideology is almost officially recognized by the regime. Franz Schurmann has formulated the contrast as one between "pure" ideology (or "theory") and "practical" ideology (or "thought").[55] The total or complete ideology of Chinese communism incorporates both of these elements. Pure ideology (i.e., Marxist-Leninist theory) constitutes the preformed ideology since it was formulated mostly before the foundation of the Chinese Communist Party. It provides a body of universal and unchanging general principles. However, Marxist-Leninist theory is incomplete: its very generality debars it from guiding action in every specific historical situation. It needs to be supplemented and complemented by ideas that emerge in concrete revolutionary practice; these ideas make up practical ideology or "thought" (which in China is "the thought of Mao Tse-tung"). Both components of ideology are necessary, for in the Chinese view "without pure ideology, the ideas of practical ideology have no legitimation. But without practical ideology, an ideology cannot transform its *Weltanschauung* into consistent action. Though all revolutionary movements must have an ideology, not all of them have evolved practical ideologies through which effective organization can be created." [56]

Practical ideology in the Chinese context closely approximates our sense of *ad hoc* ideology. To distinguish further the two interrelated aspects of Chinese communist ideology, Schurmann employs the well-known, but troublesome, sociological distinction between *values* and *norms*. While pure ideology establishes values or general "moral and ethical conceptions about right and wrong," practical ideology provides norms or "rules which prescribe behavior and thus are expected to have direct action consequences." [57] There is thus a sort of ends-means connection between the values of pure ideology and the norms of practical ideology, which we have preferred to construe here as the distinction between the *ultimate goals* and the *strategy* of revolution. For a long time the "thought of Mao Tse-tung" was considered the strategy of the Chinese Revolution. The term "theory" was reserved for the pure or preformed ideology of Marxism-Leninism. Thus, after 1927 Chinese communist ideology began to diverge gradually from Soviet communist ideology, not on the plane of pure ideology, but on that of practical ideology. The later developments of this divergence have largely determined the ideological aspects of the Sino-Soviet dispute that emerged openly in the early 1960's.

However, with the Cultural Revolution there has surfaced a latent tendency within Chinese communism: to raise the thought of Mao Tse-tung to the level of theory or pure ideology. In the 1969 Constitution of the Chinese Communist Party, Mao's thought is considered a "new historical contribution in the continuum extending from Marxism and Leninism into the future and is granted the same ideological importance." [58] Chinese communist ideology has thus traversed three basic stages: (1) an early stage, in which preformed ideology, Marxism-Leninism, dominates; (2) a second stage, in which the thought of Mao Tse-tung increasingly complements Marxism-Leninism; and (3) a third stage, in which Mao's doctrines incorporate both theory and thought, both pure ideology and practical ideology. The *ad hoc* ideology developed through long years of practice has culminated in a true and proper "Sinification of Marxism."

The Cuban Revolution deviates rather sharply from the pattern of twentieth-century revolutions, especially communist ones, because of the extreme weakness of its preformed ideology. The ideology of Castroism as it developed after the seizure of power is an amalgam of Marxist-Leninist themes and Castro's personalized interpretation of the meaning of his revolution. As Theodore Draper points out: "Most revolutionary movements have had what might be called 'anticipatory' theories. Castroism has rather had only a 'retrospective' theory in the sense that only after taking power did it begin to ask itself what it had done and how it had been done." [59] The thesis that Castro was a communist "all along" has never been substantiated, despite his 1962 claim that he was and would die a "Marxist-Leninist." There is little doubt that Castro moved further and further to the left as he felt more and more embarrassed about his regime's lack of a coherent ideology and a party dedicated to it. The Cuban leader is not an intellectual or an ideologist [60] and his personal qualities have always dominated the Cuban Revolution. However, he sensed the need to justify the revolution in ideological terms (and to win friends and influence people among the communist regimes), and this led to the enthronement of a variety of Marxism-Leninism as the official ideology.

Part of the quest for an ideology was spurred on by Castro's chief lieutenant, Ernesto "Che" Guevara. But even he, at the time he joined Castro in 1956, was a "young man of certain intellectual and revolutionary inclinations but with no precise ideological position, and this was still true in January 1959." [61] Guevara seems to have felt the need for ideology more acutely than his chief and developed his variant of Marxism-Leninism somewhat sooner. Despite this evidence, the weakness of preformed ideology vis-à-vis *ad hoc* ideology does not mean the complete absence of the former. Castro seems to have subscribed to a rather vague ideology of constitutional democracy in his early revolutionary activities. He abandoned this ideology quietly and unceremoniously from 1954 to 1959 without openly embracing a more radical one. Furthermore, some of the intellectuals ranged against Batista espoused radical ideologies; and there was a tradition, if not an ideology, of revolutionary nationalism going back to José Martí, whom the Castro regime has enshrined as one of its earliest prophets.

> The Fidelista claim of speaking for Martí survived the military phase of the Revolution and became a public assertion of the revolutionary regime. To paraphrase Ernesto Guevara . . . the Fidelistas have resurrected the movement that Martí led in behalf of Cuban independence

and that American intervention destroyed. Castro declared that his socio-economic blueprints for Cuba expressed the ideal of *humanismo*—a direct reference to Martí's thesis that *patria* and *humanidad* were synonymous.[62]

Though the Cuban (and the English) Revolution remind us not to overestimate the role of preformed ideology in the coming of revolution, later developments in either case reinforce our strong association of ideology and revolution.

A brief look at just four revolutions is enough to show some possible relationships between preformed and *ad hoc* revolutionary ideology. With some revolutions, preformed ideology is very important in the early stages and then gives way somewhat to *ad hoc* ideology, which may in the end dominate the scene. Other revolutions display a vague ideological legitimacy to supplement an inadequate *ad hoc* ideology. Still others develop competing ideological strains which end up with one of them winning a provisional victory. These variations suggest that revolutions can be ranged on a continuum from the "no-ideology" of vulgar Realism to the "all-ideology" of certain conspiracy theories, with innumerable permutations in between.

Esoteric and Exoteric Ideology

In a discussion of Marxism, Vilfredo Pareto distinguished three possible levels of ideology. The first or "hermetic doctrine" was the personal ideology of Marx and Engels and perhaps their closest collaborators. The second or "esoteric doctrine" was restricted to a small circle of learned disciples. The third or "exoteric doctrine" was designed for mass propaganda and public meetings and did not always jibe in every detail with the esoteric doctrine. Since Pareto doubted the social impact of the hermetic doctrine or ideology and since our present concern is not with what Marx or Rousseau "really meant," we can forget about the hermetic doctrine. Rather we are interested in the relations between esoteric and exoteric levels of ideology. With respect to Marxism, the precise level of ideology involved varied according to the "degree of culture and the intensity of the passions of the exegetes of Marx." [63] The exoteric ideology is much simpler and easier to comprehend, for "the exegesis of the ignorant is always much more logical and clear than that of students, because the first do not see the impossibility of the rigorously logical consequences of the doctrine. . . ." [64] The initiates on the other hand twist and turn to avoid the logical tangles that threaten on every side. Thus, the intellectual structure produced is often gothic in its complexity. There is a clear analogy here to what happens in religion when the plain man accepts the miracles of the Bible as literal truth, while the erudite with some scientific knowledge goes through all sorts of intellectual convolutions to come up with alle-gorical interpretations.

Since exoteric ideology is intended for mass consumption, so to speak, there is a common tendency to deny that the esoteric ideology really exists as a motivating force. Such an argument is found in Her-mann Rauschning's aptly titled *The Revolution of Nihilism*. There the au-thor, himself a disillusioned ex-member of the Nazi Party, insists that Nazi doctrine "is meant for the masses. It is *not* part of the real mo-tive forces of the revolution. It is an instrument for the control of the masses. The elite, the leaders, stand above the doctrine. They make use of it in furtherance of their purposes." [65] Instead of ideology, the true motivation of the Nazi elite is an irrational drive toward revolution for the sake of revolution: "the aim of National Socialism is the complete revolutionizing of the technique of government, and complete domi-nance over the country by the leaders of the movement." [66] Though Rauschning wisely stressed that this supposedly nihilistic (i.e., nonideo-logical) revolution was without historical precedent, he raises some im-portant questions. His reasoning suggests that the elite's ideological ma-nipulation of the masses is putative proof that the elite is itself ideologically cynical.

However, the gap between ideological propaganda for the masses and the motivations of the elite is not necessarily unbridgeable. The no-tions of esoteric and exoteric ideology imply that some simplification and manipulation is inevitable when ideologically sophisticated elites try to present their case to unsophisticated mass publics. This may in-volve a certain cynicism—but not the cynicism of a totally Machiavel-lian nature. As Gabriel Almond's study of communism during the Sta-linist period points out: "From the very formation of the Bolshevik movement, it has been recognized that in the era of capitalism the greater part of the working class and of other Communist audiences are unable to assimilate the Marxist-Leninist dialectic." [67] One result of this is that "at the level of mass appeal, the Communist movement por-trays itself in ways which are adopted to specific social and political set-tings." [68] For a variety of reasons, the full-blown ideology of Marxism-Leninism has to be watered down before it can be swallowed by suf-ficiently large numbers of people. This means focusing on specific problems that trouble them without much attempt to link these exo-teric concerns with the esoteric ideology of the party militants. Thus, at the exoteric level, the ideology of communist movements reflects the idiosyncrasies of time and place, while at the esoteric level, it gravitates around one or another strain of Marxism-Leninism.[69] In fact, not only do many candidates for party membership remain at the exoteric level, a goodly number of full party members "are never fully assimilated to the esoteric doctrine and practice of the Party. In this sense they are unstable party elements." [70]

What we have called the "exoteric ideology" is not ideology in the strictest sense, but rather is a translation and application of the true or esoteric ideology. Even though simplified and often distorted, the exoteric ideology nevertheless derives its sense from the esoteric ideology, though not everyone will perceive this connection. There is, of course, some point beyond which we can no longer speak of levels of the *same ideology:* two different ideologies are operative. But before reaching that conclusion, we must make sure that all possible connections between the two have been broken. Ideologies not only serve to provide programs and strategies related to broad principles, they also structure people's perceptions of the circumambient political world. Events are provided with a context of meaning that escapes those not affected by the ideology. When perceptions begin to take on an ideological cast, the individual is at least on the exoteric level of ideology and may later proceed beyond it.

Nevertheless, the gap between the exoteric and esoteric ideologies has serious risks for a revolutionary elite, especially after they come to power. The esoteric ideology's greater complexity may reveal that the road to utopia is rather long and full of detours. However, much of this realism may be lost as the esoteric doctrine is transmuted into a simplified, and perhaps demagogic, exoteric catechism for the masses. When the masses or their champions come to demand immediate delivery of the promised benefits of the catechism, the revolutionary elite will be hard pressed to hold them off with recitals of the harsh facts of life. We have already seen in Chapter V how this dilemma usually leads to the strengthening of the radical dictatorship. The exercise of sovereign power generally proves to be a sobering experience.

KEY THEMES IN MODERN REVOLUTIONARY IDEOLOGY

Progress

Some notion of progress is a logically necessary ingredient of a truly revolutionary ideology. It is sometimes held that the essential modernity of revolution stems from the essential modernity of the idea of historical progress. Though earlier cultures glimpsed this idea and Christianity prepared the way for it, only with the European Renaissance and Enlightenment did the idea of progress take on its modern form. Before that time, history was construed as the reiteration of a basic cyclical paradigm. Events possessed significance if and only if they somehow replicated a model event situated in mythical time. Mircea Eliade has traced the survival of the "myth of the eternal return" both in the sophisticated cyclical philosophies of history of Spengler, Toynbee, and Sorokin as well as in the belief of popular strata such as the peasants.[71] He even points out that groups that still "obstinately adhere to an anhistorical position" are thereby "exposed to the violent attacks of all revolutionary ideologies." [72] In a broader sense the cyclical view of history is congenial to the conservative mentality because it denies that there can really be anything new (and ostensibly better) "under the sun." We can readily appreciate Hannah Arendt's insistence that "the notion that the course of history suddenly begins anew, that a story never known or told before, is about to unfold" is "inextricably bound" to the modern concept of revolution.[73]

However, even to admit that there is authentic novelty in history is not to produce a theory of progress: that would be to confuse "the breaking down of the barriers by which advance is made possible with advance itself." [74] The notion of progress entails *an increase of value made possible by change*. There is greater realization of some key value (or set of values) at a later date than at an earlier date. The increase of value may be smooth and steady, as in theories of unilinear progress; it may be erratic, as in theories of undulating or wavelike progress; or it may be limitless, as in theories of infinite progress. All of these variations agree that over time the general direction of change is bringing with it a discernible increase of value. Different doctrines of progress use different criteria to measure progress. Freedom, happiness, equality, knowledge, material welfare, altruistic sentiment, technological advance, peace, social harmony—one, all, or any combination of these and other things may figure in the list. In any event, a revolutionary ideology must state or imply that only revolution can bring about the breakthrough that will allow the march of progress to proceed apace.[75]

We cannot analyze how the notion of progress operates in all revolutionary ideologies. Its importance, however, has increased over time; for if "a vague confidence in progress had lain behind and encouraged the revolution of 1789," it is true that "in the revolution of 1848 the idea was definitely enthroned as the regnant principle." [76] Going back to the English Revolution it is, of course, more difficult to show the importance of progress in the ideologies of the time. Many of the most radical groups did not follow the essentially secular idea of progress,[77] but were captivated by "millennial dreams" of direct divine intercession. Nevertheless, ideas such as the superiority of the "moderns" over the "ancients," the prestige of natural science, the increase of human "felicity" through technology (Francis Bacon), etc.—which were later to fuse into coherent doctrines of progress—pervaded the intellectual milieu of Stuart and Cromwellian England. According to Robert K. Merton, "It was this faith in progress which, becoming progressively marked in seventeenth century England, exerted a great influence upon the positive estimate of change. GEORGE HAKEWELL, BACON, HOBBES, BOYLE, GLANVILL and many others turned from the conviction that the world was degenerate and designed for destruction to the belief in an imminent and unequalled brilliant future." [78]

One objection against considering the notion of progress as crucial to the ideology of the French Revolution lies in the fact that Rousseau, reputedly "the philosopher of the Revolution," seemingly repudiated the notions of progress current in the decades before the outbreak of the revolution. In his early works *A Discourse on the Arts and Sciences* and *A Discourse on the Origin of Inequality Amongst Men,* Rousseau argued that the vaunted achievements of modern civilization were attained at the cost of increased misery, corruption, and anxiety for the masses of men. Progress thus was no more than a cruel joke enjoyed at the expense of the people. In the *Social Contract,* however, Rousseau, while not renouncing his criticism of the luxurious frivolity of his time, offers a revised estimate of the moral potential of human society: "This passage from the state of nature to the civil state produces a very remarkable change in man by substituting justice for instinct in his conduct and by giving his actions the morality they lacked before. It is only then with the voice of duty succeeding to physical impulse and the law of appetite that man, who until then only considered himself, is forced to act on other principles and to consult his reason before listening to his inclinations." [79] To achieve the kind of society Rousseau has in mind in his *Social Contract* is not easy, though its achievement would constitute an immense progress over existing societies. It is in this sense that people like Robespierre endowed Rousseau's ideas with a revolutionary significance that their author shied away from.

More representative of the general train of Enlightenment thought is Condorcet's *Sketch for a Historical Picture of the Progress of the Human Mind,* composed ironically while the author was in flight from the revolutionary regime he had helped to erect. Towards the end of the book we find a passage that shows how faith in revolutionary progress sometimes serves as faith in God did for the early Christian martyrs: "How consoling for the philosopher who laments the errors, the crimes, the injustices which still pollute the earth and of which he is often the victim [,] is this view of the human race, emancipated from its shackles, released from the empire of fate and from that of the enemies of its progress, advancing with a firm and sure step along the path of truth, virtue and happiness!" [80] In Condorcet's view the violence of the French Revolution resulted from the depths of iniquity and superstition in which France had been mired. This violence, however, merely reflected the birth-pangs of a new society which would allow progress to proceed in a more steady fashion.

Marxism and other modern revolutionary doctrines have taken up the threads of Enlightenment progressivism. To Marx, history was a series of stages which would culminate in the ultimate revolution that would constitute "a leap from the realm of necessity to the realm of freedom." The classless, stateless, communist society of the future is the end-product of historical progress. There man would be liberated from the bondage of exploitation and the despair of alienation. "He would consequently be emancipated from the twin tyranny of need and specialization, from his age-old imprisonment in a life of labor and from the various enslaving forms of division of labor inherent in that life. The radically new mode of production coming in post-history would be the free creativity of individuals producing in cooperative association." [81] Marx felt that proving the necessity of this direction of progress was his unique achievement. Others had demonstrated the economic nature of classes and documented the class struggle. He alone, however, had shown that classes were a transient historical phenomenon related to specific phases in the development of technology and that the class struggle would lead to the dictatorship of the proletariat, which in turn would be a transitional link to the classless society.[82]

Utopia

The concept of utopia used in this study [83] falls somewhere between Mannheim's broad idea of any coherent mental complex that serves to break down the existing order and the specific literary genre that describes an ideal and perfect society in substantial detail. Within these limits two sorts of utopia can be distinguished: one of these may be found in revolutionary ideologies, while the other serves purposes of a nonrevolutionary nature. Works of this latter type, which have been called "classic utopias" [84] by Judith Shklar and "utopias of escape" [85] by Lewis Mumford, are works of imagination written to entertain, edify, or perhaps to embarrass the educated elites of early modern Europe. A utopia of this sort offers "escape or compensation; it seeks an immediate release from the difficulties or frustrations of our lot." [86] Accordingly it is almost completely wanting in " 'activism' or revolutionary optimism or future-directed hope. . . ." [87]

In contrast to classic utopias or utopias of escape are "utopias of reconstruction," which involve a "vision of a reconstructed environment which is better adapted to the nature and aims of the human beings who dwell within it than the actual one; and not merely adapted to their actual nature, but better fitted to their possible developments." [88] The switch from classic utopias to utopias of reconstruction was instrumental in the development of modern revolutionary ideologies. In fact, the decline of the classic utopia "did not mark the end of hope; on the contrary, it coincided with the birth of historical optimism." [89] Though the utopia of reconstruction may be reformist rather than revolutionary, its "action-relatedness" is what makes it suitable for a place in revolutionary thought. While Karl Marx applied the pejorative "utopian" to hopes that a detailed blueprint of the new society would win the immediate rational assent of the ruling classes, we have just seen that his own sketchy views of the future communist society must be ranked as a "utopia of reconstruction." [90]

The level of explicit utopianism amongst revolutionary ideologies varies from almost zero to very considerable. Several more or less obvious points should clarify this. (1) One difference between a more radical and a less radical revolutionary ideology may be the former's higher degree of utopianism. This simply means that the highly utopian ideology will be highly radical because the utopia's perfected social organization is likely to require profound changes in the stratification systems of the existing society. (2) Highly utopian ideologies emerge during the course of revolutions and cause a breach amongst the various groups of revolutionaries. This is one of the differences between the ultrarevolutionary factions and the radicals discussed in Chapter V. (3) As not all utopias are revolutionary, not all revolutionary ideologies are utopian. This will appear paradoxical only to those who follow Mannheim and define utopia loosely and by essentially functional criteria. Though in one sense all political theory is "utopian" insofar as it seeks to establish the "good society" on the most "harmonious" terms,[91] it is better to rely on a narrower notion of utopianism such as social perfectionism, which according to Ralf Dahrendorf holds that "conflict over values or institutional arrangements is either impossible or simply unnecessary. Utopias are perfect—be it perfectly agreeable or perfectly disagreeable —and consequently there is nothing to quarrel about." [92] Accordingly, certain revolutionary ideologies fail the test of utopianism, because although they foresee categorical improvements to be made and believe in progress, they do not envisage the immediate or eventual attainment of perfect social harmony.

Thus, we cannot properly describe the ideology of Cromwellians or even the Levellers as utopian.[93] In fact, many moderates and even some radicals profess ideologies that are essentially nonutopian. However, another way of stating our earlier contention that the more modern revolutions are more radical than the earlier ones is to state that their ideologies are more utopian than their predecessors. Ideas that made Winstanley appear exotic in 1650's or Babeuf bizarre in the 1790's are commonplace assumptions of some twentieth-century revolutionary ideologies. Part of this may be explained by the industrial revolution itself and the potential of modern industrial societies. Herbert Marcuse may represent the attitude of many modern revolutionaries when he complains that "what is denounced as 'utopian' is no longer that which has 'no place' and cannot have any place in the historical universe, but rather that which is blocked from coming about by the power of the established societies." [94]

Nationalism

In Chapters I and IV we associated the development of nationalism with the fundamental causes of revolution and gave examples from the English, French, and other revolutions of how nationalist themes were interwoven with the rejection of the existing social and political order. Though nationalism can play an important part in revolutionary ideologies, it itself is not an ideology. According to Carl J. Friedrich, nationalism is "primarily a sentiment or body of feelings associated with the sense of self-identity of particular nations. It is typically devoid of any specific notions concerning the political or social order as such, except to insist that the order should be in keeping with 'national traditions.' This term is usually so vague as to have no specific institutional content, until converted into a specific ideology." [95] Nationalism is simply too diffuse to qualify as an ideology and is found associated with a wide variety of ideological standpoints. In the last century liberalism was often the ideological complement of nationalist movements; in the present century socialism (in a wide variety of expressions) has taken its place, with a brief flurry of fascistic movements in the interwar period.

Thus, the often-heard remark that this or that political movement is nationalist tells us rather little about it. If a revolutionary movement is nationalist, it must be other things in addition and these may be of the highest interest. We have already found that whether nationalism becomes revolutionary depends largely on the structure of the existing society. If the barriers of class or caste, religion or community interfere with that sense of oneness we associate with nationalism, the nationalist elite will tend to become radicalized. Their nationalism makes them revolutionaries. But it does not always have to be this way. A group may be revolutionary and internationalist, and yet realize that a purely internationalist ideology is ineffectual in the given milieu. This is one difference between the Marxism of Marx and Lenin's transformation of it. Marx had put the case rather strongly in the *Communist Manifesto:* "The workingmen have no country. We cannot take from them what they have not got." [96] He further went on to suggest that economic interdependence fostered by the bourgeoisie was effacing national differences and that "the supremacy of the proletariat will cause them to vanish still faster." [97] Marx's strict internationalism was also at issue in his quarrel with the more nationalistic anarchist leader Bakunin. Clearly Marx's underestimation of the force of nationalism is one of the weakest points of this thought.

Operating in the multinational Russian Empire, Lenin was forced to come to terms with a variety of resurgent nationalisms. This is why in 1913 he commissioned a young Georgian, known as Stalin, to prepare a detailed report on the "national question." [98] The Bolshevik position became one of support of the "right of nations to self-determination." Though after 1917 this was observed mostly in the breach, it made Marxism-Leninism far more sensitive to the forces of nationalism than Marx had been. Lenin gave nationalism a sort of revolutionary respectability it had previously lacked. In fact, even "bourgeois nationalism" was to be supported if it was truly aimed against Western imperialism.

This rehabilitation of nationalism has been carried still further in China. In an important ideological statement of 1940, "On New Democracy," Mao Tse-tung expressed attitudes that have long survived the "new-democratic" formula of a broad class alliance in the "antifeudal, antiimperialist" (but pre-socialist) "democratic" revolution. While acknowledging that China still had much to learn from "progressive" countries, he warned against uncritical borrowings:

> So-called "wholesale Westernization" is a mistaken viewpoint. China has suffered a great deal in the past from the formalist absorption of foreign things. Likewise, in applying Marxism to China, Chinese Communists must fully and properly unite the universal truth of Marxism with the specific practice of the Chinese revolution; that is to say, the truth of Marxism must be integrated with the characteristics of the nation and given definite national form before it can be useful. . . . China's culture should have its own form, namely, a national form.[99]

There is in Mao's statement something more than a mere recognition of the near-truism that one must always take specific conditions into account. A definite defensive posture emerges regarding Chinese culture, which has been denigrated not only by the imperialists but also by those Chinese, Marxist as well as non-Marxist, who see national salvation only in unqualified Westernization. Though developments since 1940 have reinforced the stress on Chinese nationalism, it is nationalism interpreted and applied in a particular way.

Because of the ubiquity and strength of nationalist sentiment in recent times, it is hard to see how revolutionary ideologies (or for that matter, counterrevolutionary ideologies) can avoid being impregnated with nationalistic ideas.[100] What we want to know about, therefore, is how nationalism becomes fused or confused with Marxism or Marxism-Leninism, Jacobinism (France, Mexico), and other doctrines in various contexts. If everybody is somehow something of a nationalist, we have to go beyond nationalism to learn what makes them different. Three questions will help to do this.

The first question concerns the relation between nationalism and internationalism (or supranationalism) in revolutionary ideology. In Chapter III, although we questioned the theses of a general revolutionary crisis in the seventeenth century and of a democratic or "Atlantic" revolution in the eighteenth century, we found that the major revolutions tend to develop what we might call "world-revolutionary" tendencies or what Hans Morgenthau calls "nationalistic universalism." [101] There were ideological strains in the English Revolution that called for an anti-Catholic and antimonarchist crusade in Europe; and radicals in the great French Revolution thought to carry the blessings of the revolution throughout Europe and the world. Even in the French Revolution of 1848, one of the major issues dividing moderates and radicals was the latter's hankering for a war of liberation to free Poland.

For Lenin, too, nationalism was never an end in itself. As he put it in a draft report on nationalism and colonialism for the Second Comintern Congress, "Proletarian internationalism demands, first, that the interests of the proletarian struggle in one country be subordinated to the interests of that struggle on a world scale, and, second, that a nation which is achieving victory over the bourgeoisie be able and willing to make the greatest national sacrifices for the sake of overthrowing international capital." [102] Similarly Mao has repeatedly emphasized that the Chinese Revolution is only a part, however important, of a much broader movement. Even in "On New Democracy," with its strong nationalism, he points out with pride that "the Chinese revolution has become an important part of the world revolution." [103] The Cuban Revolution, with its strong nationalism and initially low ideological level, came to advance claims to be a model for Latin America as its ideology began to take a more coherent form. In short, there need be no immediate contradiction between nationalism and revolutionary internationalism in revolutionary ideology.

Another question of utmost importance concerns whom the revolutionary ideology includes and excludes as members of the nation. We have seen, for example, the exclusion of the Norman aristocracy in the

English Revolution and the Frankish nobility in the French Revolution. In ideologies deriving from Marxism various permutations are seen, and the list of included and excluded can vary according to the precise strategic situation. The big bourgeoisie with foreign connections is first to be excluded, with other groups following behind. Exclusion does not necessarily mean the death, imprisonment, or exile of the groups in question, but rather revocation of their membership in the nation *as a class*. Ultimately the "socialist" nation should comprise no more than workers, peasants, and the intelligentsia—under "communism" even these categories will lose their signification. The progressively narrower redefinition of the nation can be gradual as was the case in China.

In 1939 Mao drew up a balance sheet of Chinese classes according to whether they were "targets" or "motive forces" of the revolution. Chief among its targets was the landlord class, followed closely by the "big bourgeoisie of a comprador character," which "directly serves the capitalists of the imperialist countries and is fed by them. . . ." [104] These two groups were definitively excluded from membership in the Chinese nation.[105] Next came the "national bourgeoisie," which has a kind of split personality oriented sometimes "above" toward the big bourgeoisie and sometimes "below" toward the revolutionary forces. In 1939 Mao considered the national bourgeoisie "a comparatively good ally of ours." (In the 1950's this was to change.) Next in line came various nonpeasant segments of the petty bourgeoisie: intellectuals and students, small merchants, artisans, and professional people. Though these groups seemed good recruits to the revolution, the bourgeois inclinations of some of them demanded hard organizational and propagandistic work to keep them loyal to the cause. The peasants themselves were divided in Leninist fashion into rich, middle, and poor peasants. An important Maoist variation was his fairly high estimate of the revolutionary potential of the rich peasants. He also went beyond Lenin's views on the poor peasants by describing them as "the biggest motive force of the Chinese Revolution, and by nature the most reliable ally of the proletariat and the main contingent of China's revolutionary forces." [106] Although the proletariat is the class "with the highest political consciousness and sense of organization," [107] it has great need of allies from other groups and strata. Finally come the "vagrants" or *lumpenproletariat,* which can act for or against the revolution and therefore require strict supervision to prevent their wandering from the revolutionary path.

Thus, revolutionary ideologies involve nationalism, but membership in the nation is often defined in ideological terms. So we can legitimately ask "nationalism for whom?" The answers to this question are quite variable. On the one hand, Castroism has been considered as more extreme than Chinese communism on the grounds of its rapid and strong measures to eliminate the national bourgeoisie as a class.[108] On the other hand, the purportedly revolutionary ideologies of African socialism tend to embrace nearly all socioeconomic categories of the population within the nation. "Class struggle" is transposed to the stage of international politics.

A final question regarding nationalism and revolutionary ideology involves the closeness of the goal of nation building itself. If the nation is old and established, nationalism itself cannot account for the radicalism of the revolutionary ideology. It is more a question of extending nationalism or what E. H. Carr called the "socialization of the nation." Other sources of discontent such as class struggle or alienation of the intellectuals are more important in the rise of revolutionary ideologies than nationalism. If the nation is more a dream than a reality, the revolutionary ideology will tend to include drastic and radical measures to hasten its realization. In this context nationalism and utopianism (in the sense we have used the latter) become different aspects of one and the same phenomenon.

CONCLUSION

In this chapter we have surveyed several concepts of ideology and tried to understand how ideology can operate in the revolutionary process. While "intellectualist" theories of history are wrong to see the conflict of ideas as the main force of all politics, we have resisted the "reductionist" tendencies of economic, sociological, or power determinism to restrict ideology to an insignificant role in revolution. While ideology is not the whole of revolution, it is a characteristic and partly autonomous part of it. This part naturally differs in various revolutions. In some, preformed ideology is enormously influential, while in others *ad hoc* ideology is paramount. In some revolutions the gap between esoteric and exoteric ideology is so wide as to make us doubt the sincerity of the revolutionary elite; in others the views of leaders and followers are fairly close. We must also be aware that in the ideologically charged atmosphere of revolution many forms of intergroup and interpersonal conflict take on an ideological covering. But even in this context ideological disputes that originated from personal or power conflicts (e.g., the Stalin-Trotsky conflict) tend to develop a dynamic of their own. Trotskyism and Stalinism survived their founders.

From a structural perspective we have seen that a revolutionary ideology must have a critical aspect, an affirmative aspect, and perhaps a strategic aspect. While revolutionary ideologies appeal to a wide variety of themes and principles, we suggested that some notion of progress is essential to provide the affirmation that things will be *better* after the revolution. Utopia also holds out the possibility of improvement, but highlights the critical aspect, by demonstrating the gap between what is, and what could and ought to be. Nationalism has become an increasingly important component of modern revolutionary ideologies, though some varieties of Marxism and anarchism can play it down considerably.

While ideology operates directly when its devotees follow its prescriptions with impressive, if imperfect, fidelity, it also works in a more oblique way. An ideology, we have suggested, is not just a system of abstract beliefs to be donned and doffed in the light of pure reason. The frequent analogies to myth and religious commitment, though sometimes misleading, reveal that the true believer in an ideology invests a good portion of his emotional energies in it. The teachings of the ideology become a part of himself and he tends to view the world through the prism it provides. Perceptions are structured according to the basic orienting themes of the ideology: certain messages and environmental stimuli may make an extraordinary impact, while others, seemingly just as important, are screened out. Revolutions manifest all the features of ideological politics in their purest and most extreme form.

NOTES

[1] Karl Marx and Friedrich Engels, *The German Ideology* (New York: International Publishers, 1960), p. 14.

[2] *Ibid.*, p. 40.

[3] *Ibid.*, p. 20.

[4] Letter to C. Schmidt, *Selected Works*, Vol. II (Moscow: Foreign Languages Publishing House, 1958), p. 486.

[5] George Plekhanov, *Fundamental Problems of Marxism* (New York: International Publishers, 1969), p. 80.

[6] *Ibid.*, p. 83.

[7] *German Ideology*, p. 40.

[8] Thucydides, *Peloponnesian War*, p. 104.

[9] *Ibid.*

[10] Hans J. Morgenthau, *Politics Among Nations*, 3rd ed. (New York: Alfred A. Knopf, 1960), pp. 87–88.

[11] *Ibid.*, p. 88.

[12] *Ibid.*

[13] Norberto Bobbio, *Saggi sulla scienza politica in Italia* (Bari: Laterza, 1969), p. 96.

[14] *Ibid.*, p. 99.

[15] *Ibid.* Pareto largely anticipated the concept of ideology associated with certain logical positivist theorists. The sociologist Geiger writes that "to the extent that statements do not reveal that they only pertain (reflectively) to the *vital relationship of a participant to*

an object, but are so phrased as to appear *as factual statements of an observer about* an object—to this extent they are ideological." Theodore Geiger, *On Social Order and Mass Society* (Chicago: University of Chicago Press, 1969), p. 144. See also Gustav Bergmann, "Ideology," in *The Metaphysics of Logical Positivism* (Madison: University of Wisconsin Press, 1967), pp. 300–25.

[16] Karl Mannheim, *Ideology and Utopia* (New York: Harcourt, Brace, & Co., n.d.), p. 194.

[17] *Ibid.*, p. 97.

[18] *Ibid.*, p. 55.

[19] *Ibid.*

[20] *Ibid.*, p. 203.

[21] *Ibid.*, p. 230. In another work, Mannheim clarifies his distinction between conservative "ideology" and simple "traditionalism." The latter is a "general psychological attitude which expresses itself in different individuals as a tendency to cling to the past and a fear of innovation," whereas conservatism proper is "conscious and reflective from the first. . . ." What has happened since the French Revolution is that "conservatism takes a particular historical form of traditionalism and develops it to its logical conclusions." *Essays on Sociology and Social Psychology* (London: Routledge & Kegan Paul, 1959), p. 99ff.

[22] *Ideology and Utopia,* p. 40.

[23] *Ibid.*, pp. 195–96.

[24] *Ibid.*, p. 196.

[25] *Ibid.*, p. 203.

[26] *Ibid.*, p. 230.

[27] *Ibid.*, p. 204. Since English society moved in directions hardly compatible with Sir Thomas More's *Utopia*, the latter would seem relegated to the scrapheap of ideologies, or at least to the list of conservative "counterutopias."

[28] See especially Chiam Waxman, ed., *The End of Ideology Debate* (New York: Simon & Schuster, 1969). For an analysis that makes distinctions between the structural and functional elements of ideology similar to those made below, see Willard A. Mullins, "On the Concept of Ideology in Political Science," *The American Political Science Review*, LXVI (June, 1972), 498–510.

[29] Dante Germino, *Beyond Ideology: The Revival of Political Theory* (New York: Harper & Row, 1968), p. 7.

[30] *Ibid.*, p. 51.

[31] See again Mullins, "The Concept of Ideology," pp. 507–10.

[32] Mircea Eliade, *Myth and Reality* (New York: Harper Torchbooks, 1968), pp. 5–6.

[33] *Ibid.*, p. 6.

[34] In certain contexts, as in millenarian movements, reinterpretations of myths can play a more dynamic role.

[35] Mircea Eliade, *Myths, Dreams, and Mysteries* (New York: Harper Torchbooks, 1967), p. 25.

[36] *Ibid.*

[37] Norman Cohn, *Pursuit of the Millennium* (New York: Oxford University Press, 1970), p. 288.

[38] In this connection the final sentences of Leon Trotsky's *Literature and Revolution* are of some interest: "Man will become immeasurably stronger, wiser and subtler; his body will become more harmonized, his movements more rhythmic, his voice more musical. The forms of life will become dynamically dramatic. The average human type will rise to the heights of an Aristotle, a Goethe, or a Marx. And above this ridge new peaks will rise." (Ann Arbor: University of Michigan Press, 1960), p. 256.

[39] R. M. MacIver, *The Web of Government* (New York: Macmillan, 1963), p. 4.

[40] *Ibid.*, p. 5.

[41] Georges Sorel, *Reflections on Violence* (Glencoe, Ill.: The Free Press, 1950), p. 57.

[42] *Ibid.*, p. 144.

[43] Ben Halpern, "Myth and Ideology in Modern Usage," *History and Theory*, I, No. 2, (1961), p. 140.

[44] Lyford P. Edwards, *The Natural History of Revolution* (Chicago: University of Chicago Press, 1970), p. 90.

[45] *Ibid.*, p. 91.

[46] *Ibid.*, p. 92.

[47] Carl J. Friedrich, *Man and His Government* (New York: McGraw-Hill, 1963), p. 98.

[48] Eliade, *Mysteries*, p. 41.

[49] A basically structural notion of ideology might stress "a philosophy of history, a view of man's present place in it, some estimate of probable lines of future development, and a set of prescriptions regarding how to hasten, retard, and/or modify that developmental direction." Joseph La Palombara, "The End of Ideology: A Dissent and Interpretation," in Waxman, *End of Ideology*, p. 320. A functionalist emphasis would hold that "In its most active form, the insistence that knowledge of society must act as an instrument of social change is known by the term 'ideology.' An ideology provides its possessor with self-justification and with claims to action. It is something to believe in and to give orientation to one's life and experience. Ideology has a function analogous to religious commitment. The commitment effects a transformation in the life of the individual and as a consequence in the lives of those about him." Raymond E. Ries, "Social Science and Ideology," in *ibid.*, 283.

[50] See note 17 in Chapter I.

[51] C. B. MacPherson, *The Political Theory of Possessive Individualism* (Oxford: Oxford University Press, 1964), p. 100.

[52] Eduard Bernstein, *Cromwell and Communism* (New York: Schocken Books, 1963), p. 131.

[53] V. I. Lenin, *Left-wing Communism: An Infantile Disorder* (New York: International Publishers, 1940), pp. 76–77.

[54] *Ibid.*, p. 29.

[55] See Franz Schurmann, *Ideology and Organization in Communist China* (Berkeley: University of California Press, 1971), Chap. I; and James C. Hsiung, *Ideology and Practice* (New York: Praeger, 1970), Chaps. 6 and 7, for analysis of the Chinese equivalents of theory, thought, and related terms.

[56] Schurmann, *Ideology and Organization*, p. 23.

[57] *Ibid.*, p. 38.

[58] Hsiung, *Ideology and Practice*, p. 284.

[59] Theodore Draper, *Castroism: Theory and Practice* (New York: Praeger, 1965), p. 58.

[60] See Chapter VIII on the concept of revolutionary ideologists.

[61] Andrés Suarez, *Cuba: Castroism and Communism, 1956–1966* (Cambridge, Mass.: M.I.T. Press, 1969), p. 39.

[62] Ramon E. Ruiz, *Cuba: The Making of a Revolution* (New York: W. W. Norton, 1970), pp. 59–60.

[63] Vilfredo Pareto, *I sistemi socialisti* (Turin: U.T.E.T., 1963), p. 476.

[64] *Ibid.*

[65] Hermann Rauschning, *The Revolution of Nihilism* (New York: Alliance Book Corp., 1940), p. 19.

[66] *Ibid.*

[67] Gabriel Almond, *The Appeals of Communism* (Princeton: Princeton University Press, 1954), pp. 65–66.

[68] *Ibid.*, p. 66.

[69] The tendency after the death of Stalin, and more so with the outbreak of the Sino-Soviet dispute, is to increasingly differentiate communist parties: the exoteric ideology is being strengthened at the expense of the esoteric ideology.

[70] Almond, *Appeals*, p. 67.

[71] Mircea Eliade, *Cosmos and History: The Myth of the Eternal Return* (New York: Harper Torchbooks, 1959).

[72] *Ibid.*, p. 142.

[73] Hannah Arendt, *On Revolution* (New York: Viking Press, 1963), p. 21.

[74] John Dewey, "Progress," in *Characters and Events*, Vol. II (New York: Henry Holt & Co., 1929), p. 821.

[75] While a revolutionary ideology must entail some notion of progress or historical improvement, "evolutionary" theories of progress very often condemn revolution as a counterproductive effort to interfere with a "natural" process that operates best, or at all, only when left undisturbed. With Herbert Spencer, not only revolution, but even mild social reforms, are apt to derail the locomotive of progress. *The Man Versus the State* (Baltimore: Penguin Books, 1969).

[76] J. B. Bury, *The Idea of Progress* (New York: Dover Books, 1955), p. 318.

[77] Christopher Dawson, *Progress and Religion* (New York: Image Books, 1960).

[78] Robert K. Merton, *Science, Technology and Society in Seventeenth-Century England* (New York: Harper Torchbooks, 1970), pp. 226–27.

[79] Jean-Jacques Rousseau, *Du Contrat Social* (Paris: Garnier, 1962), pp. 246–47.

[80] Antoine-Nicholas de Condorcet, *Sketch for a Historical Picture of the Progress of the Human Mind* (London: Weidenfield & Nicolson, 1955), p. 201.

[81] Robert Tucker, *The Marxian Revolutionary Idea* (New York: W. W. Norton, 1969), p. 220.

[82] Letter to J. Weydemeyer, in *Selected Works*, Vol. II, p. 452.

[83] In Chapter II we consider utopia as "the notion of a future or possible society whose organization is so perfected that injustice, social conflict, misery, superstition, criminality, and oppression have been forever eliminated."

[84] Judith N. Shklar, "The Political Theory of Utopia: From Melancholy to Nostalgia," in *Utopias and Utopian Thought*, ed. Frank Manuel (Boston: Beacon Press, 1967).

[85] Lewis Mumford, *The Story of Utopias* (New York: Viking Press, 1971).

[86] *Ibid.*, p. 15.

[87] Shklar, "Political Theory of Utopia," p. 106.

[88] Mumford, *Story*, p. 21.

[89] Shklar, "Political Theory of Utopia," p. 107.

[90] Marx refrained from much explicit description of future communism for two reasons: (1) he thought it unscientific to relate the details of a society that would emerge only after the cataclysmic shake-up of the revolution; (2) he considered his main personal mission rather to lay bare the self-destructive dynamic of capitalism in order to facilitate the coming of the proletarian revolution.

[91] For a defense of utopianism in a rather broad sense, see George Kateb, *Utopia and its Enemies* (New York: Schocken Books, 1972).

[92] Ralf Dahrendorf, *Essays in the Theory of Society* (Stanford: Stanford University Press, 1968), p. 109.

[93] With the former it is probably the residual effect of Calvinism with its emphasis on human sinfulness and corruption that impeded the development of utopianism. The

raw human material of society will not admit of social perfectionism. See R. H. Tawney, *Religion and the Rise of Capitalism*, Chap. IV.

[94] Herbert Marcuse, *An Essay on Liberation* (Boston: Beacon Press, 1969), pp. 3–4. In Mannheimian terms, Marcuse envisages the transformation of "absolute utopias" into "relative utopias."

[95] Friedrich, *Man and His Government*, p. 90.

[96] Karl Marx and Friedrich Engels, "The Communist Manifesto," in *Basic Writings on Politics and Philosophy*,   ed. L. S. Feuer (New York: Garden City, N.Y.: Anchor Books, 1959), p. 26.

[97] *Ibid.*

[98] Bruce Franklin, ed., *The Essential Stalin* (Garden City, N.Y.: Anchor Books, 1972), pp. 59–84.

[99] Mao Tse-tung, "On New Democracy," in *Selected Works*, Vol. III (New York: International Publishers, 1954), p. 154.

[100] New Left and neoanarchist thought is a possible exception, but these movements have not registered great success in attaining mass support.

[101] "For the claim to universality which inspires the moral code of one particular group is incompatible with the identical claim of another group; the world has room for only one, and the other must yield or be destroyed. Thus, carrying their ideals before them, the nationalistic masses of our time meet in the international arena, each group convinced that it executes the mandate of history. . . ." *Politics Among Nations*, p. 259.

[102] V. I. Lenin, *On Politics and Revolution* (New York: Pegasus Books, 1968), p. 318.

[103] Mao Tse-tung, "On New Democracy," p. 115.

[104] Mao Tse-tung, "The Chinese Revolution and the Chinese Communist Party," in *Selected Works*, Vol. III, pp. 88–89.

[105] Because of the "mentalist" character of Chinese communism, it is possible for individual members of an "enemy" class to confess their sins and be reeducated as "useful" members of the new society.

[106] Mao Tse-tung, "Chinese Revolution," p. 93.

[107] *Ibid.*, p. 95.

[108] Draper, *Castroism*, p. 88.

VII

THE PROTAGONISTS OF REVOLUTION

IN the broadest sense the protagonists of revolution are to be found in the categories of classes (or strata), elites, crowds, and individuals (top leaders). In the following discussion it must be borne in mind that ours is a study of revolutions and not so much of revolutionary movements or revolutionists *per se*. Our major concern thus is with the great, not-so-great, and even abortive revolutions. Consideration of revolutionary movements and self-professed revolutionaries in nonrevolutionary settings is of interest to us only insofar as information about them illuminates our specific interests.

CLASSES

Workers and Peasants

Up to now our conclusions regarding the role of entire classes and of class struggle in revolution have been somewhat guarded and skeptical. We have (1) criticized the use of the term "class" when noneconomic modes of stratification are involved; (2) emphasized the complexities of the cleavage patterns that give rise to revolutions; (3) found that the role of classes varies from revolution to revolution and that of class struggle, from phase to phase in the revolution; and (4) agreed with others that the attitude of peasants is a crucially important variable in the outcome of revolutions. It is time to probe some of the complexities of these issues a little deeper.

Alexis de Tocqueville was a "participant-observer" of the French Revolution of 1848. Though his *Recollections* are basically hostile to the revolution, his analysis of its protagonists has often been cited because of striking resemblances to Marx's views on the same revolution.[1] There is a strong temptation to infer from this convergence of views that their substance is correct and perhaps valid for other revolutions as well. Tocqueville sets out by dispelling any idea that conspiracy played a major role in the collapse of the French monarchy in February, 1848. Revolutions of this type, which are "accomplished by means of popular uprisings," [2] are "spontaneous" outcomes of long and deeply germinating factors. The self-proclaimed originators and leaders of insurrection "originate and lead nothing; their only merit is identical with that of the adventurers who discovered most of the unknown countries. They simply have the courage to go straight before them as long as the wind impels them." [3]

The salient character of this revolution was that it constituted "the revolt of one whole section of the population against another." [4] According to French tradition Tocqueville designated the main protagonists as the people and the bourgeoisie (i.e., the components of the old Third Estate before 1789). In other revolutions, such as those of 1789 and 1830, the bourgeoisie both directed and profited from the action of the popular masses. The February Revolution of 1848 was different, for it "seemed to be made entirely outside the bourgeoisie and against it." [5] Rather it gave "omnipotence . . . to the people properly so-called—that is to say, the classes who work with their hands—over all others." [6] This is what gave the revolution a social character that contrasted sharply with the essentially political aims of its predecessors: it aimed instead at "altering the order of society." [7] It represented "a struggle of class against class, a sort of Servile War," [8] because the "workmen" sought to break out of the confinements of their existing mode of life and move towards what to Tocqueville seemed a wholly chimerical realm of universal prosperity and absolute justice. He located the source of these delusions in the "Socialistic theories" which he considered the "philosophy of the Revolution of February" and which "later kindled genuine passion, embittered jealousy, and ended by stirring up war between the classes." [9]

A brief look at the shortcomings of Tocqueville's interpretation of the French Revolution of 1848 may afford us some broader insights about the role of entire classes in revolution. To begin with, it seems doubtful that the trends that emerged by the late spring of 1848 were already dominant in February. We have suggested above that the brief civil war of the June days represents a successful attempt to curtail and even to reverse the hypertrophy of the revolution (Chapter V). Some months were required for the various strands of the revolution to become fully polarized. Furthermore, the term "socialism" was too effervescent to encapsulate the various strains of revolutionary thought in

1848. Similarly the elements on either side of the June barricades were too heterogeneous to be considered monolithic class blocs. Even in 1848 *le peuple* closely resembled the old *sans-culotte* artisans, day laborers, and shopkeepers more than a modern industrial proletariat. This is not to deny that the moderate "men of order" came heavily from the higher social categories or that the radicals' mass support was strong among "the classes that work with their hands." But the main weakness of Tocqueville's analysis is his deemphasis of the role of leadership both during the outbreak of the revolution and its sequel. Various oppositionist circles amongst the intelligentsia had paved the way for the revolution and gave it some coherence when the monarchy fell. A participant-observer, in other words, is not always best placed to observe the nuances and complexities that make revolutions so difficult to understand. He is liable to take crowds for classes and thereby to ignore the other protagonists of revolution.

Tocqueville observed an urban-centered revolution, whose radical aspects met with a hostile reception in the countryside. This situation in one way, as the Chinese Revolution in another, raises the question of the role of the peasantry in revolution. We have already objected that the phrase "peasant revolution" (and more ambiguously "agrarian revolution") obscures as much as it reveals in certain contexts. Nevertheless, a recent study challenges Chalmers Johnson's thesis that nationalism spurred by the "Anti-Japanese War" of 1937–45 is the main source of lingering peasant support for the Chinese communists.[10] Though not denying the force of nationalism, Mark Seldon's study of Yenan from the late 1920's through the early 1940's tries to demonstrate that the ultimate communist victory resulted from a highly distinctive peasant revolutionary movement. His main thesis is that a land or agrarian "revolution" sponsored by the communists was the basis for developments. This "revolution" consisted of a considerable land reform that eliminated landlordism, limited rich (by Chinese standards) peasants' holdings, and increased those of middle and poor peasants. Before the communists' intervention in the late 1920's, peasant social protest was vented through banditry and self-help cooperative movements.

Peasant society in Yenan and throughout Shensi province (as well as elsewhere in China) was in a state of near disorganization when the communists looked to the countryside after their defeat in the cities in 1927. It was also to this area that the decimated communist forces repaired after the fabled Long March from the south of China in 1934–35. In the early years, communist successes in peasant mobilization were somewhat erratic, though an infrastructure of guerrilla operations was set up that would be important later on. However, according to Seldon it was in the mid-1930's that the revolutionary movement really "took off":

> The communists moved swiftly to channel energies unleashed in the upheaval by coordinating it closely with drives for peasant membership and military recruitment and the establishment of local organs of government. In 1935 and 1936 violent revolution that combined a millennial vision of equality and prosperity with concrete measures to destroy the old order quickly served to swell the ranks of the party and army. Poor peasant youth, the most explosive element in the land revolution, not only supplied the manpower for local guerrilla and paramilitary units but began to assume leadership positions in the communist-sponsored mass organizations, party branches, and local government.[11]

Thus, the communists got an original foothold amongst the peasants by delivering land. They used this foothold to recruit and train new forces. All the while they stressed the concrete problems of peasant life rather than the vagaries of Marxism-Leninism. When war came they were in a good position to win the reputation of being the best defenders of China's sovereignty and pride—but the spadework had been done during the previous decade.

Indeed, when the war came they had to tone down some of the revolutionary policies that Seldon finds so popular with the peasants. Otherwise they would have imperiled the precarious alliance or "popular front" with Chiang and the Nationalists. However, as the military situation improved and the popular front disintegrated, the communists—especially after 1942—launched into more radical policies once again. Looking back, Seldon concludes that the Chinese communists "were not simply agrarian reformers. However, the ability of these revolutionaries to respond boldly and effectively to war-aggravated problems of rural society lies at the heart of their immense popular success in the Yenan period. Their appeal to the peasant was rooted in an effective program of administration and reform. The new nationalism in the countryside was linked to the revitalization of the social and economic life of the village."[12]

Was the Chinese Communist Revolution essentially a peasant revolution? The answer is more complex than the above sort of interpretation reveals, since Seldon himself admits that the Yenan model does not hold for all of China and that communist successes elsewhere must be otherwise explained. Even more problematic are the broad inferences drawn from the fact of peasant mobilization and participation. There is a rush to conclude that here indeed was a true peasant revolution. But it must first of all be remembered that a land reform, even if extensive, is not tantamount to revolution, and sometimes is quite the contrary. To speak of it as a land revolution begs more than a few questions. Peasants will often support a land reform, but do they support what the French call the *arrière-pensées*—in this case the covert ideological-political objectives—of the nonpeasant dispensers of the reform? Peasants have been swindled by city slickers for centuries, and one has the suspicion that movements and governments that invoke their name so often may be doing something similar. For the school of thought represented by Seldon, the original peasant support for land and other reforms created a moral capital that carried over into the more severe land reforms of the late 1940's, the collectivization of the 1950's, the Great Leap Forward of 1958, and indeed the Cultural Revolution of 1966–69.

Not only does this approach underestimate the impact of the war, it also minimizes the role of terrorism and manipulation —"rectification" or, less politely, "brainwashing"—that accompanied transitional phases of the Chinese Revolution. The "Yenan Way" was as much a proving ground for methods of political penetration and control as for methods of meeting the needs of the peasantry.[13] To infuse the various forms of peasant revolt characteristic of a disintegrating society with a radical revolutionary content involves ideological and organizational leadership from the outside (i.e., from a revolutionary intelligentsia whose background originally is urban rather than rural). The political power and skills of the leadership group explain at least as much of the recent history of China as does the spontaneous irruption of social and economic forces. As Franz Schurmann points out, "Revolutionary fervor had led to a considerable peasant self-organization during the early days of the soviets, but the phase beginning in 1934 seems to have come 'from the top down.'" [14] More germane to the point at issue is his finding that "by creating a new Communist party and by training a new type of leader, the cadre, the Chinese Communists were finally able to achieve what no state power in Chinese history had been able to do: to create an organization loyal to the state which was also solidly imbedded in the natural village." [15]

This aspect of the Chinese Revolution can be illuminated with the help of William Kornhauser's concept of the mass society.[16] With the disintegration of peasant society in China, some areas were ripe for the growth of a *mass movement*. According to Kornhauser the objectives of a mass movement are "remote and extreme": "they favor activist modes of intervention in the social order; they mobilize uprooted and atomized sections of the population; they lack an internal structure of independent groups (such as regional or functional units with some freedom of action)." [17] However, mass movements are liable to be penetrated, taken over, and reoriented by "totalitarian" groups and movements, which—in contrast to the mass movement—are "highly organized by an elite bent on total power." [18] What vitiates interpretations of the Chinese Revolution as a "peasant revolution" is their gross underestimate of the metamorphosis of the spontaneous peasant movement (where it did exist) when the Communist Party entered the picture. As always, this was somewhat of a two-way relationship: Chinese communism was itself indelibly transformed while it transformed peasant movements.[19] The nature of the resulting political movement eludes those who profess to see only the original mass movement throughout, as well as those preoccupied with an unchanging communist conspiracy. In any case, the history of the Chinese People's Republic bears little resemblance to what (if anything) an unadulterated peasant movement would have achieved.

Though superficial similarities between the Cuban and Chinese revolutions have prompted the false conclusion that Fidel Castro pragmatically made a "Chinese-style" revolution without benefit of Chairman Mao's strategic writings, the Cuban Revolution presents a less troublesome picture than the Chinese on the nature and extent of peasant involvement. The cause of the confusion is that Castro fought a guerrilla war for three years in the remote Sierra Maestra mountains before he entered Havana in January, 1959. This is supposed to exemplify the formula of the "encirclement of the cities." However, the Cuban Revolution is in reality an intermediate type between the Eastern (Chinese) and Western models of revolution. Its retention of certain "Western" features derives mainly from its relatively high level of urbanization, industrialization, and standard of living compared to most Third World countries. The chief deviation from the Eastern prototype is that Castro did not fight a truly protracted civil war that involved large conventional forces as well as small guerrilla units. There was no mass party tightly linked with a mass army in the Chinese or Vietminh manner. The imperialist "enemy" was not a direct party to hostilities. Perhaps most significantly, the Batista regime was not really defeated; it *collapsed* for largely internal reasons, some of which had precious little to do with Castro's and Che Guevara's daring escapades. The nature of Castro's triumph, as well as his early moderation, seem to belong more to the Western than to the Eastern style of revolution.

During the struggle against Batista, Cuban peasants were not the major components of Castro's forces. Nor were they completely responsive to the operations of his guerrillas. They were at the most *benevolently neutral*. "The peasantry never had in its hands any of the levers of command of the revolution, before or after the victory. The revolution was made and always controlled by declassed sons and daughters of the middle class." [20] As peasants did not flock in droves to Castro's banner, his fighting force was infinitesimally small in relation to even the earliest contingents under Mao. Furthermore, "the character of an army is established by its leadership and cadres, which remained almost exclusively middle class throughout, and not by its common soldiers—or every army in the world would similarly be an army of the peasants and proletariat." [21] Though we should not forget the "feedback" effect of the mass upon the elite (there was less of a mass in the Cuban case than in the Chinese), Draper's analysis reinforces our stress on the pivotal role of leadership. Peasant involvement in revolution, perhaps more than that of any other social group, requires a binocular perspective on both elite and mass. If this is done, we can see that even if a revolution is not a peasant revolution because its leaders hail from the middle classes, we should not conclude then that it was a middle-class revolution in the sense of benefiting that class. Quite the contrary; for as Draper points out, "Middle class leaders and leaders of the middle class are not the same thing." [22] All of this should produce a wariness against laying too much emphasis on class analysis in the study of revolutions: a person's middle-class or peasant or proletarian background sometimes is less important than the fact that he is *déclassé* and young.

In general terms, five distinct roles in revolution seem possible for the peasantry: (1) *active or passive hostility,* in which peasants remain resentful or impervious to the appeals of an urban-based revolutionary movement (examples: France in both 1848 and 1871; China, 1911) or in which, somewhat differently, they reject the call to arms of rural-based guerrillas seeking to launch a "peasant" revolution (Guevara's fate in Bolivia, 1967); (2) *benevolent neutrality,* in which the peasants may feed or shelter revolutionaries but do not join the movement *en masse* (Cuba, 1956–59); (3) *independent nonrevolutionary action,* in which the peasants act moderately and seek reforms while a more blatantly revolutionary struggle rages in the cities (certain areas in Mexico after 1910; Central Europe, 1918–19); (4) *independent revolutionary action,* in which the peasants take direct action to make drastic changes in rural society—this action may prove hard to blend with the policies of a concomitant urban movement and a clash is unavoidable (France, 1789; Russia, 1917; Spain, 1936–37); (5) *penetration, takeover, and consolidation of autochthonous peasant movements by outside revolutionary cadres,* especially in the form of a party in which leaders superimpose ideology and organization upon rural protest (China, 1927–49). While these five roles seem to exhaust the possible responses of peasants to revolution in the global society, a closer look at regional diversities in agrarian structure reveals a more differentiated picture, with several subtrends underlying the more general one (e.g., peasant counterrevolution in La Vendée in France).

Several factors influence which of the above roles is prevalent in a given peasantry during revolution. An obvious factor will be the strength of the traditional culture among the peasantry: where the traditional mode of life and thought remains a coherent interpretation of the world for the peasant, he is unlikely to be swayed by the message of revolution. Another factor is rapid change in the land-man ratio, which can be disturbed both by a variety of demographic trends and by the encroachments of big landlords. In parts of Mexico before the Revolution of 1910, "it was not the balance between latifundios and indigenous communities, but the usurpation of those communities by the land-hungry *haciendados* [big landowners] and despoliation of indigenous peasants which set off what may have been one of the bloodiest revolutions of modern history." [23] A third factor is leadership, both that of authentic peasants and that of outsiders. Perhaps a proper balance between these two types of leadership is the best prescription for turning peasant protest into truly revolutionary directions. However, the more purely peasant-based and peasant-led a movement remains, the more likely is it to remain in the confines of revolt: its animus will be to restore, repair, or revenge something rather than to rebuild the foundations of the social and political order

Crisis Strata

In Chapter III we suggested that Sigmund Neumann's concept of "crisis strata" is often a more useful intellectual tool in the study of revolutions than the concepts of class and class struggle. Crisis strata are those groups whose status, economic position, or political role undergoes such a rapid alternation that many members of these groups become susceptible to extremist or revolutionary appeals. Even this formulation may be too crude to capture the complexities of the revolutionary situation. Whole social strata rarely have identical interests and sentiments, and thus divisions within the same broad stratum can often be significant. Rising and declining gentry are both gentry, but their political behavior differed substantially in the English Revolution. The Third Estate included millionaires and paupers in pre-revolutionary France. Even the bourgeoisie at that time was divided into a manufacturing-commercial section and a legal-professional section, whose roles in the revolution differed substantially. The blanket term "working class" has been stretched to include all sorts of queer fish; but the more precise formulations distinguish between the labor aristocracy, the average worker, and the *lumpenproletariat.*

The concept of crisis strata can help us to understand better the precise role of peasants in revolution. First, however, it is necessary to remove some of the ambiguity surrounding the notion of "peasant." According to George Foster:

> When settled rural peoples subject to the jural control of outsiders ex-change a part of what they produce for items they cannot themselves make, in a market setting transcending local transactions, then they are peasants. We see peasants as a peripheral but essential part of civiliza-tions, producing food that makes urban life possible, supporting (and subject to) the specialized classes of the political and religious rulers and the other members of the "Great Tradition," which gives continuity and substance to the sequences of advanced culture, and which lies in con-tradistinction to the "Little Tradition"—which characterizes villagers themselves.[24]

This formulation incorporates several points that have characterized anthropological study of the peasant. A major emphasis of the formu-lation is that peasant societies are part of the higher civilizations and thus that agriculturists who retain tribal organization and live in rela-tive autarchy are *not* peasants. On the other hand, the term "peasant" is withheld from farmers whose market-orientation is so complete as to make them "agricultural entrepreneurs." Though peasants are partially dependent on market exchange, their cultivation is part of a broader "way of life" and is much more than a mere "livelihood." Thus in the typical peasant household (in contrast to capitalist farming) "the objec-tive arithmetical calculation of the highest possible net profit in the given market situation does not determine the whole activity of the farming unit. . . ."[25]

Since a variety of economic roles characterize rural society, dis-agreement is frequent as to which social categories are to be considered as true peasants. Especially troublesome are the landless agricultural la-borers found either on large traditional latifundia and plantations, or on modern large-scale "industrial" farms. While many serfs would qualify also as peasants, those who are bound to the exclusive personal service of the seigneur rather than to the land *per se* probably do not. In modern times the economic differentiation of rural society has given rise to several distinct strata. In contrast to the large landowners at the summit of the rural socioeconomic pyramid and to the landless labor-ers at the base are the peasants, properly speaking (i.e., the rich, poor, and middle peasants). However, H. Alavi warns us that such a termi-nology gives the impression of a simple ranking according to wealth, whereas middle peasants, for example, really "belong to a different sec-tor of the rural economy"[26] vis-à-vis the rich and poor peasants. The so-called rich peasants are in effect *capitalist farmers* who own sizable plots of land and employ significant outside help. The so-called middle peasants are mostly *independent small-holders* who own their own land and only marginally employ labor other than their own family. The so-called poor peasants are *sharecroppers and small tenants* of the big land-owners and (in some views) also the landless laborers who work for landlords or rich peasants. Such categories retain some validity, even though a peasant "may be at one and the same time owner, renter, sharecropper, laborer for his neighbors and seasonal hand on a nearby plantation." [27]

According to Eric Wolf, the "rich peasants" are unlikely to become interested in revolt or revolution because of their essentially satisfactory position in economy and society. On the other hand, poor peasants and many landless laborers are too much under the watchful control and economic dominance of landlords to undertake insurrection. It is thus the middle peasants (and perhaps some poor peasants in remote areas) that will be most active in revolt or revolution. The middle peasants are a *crisis stratum,* for despite and somewhat because of their strong traditionalism, they are "relatively the most vulnerable to economic changes wrought by commercialism." [28] Furthermore, the middle peasants are most subject to influences from the growing urban working class, because some members of their families may have migrated to cities in search of work. H. Alavi agrees that the middle peasants are important in revolution (especially in the early days), but looks to the specific features in each revolutionary context that account for their activism. In Russia, "the main peasant struggle in 1917, as before in 1905–07, was that of the middle peasants against landowners for the cut-off lands and for the abolition of the surviving feudal restrictions." [29] Nevertheless, when Alavi concludes that the important role of the peasantry in the Russian Revolution was essentially "indirect" and that any "alliance" with the Bolsheviks was "from the side of the peasantry, undeclared, unorganized and without a clear direction," [30] he supports our limitations upon the revolutionary proclivities of peasants—even the active crisis strata among them.

In Spain, and particularly southern Spain, before the civil war of the late 1930's, the rural social structure displayed the rather widespread configuration of large landowners, rich peasants employing some labor, middle peasants who owned their farms, poor peasants in the form of sharecroppers and small tenants, and at the bottom landless laborers. In southern Spain, where agrarian revolution characterized the mid-1930's, the group of landless laborers was much larger than elsewhere in Spain and was made up of permanent and day laborers. More so than the middle small-holding peasants and even the sharecropping or tenant poor peasants, the day laborers were a true crisis stratum: "the misery and insecurity of most day laborers in dry-farming regions was so great as to convert them into the only inherently revolutionary group in Spanish rural society." [31] It is thus no surprise that in the first three decades and a half of this century the Anarcho-syndicalists, the most demonstratively revolutionary political formation in modern Spanish history, "tended to achieve their greatest success in regions where day laborers were overwhelmingly predominant. . . ." [32]

With decreasing intensity the rich, middle, and poor peasants had a stake in the existing order. Even sharecroppers and small tenants had something to lose and retained a certain foothold in the rural status hierarchy. The landless laborers, on the other hand, were the first group to feel the effects of the endemic weaknesses and cyclical fluctuations of agriculture in Spain. There was, for example, a vicious cycle of excessive population growth and rural unemployment and underemployment: "human pressure on the land constantly increased in absolute terms, although the proportions of the population engaged in agriculture constantly declined." [33] Despite a certain prosperity during World War I, agriculture in Spain was in an increasingly depressed condition in the next two decades. In 1936, the year in which Franco's counterrevolution fully precipitated the revolutionary tendencies in Spain, record-breaking rainfall had produced extensive crop damage. Landless laborers were amongst the most zealous revolutionaries.

Thus, terms such as the *peasantry*, the *gentry*, the *bourgeoisie*, and others must be broken down into more precise notations so that we can see if some smaller groupings are so crucial to the revolutionary process as to merit the label of "crisis strata." While the middle peasants, for example, may be the most active political force in some contexts, rich peasants, middle peasants, poor peasants, or landless laborers may be strategically important in others.

ELITES

Elite theory is founded on the rule that all politics is an affair of the coherent minority dominating the incoherent majority. Revolutions provide both a confirmation and a qualification of this rule. We have warned against taking the terms the *people*, the *masses*, or the *majority* too seriously in the context of revolution. It is often difficult to identify what is meant by these terms in the specific case, and more difficult still to gauge attitudes during a revolutionary crisis. Though simplistic conspiracy theories err in ascribing almost magical powers to a hidden coterie of wire-pullers, elites are often directly or indirectly responsible for action attributed to spontaneous mass action. Political elites are groups of men usually of mixed, though not random, social composition, who achieve a fair measure of ideological and organizational coherence that allows them to play a disproportionate and often determinant role in revolution.

The Intelligentsia

Having discussed the critical function of intellectuals in eroding the legitimacy of the pre-revolutionary regime, we must take a further step and see if this preparatory function is followed by a more active leadership role. Unfortunately the terms *intellectuals* and *intelligentsia* are controversial and usage varies according to time and place. Lipset has pointed to three subgroups within the generic category which includes "all those who create, distribute, and apply *culture,* that is, the symbolic world of man, including art, science, and religion." [34] Intellectuals in the purest sense are the *creators* of culture: "scholars, artists, philosophers, authors, some editors, and some journalists." These are seconded by the *distributors* of culture: "performers in the various arts, most teachers, most reporters." The third "peripheral" group includes those like doctors and lawyers "who apply culture as part of their job." [35] (We would add some clergymen to the first and second groups and some military officers to the second.) The American usage of "intellectuals" is generally restricted to the creators and distributors of culture, while in Europe and most other places "the intelligentsia" stands for all three groupings. Students thus are often considered among the intelligentsia abroad, while widespread higher education in America enjoins more selective criteria and omits students from the ranks of intellectuals. The difference is not merely semantic because in many places the intelligentsia has many of the attributes of a status group, which enhances the political influence of groups such as students who are considered part of the group. College students in America are thought to be in a kind of limbo preparatory to going on to some achieved or ascribed status position.

Two factors—one fairly constant, one more variable—dispose intellectuals and even the intelligentsia toward revolutionary activism. One is associated with the essentially critical nature of intellectual activity discussed in Chapter IV. Such persistent questioning may reach proportions difficult to restrain within the bounds of mere speculation. As Lewis Feuer points out: "The rise of an intellectual class often means . . . a proliferation of thinkers who do not become doers. Thinking that does not culminate in action is, from the biological standpoint, a psychological anomaly. The very situation of the intellectual thus carries with it a high degree of frustration. . . . The frustration of the intellectual breeds its counterpart of heightened energy." [36] Political activism becomes a catharsis for the pent-up frustration resulting from "pure" intellectual activity: "the intellectual then tends to dictatorial, impatient, and ruthless modes of action." [37] How many intellectuals have wholly refrained from fantasizing themselves as the great lawgiver who will right society's wrongs and cure its ills? The distribution of opinions amongst the intelligentsia is rarely a microcosm of that amongst the general public; it is often skewed to the left, sometimes to the right, and sometimes both to the left and the right. Activism is more highly correlated with extremism than with moderation, and "the situation of the intellectual tends to make him into an ideologue." [38]

A more variable element is the opportunity that a society provides for its intellectuals to find gainful and satisfying employment. In many countries there has been an oversupply of intellectuals trained in legal and humanistic disciplines. Since the number of suitable posts is small (as is the case in many underdeveloped countries), there develops an "intellectual proletariat," which feels its great dissatisfaction with the status quo confirmed and intensified by unemployment, underemployment, or, perhaps even worse, "unworthy employment." No doubt there is even a kind of "intellectual *lumpenproletariat*," whose lack of success or employment results in the main from purely personal shortcomings. Marx and Engels considered such types as fertile recruiting grounds for the hated banner of Bakunin's revolutionary anarchism: "a bunch of déclassés, the dregs of the bourgeoisie . . . lawyers without clients, doctors without patients and without knowledge, pool room students, commercial travelers and other salesmen and particularly journalists of the small press." [39] However, the choice of revolutionary politics as a vocation of the intelligentsia is not always or mainly spurred by a lack of better prospects. What Edward Shils found for underdeveloped countries holds for other settings as well: "some of the intellectuals who graduated in the years of nationalistic fervor did not even attempt seriously to enter upon a professional career but went directly into agitational and conspiratorial politics." [40] A commitment of this sort is made on ideological or moral grounds; and the activist or revolutionary intellectual, especially of middle-class background, may be supported by family or friends even if they deplore his politics.[41]

The leadership of most revolutions and revolutionary movements is recruited from among the intelligentsia and sometimes from among intellectuals in the narrowest sense. Whether this preeminence is a virtual monopoly depends upon particular conditions and its extent can vary over time. Though nonintellectual notables, workers, peasants, and petty bourgeoisie win leadership positions in various revolutions, there is no need here to document the well-known role of intellectuals. However, a brief excursus on the Chinese Communist Revolution seems useful in the light of our conclusions about the peasants. An early (1951) study made of the Kuomintang and communist elites found that "to a notable extent, both leadership elites were composed of culturally alienated intellectuals—men and women of well-to-do families who had removed themselves from the orthodox stream of their society's traditional culture." [42] Furthermore, both elite groupings largely derived from families descending rather than ascending on the social scale. However, as time wore on the two elites became not only polarized in ideology, there was also an increasing divergence in social composition. On the communist side, "the rise of Mao to power and the emergence of Soviet areas in the hinterland were accompanied by the replacement of intellectuals of middle-class and upper-class backgrounds by sons of peasants." [43] Meantime, the Kuomintang became ideologically and sociologically more business-oriented.

One explanation of the "plebeianization" of the communist elite was its geographical base in rural China: the Chinese Red Army eventually absorbed large numbers of peasants, whose rise in military terms was simultaneously a rise in political terms. To conclude from this, however, that the "Communist Party managed to transform itself from an intellectually oriented organization into a rural mass oriented one" [44] underestimates the persistent ideological magistracy of the "old" intelligentsia and the transformation a peasant undergoes in a revolutionary army. Subjected to indoctrination perhaps from his early youth, he ends up as something vastly different from a traditional peasant; as Regis Debray points out: "Revolutionaries make revolutionary civil wars; but to an even greater extent it is revolutionary civil war that makes revolutionaries." [45]

Student movements deserve special attention as a subgroup of the intelligentsia, as they are often the spearhead of revolutionary movements. It is necessary to go beyond the clichés about youth and idealism, youth and extremism, youth and impatience to sense the importance and character of student movements. First of all, student movements and youth movements must be distinguished: the latter are more diffuse and likely to remain apolitical, if not antipolitical (at least in the short run). In a very different and narrower sense, "youth movements" are organizational adjuncts to mass political parties which are firmly in control. Because of the special dynamics of a student movement Lewis Feuer has carefully defined it as "a combination of students inspired by aims which they try to explicate in a political ideology, and moved by an emotional rebellion in which there is always present a disillusionment with and rejection of the values of the older generation; moreover the members of a student movement have the conviction that their generation has a special mission to fulfill where the older generation, other elites, and other classes, have failed." [46]

To the oppositional disposition that a student movement shares with other segments of the intelligentsia, we must add a motivation stemming from the acute psychological trauma of the conflict of fathers and sons. Other parts of the intelligentsia feel the same sense of special mission (elitism) to save the noble, but downtrodden masses (populism) through a withdrawal of legitimacy from the existing order (alienation). Radical student movements, however, betray tendencies toward *terrorism* and *suicidalism* that depend more on psychological than on social and cultural conditions. Thus, "a youth-weighted rate of suicide is indeed characteristic of all countries in which large-scale revolutionary student movements are found." [47]

Student movements therefore manifest a high level of *irrationalism* (i.e., behavior that is irrelevant to or counterproductive of stated goals), which is produced by repressed guilt feelings spawned by generational conflict.[48] This irrationalism provides a formidable emotional reservoir that gives rise to all sorts of extremist and revolutionary manifestations. In Feuer's view, ideology is more the rationalization than the origination of these tendencies: "it is the state of mind and feeling which impels a person to the revolutionary experience for its own sake." [49] The red thread that leads through a labyrinth of ideological fickleness is an emotionally fed and total rejection of things as they are. Student movements of this sort are not generally self-sufficient; they attach themselves to a "carrier" movement of more grandiose dimensions (i.e., mass movements oriented towards peasants, workers, or ethnic groups).[50] If this elite succeeds in superimposing itself upon the mass, the resulting synthesis is a movement more irrationalist, more extremist, or more revolutionary than before. This is so because a student movement, of necessity, "imparts to the carrier movement a quality of emotion, dualities of feeling, which would otherwise have been lacking." [51]

Nevertheless, psychological forces alone cannot account for the large size and hyperradicalism of student movements in certain countries. Feuer suggests that the likelihood of a revolutionary and elitist student movement bears a close relationship to the cultural and intellectual backwardness of the country.[52] Nineteenth-century Russia and twentieth-century China seem to support this thesis, though events in Germany, France, and the United States in the late 1960's suggest qualifications. In the two former cases there emerged a widespread kind of *noblesse oblige* complex, which transfixed many students and induced sacrifices that seem to have had a masochistic basis in the depths of the unconscious. On the surface, however, "a student movement always looks for some lowly oppressed class with which it can psychologically identify itself." [53] Peasants have often been the ostensible beneficiaries of these attentions; and if the advances are reciprocated, the revolutionary potential of a country is raised substantially. The ideal incubator of a revolutionary student movement is a transitional society in which there is at least a modicum of response from the soon-to-be-redeemed class or classes. Under full traditionalism, peasants are more likely to repudiate student revolutionaries; and, more simply, there may be no large universities to serve as a basis for the movement.

Ironically, those qualities that propel student movements to the forefront of revolutionary movements in nonrevolutionary settings are the same ones that limit their role in successful revolutions. Their compactness, for example, gives them organizational coherence, but allows the authorities to watch them and sometimes to suppress them. In addition, their revolutionary zeal may become fruitless impetuosity leading to premature insurrection or gratuitous terrorism that actually strengthens the hand of the old regime. Since participation in student movements coincides with a most crucial and volatile stage in human development, mere aging of students tends to deprive the wider revolutionary movement of long-range leaders of experience and reliability. Student movements produce amateur revolutionaries, only some of whom become professional revolutionaries.

It is thus no surprise that student movements have played an extremely variable role in actual revolutions. They can have a *deferred* or *immediate* impact on them. Although with a deferred impact, no student movement takes part in the ultimate seizure of power, in the not too distant past a radical student movement made two major contributions: (1) it accelerated the delegitimization of the regime—the "desertion" of the intellectuals; (2) some of its members withstood the lures of the establishment and remained lifetime professional revolutionaries. Without the early experience they might not have taken this path. Both the Russian and Chinese radical student movements had this sort of deferred impact. Russian students were in the vanguard of the revolutionary movement in the last decades of the nineteenth century and were quite active in the abortive revolution of 1905.[54] Afterwards, however, changes in educational policy and in the social background of students so altered their political inclinations that they ended up as a "relative bastion of patriotism and order against the Bolshevik trend." [55]

One of the watershed events of modern Chinese history was the May 4th Movement of 1919, in which a massive upsurge of nationalistic sentiment among students and educators launched many a revolutionary career that would culminate three decades later with the foundation of the Chinese People's Republic. In contrast to Russia, however, Chinese student movements also had an immediate impact on the communist victory through opposition to the Nationalist government and sometimes through defection to the communist forces in the countryside. A. Doak Barnett reported in 1948 that "students are the most vocal opposition group within Nationalist China today," [56] and detected that there was "an increasing alienation of students from the Central Government and a definite shift to the Left, in the sense that more and more students are showing sympathy towards the Chinese Communist Party, and now regard Communist takeover as the only alternative to what they consider an intolerable situation." [57] And almost two decades later, it is hard to dispute Franz Schurmann's contention that "however much it was manipulated from above in the interests of the power struggle, the Cultural Revolution must be accounted the greatest student movement in history." [58] Student movements have played a less imposing role in other revolutions.

Another subgroup of the intelligentsia that is of special interest to the study of revolution in recent times is the officer corps or "military intelligentsia." While the Western experience has often revealed a contrast between the conservatism of the professional military elite and the "pure" or "civilian" intelligentsia, the history of underdeveloped countries provides a somewhat different picture. Because of their education, the officer corps must often be included in the ranks of a country's meager intelligentsia. An early instance of this situation is seen in the Decembrist uprising in Russia in 1825, which was an abortive attempt of military intellectuals to launch a revolutionary coup. In more recent times the "military intelligentsia has emerged as the most universal revolutionary phenomenon" in those non-Western countries that were not formally colonial possessions, while the "pure" or civilian intellectual has characterized those areas where colonialism prevented or restricted the rise of an independent military.[59] However, as these countries became independent they developed military forces as an attribute of sovereignty, thus creating a bifurcation of the civilian and military intelligentsias, which has often culminated in one or more military coups.

While many of these fall short of being truly revolutionary, others seem to cross that elusive threshold. The military intelligentsia everywhere has tendencies to fancy itself the incarnation of the actual or possible "nation" and may conclude that revolutionary measures are the only way to realize the promise of nationhood. In addition to nationalism, Morris Janowitz has perceived three further themes in the ideology of the military in underdeveloped countries. Each of these if pushed far enough according to historical conditions seems potentially revolutionary.[60] The first is a strong puritanical ethos which disdains the corruption and conspicuous consumption of other elite groupings. This may produce a sense of alienation that closely resembles the "desertion of the intellectuals" before the great Western revolutions. Second, there is an acceptance and often a preference for collectivist economic institutions. Since modern collectivism involves "preceptive planning" or a "command economy," there are definite analogies with the military's experience with chain-of-command decision making. This attitude will be the more revolutionary the less the country's economy has achieved collectivism. Finally, there is what Janowitz calls the "antipolitics" outlook of the military elites. This involves a repudiation of politics-as-usual with its attendant wheeling and dealing. The military stereotypes all politicians as either self-servers or incompetents, who must be swept aside before the grave national problems can begin to be tackled effectively. This last point seems to explain why so often military regimes are set up where strong revolutionary political parties have failed to take root.

However, while the military intelligentsia may become revolutionary, its revolutionary style differs in important ways from that of the "pure" intelligentsia. Here too the experience of the Decembrists was a harbinger of things to come. This military conspiracy was divided into a more radical wing, the Southern Society; and a more moderate wing, the Northern Society. Paul Pestel, the guiding spirit of the whole movement, was the leader of the Southern Society. Despite differences between the two societies, they both favored drastic political, and less drastic social, changes that necessitated violent overthrow of the existing regime. Furthermore, one theme common to them both was the "desire to avoid a revolution involving the masses. Possible civil war, anarchy, and general chaos seriously worried Muraviev [a leader of the Northern Society], as well as Pestel, who hoped to prevent it by a strong, dictatorial provisional government. Both societies hoped that the revolution could be carried out by a small military group. . . ."[61] Since this notion of the revolution has appealed to other military intelligentsias, it seems that this blatant elitism contrasts with the more populistic inclinations of the "pure" intelligentsia. The pure intellectual thrives on delusions of popular spontaneity, and his self-effacing adulation of the workers and peasants is too complex an affair to be written off as mere duplicity. The military intelligentsia is often strikingly frank in its professions of tutelary or paternalistic elitism. It is this sort of difference that makes the fusion of the two intelligentsias in Chinese communism all the more remarkable. The Cultural Revolution and its aftermath has qualified but not overturned this judgment.

Cliques and Parties

Revolutionary *cliques* is a catchall category for small formations of the intelligentsia whose diminutiveness, organizational looseness, or ideological vagueness excludes them from the category of genuine political parties. Included under the rubric of cliques are such things as clubs, secret societies, and small conspiracies. Samuel P. Huntington has compared these "antisystem" groups to the legislative cliques that operate within the system: both are creatures of the period before the expansion of political participation induced the birth of modern-style mass parties. Thus both are "also initially divorced from ties with any substantial social force. The intellectuals and others in them form and reform in a confusing series of permutations and combinations which are no less factions for being equipped with ponderous names and lengthy manifestoes. They are the civilian equivalents of the secret juntas and clubs formed by military officers intent on challenging the existing traditional order." [62] Though the specific type of revolutionary clique or faction Huntington has in mind almost always has proved an exercise in futility for lack of a mass basis, sometimes more formidable cliques can play a more substantial role. They can, perhaps without realizing it, help to precipitate the revolution, or, more importantly, can rush into the vacuum of power presented by the collapse of the old regime. The leaders of the Country around 1640 in England and the Patriots in France around 1789 were cliques in this broadened sense.

Clubs and secret societies can provide a political infrastructure that compensates somewhat for the lack of real political parties. Overreaction against simplistic conspiracy theories has impeded a fair evaluation of the role of the Masons in French revolutions of 1789 and 1848, and in the March, 1917, revolution in Russia. Even the Chinese communists had some truck with secret societies before moving against them. More significantly, cliques grouped around the periodicals *Le National* and *La Réforme* were extremely important during and after the February Days in the France of 1848. The provisional government proclaimed on February 25th had eight of its eleven members coming from the editorial staffs of these two journals. If these two cliques did not exactly plan the downfall of the monarchy, their oppositionist activities were clearly precipitating factors. While it is often wrong to leap to the conclusion that oppositionist cliques are directive nerve centers of the revolution, in certain cases such as that of the Jacobins there are strong grounds for such a view. Here the clique is hard to distinguish from an authentic revolutionary party.

Another type of clique made famous by the Cuban Revolution is the small guerrilla band. This is not so much a pre-party phenomenon in the historical sense, but an extraparty, and to some extent an antiparty one. In Batista's Cuba the Communist Party (Partido Socialista Popular–PSP) was not wholeheartedly behind the guerrilla strategy adopted by Castro. In part, it was "reformist"; in part it felt that the true focus of the revolution, should it come, would be urban. Generalizing from Castro's experience, Regis Debray maintains that the revolutionary vanguard may be a nonparty band of guerrillas predominantly of bourgeois background.[63] What is important is to make the revolution in the quickest and most effective way, even if this temporarily ignores the primary role of the party and therefore deviates sharply from the Russian and Chinese experience. Since present-day political and military conditions make the victory of a spontaneous mass insurrection against well-trained troops almost impossible, guerrilla warfare becomes the only resort of committed revolutionaries. The chief consequence of this is that according to Debray: "The vanguard party can exist in the form of the guerrilla *foco* itself. *The guerrilla force is the party in embryo.*" [64] (Italics mine.)

Nevertheless, it is clear that the success of the strategy of guerrilla bands in Cuba was due to highly specific conditions. There is no guarantee that elsewhere the armies of the established regime will either crumble from internal decay or become demoralized through the frustrations of counterinsurgency warfare. Learning this lesson cost Che Guevara his life in the wilds of Bolivia in 1967. Leading a motley band of guerrillas, he hoped to duplicate what he felt was the Cuban experience in the Bolivian context. However, he failed to reckon with two considerations: (1) the political position of the Barrientos regime was considerably stronger than Batista's was in the late 1950's. The latter "collapsed" under the relatively light pressure of the Castro movement, because it had frittered away considerable previous support. In contrast, the Bolivian regime retained some residual allegiance even among peasant groups. (2) Since Cuba was a fairly well-developed, linguistically homogeneous society, the culture gap between the Fidelista guerrillas from the intelligentsia and the local population in Oriente province was relatively small. In Bolivia this culture gap was far broader, leading to insufficient response and slight indirect aid from the natives and ultimately inducing the betrayal that resulted in Guevara's capture and execution.[65]

A final and most important elite group is the modern revolutionary party. As we have pointed out, modern political parties did not really operate in the English or French revolutions. On the other hand, "every major revolution of the twentieth century has led to the creation of a new political order to structure, to stabilize, and to institutionalize the broadened participation in politics. It has involved the creation of a political party system with deep roots in the population. In contrast to all previous revolutions, every twentieth century revolution has institutionalized the centralization and the expansion of power in a one-party system." [66]

The revolutionary party does not necessarily antedate the outbreak of the revolution. In Mexico it took nearly two decades for the dominant revolutionary party to take shape. However, the fact that prior to its emergence the Mexican Revolution resembled a traditional "time of troubles" as much as a modern revolution lends substance to the importance of the political party under modern conditions. Likewise the impressive numerical growth of the Bolsheviks occurred *after* March, 1917; that of the Spanish Communist Party *after* Franco's coup; and that of the Yugoslav communists *after* the Nazi invasion of 1941. In such cases one is reminded of the adage of the acorns and the oak trees. Only Cuba provides a partial exception to this rule: the Fidelista Communist Party of Cuba that emerged after a series of fissions and fusions in October, 1965, does not seem to have the same importance as single parties in other modern revolutionary regimes.

The main function of the modern revolutionary party is to link the revolutionary elite or cadres with segments of the broader population. This linkage is essentially one of control, with some feedback from the rank and file. Historically, revolutionary leaders have developed three basic models of the party's relationship to the masses: the *Blanquist,* the *Leninist,* and the *populist.* The Blanquist model, based upon the ideas of the nineteenth-century French revolutionary Auguste Blanqui, is the most forthrightly elitist of the three. It considers the masses too lethargic or brainwashed to rise up in spontaneous revolution against the system. Though the masses are the ultimate beneficiaries of the revolution and will be the rulers of the new society, they will initially play an essentially passive role in the revolution and especially in its preparation. It is thus up to the dedicated revolutionary elite to lead the masses for their own good. The revolutionary party is essentially an illegal, conspiratorial organization. However, since it has the capacity to broaden its ranks during the revolutionary struggle and the seizure of power, it cannot be ranked as simply another revolutionary clique. Many revolutionary parties which have gone on to greater things have passed through an early, essentially Blanquist, phase.

The Leninist model, which in practice often seems to veer towards Blanquism, differs from it because it proclaims and achieves a more symbiotic relationship between the party elite and the mass base. Agitation, propaganda, and even some recruitment among the masses are deemed essential to the vitality of the revolution and its vanguard party. Before the seizure of power the Leninist party carries on both legal and illegal activities, emphasizing either as the tactical situation dictates. Both the Soviet and Chinese communists offer varieties of the Leninist approach, though where the Soviets sometimes veer toward Blanquism, the Chinese have occasional fits of populism. The populist conception of the revolutionary party plays down a bit the predominance of the party's inner circle and leading cadres. It hopes to upgrade the participation of "mass organizations" in the party and to retain certain powers of initiative and veto with the lower echelons of the party organization. The heart of the difference between the Leninist and populist conceptions of the revolutionary party comes out in Rosa Luxemburg's polemic against Lenin in 1904. Accusing the Bolshevik leader of "Blanquism," she maintained that "except for the general principles of the struggle, there do not exist for the Social Democracy detailed sets of tactics which a Central Committee can teach the party membership in the same way as troops are instructed in their training camps. Furthermore, the range of influence of the socialist party is constantly fluctuating with the ups and downs of the struggle in the course of which the organization is created and grows." [67] Since the fluidity of circumstances demanded tactical flexibility, Luxemburg felt that Lenin's stress on iron discipline and restrictive party membership were both unnecessary and undemocratic. But polemics aside, our general stress of leadership in revolution reminds us that the differences between Blanquist, Leninist, and populist notions of the revolutionary party are often elusive matters of degree: strong leadership there must be!

CROWDS, COLLECTIVE BEHAVIOR, AND REVOLUTION

From the study of crowds, revolutionary and otherwise, has developed a subdiscipline of social science known as the study of "collective behavior." Its focus is on phenomena that seem to differ drastically from "normal" social and political processes. Panics, crazes, rumors, crowds, and social movements—all catch the observer's eye because of their relative spontaneity, instability, and even irrationality. Collective behavior thus contrasts with the structured roles and predictable responses of more established social institutions. Although some recent thought tends to minimize the discontinuity and dissimilarity between "normal" social behavior and collective behavior, revolutionary times in all accounts exhibit a wide variety, high intensity, and extreme frequency of collective behavior. Thus the study of collective behavior can elucidate the study of revolution, while the study of revolution can elucidate the study of collective behavior.

What follows in this section does not purport to be a complete analysis and explanation of the forms of collective behavior that are found in revolution. The emphasis here is on the structure and internal dynamics of crowds and social movements as they display themselves in the revolutionary situation. Although it is wrong to identify crowd behavior and social movements with the totality of revolution, some of the etiology of the phenomena treated below is found in the discussion "The Social Psychology of Revolution" in Chapter IV. There we surveyed theories about the various needs and frustrations that impel men to join revolutionary crowds or social movements and to engage in violence to express their anger, to redress their felt grievances, or to shape a new society. For this reason we assume below that the long and middle-term causes of revolution have done their work to exacerbate the forms of social conflict delineated in Chapter III and to heighten the sense of relative deprivation experienced by certain social strata. It is only within these parameters that the structural and dynamic features of crowds and other types of collective behavior can be discussed on their own as aspects of the revolutionary process.

Revolutionary Crowds

The field of collective behavior has developed largely as a critical response to the work of Gustave Lebon. Of greatest interest to us are his *The Crowd* (1895) and *The Psychology of Revolution* (1913). Two grave weaknesses limit the usefulness of these works for students of revolution and of collective behavior. First, Lebon allowed his ideological hostility to the French Revolution and modern "mass society" to distort his conclusions. He thus exaggerated the irrationality, violence, and destructiveness of crowds both in the French Revolution and beyond it.[68] Second, Lebon's obsession with the crowd phenomenon caused him to stretch the application of crowd psychology to tiny groups (juries, for example), as well as to broad social strata. He included political and religious sects, occupational groups, and social classes under the rubric of "homogeneous" crowds.[69] While members of broad social aggregates sometimes respond to the same stimuli, Lebon was mistaken to reduce all collective behavior to crowd behavior and to reduce so much of social behavior to collective behavior.

In *The Crowd,* in which he expounds the general principles of crowd behavior, Lebon advances an extreme version of the contagion theory of crowds. Contagion in the crowd annihilates the individual's conscious personality and liberates the unconscious, animalistic part of the mind. This atavistic reaction obliterates whatever intellectual, moral, and even social differences that distinguish men taken in isolation. Thus the emergent crowd mentality is not a mere average of the traits of its members, but their lowest common denominator (which according to Lebon varies according to race). More pointed is his conclusion that "by the mere fact that he forms part of an organized crowd, a man descends several rungs in the ladder of civilization. Isolated, he may be a cultivated individual; in a crowd he is a barbarian—that is, a creature acting by instinct." [70] The behavioral properties of a crowd, therefore, cannot be inferred from the personal idiosyncrasies of its components. This annihilation of the conscious personality Lebon equates with what happens under hypnotism: the individual abdicates will and conscience to an external force. In ordinary hypnosis one submits to the will of the hypnotist; in the crowd situation one submits to the general mentality of the crowd and its leader. Like the hypnotic subject, the crowd's members are highly susceptible to suggestion, which causes them to behave in exaggerated, extreme ways. [71]

In *The Psychology of Revolution* Lebon applies his crowd psychology to the French Revolution. However, he departs in several respects from the views of *The Crowd,* and these points of difference bring him closer to Taine and away from exclusive emphasis on the contagion theory of crowds. He now detects another smaller grouping which plays a "capital part in all national disturbances." This grouping comprises a "subversive social residue dominated by a criminal mentality. Degenerates of alcoholism and poverty, thieves, beggars, destitute 'casuals,' indifferent workers without employment—these constitute the dangerous bulk of the armies of insurrection." [72] By so stressing the prevalence of criminal or aggressive types in revolutionary crowds, Lebon shifts his emphasis away from mere contagion to the convergence theory of crowds. Convergence theory maintains that crowds "displaying antisocial behavior" are "made up of a special collection of individuals who have converged on the scene, possessed of a set of errant impulses not shared by the population at large." [73]

Because of his overextended notion of the crowd phenomenon, Lebon considered crowd behavior as the alpha and the omega of the revolutionary process. Not only did he reduce forms of institutional and collective behavior to manifestations of crowd behavior, he ignored behavioral differences between various types of true crowds. Theoretical refinements and empirical research since his time have sought to remedy these defects. In the first place, it is generally accepted that small "room-size" groupings and those too large to gather in one place should not be called crowds. [74] Nor should highly institutionalized formations such as parliamentary assemblies be so termed, even though they may occasionally succumb to panic and other forms of collective behavior. Roger Brown's typology of crowds represented below encompasses the sorts of crowds found both in the revolutionary and non-revolutionary setting.[75] However, the revolutionary setting would be characterized by *aggressive* and *acquisitive* crowds, as well as a greater tendency of one type to pass into another—for example, acquisitive (perhaps food-seeking) crowds pass into aggressive (perhaps scapegoat-hunting) crowds, or either of these into *escape* crowds when panic breaks out because of an encounter with security forces or other crowds. Indeed, all forms of collective behavior are more volatile in the revolutionary situation. These crowds are identical neither in composition or behavior.

The contagion theory of crowds, as modified or not by some emphasis on convergence, has been challenged by a more sociological and less psychological approach called "emergent norm theory." While in its own way excessive, norm theory sensitizes us to some features of revolutionary crowds that Lebon and others have overlooked or underestimated.[76] (1) Crowds are usually characterized by a considerable diversity of activity and participation, running from passively favorable observation up to the operations of the active minority. Upon closer inspection, in other words, Lebon's monolith dissolves into a conglomeration of variably committed and occupied clusters of individuals. (2) Norm theory deemphasizes the common emotional bond of the crowd

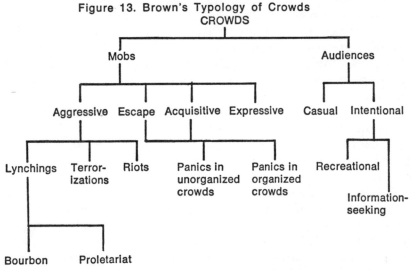

Figure 13. Brown's Typology of Crowds

SOURCE: Roger W. Brown, "Mass Phenomena," *Handbook of Social Psychology*, Vol. II, ed. Gardner Lindzey (Cambridge: Addison-Wesley, 1956), p. 841.

and underscores rather the emergence of a normative consensus, which enjoins the individual's conformity. This implies that there is a greater amount of conscious, even rational, choice involved in the crowd's behavior than contagion theory will allow. (3) The effectiveness of the emergent norms is similar for both agitated and quiescent situations, while contagion theory is concerned almost exclusively with the former. (4) While contagion theory stresses communication of the overriding emotional and activist impulse of the crowd, norm theory sees a complex array of communications concerned with achieving a common definition of the situation, justifying the crowd's action, and "dispelling conventional norms." [77] Since revolutions certainly involve normative change, crowd action may violate conventional norms, not so much through fanatical zeal or criminal elements, but because the emergence of a new set of norms is still in an inchoate, irregular state. (5) According to contagion theory the crowd should become more and more excited and indiscriminately violent and aggressive. Norm theory, however, suggests a discernible set of *limits* deriving from the norms prevalent in a given crowd. Evidence of such prescriptive limits in revolutionary settings is seen when crowds that massacre are scrupulously honest about the victims' possessions, when crowds bent on looting avoid bloodshed, or when crowd destructiveness is punctiliously selective and careful in its objects. This would indicate less the collapse of all civilized values than the suppression of some in favor of other new ones. (6) Finally, while contagion theory finds the crowd's anonymity conducive to contagion and individual irresponsiblity, norm theory maintains that "social identity" is the backdrop of emergent norms and that therefore "the control of the crowd is greatest among persons who are known to one another." [78]

Exclusive emphasis on contagion, convergence, or norms gives rise to a framework too narrow to do justice to the problem of revolutionary crowds. Nevertheless, each approach can claim some empirical confirmation.[79] For example, Georges Lefebvre's study of revolutionary crowds at the outset of the French Revolution offers support to norm theory by pointing out that "there is no revolutionary crowd unless an appropriate collective mentality has been previously formed." [80] An important part of this "collective mentality" consists of a new set of normative preconceptions, indeed of stereotypes, as when the popular image of the aristocratic seigneur is transformed from one of authority to one of an enemy of the people. The new stereotype is so strong that it obscures whatever redeeming features an individual seigneur may possess.[81] Furthermore, norm theory's stress on the "continuity between normal *group* behavior and crowd behavior" [82] seems vindicated by Lefebvre's finding that there is "no distinction between the mental operations" of revolutionary crowds and those produced by the interactions of "daily collective life." The two phenomena are alike, and the crowd "merely speeds up the rhythm." [83]

Lefebvre also assigns an important role to contagion because he recognizes that the "aggregate, by its very size, destroys the will to resist." In language that resembles the tamer assertions of Lebon he asserts that the weakening of individual responsibility in the crowd is partially *unconscious:* "As the individual more closely assimilates the collective mentality, he becomes its instrument, and his activities cease to be autonomous." [84] Taking his cue from Lefebvre, George Rudé finds that those revolutionary crowds which have "collected in direct response to leaders" illustrate the principle of convergence. In this case the participants are previously committed to the aims of the ensuing demonstration. Accordingly, the "collective mentality of the crowd corresponds closely to that of the groups of individuals forming it." [85] Two preliminary conclusions seem warranted on the basis of studies of the French and other revolutions: (1) contagion, convergence, and emergent norms can all play some role in revolutionary crowds; (2) since revolutionary crowds differ in important ways, contagion or convergence or emergent norms may be the decisive factor in any given crowd.

Revolutionary crowds differ in the first place according to the relative amounts of spontaneity and of planned and directed organization that mark them. They also differ regarding the strength of political or economic considerations in the crowd's collective mentality. While some revolutionary crowds are evidently spontaneous in the sense of being unplanned and having solely on-the-spot leaders, other formations resemble "organized military formations" [86] so closely that perhaps the term "crowd" should not be applied to them at all. In the French Revolution, capture of the Bastille and the disturbances leading to the fall of the monarchy in August, 1792, or to the ouster of the Girondin deputies in May–June, 1793, did not depend "on unarmed (or largely unarmed) revolutionary crowds, but on the deployment of a centrally organized armed force. . . ." [87] More reminiscent of our preconceptions of spontaneous crowd behavior is the demonstration of June 20, 1792, when a "peaceful procession of citizens headed by their acknowledged leaders" was transformed into a "riotous and spontaneous challenge to the authority of the king in person." [88] It would likewise be wrong to confuse the milling and effervescent crowds that toppled the Tsarist regime in March, 1917, with the well-orchestrated Bolshevik uprising in November of that year. With the spontaneous crowd there is little forethought as to the purposes of the outburst, and it is the intervention of some, perhaps fortuitous, event that transforms the crowd's behavior.[89] With the organized quasi-military crowd we find groups of political leaders who either in person or, more commonly, through a network of subleaders, direct the operations of a mass of adherents, supporters, and others. Not surprisingly, organization varies so much that poorly organized crowds and spontaneous crowds that call forth on-the-spot leaders or are "taken over" by late-comers are hard to tell apart.

Overlapping somewhat the distinction between spontaneous and organized revolutionary crowds is that between economically motivated and politically motivated crowds. Spontaneity is highly correlated with economic motivation and organization with political motivation. The economically motivated crowd responds spontaneously, for example, to the near-famine conditions associated with revolution. For the French Revolution "the most constant motivation of popular insurrection. . . , as in the eighteenth century as a whole, was the compelling need of the *menu peuple* for the provision of cheap and plentiful bread and other essentials, and the necessary administrative measures to ensure it." [90] Furthermore, the revolutionary context promotes changes in the operations of economically motivated crowds despite some continuity with the food riots of the classic urban mob. In the first place, the collective mentality of the crowd is more highly politicized in the revolutionary context and the veneer of ideology is considerably thicker than in more traditional settings. Thus, economic motivation is more likely to spill over into political motivation and thereby to make a lasting effect on the course of the revolution. Activities of economically motivated crowds can serve elites both at the time of the original collapse of the old regime, and later during the factional fights between radicals and moderates. (On occasion it is counterrevolutionary elements that reap the greatest benefit from this sort of turmoil.) Politically motivated crowds are more explicitly ideological than economically motivated crowds and are far more concerned with influencing the balance of political power. While the economically motivated crowds tend to react *ad hoc* to rising prices, lower wages, shortages, etc., political crowds tend to be planned, organized, and led. Nevertheless, the distinction should not be pushed too far, because both sorts of crowds are likely to have some political impact in the highly charged atmosphere of revolution. Yet it is possible to say, for example, that one difference between the French Revolution of 1848 and its great predecessor was the more extensive and intensive political motivation of its crowds.

The motivations and behavior of revolutionary crowds are intimately associated with their structure. Brown has presented us with a gradation of structure of crowd participation in terms of nature and intensity of individual activity.[91] A modified version of his analysis is represented graphically and discussed below.

(1) The *fanatic activists* are those who profess deep attachment to the ideology and goals of the revolution. Their commitment to direct action derives either from ideology itself or from more or less pathological character traits. Some fanatic activists enjoy the violence of revolutionary crowds as an end in itself. Despite certain modern or "revisionist" theories of the crowd, a portion at least of fanatic activists resembles the stereotypes of Taine and Lebon. As Brown himself suggests, their "brutal behavior in the mob is not completely discontinuous with their personal lives. . . ." [92] Some of these, however, are simply doing the dirty work for leaders in the background whose motivations are more complicated.

(2) Next come the *cautious,* whose revolutionary activism or violent predispositions are initially held in check by fear of punishment or retaliation. They are emboldened by the size and perhaps the anonymity of the crowd to strike their blow for freedom or just to strike their blow. As there is less premeditation in their actions than in those of the fanatical activist, contagion probably explains much about their behavior.

(3) The *suggestible* are those persons who are neither very revolutionary nor very criminal, but are "very susceptible to a certain kind of leadership." [93] Perhaps Freud's theory of the leader as father-substitute

Figure 14. Levels of Participation in Revolutionary Crowds
(Based on Brown's Analysis)

is especially or exclusively applicable to the hypersuggestible types. At any rate the suggestible person does not initiate crowd violence but follows rather blindly the lead of others. He also may prove more reliable to the activist leaders than cautious persons, for he is less liable than they are to take fright and flee the scene.

(4) The *yielders* to a degree resemble the suggestible, but respond less to leaders than to the crowd as a whole. But it is less emotional contagion that spurs the yielders on than a judgment that "since the whole crowd show by their acts that they wish the deed to be done, it must be right after all," and that "since so many people will benefit by this act, to perform it is a public duty and a righteous deed." [94] When such convictions are well distributed in the crowd and are more than simple rationalizations after the fact, we can speak of an authentic case of emergent norms.

(5) The *passive supporters* are benevolently neutral persons close to the main body of the crowd. Though not actively engaged, they are "not averse to enjoying the show or even shouting encouragement." [95] Standing on the sidelines, so to speak, their passive support can sometimes be a precondition for the eruption or prolongation of mob action.

(6) The *coerced* comprise both passive supporters and clear opponents of the crowd, who are physically forced to join its ranks and sometimes to take part in its more extreme activities. It is quite possible that some initially coerced persons will later on voluntarily join in the crowd's activities through contagion or other mechanisms. Most, however, would probably run away if they could.

This distinction between the six types of participation in the crowd also implies a sequential pattern that is sometimes followed. The fanatic activists are the first on the scene and serve as the nucleus for a process of accretion that then brings in the cautious and the suggestible. Next to join are the yielders, since their mental reaction is less immediate; finally come the coerced, who are afraid to flout the wishes of an already large and overheated mob. Something like this scenario has been reenacted in numerous instances in nearly all revolutions, but it would be hazardous to make it into a hard and fast rule.

Collective Behavior Beyond the Crowd

Two other forms of collective behavior which merit treatment because of their relation to both crowds and the wider revolutionary process are the *panic* and the *social movement*. A panic is a rapid, near-hysterical reaction of escape or self-defense based on a real or imagined threat to life, property, or welfare. While some conceptions of panic focus on the escape or "flight" phenomenon, collective defense highly disproportionate to the real extent of threat should also be included in the category. Thus various sorts of political "scares" can be deemed an instance of panic. George Lefebvre has studied *la grand peur* of 1789 in the early days of the French Revolution.[96] The main theme of this "big scare" was a generalized hysterical belief that "brigands" were about to emerge on the scene and steal the still unharvested grain. Previously, fear of brigands was widespread but localized. The general and rapid spread of this panic, *la grand peur* proper, was greatly facilitated by the unsettled political conditions and general uncertainty of the revolutionary situation. It was thus easy to link the dreaded brigands (who rarely materialized) with a somewhat more substantial "aristocratic plot" against the movement for reform. In fact, certain conservative historians see this politicization of the panic as putative evidence that there was indeed a plot—but one hatched by the revolutionaries to discredit their opponents.

This latter thesis is unproven and seems unlikely, but more significant are some of the side effects of the panic in many parts of France. As Lefebvre points out, "A vigorous reaction succeeded instantaneously to the panic, in which the military ardor of the revolution is discerned for the first time and which furnished the occasion for national unity to manifest and fortify itself. Then, above all in the countryside this reaction is turned against the aristocracy: by rallying the peasants it made them conscious of their strength and reinforced the attack which was proceeding to ruin the seigneurial regime." [97] A similar panic or "Catholic scare" gripped many Protestant Englishmen just before the outbreak of the civil war in the 1640's: it was feared that Catholicism would be restored as the state religion, most likely by an invasion of Papist Irishmen. Accordingly, Trevelyan speaks of "the rumour of papist massacre often as wild as the silliest story that ever gulled Marat's Paris" as one of the "furies that drove the blind multitude to battle on behalf of nobler men and higher projects than any of which they themselves were aware." [98] Rumors and panics are of importance in all revolutions, because the revolutionary situation harbors those preconditions that give rise to them. A breakdown of conventional certainties, a vast influx of contradictory information, anxieties about one's life or welfare, deliberate rumor-mongering, etc.—these all contribute to a lowering of critical faculties and to a rapidity of reaction unknown in more serene circumstances. Thus, the ramifications of panic behavior can lead to permanent mobilization of elements of the population and to boundless credulity in all sorts of planted rumors. These may serve the purposes of various revolutionary factions and speed up the revolutionary process.

If collective behavior involves a low level of structure of institutionalization, social movements rank as the least characteristic form of collective behavior. They possess some structure and tend to become institutionalized. Killian had designated four important features of social movements: (1) *shared values* (i.e., a set of goals related to a somewhat amorphous ideology); (2) a sense of *membership* or "we-ness," which marks off the movement from hostile or indifferent outsiders; (3) *norms* that govern both the internal and external relations of the group; and (4) a *structure* that articulates a division of labor between leaders and followers.[99] Since this structure is more fluid than that of a modern mass party or interest group, a social movement is about equidistant from such groups on the one hand and from the behavior of discrete individuals following some fad on the other. Though a social movement often draws its members from a variety of social groups and strata, it is likely to appeal disproportionately to certain ones. If we recall, for example, that neither the Fifth Monarchist movement nor the *sans-culotte* movement was a political party (or a coherent social class), we will have a rough idea of the intermediate character of social movements.

Explanations of the rise of social movements focus on two distinct levels of analysis: at the systemic level, social movements are considered to result from the strains of dysfunctions in a social system, which prevent the resolution of problems and disputes within the usual channels. The social movement is a symptom of and perhaps a partial cure for grave social ills. Many social scientists thus advise us to look beyond the allegedly crackpot exterior of these movements and to view them instead as a feasible response to social malaise.[100] At the individual level, some analysts contend that social (or mass) movements have an exceptional appeal to distinct psychological types. Eric Hoffer concludes that "a rising mass movement attracts and holds a following not by its doctrines and purposes but by the refuge it offers from the anxieties, barrenness and meaninglessness of an individual existence. It cures the poignantly frustrated not by conferring on them an absolute truth or by remedying the difficulties and abuses which made their lives miserable, but by freeing them from their ineffectual selves."[101] However, as we shall see in the next section, the most adequate explanation of social phenomena such as social movements steers a middle path between *sociologism*—the denial of the relevance of psychological data—and *psychologism*—underestimation of the social and cultural factors impinging upon individual behavior.

Our employment of the expression "revolutionary movement" has almost always meant something much broader than a single social movement. A given revolution will usually embrace several distinct social movements—to say nothing of other forms of collective, institu-

tional, elite, and individual behavior. This is not to deny the importance of social movements in revolution. By turning loyalties to the
in-group they can deprive the old regime of the allegiance of considerable numbers of people. Even more important is the mobilization of
members of a social movement for revolutionary action: organization,
even if rudimentary, can be a determining variable in any confrontation of forces. For example, social movements are often associated with
crowd behavior. From one viewpoint, a crowd may be a "stage in the
development of a social movement," as when the spontaneity of the
early moments of the revolution gives way to higher levels of organization. We have already observed the three-phase process of crowd, to
popular councils, to governmentalization of same with regard to the
Parisian sections and the Moscow and Petrograd soviets. From another
viewpoint, because of tactical considerations "crowd behavior may be
deliberately fostered by the leaders of a social movement," and thus
"crowds may constitute subordinate parts of the social movement." [102]

A REVOLUTIONARY PERSONALITY?

Before considering the question of a revolutionary personality, a
preliminary question must be explored. For if individuals qua individuals play a negligible role in revolution, then personality or character
traits or syndromes are of marginal interest to us. We are thus, perhaps
without wishing it, confronted by that perplexing and abiding problem
of social science and the philosophy of history: the role of the great
man or "hero."

A stimulating treatment of the great man is found in Sidney
Hook's *The Hero in History*. There Hook gives scientific determinism its
due by conceding that grandiose trends such as the development of
capitalism, the industrial revolution, etc., would have taken place regardless of the role of great men. Furthermore, there are "situations in
the world no hero can master," and these are often to be found "at the
end of prolonged periods of distress and oppression, as in the great
revolutionary upheavals." [103] Despite these ineluctable trends, Hook—
like Machiavelli—finds that genuine historical alternatives exist, which
have "mutually incompatible consequences that might have redeter-
mined the course of events in the past, and that might redetermine
them in the future." [104] And also like Machiavelli he suggests that
which alternatives prevail can be determined by the action of important
individuals. We can think of the great man or hero as one who makes a
difference or, more elaborately, as one exercising "preponderant influ-

ence in determining an issue or event whose consequences would have been profoundly different if he had not acted as he did." [105]

Hook's important distinction between the *eventful man* and the *event-making man* has striking analogies with our earlier contrast between moderate and radical revolutionary leaders in Chapter V. The merely eventful man is one whose historical action does make a difference, but in a rather passive way. He has been catapulted into a *position* where he seemingly can alter the course of events. Yet he is an actor who makes the least of the opportunities afforded him and is usually in the tow, if not the pay, of a particular social group. His personal mark upon the historical process is relatively indistinct, as he tends to be a medium for social forces that speak in and through him.[106] The event-making man, however, influences the historical process in a more remarkable and personalized way: "it is the *character* of the individual which chiefly distinguishes the eventful man from the event-making man." [107] Therefore, the event-making man is an eventful man whose actions proceed from "outstanding capacities of intelligence, will, and character rather than accidents of position." [108] For this reason the student of revolution cannot afford to neglect the personalities of leaders of specific revolutions, nor can he dismiss beforehand the possibility that these leaders share common personality traits.

In his critique of Trotsky's views on the Russian Revolution, Hook ranks revolutions in that class of social phenomena whose outbreak is the result of irresistible forces. "We can tell that it is coming, we can predict its approach though not what particular event will set it off. We can predict . . . the advent of a revolution or a war but *not always what its upshot will be. That upshot may sometimes depend upon the characters of the leading personalities.*" [109] Thus, the "collapse" element of so many revolutions is not the work of any particular oppositionist hero. But this very collapse may initiate a relatively "open" period wherein someone with the right qualities can influence the course and perhaps the survival of the revolution. In fact, Hook's description of the event-making man seems to hold for radical revolutionary dictators such as Lenin, Cromwell, Mao, Castro and, less clearly, Robespierre. Such personages excel in freeing themselves from the close tutelage of the social group they supposedly represent. They especially succeed in (1) playing off various social interests against each other, (2) gaining control over the military (and security) forces, and (3) using a "machine" to "take over and administer social functions, pulverize opposition, and consolidate military influence." [110] It is this capacity of the revolutionary leader as event-making man to bend his allies and instruments to his will that allows him to "make history."

These possibilities for truly decisive action are somewhat different in each revolution and should in no way be exaggerated. The great man is highly dependent on his lieutenants and they in turn on others below them. Events initiated by revolutionary leaders often exceed or fall short of their expectations. And yet, their influence is too important to neglect.

The Psychoanalytic Approach

The conclusion that the personality of top revolutionary leaders can be of great importance at certain junctures of the revolutionary process does not entail the existence of a specific revolutionary personality. To establish the latter one must appeal to a particular psychology of personality. The only approach to personality that up to now has much of substance to say about the character of revolutionary leaders is Freudian (and neo-Freudian) psychoanalysis. Next to the works of Freud himself in influence are the works of Harold D. Lasswell and Erik Erikson, who have applied and qualified certain of Freud's ideas.[111] However, the small number of "psycho-biographies" and comparative ventures suggests that any final answer on the question of a revolutionary personality is some years away. It may well turn out (though we will assume the contrary below) that all we can say about the personalities of revolutionary leaders is comprised in the psychology of political leadership in general. Research then would have concluded that the distribution of personality traits and types among top revolutionary leaders follows a curve roughly similar to that for the broader class of political leaders. But before we can really grasp the issues at stake it is essential to have a brief compendium of the application of psychoanalytic concepts to politics.

Following Lasswell, all psychoanalytic approaches to politics see three basic steps: (1) *private motives,* as these are understood by psychoanalysis; (2) their *displacement onto public objects* or politicization; and (3) their *rationalization* in terms of public interests (i.e., an ideological covering).[112] This suggests that political behavior is often an externalization of problems which have troubled the leader from his earliest days, but that he obscures the true nature of these problems by displacement and rationalization. Given the importance of power in Lasswell's theories, it is no surprise that for him the salient traits of that specific character type, the political personality, are preoccupation with power and considerable skill in power manipulation.[113] This power-seeking personality most often seeks political power in order to "overcome low estimates of the self."[114] That many people whose bullying or self-assurance seems to reveal a lofty estimate of the self are in reality nur-

turing "inferiority complexes" is an axiom of the psychoanalytic trad-
dition. But we must now retrace Lasswell's three steps by offering a
fuller exposition of Freudian ideas.

One of Freud's most succinct statements of his core concepts is
found in his collaborative and highly controversial psycho-biography of
Woodrow Wilson.[115] There he delineates the three main "axioms" of
his system. Axiom I maintains that "in the psychic life of man, from
birth, a force is active which we call libido, and we define as the energy
of the Eros." [116] The sexual drives best exemplify the force of Eros,
though Eros itself is a broader impulsion to bring about "more and
more far-reaching combination of the particles into which living substance is dispersed. . . ." [117] In any case, the libido directly or indirectly provides the energy for the vast bulk of human exertions and
achievements. Freud's Axiom II maintains that "all human beings are
bisexual." [118] Thus, the degree of masculinity attained by an adult male
is highly influenced by infantile and childhood experiences. This bisex-
uality can produce a whole series of acute mental conflicts that affect
and sometimes ruin the lives of people. Axiom III, which reflects a
later trend in Freud's speculations, maintains that a specific Death Instinct contrasts sharply with Eros.[119] In *Civilization and Its Discontents*
Freud construes the Death Instinct as a tendency to return things to an
earlier state before life had emerged. What is more important, the "instinct of aggression is the derivative and main representative of the
death instinct. . . ." [120] And still more important is Freud's analysis of
the mechanisms of aggression: "this aggressive cruelty usually lies in
wait for some provocation, or else it steps into the service of some other
purpose, the aim of which might as well have been achieved by milder
measures. In circumstances that favor it, when those forces in the mind
which ordinarily inhibit it cease to operate, it also manifests itself spontaneously. . . ." [121] What makes both life and psychoanalysis both possible and difficult is that Eros and the Death Instinct are from the outset together in the psyche and "seldom or never appear in pure form
but are, as a rule, welded together in varying proportions." [122]

Freud's three axioms figure prominently in his articulation of the
Oedipus complex—the key to his understanding of personality development. In the Freudian schema the human mind is divided into three
fundamental parts. The most basic and primordial part is the Id, where
the instinctual forces of the libido reign supreme. The Id is *unconscious*,
though so too in part are the other aspects of the mind. The Id
operates according to the "pleasure principle" (i.e., it seeks immediate
and full gratification of libidinal desires). The Ego becomes differentiated and separated from the Id and provides the mind's main contact
with external reality. "Moreover, the ego seeks to bring the influence of

the external world to bear upon the id and its tendencies, and endeavors to substitute the reality principle for the pleasure principle. . . . The ego represents what may be called reason and common sense, in contrast to the id, which contains the passions." [123] There is thus an inherent conflict between the unconscious promptings of the Id and the Ego's recognition that moderation and modification of primal libidinal impulses are necessary to the long-term welfare of the individual. Also deriving its energies from the Id's reservoir is the third part of the mind, the Superego. The latter corresponds roughly to what we call the conscience, but Freud's explanation of how it develops is distinctive and highly controversial.

The Superego, like the Ego, develops later than the Id and is a chief result of the Oedipus complex, as it develops in the male child because of unavoidably ambivalent relationships to the father. On the one hand the father appears as an obstacle to the child's gratification of his love-impulses towards his mother. On the other hand the father himself is an object of affection, as well as a source of strength and authority to be emulated. How the individual resolves the Oedipus complex will largely determine his further psychic progress. In all this the Superego plays a vital role, because its content and function in the personality is largely determined by the way in which the individual deals with mixed hostile and aggressive, affectionate and respectful feelings he harbors towards his father. "Clearly the repression of the Oedipus complex was no easy task. The child's parents, and especially his father, were perceived as the obstacle to a realization of his Oedipus wishes; so his infantile ego fortified itself for the carrying out of the repression by erecting this same obstacle within itself. It borrowed strength to do this, so to speak, from the father, and this loan was an extraordinarily momentous act." [124] The Superego always retains the marks of its origin, for where repression is particularly rapid and intense the individual will exhibit an overdeveloped and relentless moral sense and quite probably an "unconscious sense of guilt." [125]

Thus, in the Freudian view the three-cornered conflict between the Ego, the Superego, and the Id determines personality development. In simple terms, the conflict arises because the Ego receives unconscious messages from the Id saying "Yes" to libidinal drives as well as messages from the Superego saying "No." Though Freud suggests that "all men are more or less neurotic," [126] the normal individual is one in whom there reigns a sort of "peaceful coexistence" between the three parts of the psyche. Someone who only partially succeeds in managing the conflict is a *neurotic,* and his neuroses are his inadequate mechanisms for coping with inner turmoil. Someone who fails completely at this and loses touch with reality is a *psychotic* or insane person.

Freud designates three major mechanisms for dealing with the conflict between libidinal aims and the prohibitions of the Superego. (1) *Repression* denies the instinctive desires and pushes them out of consciousness. This provides but a provisional respite and opens the door for later manifestations of the original conflict in the form of neurotic symptoms. (2) *Identification* attempts to gratify the instinctive desire by a sort of dissimulation "so that the self represents both the desiring subject and the desired object." [127] For the boy, the father is the most prevalent object of identification. (3) *Sublimation* is a kind of diversionary operation whereby the instinctive drives are partially gratified through directing them towards alternative objects. In so doing the Ego achieves some *modus vivendi* with the external world and avoids the harsh censure of the punctilious Superego. Freud even argues that sublimation is the dynamic source of the higher achievements of culture and civilization. "Its success is greatest when a man knows how to heighten sufficiently his capacity for obtaining pleasure from mental and intellectual work." [128] From the standpoint of mental health sublimation is the most, but by no means is it a wholly, successful means of handling desires that cannot be gratified in their pristine form.

It is thus towards the outcome of the Oedipus complex that Freudian psychoanalysis looks in its striving to understand both the normal and the pathological personality. Overthorough repression of the Oedipus hostility towards the father will likely produce an individual who will betray residual hostility to father-representatives who in often unconscious ways "remind" him of his true father. When real provocation is added to this gratuitous resentment, tolerable relations usually prove impossible. "As a rule such a man will find it difficult to maintain friendly relationships with other men of equal position, power, and ability, and it will be impossible for him to cooperate with persons who are superior to him in position, power, and ability: such men he is compelled to hate." [129] We can only mention here the list of personality problems that Freud relates to the Oedipus complex: narcissism or exacerbated self-love, in which the Ego itself becomes the object of libidinal interest; homosexuality (latent and open), which causes further difficulties; extreme aggressiveness and sadism, in which aggressive impulses operate completely detached from Eros; exaggerated feelings of guilt, inferiority, and paranoia—these and other phobias and manias stem from roots in the Oedipus complex.

How far these things affect politics, revolutionary and otherwise, has been the subject of much dispute.[130] We cannot hope to resolve these problems here. However, two studies have gone beyond Lasswell's thesis indicating that political leaders of various sorts are psychoanalytically distinct, by maintaining that revolutionary leaders are psychoanalytically distinct in a particular way. In short, a revolutionary personality does exist. Gustav Bychowski's *Dictators and Disciples* is a study of Julius Caesar, Cromwell, Robespierre, Hitler, and Stalin, in which the theoretical framework is imbedded in five psychological profiles and in which little attempt is made to generalize. E. Victor Wolfenstein's *The Revolutionary Personality* studies Lenin, Trotsky, and Ghandi and makes broader theoretical thrusts than the earlier work. Bychowski is a psychiatrist of the orthodox Freudian persuasion, while Wolfenstein is a political scientist influenced by Lasswell and Erikson as well as Freud. As we shall see, the main problem with such works is their application of a conceptual framework assumed to be valid to a small number of case studies. What is of interest to students of revolution, however, is precisely to test the validity of a modified psychoanalytical approach with reference to a rather larger sampling of top revolutionary leaders.[131] Nevertheless, at this stage of knowledge, almost any results deserve close scrutiny.

Though Bychowski did not explicitly study the revolutionary personality, but rather the personalities of five dictators, his subjects were all to some extent revolutionary dictators. Furthermore, his conclusion that despite diversity in background and character Caesar, Cromwell, Robespierre, Hitler, and Stalin were cut from the same psychological cloth points in the direction we wish to travel. Certain character traits of these men are "manifest and almost self-evident: excessive narcissism, aggressiveness, hatred, and lust for power. However, deeper analysis reveals that this facade conceals weakness and inferiority often based on early frustrations and on inadequate virility." [132] Furthermore, this type of leader "seems to be on the verge of a definite psychosis, a paranoia of grandeur and of persecution." [133] These selfsame traits also supply the leader with the fanaticism, self-righteousness, intuitive faculties, and powers of suggestion necessary to lead the masses in a revolutionary situation.[134] While the leader's fanatical convictions often remove him from the influence of reason and reality, he is a neurotic, not a true psychotic, and thus has not completely lost touch with the world around him. He is able to compartmentalize his neuroses and displace them so that ironically they can sometimes be a political asset rather than a liability.

As a Freudian, Bychowski is naturally led to conclude that the leader's fanaticism, will-to-power, and paranoic suspiciousness stem from his failure to cope with the traumas of childhood and adolescence. Bychowski's interpretation of the early life of Robespierre illustrates, perhaps in extreme form, how the psychoanalytic approach deals with adult political behavior. Robespierre's ideological purism, autocratic tendencies, and suspiciousness are considered to reveal "strong narcissistic and aggressive drives, as well as imperative tendencies toward sublimation and repression, toward idealization and rationalization." [135] Bychowski further suggests that his subject manifested "a great deal of latent homosexuality." [136] Accordingly, his paranoia is explained as a defense mechanism of the ego "against the impact of repressed homoerotic libido," and the fusion of this with "strong sadistic drives may account for the ruthlessness he manifested toward anyone whom he regarded as an enemy." [137] The origin of these tendencies in Robespierre resides in inadequate virility caused by inability to identify with his father. This ne'er-do-well person early abandoned his family; and his wife, Robespierre's beloved mother, died not long after. These things, coupled with his father's shady reputation, hurt the young Robespierre's pride and "caused him to react by developing an ego ideal of perfect masculinity and virtue as a compensation for the crushing awareness of his father's weakness." [138] The dependence and near-poverty of his adolescence merely exacerbated these tendencies. Bychowski finds that Robespierre would strike back against those who seemed evil or unjust in order to release his pent-up aggressiveness. When the movement culminating in the revolution came on the scene, Robespierre was ready for it, because "his great capacity for sublimation made it possible for him to express these tendencies in an ideological form that corresponded with the prevailing social and political ideas." [139]

Bychowski's study has both the strengths and weaknesses of purist approaches. It presents a highly distinctive point of view with maximum economy. Nevertheless, it is simplistic and reductionist because it explains the revolutionary leader's political behavior almost exclusively in psychological terms. Insufficient attention is devoted to broader social and political forces that might induce leaders of even normal personality to behave in extraordinary ways. This raises the question whether all the extraordinary behavior of admittedly semineurotic leaders is really an expression of deep-seated personality traits, or is crisis behavior pure and simple. Furthermore, when Freud himself points out that membership in certain sects and cults can be "expressions of crooked cures of all kinds of neuroses," [140] he raises the intriguing possibility that neurosis begins to lose its explanatory power for behavior *after* one's joining the movement. The "crooked cure" may mean that someone like Robespierre is "less neurotic" after joining the revolutionary movement and that perhaps psychopathology cannot tell the student of revolution what he wishes to know.

Since Wolfenstein's study is more sensitive to the historical circumstances around the men he chose as examples of the revolutionary personality, he avoids somewhat the charge of reductionism. Furthermore, he is more explicitly concerned with why men become revolutionary leaders in the first place than Bychowski is. What character traits disposed Lenin, Trotsky, and Ghandi to make revolution their profession is his real interest. Personality and revolutionary radicalism are closely linked, as "the less an individual is dedicated to radical social change and a total displacement of the ruling class, the less will he be likely to embody the psychological attributes of the revolutionary personality." [141] However, the emergence of a distinct revolutionary personality is conditional upon historical factors such as an "established revolutionary tradition." In alternative settings, "the role of criminal, outcast or deviant will have to substitute for the more creative and politically significant role of rebel." [142]

Though Wolfenstein's analysis follows the Freudian recipe of acute Oedipal conflicts and the Lasswellian recipe of their politicization, it also makes generous use of Erikson's notion of "identity crisis." This notion serves to extend the timetable of character development through the late teens and even beyond. According to Erikson, the identity crisis "occurs in that period of the life cycle when each youth must forge for himself some central perspective and direction, some working unity, out of the effective remnants of his childhood and the hopes of his anticipated adulthood; he must detect some meaningful resemblance between what he has come to see in himself and what his sharpened awareness tells him others judge him and expect him to be." [143] The intensity of the identity crisis is affected by historical conditions: it is "apt to be aggravated either by widespread neuroticisms or by pervasive ideological unrest." [144] The response of individuals to these acute stimuli can take various forms: (1) neurosis, psychosis, and delinquency; (2) "participation in ideological movements passionately concerned with religion or politics, nature or art"; (3) emergence from a troubled and seemingly protracted adolescence by making an original contribution to "an emerging style of life." [145] Whether a given revolutionary leader goes beyond the second response to the third would seem to depend on his personal qualities and the ideological sympathies of the observer.

Thus, Wolfenstein's revolutionary personality does not emerge automatically from the deposits of character in the early and Oedipal phases of Freud, but only after surmounting the identity crisis of late adolescence—perhaps after a period of introspective withdrawal or "moratorium" as Erikson calls it. However, some event must act as a final precipitant to launch the youth on his revolutionary career—the execution of Lenin's elder brother Alexander is the classic example of this. Some highly personal experience of government oppression or callousness thus serves to crystallize the individual's previously incoherent aims. At this point the revolutionary personality, as characterized by militant opposition to the existing regime, emerges into the clear light of day. In a process whose final steps are akin to religious conversion in their drastic quality, the revolutionary personality finds its political vocation. The Freudian influence is evident in Wolfenstein's conclusion that

> the basic attribute of this personality is that it is based on opposition to governmental authority; this is the result of the individual's continuing need to express his aggressive impulses vis-à-vis his father and the repressive action of governmental officials. The latter permits the individual to externalize his feelings of hatred—previously he had been tormenting himself because his feelings of antipathy toward his father were balanced by feelings of love, respect, and the desire to emulate him. Now the situation is much less ambivalent   [146]

We can now sketch a sort of composite syndrome of the revolutionary personality based upon the speculations of Bychowski and Wolfenstein: *the revolutionary personality*

(1) experiences the trauma of the Oedipus complex in a particularly acute form, stronger than the average for his society and his social group;

(2) weathers the identity crisis by keeping neurotic tendencies in check and by sublimating instinctive desires and aggressive impulses through working for the great cause of the revolution and through rationalization of this in a revolutionary ideology;

(3) before the seizure of power, discharges some of the repressed Oedipal hostility against the officials and establishment of the old regime, while his violent propensities acquire an ideological sanction that appeases his Superego;

(4) after the seizure of power, tends to exhibit fanaticism, autocratic behavior, and acute suspiciousness that reflect neurotic tendencies with deep roots in his character (e.g., harshness against father-representatives).

Can we accept this synopsis of the separate conclusions of Bychowski and Wolfenstein about the nature of the revolutionary personality? Unfortunately, in our view these preliminary studies raise an intriguing possibility, perhaps a promising line of inquiry, but no more. We simply need more psycho-biographies of more revolutionary leaders before reaching final conclusions. While many revolutionary leaders have inspired a goodly number of friendly and hostile biographers, only a tiny portion of these pretend the slightest acquaintance with psychoanalytical or other personality theories. One result of this is that these "straight" biographies often say very little about the childhood and adolescence of their subjects, thus depriving the social scientist of important information. In fact, shortage of information remains one of the stumbling blocks to any final resolution of the issue. This comes out most clearly in Bychowski's treatment of Cromwell. Since so little is known to date on Cromwell's early life, Bychowski is forced to declare that we can "at best imagine" his basic childhood conflicts: "In a boy of a violent disposition, nurtured in an atmosphere of puritan constraint and austerity, processes of forcible and yet insufficient repression of the oedipus complex must have undoubtedly occurred." [147] It is the "must have" here that is troublesome: since the theory prescribes a certain developmental sequence, it "must have" occurred in the case at hand. Freud gave the lead to such imaginative reconstructions in certain of his works, and people like Erikson have followed it. In fact, in most psycho-biographies an enormous load of inference is placed upon a few dubious recollections, reports, or "Freudian slips." These problems are largely owing to the fact that psychoanalysis originated as a clinical encounter between the physician and his patient, whereas psycho-biography is a species of "psychoanalysis by proxy" through media such as letters, memoirs, anecdotes, published works, etc. This drastic breach in method has not been wholly mended.

Another methodological problem concerns the levels of analysis of various approaches to the study of revolution.[148] We have already termed approaches that focus exclusively on the individual as a social monad "psychologistic," and those that take account only of grandiose sociocultural trends as "sociologistic." Sometimes, of course, it is possible for individually oriented and collectively oriented explanations of the same phenomena to be equally fruitful, simply because the viewpoints and interests of inquiry are different. "In the individual-psychological universe of discourse, society and culture are simply means for the implementation of subjective needs and psychic mechanisms, just as in the collective-sociological universe of discourse individual psychic structures are simply means for the implementation of collective needs and mechanisms of the socio-cultural system." [149] The "pure" psychologist considers social and cultural conditions virtually as givens and investigates individual motivation as the dynamic explanatory factor in his field; the "pure" sociologist takes personality needs more or less as givens and addresses himself to the broader social and cultural trends. From the pure psychologist's viewpoint, phenomena such as "nationalism, class struggle, resistance to oppression, idealism" are taken as "psychologically *instrumental* motives," which make the expression of certain needs both congenial to the ego and acceptable to society.[150] From that of the "pure" sociologist, the diversity of individual needs and motivations is seen "as the raw material from which a social process, spontaneous or traditional, can crystallize just as a variety of fuels, when thrown into the same furnace, can heat the same boiler." [151]

In the study of revolution, however, it is not so easy to keep these different levels of analysis, individual and sociocultural, apart. This is especially so because of our conclusion that the actions of revolutionary leaders can affect the overall course of revolution. We are thus forced to avoid wholly systemic or wholly individualistic explanations. What the quest for the revolutionary personality has caused in Bychowski and to a lesser extent in Wolfenstein is a one-sided or psychologistic account of the revolutionary process. This remains true even though both writers disclaim any attempt at explanatory completeness. Unfortunately, there is no foolproof formula to give individuality its appropriate place against the background of complex social forces. Despite these problems, the work of Bychowski, Wolfenstein, and others inclines one to think that some sort of revolutionary personality exists. Psychological information helps to explain why some leaders become "event-making" men, while others remain merely "eventful" men. While excesses stemming from ideological or methodological distortion vitiate the psychological portraits drawn of many revolutionary leaders, it is hard to avoid talk of neurosis when dealing with a Marat, Stalin, or even a Robespierre. If revolutions are "abnormal" in the sense discussed in Chapter IV, it seems likely that they will give vent to some behavior that is "abnormal" in the very different sense of modern psychology. [152]

Kinds of Revolutionaries

Whatever the ultimate answer to the question of *the* revolutionary personality, there seems greater consensus about classifying upper-echelon revolutionaries according to the roles they play. Common classifications incorporate both psychological and sociological criteria. Brinton, for example, briefly describes the "gentlemen-revolutionists," the "failures," the "lunatics," the "idealists," and others. Serviceable typologies could also be derived from psychological types or even from literature. However, the convergence of the tripartite typologies of political and social movement leaders formulated by Harold Lasswell, Eric Hoffer, and others reflects what seems to be a natural division of labor amongst the roles of the revolutionary elite. Though Lasswell is concerned with political leaders in general, his discrimination between *theorists, agitators,* and *administrators* is easily applied to revolutionary leaders. Our conviction of this is strengthened when we note the similarity of Eric Hoffer's *men of words, fanatics,* and *practical men of action,* and of Lewis M. Killian's *intellectual leaders, charismatic leaders,* and *ad-*

ministrative leaders.[153] Despite certain differences among these three typologies of leadership, we will adopt a slightly modified version of Lasswell's approach and draw freely upon the other two for supportive material.

The role of the *ideologist* (theorist, man of words, or intellectual leader) in the revolutionary process is not so much to articulate general principles of political philosophy as to apply them to the existing political and social order. He employs ideas to hasten the collapse of the old order and to justify the erection of a new one by (1) delegitimizing the leaders and institutions of the old regime, (2) thereby creating a "hunger for faith in the hearts of those who cannot live without it," (3) then "furnishing the doctrine and slogans of the new faith," and (4) "undermining the convictions of the 'better people' " and sapping their capacity to resist the "new fanaticism." [154] We are not talking here of the influence of Calvin on the English Revolution, Rousseau on the French Revolution, or Marx on the Russian or Chinese revolutions—this influence is real but too far removed. Rather we mean actual participants in the specific revolutionary process or movement.

The ideologist's role is not necessarily compatible with some of the later needs of the nascent or successful revolutionary movement. Some ideologists may fit the pattern of Hoffer's creative man of words, who "no matter how bitterly he may criticize and deride the existing order, is actually attached to the present. His passion is to reform not to destroy." [155] Because of his education and background, the ideologist does not usually excel in the exploits of day-to-day political activism. Training and character dispose him to make distinctions, qualifications, and exceptions—traits that can lead to hesitation, doubt, or moderation. He may be sure enough of his principles, but less sure of how to implement them. Also he may balk at the notion that the ends justify the means. Such behavior seems an outmoded luxury during the more critical phases of a revolution; and consequently the ideologist is likely to recede into the background in favor of other, more forceful, leadership types. The fate of two leading ideologists of the French Revolution illustrates this clearly. The Abbé Sieyès, we have seen, wrote the highly influential tract *What is the Third Estate?* on the eve of the Revolution. He was active in the early days of the National Assembly and influenced more demonstrative leaders such as Mirabeau. However, as the revolution took a more radical turn, Sieyès seemed to see the handwriting on the wall and virtually retired from active politics for some three years. He made something of a comeback after the fall of Robespierre and was later instrumental in bringing Napoleon Bonaparte to power. But his survival, surprising in any event, was conditional upon his withdrawal from the political forefront. He lacked the agita-

tional skills to retain influence during the radical ascendency. Condorcet, perhaps the last of the *philosophes,* was a moderate associated with
the Girondists and ran afoul of the Jacobins. He died while hiding
from certain death at the hands of his more extreme political adversaries. Condorcet's evolutionary progressivism was too tame for the radical
leaders. Despite the harsh treatment ideologists sometimes receive,
their role is crucial; for even if the masses do not understand their
more recondite pronouncements, they are sources of prestige who can
be invoked to defend various positions.[156]

A different type of revolutionary leader is the *agitator* (fanatic or
charismatic leader). His specialty is mobilizing and, to a lesser extent,
organizing people for revolutionary action. Lasswell sees this type as
"obviously well adapted to crises of revolution and war in a society
where automatic obedience cannot be taken for granted." [157] Hoffer
more bluntly suggests that "chaos is his element. When the old order
begins to crack, he wades in with all his might and recklessness to blow
the whole hated present to high heaven." [158] His skills are strongly verbal and oratorical: he translates the rarefied theories of the ideologist
into the medium of popular discourse by simplifying, sloganizing (and
probably distorting) their content. In a certain sense he incarnates the
philosophical premises of the revolutionary movement by making them
concrete and specific. If the revolutionary ideology includes strategic
principles, he selects the appropriate ones and provides for their tactical implementation. He does this as much by action and example as by
words.

The agitator's hold over his immediate followers and sometimes
over broad masses has often been described in terms of Weber's notion
of charismatic leadership.[159] His followers endow him with extraordinary and highly personal qualities of leadership. We have seen that
leaders of messianic movements are seen to possess charisma in the literal religious sense of a special relationship to God; in modern revolutions the agitator *may* possess charisma in the sociological sense of commanding blind devotion to his person. Since one form of Weber's types
of authority—that is, tradition—has broken down in the revolutionary
situation and the second, rational-legal authority, has not yet taken
hold, charismatic authority may provide a provisional alternative to
utter chaos. Lasswell is probably correct in asserting that agitators develop from a distinctive personality type which places a "high value on
the 'emotional response' of the public." [160] In Freudian terms, "agitators as a class are strongly narcissistic types"; [161] as such, they have an
overweening need for acclamation which the role of agitator is well
suited to supply. In any case, the agitator would seem a better subject
for psychoanalytical approaches than the other two types of revolu-

tionary leader. Hoffer's description has a different orientation: his "fanatics" derive mostly "from the ranks of non-creative men of words." [162] Career and artistic frustrations help to produce an individual with a grudge against the system which fails to acknowledge his true worth. Jean Paul Marat and Adolf Hitler are almost perfect examples of this type.

The *administrator* (or practical man of action) is a revolutionary leader whose talents run in somewhat different channels: "he is willing and able to concern himself with the less dramatic and less heroic facets of the movement, the mechanics of organization, finances, and diplomacy." [163] Furthermore, he is less transfixed than the ideologist or agitator by the long-term goals of the revolution, and more preoccupied with consolidation of what has already been accomplished. While the agitator relies upon and thrives upon mobilized enthusiasm, the administrator represents the tendencies to institutionalize the revolution. He is especially adept at harnessing breakthroughs in technology and in organizational techniques to defend and preserve, if not to extend or export, the revolution. Killian even suggests that it is the administrative leader "who is most likely to betray the ideals of the revolution in the effort to consolidate the power following the initial victory." [164] It is clear that some of the tensions in the Robespierrist Committee of Public Safety were spawned by the contrast between administrators such as Lazare Carnot and Robert Lindet, and agitators such as Robespierre and Saint-Just.

The differences between these three types of revolutionary leaders have led to the conclusion that each is peculiar to a distinct phase of the revolution, which requires his specific skills and qualities. The ideologist prepares the way for the revolutionary movement; the agitator mobilizes for the seizure of power; and the administrator moves in to consolidate that power.[165] While there is a certain logic to this sequence, it seems to presuppose the sort of three-phase rhythm we have called into question in Chapter V. The agitators, for example, may stage a comeback at the expense of administrators when an antientropic campaign is launched. Furthermore, it is difficult to fit some revolutionary leaders into the exclusive pigeonhole of ideologist, agitator, or administrator. Leaders such as Mao, Cromwell, Tito, or Ho Chi Minh have weathered too many political storms for us to deny their ability to do several things well. Such men display the talents of administrator as well as agitator. And if instead of a chronological pattern, we resort to a functional division of labor and say that the agitator "supplies and symbolizes the values," the administrator "promotes" them, and the ideologist "elaborates them and justifies them," [166] we must then reserve a special title such as "the protean revolutionary" for those like Mao and Lenin who come close to being complete or all-around revolutionary leaders. This is the more remarkable because ordinarily the "three types of leadership roles demand skills and attitudes which are not only different but are sometimes conflicting." [167]

One way to get the most out of our leadership trichotomy is not only to distinguish between "protean," "composite," and "specialized" types, but also to develop a scale to rank performances in the various sectors of activity. Then we can say that a given revolutionist is "primarily" an ideologist, agitator, or administrator without neglecting the other aspects, if any, of his contribution to the revolution. To illustrate, let us somewhat impressionistically allot one point for poor performance, two for mediocre, three for good, and four for outstanding performance in our three activities to a list of important revolutionists from several revolutions.

Figure 15. Revolutionaries Ranked According to Role Proficiencies

	Ideologist	Agitator	Administrator	Composite
Cromwell	1	2	4	7
Robespierre	2	3	2	7
Sieyes	3	1	2	6
Lenin	4	3	4	11
Trotsky	4	4	2	10
Stalin	2	3	4	9
Bukharin	3	2	1	6
Mao Tse-tung	4	3	4	11
Chou En-lai	1	2	4	7
Castro	1	4	2	7
Guevara	2	4	1	7

As we have selected some of the best-known revolutionists, the composite scores are artifically high because their very reputations imply composite skills. More obscure revolutionists would tend to be more specialized and mediocre in their specialization.

CONCLUSION

We have analyzed the protagonists of revolution under four basic categories. The fundamental patterns of social stratification are involved in our discussion of classes and crisis strata. Though we have concluded that whole social classes such as workers or peasants are much too diversified to play a uniform, consistent role in revolutions, when we allow for substantial regional variations and for external leadership, class analysis can make an important contribution to our knowledge of specific revolutions. Similarly, when we broaden our notion of social stratification from classes to crisis strata, we are better able to understand how basic social structure interacts with changing, conjunctural factors to dispose particular groups (perhaps segments of broad strata) towards a revolutionary solution of their problems.

Such an understanding of the complexities of social structure, when joined with awareness of the role of political elites, should discredit once and for all theories that make an undifferentiated "the people" or "the masses" the main protagonist of revolution. Political elites—especially the various subdivisions of the intelligentsia—play a crucial role in revolutions. Without their leadership no revolution could come close to success. Student movements, guerrilla bands, and revolutionary political parties can make an impact far beyond what their often small numbers would indicate. If ideology and organization are important aspects of revolution, the importance of elite formations seems assured. They create and propagate revolutionary ideologies and direct the various organizational manifestations of the revolutionary movement. While the exact weight of the elite may vary somewhat in different revolutions, it is always imposing.

Our discussion of crowds and collective behavior calls attention to that side of revolutionary politics that is not encompassed in the more patterned behavior of distinct social groups or organized political formations. Though classic theories of crowd psychology were wrong to construe revolution almost exclusively in terms of nonrational crowd behavior, as one form of revolutionary action crowd behavior *can* turn the balance in one direction or another at certain decisive points. Related phenomena such as panics and social movements also can have serious political consequences in the highly volatile atmosphere of revolution.

Much of the "grand theory" of revolution deals with complex formulas of social change, modernization, growth of the state, and so on; nevertheless, a true sensitivity to the uniqueness of revolutions leaves some room for the influence of dynamic leaders. The more effective of these leaders leave an impress on the revolution that no one else could have duplicated. While the returns are not yet in, there is a good chance that some of these leaders share sufficient personality traits that one or several types of revolutionary personality with a distinctive pattern of development can be articulated. Only further research will tell.

But perhaps the main implication of this chapter is methodological rather than substantive: that is, a truly rigorous and comprehensive understanding of the revolutionary process is only possible in a synthetic view of nearly all the disciplines and subdisciplines of social science. The historian, political scientist, sociologist, anthropologist, individual and social psychologist, and economist can all tell us things we wish to know about the various protagonists of revolution.

NOTES

[1] Alexis de Tocqueville, *Recollections* (New York: Meridian Books, 1959).

[2] *Ibid.*, p. 34.

[3] *Ibid.*, p. 35.

[4] *Ibid.*, p. 151.

[5] *Ibid.*, p. 74. Cf. Marx's analysis: "None of the numerous revolutions of the French bourgeoisie since 1789 was an attempt against *order*, because each left intact the rule of the class, the slavery of the workers, and the bourgeois order, no matter how often the political form of that rule and that slavery changed. June had laid hands on that order. Woe to that June!" "The Suppression of the June, 1848 Revolution," in Karl Marx, *On Revolution*, ed. S. K. Padover (New York: McGraw-Hill, 1971), pp. 148–49.

[6] Tocqueville, *Recollections*, pp. 73–74.

[7] *Ibid.*, p. 150.

[8] *Ibid.*

[9] *Ibid.*, p. 78.

[10] Mark Seldon, *The Yenan Way in Revolutionary China* (Cambridge, Mass.: Harvard University Press, 1972). Cf. the brief exposition of Johnson's thesis in Chapter IV above.

[11] Seldon, *Yenan Way*, p. 88.

[12] *Ibid.*, p. 277.

[13] The Chinese peasantry have neither directed the Chinese Revolution nor gotten what they originally *wanted*: this says nothing whatever about the issue of whether they have gotten what they *need*. See Isaiah Berlin, *Two Concepts of Liberty* (Oxford: Oxford University Press, 1963) for some of the philosophic issues involved.

[14] Franz Schurmann, *Ideology and Organization in Communist China* (Berkeley: University of California Press, 1971), p. 415.

[15] *Ibid.*, p. 416.

[16] See Chapter IV, "A Catalytic Theory of Revolutionary Leadership."

[17] William Kornhauser, *The Politics of Mass Society* (New York: The Free Press, 1963), p. 47.

[18] *Ibid.* We have avoided the term "totalitarian" up to now because of the controversial and elastic meaning of the concept to which it refers. Major difficulties of the concept include its overemphasis on secret police terrorism and its underemphasis of the resilience of social groups and institutions to attempted take-over or penetration. For a classic statement, see Carl J. Friedrich and Z. K. Brzezinski, *Totalitarian Dictatorship and Autocracy* (New York: Praeger, 1956); and for a critique, see Carl J. Friedrich, Michael Curtis, and Benjamin R. Barber, *Totalitarianism in Perspective: Three Views* (New York: Praeger, 1969).

[19] Cf. William Kornhauser's remark that "members of the elite are recruited from the mass and continue to be exposed to the values of the mass, so that even they tend to accept populist values." *Mass Society*, p. 60. However, this point must not obscure the equally important one that large numbers of *déclassés* from the higher strata also become important figures in mass or "totalitarian" movements.

[20] Theodore Draper, *Castro's Revolution* (New York: Praeger, 1967), p. 13.

[21] *Ibid.*

[22] Theodore Draper, *Castroism: Theory and Practice* (New York: Praeger, 1965), p. 111. "Castroism is not a peasant movement or a proletarian movement any more than it was a middle-class movement. The *déclassé* revolutionaries who have determined Cuba's fate have used one class or another, or a combination of classes, for different purposes at different times. Their leader functions above classes, cuts across classes, or maneuvers between them." *Ibid.*, p. 113.

[23] Gerrit Huizer, "Emiliano Zapata and the Peasant Guerrillas in the Mexican Revolution," in *Agrarian Problems and Peasant Movements in Latin America,* ed. R. Stavenhagen (Garden City, N.Y.: Anchor Books, 1970), pp. 397–98. Also John Womack, Jr., *Zapata and the Mexican Revolution* (New York: Vintage Books, 1969).

[24] George M. Foster, "Introduction: What is a Peasant?," in *Peasant Society: A Reader,* ed. J. Potter, M. N. Diaz, and G. M. Foster (Boston: Little, Brown & Co., 1967), p. 6.

[25] Basile Kerblay, "Chayanov and the Theory of the Peasantry as a Specific Type of Economy," in *Peasants and Peasant Societies,* ed. T. Shanin (Baltimore: Penguin Books, 1971), p. 153.

[26] Hamza Alavi, "Peasants and Revolution," in *The Socialist Register 1965,* ed. R. Miliband and J. Saville (New York: Monthly Review Press, 1965), p. 244.

[27] Eric R. Wolf, *Peasant Wars of the Twentieth Century* (New York: Harper & Row, 1969), pp. 289–90.

[28] *Ibid.*, p. 292.

[29] Alavi, "Peasants and Revolution," p. 249.

[30] *Ibid.*, p. 251.

[31] Edward Malefakis, *Agrarian Reform and Peasant Revolution in Spain* (New Haven: Yale University Press, 1970), p. 98.

[32] *Ibid.*, p. 129.

[33] *Ibid.*, p. 104.

[34] Seymour M. Lipset, *Political Man* (Garden City, N.Y.: Anchor Books, 1963), p. 333.

[35] *Ibid.*

[36] Lewis S. Feuer, *Marx and the Intellectuals* (Garden City, N.Y.: Anchor Books, 1969), p. 61.

[37] *Ibid.*, p. 61.

[38] *Ibid.*

[39] Quoted in Max Nomad, *Aspects of Revolt* (New York: Bookmen Associates, 1959), p. 160.

[40] Edward Shils, "The Intellectuals in the Political Development of New States," in *Political Change in Underdeveloped Countries,* ed. John H. Kautsky (New York: John Wiley, 1964) p. 205.

[41] *Ibid.*

[42] Robert C. North and Ithiel de Sola Pool, "Kuomintang and Chinese Communist Elites," in *World Revolutionary Elites,* ed. Harold D. Lasswell and Daniel Lerner (Cambridge: M.I.T. Press, 1966), p. 320.

[43] *Ibid.*, p. 389.

[44] *Ibid.*, p. 417.

[45] Regis Debray, *Revolution in the Revolution?* (New York: Grove Press, 1967), p. 111.

[46] Lewis S. Feuer, *The Conflict of Generations* (New York: Basic Books, 1969), p. 11.

[47] *Ibid.*, p. 5.

[48] See "The Psychoanalytical Approach" below for the Freudian backdrop of this type of analysis.

[49] Feuer, *Conflict*, p. 35.

[50] *Ibid.*, p. 8.

[51] *Ibid.*

[52] *Ibid.*, p. 22.

[53] *Ibid.*

[54] Sidney Harcave, *The Russian Revolution of 1905* (New York: Collier Books, 1970), pp. 100–01.

[55] Feuer, *Conflict*, p. 117.

[56] A. Doak Barnett, *China on the Eve of Communist Takeover* (New York: Praeger, 1968), p. 43.

[57] *Ibid.*, p. 47.

[58] Schurmann, *Ideology and Organization*, p. 582.

[59] Harry J. Benda, "Non-Western Intelligentsias as Political Elites," in *Political Change*, ed. J. Kautsky, p. 244.

[60] Morris Janowitz, *The Military in the Political Development of New Nations* (Chicago: University of Chicago Press, 1967), pp. 64–65.

[61] Anatole Mazour, *The First Russian Revolution, 1825* (Stanford: Stanford University Press, 1965), p. 97.

[62] Samuel P. Huntington, *Political Order in Changing Societies* (New Haven: Yale University Press, 1970), p. 414.

[63] Debray, *Revolution in the Revolution?*, pp. 111–12.

[64] *Ibid.*, p. 106.

[65] See Richard Gott, *Guerrilla Movements in Latin America* (Garden City, N.Y.: Anchor Books, 1972), Chap. V.

[66] Huntington, *Political Order*, p. 315.

[67] Rosa Luxemburg, *The Russian Revolution and Leninism or Marxism?* (Ann Arbor: University of Michigan Press, 1961), p. 88.

[68] Not surprisingly, some of the criticism of LeBon is no less ideological than his own work.

[69] Gustave LeBon, *The Crowd* (New York: The Viking Press, 1960), p. 156.

[70] *Ibid.*, p. 32.

[71] In LeBon's day, the limitations posed to hypnotic suggestion by the subject's deepest moral convictions were not fully recognized. Quite naturally, LeBon's overestimate of the power of hypnosis carried over into his views on crowd suggestibility.

[72] Gustave Lebon, *The Psychology of Revolution* (Wells, Vt.: Fraser Publishing Co., 1968), p. 70. This description of a protagonist of revolution calls to mind how Marx wished to keep the *lumpenproletariat* at arms distance from the revolutionary movement. Bakunin, flying in the face of both Marx and (by implication) LeBon, proclaims that "I have in mind the 'riff-raff,' that 'rabble' almost unpolluted by bourgeois civilization, which carries in its inner being and in its aspiration . . . all the seeds of the socialism of the future, and which alone is powerful enough to inaugurate and bring to triumph the socialist revolution." Mikhail Bakunin, *Bakunin on Anarchy* (New York: Vintage Books, 1972), p. 294.

[73] Stanley Milgram, "Crowds," in *Handbook of Social Psychology*, 2d ed., Vol. IV, ed. Gardner Lindzey and E. Aronson (Reading, Mass.: Addison-Wesley, 1969), p. 533.

[74] Roger W. Brown, "Mass Phenomena," in *Handbook of Social Psychology*, Vol. II, ed. Gardner Lindzey (Cambridge: Addison-Wesley, 1956), p. 834.

[75] *Ibid.*, p. 841.

[76] For the following six points, see Milgram, "Crowds," and Ralph H. Turner, "Collective Behavior," in *Handbook of Modern Sociology*, ed. Robert E. L. Faris (Chicago: Rand McNally, 1964).

[77] Milgram, "Crowds," p. 554.

[78] *Ibid.*, p. 555.

[79] Since revolutionary crowd phenomena have been most closely studied for the great French Revolution, the following discussion is based on research for that era. However, the general principles are largely transferable to other contexts, although the precise importance of crowds in revolutions will vary according to factors such as rural-urban configuration, etc.

[80] Georges Lefebvre, "Revolutionary Crowds," in *New Perspectives on the French Revolution*, ed. Jeffrey Kaplow (New York: John Wiley, 1965), p. 180.

[81] *Ibid.*, p. 182.

[82] Turner, "Collective Behavior," p. 392.

[83] Lefebvre, "Revolutionary Crowds," p. 188.

[84] *Ibid.*, p. 189.

[85] George Rudé, *The Crowd in the French Revolution* (New York: Oxford University Press, 1969), p. 219.

[86] *Ibid.*, p. 122.

[87] *Ibid.*, p. 198.

[88] *Ibid.*, p. 220.

[89] Lefebvre was careful to point out that "pure" spontaneity was relatively rare "because an intermental action and a formation of a collective frame of mind had already taken place." *Ibid.*, p. 175.

[90] Rudé, *French Revolution*, p. 200.

[91] Brown, "Mass Phenomena," pp. 846–47.

[92] *Ibid.*, p. 846.

[93] *Ibid.*, p. 847.

[94] Floyd Allport, *Social Psychology* (Boston: Houghton Mifflin, 1924), p. 313.

[95] Brown, "'Mass Phenomena," p. 847.

[96] Georges Lefebvre, *La Grand Peur de 1789* (Paris: Armand Colin, 1970).

[97] *Ibid.*, p. 247.

[98] G. M. Trevelyan, *England Under the Stuarts* (London: Methuen & Co., 1965), p. 192.

[99] Lewis M. Killian, "Social Movements," in *Handbook of Modern Sociology*, p. 431.

[100] Hans Toch, "Social Movements," in *Handbook of Social Psychology*, 2nd ed., Vol. IV, p. 586.

[101] Eric Hoffer, *The True Believer* (New York: Mentor Books, 1958), p. 44. Hoffer probably underestimated the degree to which some, perhaps most, social movements do serve to give meaning to the lives of their members and to better their lives in some rather concrete and material ways. Stated differently, social movements can attract different people for different reasons.

[102] Killian, "Social Movements," p. 432.

[103] Sidney Hook, *The Hero in History* (Boston: Beacon Press, 1967), p. 174.

[104] *Ibid.*, p. 114.

[105] *Ibid.*, p. 153.

[106] Hook mentions the "moderates" Kerensky and Lafayette. We might add Lamartine in the French Revolution of 1848, Sun Yat-sen in China, Francesco Madero in the Mexican Revolution, and Manuel Azaña in the Spanish Revolution.

[107] *Ibid.*, p. 220.

[108] *Ibid.*, p. 154.

[109] *Ibid.*, p. 113.

[110] *Ibid.*, pp. 167–68.

[111] See Harold D. Lasswell, *Psychopathology and Politics* (New York: Viking Press, 1960); and *Power and Personality* (New York: Viking Press, 1962); Erik Erikson, *Young Man Luther* (New York: W. W. Norton, 1962).

[112] Lasswell, *Psychopathology*, p. 124.

[113] Lasswell, *Power*, p. 57.

[114] *Ibid.*, p. 39.

[115] Sigmund Freud and William C. Bullitt, *Thomas Woodrow Wilson* (Boston: Houghton Mifflin, 1967). Whatever the role of Freud in the later chapters of this book, Chapter I is authentically Freud or Freudian.

[116] *Ibid.*, p. 36.

[117] Sigmund Freud, *The Ego and the Id* (New York: W. W. Norton, 1962), p. 30.

[118] Freud and Bullitt, *Wilson*, p. 36.

[119] *Ibid.*, p. 38.

[120] *Civilization and its Discontents* (Garden City, N.Y.: Anchor Books, n.d.), p. 75.

[121] *Ibid.*, p. 61.

[122] Freud and Bullitt, *Wilson*, p. 38.

[123] *The Ego and the Id*, p. 15.

[124] *Ibid.*, p. 24.

[125] *Ibid.*, p. 25.

[126] Freud and Bullitt, *Wilson*, p. 42.

[127] *Ibid.*, p. 43.

[128] *Civilization and its Discontents*, p. 20.

[129] Freud and Bullitt, *Wilson*, p. 44.

[130] In what follows we must bear in mind the chastening remarks of Lucien Pye that "in spite of the enthusiasm of those who are ready to try to enrich political science with Freud's psychoanalytical contributions, . . . the results are often awkward, and at times grotesque." "Personal Identity and Political Ideology," in *Psychoanalysis and History*, ed. Bruce Mazlish (New York: Grosset & Dunlap, 1971), p. 151.

[131] Only thus can the framework itself be adequately tested. This would involve studies of the top leaders of the various revolutions from a psychoanalytical point of view, a comparison of the results obtained, and a final decision as to whether the Freudian or some other scheme is best equipped to deal with the problem.

[132] Gustav Bychowski, *Dictators and Disciples* (New York: International Universities Press, 1969), p. 245.

[133] *Ibid.*, p. 247.

[134] *Ibid.*, p. 246.

[135] *Ibid.*, p. 112.

[136] *Ibid.*, p. 113.

[137] *Ibid.*

[138] *Ibid.*, p. 112.

[139] *Ibid.*

[140] Freud, *Group Psychology and the Analysis of the Ego* (New York: Bantam Books, 1960), p. 95.

[141] E. Victor Wolfenstein, *The Revolutionary Personality* (Princeton: Princeton University Press, 1971), p. 21.

[142] *Ibid.*, p. 23.

[143] Erikson, *Luther*, p. 14.

[144] *Ibid.*

[145] *Ibid.*, pp. 14–15.

[146] Wolfenstein, *Revolutionary Personality*, p. 308.

[147] Bychowski, *Dictators*, p. 69.

[148] See the essays by E. Gellner, J. W. N. Watkins, and A. M. MacIver in May Brodbeck, ed., *Readings in the Philosophy of the Social Sciences* (New York: Macmillan, 1968).

[149] George Devereux, "Personality and the Social System as Levels of Analysis," in *Personality and Social Systems,* ed. N. J. Smelser and W. T. Smelser (New York: John Wiley, 1963), p. 27.

[150] *Ibid.,* p. 30.

[151] *Ibid.*

[152] This conclusion is not necessarily shared by psychiatrists: one of them writes that the "idea of mental illness is of very limited usefulness in delineating the revolutionary personality. We should be concerned with psychodynamics rather than psychopathology." Zebulon C. Taintor, "Assessing the Revolutionary Personality," in *Revolution and Political Change,* ed. Claude E. Welch and Mavis B. Taintor (No. Scituate, Mass.: Duxbury Press, 1972), p. 249.

[153] Hoffer, *True Believer;* and Killian, "Social Movements."

[154] Hoffer, *True Believer,* p. 128.

[155] *Ibid.,* p. 131.

[156] Killian, "Social Movements," p. 443.

[157] Lasswell, *Personality,* pp. 88–89.

[158] Hoffer, *True Believer,* p. 131.

[159] It is important in this context to avoid further trivialization of the term "charisma": in recent times nearly every political leader is alleged to exude charisma by the bucketful. James V. Downton, Jr. warns us that it is "fallacious to equate charismatic leadership with popular leadership. . . ." More particularly, "while a sector of a leader's following may be committed on a charismatic basis, a sizable number may follow because the leader proposes to solve their problems or threatens to terrorize them for disobedience." *Rebel Leadership* (New York: The Free Press, 1973), p. 217. Downton advocates a broad notion of "personal leadership," which encompasses "transactional leadership" (a leader's capability to dispense benefits and sanctions), "inspirational leadership" (the ability of a leader to clarify values and give meaning to suffering), and properly "charismatic leadership" (the leader's ability to lessen psychic tensions in the follower). A leader might exercise one, two, or three of these forms of leadership. In terms of our trichotomy of ideologists, administrators, and agitators, it is the last who would be most likely to have a following because of charisma. The correlation of "inspirational leadership" with the ideologists and of "transactional leadership" with the administrators would likewise seem to be quite high. Nevertheless, Downton's emphasis on the multilateral basis of most leadership phenomena seems valid. See also James C. Davies, "Political Charisma and Revolution," to be published in a collection of essays edited by Mattei Dogan.

[160] Lasswell, *Psychopathology*, p. 78.

[161] *Ibid.,* p. 125.

[162] Hoffer, *True Believer,* p. 131.

[163] Killian, "Social Movements," p. 442.

[164] *Ibid.*

[165] Hoffer, *True Believer,* p. 120.

[166] Killian, "Social Movements," p. 442.

[167] *Ibid.,* pp. 442–43. See Lasswell's distinction between "specialized" and "composite" political types. *Psychopathology*, p. 54.

VIII

CONCLUSION:
COUNTERREVOLUTION
AND REVOLUTION

COUNTERREVOLUTION

LIKE nearly all the major concepts evoked by the study of revolution, the concept of counterrevolution is a fruitful source of ideological contention. The adjective "counterrevolutionary" has been applied to everything ranging from traditional conservatism and fascism up to whatever happens to diverge from someone's idea of what is truly and virtuously "revolutionary." For our purposes it is best to think of counterrevolution as closely related to revolution: counterrevolution is an oppositionist political response to an imminent, early, or advanced revolution. There must exist some authentic imposing revolutionary threat either in one's own country or accessible to it in order to generate counterrevolutionary thought and behavior. In other instances where a "rightist" political movement exists, without a revolutionary situation, we are confronted with a *conservative, reactionary,* or *fascist* movement as the case may be. The first two major sections of this chapter will attempt to make these terms precise enough to justify the narrow connotation of counterrevolution we are suggesting.

A counterrevolution, therefore, is a definite sociopolitical movement that aims to forestall, arrest, or reverse an authentic revolutionary process. The real or feigned panic of conservatives about the danger of revolution is not truly counterrevolutionary unless we can also identify a serious movement toward revolution. Thus, a goodly number of right-wing movements are not counterrevolutionary, though they would be if a revolutionary situation did develop. An obvious conclusion from this is that to some extent study of the causes of revolution is *ipso facto* a study of the causes of counterrevolution. Accordingly, our encounter with the complexity of revolution suggests similar complexity for counterrevolution, especially with respect to the diverse sources of support for counterrevolution. In fact, the unwieldiness and turbulence of the counterrevolution may well exceed the disarray among the revolutionaries.

The lack of ideological and organizational unity amongst the counterrevolutionary forces is particularly evident in the French and Russian revolutions. In France, the label "royalist" covered a spectrum from fairly liberal constitutional monarchists *(monarchiens)* to the "absolutists" who wished to restore the old regime intact as it existed before 1789. There was such a lack of coordination between regional counterrevolutionary movements that several seemingly good opportunities to topple the revolutionary regime were lost.[1] In the Russian Revolution the succession of counterrevolutionary military leaders—Denikin, Kolchak, Yudenich, Wrangel—was one of the mildest symptoms of the disorder reigning amongst the counterrevolutionary forces. The different breeds of revolutionaries at least have some sort of "revolutionary myth" to bind them together, while counterrevolutionaries oppose the revolution from a variety of standpoints.[2] In strategic terms, seizure of the capital city (in Western revolutions) gives the revolutionaries a central base of command and communications, while the counterrevolutionaries are generally forced to operate in the periphery. This latter disadvantage can be overcome. Though Madrid and Barcelona remained in Loyalist hands, Franco succeeded in imposing an impressive unity of command and organization among the Spanish counterrevolutionaries. For once, it was the revolutionary side that was most plagued by political, regional, and ideological discord.

Three important factors help to determine the exact shape and strength of counterrevolutionary movements: regionalism, religion, and foreign intervention. Diverse regional response both to revolution and counterrevolution is a feature of all revolutions. During the so-called First Civil War (1642–46) in England, the counterrevolutionary forces of the king controlled vast areas of northern and western England, while the parliamentary forces dominated in the eastern and southern counties. In France in the peak year of 1793, the counterrevolution was strongest in parts of western and southern France, while central and eastern France were more or less loyal to the revolutionary government in Paris. In the Russian civil war the Bolsheviks retained control of most of the heartland of European Russia, while a series of thrusts against them won wide areas of the periphery in the Ukraine, Siberia, the Caucasus, and the Donetz Basin. In the Spanish civil war the Nationalists established control with relative ease in most of northern and western Spain and by the end of the war in 1939 had confined the Loyalists to the quadrant of southeastern Spain.

Although part of the exact regional balance of power in the civil war situation is due to raw military consideration and quick action, the economic and cultural aspects of regional diversity influence whether the counterrevolutionary movement finds a hostile, chilly, or warm reception. In England the areas under Parliamentary control were "richer, more populous, generally more advanced both in agriculture and industry, the Royalist ones sparser, poorer and more backward." [3] Though regions are rarely monolithic, politically or otherwise, the counterrevolution in England was certainly stronger in those areas where modernization was most retarded. Similarly in France the great counterrevolutionary war of La Vendée took place in the most backward agricultural areas: "The segments of western France's society which supported the Revolution were those which urbanization had enveloped; the segments in which opposition appeared were those which urbanization had touched but little." [4] More specifically, counterrevolutionary sentiment in France was most widespread and intense in those subregions where the contrast between the intruding forces of modernization and the forces of tradition was most blatant.[5] The "purer" areas where modernization was well advanced or where it was virtually unknown experienced the counterrevolution at a reduced rate of involvement. Thus, for the English and French revolutions, rural regional characteristics and economic backwardness are highly correlated with counterrevolution.

Other counterrevolutions display regional variability, but with alternative cultural and economic features. In the Spanish Revolution, some of the most backward agricultural regions turned a deaf ear to the counterrevolution and enthusiastically supported advancement of the revolution. If we ignore hostility to the counterrevolution on the grounds of cultural or ethnic separatism (the Basques and the Catalans), it was the better-off agricultural regions that hailed the Franco uprising. Since the Spanish Revolution seemed headed in a collectivist direction, it had to appear somewhat threatening to small-holding peasants. Agriculture in northern Spain was precisely of this small-holding sort. In most of the South, the agrarian system was one "in which landless workers predominated. No land was transferred to this class, whose dependence on the large owners increased as the latter took over the disentailed properties. As the population grew, the lot of the workers probably worsened." [6] The different agricultural systems of the different regions of Spain, in other words, tended to produce peasants disposed either to revolution or to counterrevolution. Thus, the economic and other aspects of regionalism have a profound impact on both revolution and counterrevolution.

Religion can also be a potent source of counterrevolutionary activity. All revolutions attack the established or orthodox religious institutions, if not religion as such. The English Revolution was not entirely misnamed when it was called the "Puritan Revolution." Though no one contends that the king's support was exclusively religious, religious preferences and attachments were of some significance in the counterrevolution. Catholics, though persecuted for over a century, could expect harsher treatment from the revolutionary side. Similarly, the supporters of the Church of England must have blanched at the abolition of the episcopacy and the execution of Archbishop Laud. Religious (as distinguished from political) Presbyterians often turned against the revolution, when its religious reforms became insufferable to them. In the French Revolution, the Civil Constitution of the Clergy, which made priests into state functionaries, more than any other reform made the revolution anathema to numbers of French Catholics. The draconic anticlerical and sometimes antireligious measures of the Russian, Mexican, and Spanish revolutions have assaulted the religious sensibilities of the faithful. In the last case, "Throughout Republican Spain, churches and convents were indiscriminately burned and despoiled. Practically nowhere had the Church taken part in the [Franco] rising. . . . But the Churches nevertheless were attacked, as outposts of upper or middle-class morality and manners. Destruction rather than loot was the aim." [7] The point here is not terrorism, destruction, or loss of life: there is often little to choose between the White Terror of counterrevolution and the Red Terror of revolution. It is rather the impact of such deeds on the religiously inclined. To them there is a categorical difference between the destruction of sacred objects and persons and those that are merely profane. The counterrevolution must benefit from a sense of religious outrage. [8]

Revolutions provoke foreign intervention on both the counterrevolutionary and the revolutionary side. The range of impact of counterrevolutionary intervention is considerable, and its modes vary from direct massive military intervention to little more than public commiseration with the "victims" of revolution. The English Revolution saw a minimum of foreign intervention, largely because so much of Europe was in the throes of instability associated with the Thirty Years War. Charles' widow was a French Catholic princess and received subsidies from the French government, but the war before 1648 and the Fronde afterwards kept the regimes of Richelieu and Mazarin too busy at home to contemplate full-scale intervention across the Channel. Foreign help of various sorts was forthcoming to counterrevolutionary émigrés and agents in the French Revolution; but a balance sheet of this often clumsy, inadequate, ill-timed intervention would probably show that it helped as much as it harmed the cause of the revolution. Allied intervention against the Bolsheviks has been trumped up considerably in Soviet historiography, nevertheless its ultimate impact was probably less beneficial to the White cause than similar help to French counter-revolutionaries. Nazi and Italian fascist "volunteers" were of substantial help to Franco, but their role in determining the ultimate outcome of the Spanish civil war has often been exaggerated for propagandistic reasons. On the other hand, a model instance of successful foreign intervention in behalf of a counterrevolution occurred when the invading Romanian Army eventually supplied the *coup de grace* to Bela Kun's Soviet regime in 1919.

Direct military aid in behalf of counterrevolution can easily boomerang. We have already noted how the presence of the foreigner can trigger a nationalist resentment that the revolutionary leaders can exploit. One is tempted to say that if foreign intervention did not exist, it would have to be "invented." The inflation of the foreign danger has seemed to aid the beleaguered revolutionary regime on more than one historical occasion. If direct military intervention is the chosen medium, rapid, massive intervention has proven more successful than gradual, halting involvement. There is, however, a variety of alternative types of aid to counterrevolution. Money is the most important of these, since many counterrevolutionary movements seem short on financial resources. The British expended rather substantial sums during the French Revolution, and one does not have to be an extreme leftist to acknowledge the counterrevolutionary intent of much of United States foreign aid programs. Diplomatic support and shared intelligence can also be rendered to counterrevolutionary elements by foreign powers. All of these things must be operated with uncommon finesse to prove an unmixed blessing to the counterrevolution.

Protagonists of Counterrevolution

Quite often, the protagonists of counterrevolution comprise a cross section of the populace nearly as complex and socially representative as that of the revolutionary coalition. It is more than a question of a "handful of aristocrats" and "superstitious priests." In fact, in some revolutions vast numbers of people turn against the revolution, though all talk of majorities is dangerous in the context of revolution and counterrevolution. One consequence of the diversity of counterrevolutionaries is that they cannot compose differences sufficiently to strike a knockout blow against the revolutionary regime. Nevertheless, certain social groups are more responsive to counterrevolutionary appeals than others.

Though members of the aristocracy, gentry, or other privileged status groups can be found among the revolutionaries, there are good reasons why large numbers from these groups will follow or lead the counterrevolution. Concerning this problem the English and the Chinese revolutions provide us with two polar cases. In England many aristocrats and gentry were on the side of the revolution, though with less enthusiasm in the later stages. In China, on the other hand, the vast bulk of the gentry were counterrevolutionary, although some members of the gentry did support the communists. The strength of counterrevolutionary sentiment among the higher status groups reflects the character of each revolution: the more moderate the revolution, the weaker the counterrevolutionary response of the higher status groups. Nevertheless, these groups are disposed to counterrevolution, for even the mildest revolutions make inroads on the status system. They are also vulnerable on the economic and political fronts: as large landowners, aristocrats and gentry may be the targets of change in the structure and distribution of agrarian property; and as high political and military officials, they may be deprived of their positions during the course of the revolution. Though an aristocracy may not always be a "ruling class" in the Marxian sense of ownership of the main means of production or in Mosca's sense of monopoly of political power, it is often the titular and ceremonial leader of society. Accordingly, aristocrats symbolize the existing order, even if the political and economic grievances that move the revolutionaries are only indirectly the result of aristocratic interests and institutions. They are the most visible incarnation of the total evil of the old regime.

For these reasons aristocrats and lesser notables figure prominently in the ranks of counterrevolutionaries and among those émigrés who flee perhaps to fight another day.[9] Where tradition is strong, or because of their military or educational qualifications, aristocrats and gentry are placed or place themselves in the vanguard of counterrevolutionary movements. Sometimes their very prominence obscures the complex nature of the movement they lead, and revolutionary propaganda has a clear interest in overdramatizing their machinations. Thus, Charles Tilly has concluded that the role of aristocrats in the counterrevolution of La Vendée was smaller than commonly supposed.[10] Conspiracy—in which notables and aristocrats are frequently thought to play a part—is a viable partial explanatory category for counterrevolution, as similar ideas are for revolution, only when the proper safeguards against simplistic conspiracy theories are taken. In both revolution and counterrevolution there often is an element of mass spontaneity which we must neither exaggerate nor ignore, but find the proper balance for in each historical case.

Peasants often play a significant role in the counterrevolutionary movement. There seem to be three major factors involved. We have already seen that the structure of agrarian tenure in relation to the trend of economic development is an important consideration in revolution. Under certain conditions the independent peasant proprietor will favor revolution because he wants more land or the abolition of remaining seigneurial privileges. On the other hand, a free-holding peasantry that has benefited from earlier land reforms may see revolution as a threat to what they already possess. They will tend to support the counterrevolution. Landless agricultural laborers, sharecroppers, and those who rent their land from big landlords tend to favor revolution, but not necessarily so. An important determinant seems to be the relationship of landlord and peasant. If it is perceived as exploitative, the peasants may favor the revolution; but if a certain paternalistic ethos remains, the peasant may preserve a solidary relationship with the landlord and follow (or perhaps lead) him into counterrevolution. Again this result is most likely where rationalization for a market economy has not advanced enough to overturn an earlier way of life.

A second factor predisposing peasants to counterrevolution is religion. Peasants are usually the most fervently religious group in the country, even if their orthodoxy is sometimes questionable. Skepticism, agnosticism, and secularism take root more readily in the urban milieu. The religious measures of the revolution may therefore spur peasants to join the counterrevolution. This seems especially true in La Vendée: "to the extent that the rebellion of 1793 can be said to have articulated aims and ideology, they were cast primarily in religious terms." [11] Both in La Vendée and the Carlist area of Spain [12] the counterrevolutionary civil war took on the aspect of a holy war or crusade.

The third factor is less concrete and more variable. It is the existence of a peculiarly peasant view of the world that supports tradition against the challenge of innovation. Despite the differences between various peasant societies, Robert Redfield has found a common core of peasant attitudes and values which includes "an intense attachment to native soil; a reverent disposition to habitat and ancestral ways; a restraint on individual self-seeking in favor of family and community; a certain suspiciousness, mixed with appreciation of town life; a sober and earthy ethic." [13] Most of these traits are highly incongruous with modern revolutionary ideologies. Reverence for ancestral ways seems the antithesis of the revolutionary theme of progress. Stress on family and (local) community eludes such categories of revolutionary thought as the individual, the class, the nation, or humanity at large. Suspiciousness of the town has often been extended to urban revolutionaries and their preachings. No revolutionary ideology can be described as a "sober and earthy ethic." Unless broken down by various currents of change, the peasant view of the world disposes towards traditionalism and the status quo rather than towards drastic change. This world view often puzzles outsiders—revolutionaries and others—who see the evident peasant interest as throwing off the yoke of exploitation that benefits the upper social strata. But the puzzlement results from ignoring the total picture of the peasant way of life. It is not always or merely that the peasantry has been duped by the aristocracy or the gentry: they have quite their own reasons, good or bad, for ignoring the revolution or supporting the counterrevolution.

Also important in certain counterrevolutions are elements of the officer corps of the old regime. To grasp the full significance of this, Katherine Chorley's strictures about the pivotal role of the military must be kept in mind: "In a revolutionary situation the attitude of the army is . . . of supreme importance. It is the decisive factor on which will depend success or failure. The army's attitude will be determined in part by the corps of officers and in part by the rank and file. The evidence suggests that widespread dissatisfaction among officers is generally sufficient in practice to paralyse the striking power of the army." [14] This statement suggests that if the officer corps were uniformly counterrevolutionary and exercised effective command over the lower ranks, a revolution would either be nipped in the bud or overthrown in a *brief* counterrevolutionary insurrection. Obviously one or both of these conditions were lacking in the English, French, Russian, Spanish, Mexican, and other revolutions. Statistics about two of these revolutions should underscore the basic conclusion. In the Russian Revolution it is estimated that about 50,000 officers of the old regime served in the Red Army during the civil war.[15] Just over half (4660 out of 9000) higher officers in the Spanish Peninsular Army went over to the Nationalists; the rest remained loyal to the Republican regime.[16] The result in either case was three years of bloody civil war. Unless the counterrevolution can count on substantial support from part of the old officer corps, its chances of success seem dim.

Quite naturally the counterrevolution splits the officer corps into three basic categories: (1) those who remain loyal to the revolutionary regime; (2) those who through conviction go over to the counterrevolution; and (3) those who adapt themselves to given conditions and change sides one or more times, the opportunists.[17] Since high military rank in certain societies is a near-monopoly of the upper status groups or classes, many officers merely share the repugnance that the revolution arouses in privileged groups. But the situation is often not so simple as this. Sometimes the composition of the officer corps may be undergoing rapid change. Increased mobility in the global society or the need to replenish the ranks depleted by war account for the rise of new men, often with new ideas, into the officer corps. The end result is a politically heterogeneous or nondescript officer corps, as in Republican Spain: "Every political ideology . . . was represented within the officer corps by the early 1930's. Officers who admired the extreme left were few in number. . . . Those drawn towards the extreme right or ideas of nationalist authoritarianism were more numerous, but they were a definite minority. Most officers were either vague moderate pro-republican 'liberals'—using the term liberal in a loose way—or had no exact convictions at all." [18]

There is also a tendency in many, if not all, countries for the military to consider themselves the custodians of the national interest: protectors of the integrity and majesty of the state above and beyond politics and narrow partisanship. To many officers, Republican concessions to Basque and Catalan regionalism seemed to presage the dismemberment of Spain, and they consequently joined the counterrevolutionary movement of 1936. Sometimes this nationalist pride works in favor of the revolution, as when former Hapsburg officers rallied to the Soviet regime of Bela Kun because of their outrage at the "dismemberment" of Hungary. Thus, whether many officers opt for or against the revolution is not always a question of clear-cut ideology or social prejudice, but of their perception of the national interest in the given domestic and international situation.

The clergy are sometimes an important factor in the counter-revolution. There are even cases in La Vendée or Spain in which priests have left the pulpit to take up arms against the revolution. Revolutions run afoul of the Church for reasons of both power and ideology. The revolution is likely to attack the economic position and the political influence of the Church as part of the institutional setup of the old regime. Not surprisingly, the upper echelons of the church hierarchy will take umbrage at this. Also the revolutionary ideology may make claims that are hard to reconcile with the teachings and dogmas of the Church. This is likely to alienate elements of the lower clergy, who might otherwise go along with the social and political changes ushered in by the revolution. Of course, some clergymen will always side with the revolution, as did the more Puritan ministers of the Church of England; the "Constitutional" priests in France; and for reasons of regional nationalism, the Basque clergy in Spain. The exact balance between pro-revolutionary and counterrevolutionary contingents of the clergy will naturally reflect the intensity of the attack upon organized religion. Things often reach such a pitch that the mere holding of religious services is considered (by all parties) a counterrevolutionary act.

Types of Counterrevolution

Our decision to limit the concept of counterrevolution to a response to an actual revolution has typological implications. One typology is essentially chronological, though the time element brings a number of structural differences along with it. Accordingly, a counterrevolution may precede the actual outbreak of the revolution—a *preemptive counterrevolution;* or it may occur almost concomitantly with it—*reactive counterrevolution;* or it may be deferred until the revolution has become rather firmly established—*delayed counterrevolution.*[19]

The preemptive counterrevolution is the most difficult of our three basic types to identify. This is so because we stipulated that the threat of revolution must be real and imminent before we can speak of counterrevolution. But many right-wing movements have exploited fears of revolution, while in fact the objective chances of successful revolution from the left have in retrospect proven virtually nonexistent. In many interpretations of the rise of fascism, a notion of preemptive counterrevolution seems to be involved, but these same interpretations deny that a truly revolutionary situation existed in Italy in 1922 or Germany in 1933. From our standpoint, such assertions are contradictory. Either fascism is not counterrevolutionary or there was indeed a revolutionary situation involved. Without anticipating the discussion below, we can say that many Germans and Italians joined, supported, or tolerated the Nazi and fascist movements—not because they feared the imminent revolutionary triumph of Bolshevism, but because they were sick and tired of the economic and political disorder that troubled the two countries.[20] From this perspective a defensive "law and order" approach is not necessarily counterrevolutionary; it depends on the existing conditions.

A common instance of preemptive counterrevolution occurs when the existing regime moves to forestall the "importation" of revolution from a foreign revolutionary center. In this situation the demonstration effect of a successful revolution has made the outbreak of revolution at home a real possibility—we assume that this would not happen if conditions at home were not already ripe for radical groups to take the revolutionary cue. Domestic revolutionaries have responded in this way to the outbreak of the French Revolutions of 1789 and 1848, as well as to the Russian Revolution. However, we must always distinguish between mere civil disturbances and movements of a much deeper resonance. In a rather different context we know that the preemptive counterrevolution serves as a precipitant or accelerator of the revolution itself. King Charles' raising of his standard in Nottingham in August, 1642, and the military rising in Spain in July, 1936, can be seen in this light. In these cases, while the overall revolutionary process was operating before the launching of hostilities, the revolution had not yet broken out in an unequivocal way. It is usually the government or the army that takes the initiative in preemptive counterrevolution, because conditions are too ambiguous for other groups to act with decision. These groups will generally join in, if the counterrevolutionary probing action does indeed reveal an authentic revolutionary threat.

A reactive counterrevolution differs from the preemptive type in that much of the element of premeditation is missing. It follows immediately upon the heels of a genuine political thrust by the revolutionary movement. The counterrevolutionary response is almost reflexive in nature. Revolution and counterrevolution proceed in a dizzying pace of move and countermove. The Kornilov putsch in September, 1917, is a good example of an early counterrevolutionary thrust in the Russian Revolution, even though it was not necessarily as "reactionary" as some of the later White movements. Since the reactive counterrevolutionary movement emerges before the revolutionary regime has really consolidated its power throughout the country, a counterrevolutionary drive on the capital city—the revolutionary epicenter—is an overriding strategic goal of the movement. It is held, probably correctly, that ouster of the revolution from its base (in Western revolutions) will lead to the general collapse of the revolution.

The reactive counterrevolution is likely to be more spontaneous than either the preemptive or delayed types. The former is calculated, and the latter occurs when attitudes towards the revolution have had a chance to crystallize. With the reactive counterrevolution there is a basic mental uncertainty for many people, and some middle-of-the-roaders still hope for a broad national reconciliation. This factor makes it difficult sometimes to distinguish between the moderate revolutionaries (who soon are considered outright counterrevolutionaries by the radicals) and the less intransigent counterrevolutionaries. Nevertheless, there are differences of both a symbolic and more substantial nature. The moderate revolutionaries accept the myth and rhetoric of the revolution, while the counterrevolutionaries cannot bring themselves to utter the stock phrases of the moment. For them the situation requires reforms, not revolution. There are also specific issues that separate the two formations: to compromise on these would be to betray one's convictions. The process of polarization often wipes out this intermediate zone where, to outsiders, accommodation seems eminently feasible. The radicals replace the moderates on the revolutionary side, and (somewhat less dramatically) intransigent or "integral" counterrevolutionaries shove the flexible ones aside.

The delayed counterrevolution occurs after the revolutionary regime has established a substantial degree of control over the country. The delay of the counterrevolution has three possible causes: (1) an earlier attempt was so decisively crushed by the fledgling revolutionary regime that some time for recuperation and regroupment of counterrevolutionary forces was required; (2) the early moderation of the revolution did not provoke an immediately serious counterrevolutionary movement, but its later radicalism has proven the last straw for various sectors of society; and (3) foreign governments have taken some time in making up their minds to aid the counterrevolution enough to make it a going concern. That these explanations are not exclusive is seen in the case of La Vendée, in which the second and third factors were of some importance. We must also realize that before the development of mass communications, the full impact of a revolution (and thus its capacity to arouse counterrevolution) was often spread by a gradual capillary action. Its immediate effect in peripheral areas was considerably less than revolutionary. In the eighteenth century La Vendée was rather a remote region, and it was awhile after 1789 that the progress of the revolution drastically impinged on local problems.

Delayed counterrevolutions have registered few historical successes, and a major reason for this is the delay itself. The revolution normally has become semiestablished, supported by a myriad of new ideals and interests. Its internal security apparatus is always more impressive than that of the old regime. The English Restoration therefore seems more a testimony to the vacuum of leadership after Cromwell's death and to the overall moderation of the revolution than it does to the strength of a distinctive counterrevolutionary movement. Royalist risings in the 1650's were little more than minor irritations, even though Royalist sentiment was fairly strong. The French Restoration was imposed from the outside after Napoleon's crushing defeats. One also suspects that if the Spanish Nationalists had delayed a year or so, the mounting revolutionary wave would have made the conditions for a successful counterrevolution much more difficult, if not impossible.

FASCISM: REVOLUTION OR COUNTERREVOLUTION?

The Quintessence of Fascism

In the previous chapters our discussion has been of revolutions that can be described as coming from the "left" (i.e., revolutions that criticize the old regime from an ideological standpoint that stresses egalitarianism, rationalism, progressivism, and pacificism. We must nevertheless give a qualified yes to the question of whether fascism can be considered revolutionary. To see what is at issue we must first revert back to our original definition of revolution presented in Chapter I:

> A revolution is an acute, prolonged crisis in one or more of the traditional systems of stratification (class, status, power) of a political community, which involves a purposive, elite-directed attempt to abolish or to reconstruct one or more of said systems by means of an intensification of political power and recourse to violence.

If a political convulsion meets the standards suggested in this definition, it is a true and proper revolution. If a political movement aims to bring about the types and magnitude of change described in Chapter III, it deserves the label "revolutionary." If an ideology has the type of critique, affirmation, and strategic guidance we have associated with revolutionary ideologies, then it too is revolutionary. To begin to understand why this can be, we must explore the meaning of several key ideas more closely than we have done up to now.

We have occasionally employed the terms "conservative" and "reactionary" in a commonsense functional way: conservative, to suggest the desire to preserve the status quo perhaps with slight changes; and reactionary, to suggest the restoration of a status quo that has undergone considerable change. Conservatism and reaction would thus be milder and more extreme versions of a preference for the old order of things: both are antirevolutionary. However, conservatism also refers to a *body of political doctrine*,[21] while there is no substantive political doctrine of reaction*ism*. Thus, a substantive theory of "Conservatism" maintains that it is a set of political principles—a syndrome—that provides a general orientation towards man, society, history, and values.[22] One implication of this approach is that Conservatives may not be defenders of the established order: while "adjusted" Conservatives find essential congruity between their principles and their society, "alienated" Conservatives are highly critical of societies saturated with liberal or radical values and organized accordingly. People like T. S. Eliot or George Santayana felt morally, spiritually adrift in liberal capitalist society, precisely because they were philosophic Conservatives.

If we push the substantive theory of Conservatism to what may be untenable extremes, what seems paradoxical following common usage, a "Conservative revolution," becomes at least a logical possibility. Fritz Stern's conclusions about Germany have analogies in almost every Western country: "The term conservative revolution . . . denotes the ideological attack on modernity, on the complex of ideas and institutions that characterize our liberal, secular, and industrial civilization. . . . Our liberal and industrial society leaves many people dissatisfied—spiritually and materially. The spiritually alienated have often turned to the ideology of the conservative revolution." [23] While there is no example of an actual revolution with a Conservative ideology, some of its advocates—not all—have looked with great sympathy upon fascist movements as the best or only alternative to liberal "chaos" or Bolshevist "tyranny." [24]

If a nonliberal, nondemocratic, non-Marxist, nonanarchist revolution is at least a logical possibility, the question of the nature of fascism assumes strategic importance for the student of revolution. Does fascism seek to build a new society by revolutionary means, or merely to preserve or restore an old one by a variety of sham concessions to twentieth-century political necessities? Discussion of fascism is especially hampered by loose terminology. The literature in which fascism is something more than a political swearword has three major foci: (1) fascism as an ideology, (2) fascism as a social movement, and (3) fascism as a political regime. Failure to distinguish between, and show the relation between, these three aspects of fascism has led to confusion and false schematisms. An initial problem is the fairly widespread denial of any ideological substance to fascism at all.[25] In this view fascism is pure pragmatism—all nebulous *ad hoc* ideology with almost no preformed ideology. Our own view accords more with those maintaining that "there is in fact a fascist ideology which cannot be successfully analyzed as the rationalization of the interests of any given social class. It is a political ideology, usually articulated by declassed intellectuals, which becomes an animating force for a mass movement of solidarity. . . ." [26]

The distinction between fascism as a mass movement and fascism as a political regime has two sides: (1) all social movements are altered somewhat when they take political power—without certain ideological or organizational concessions to reality, Lenin, Hitler, Castro, Mussolini, and others could not have maintained themselves in power; and (2) social scientists often have such a broad notion of fascism that all sorts of social movements and political tendencies fall under its umbrella. Without envisaging some sort of basic fascist political regime as the projection of the movement and the ideology, it seems wrong to term any movement "fascist." Similarly, the tendency to lump all non-Marxist authoritarian political regimes under the rubric of fascism is easy to fall into if one ignores the backdrop of ideology and social movement (e.g., when the Salazar regime in Portugal or the "regime of the colonels" in Greece is termed "Fascist"). The phenomenon of fascism is difficult to grasp; it is impossible to do so if we ignore any of its three aspects.

Fascism, then, is a social movement armed with an ideology that leads towards the establishment of a particular sort of authoritarian political system. The characteristic traits of fascism are charismatic leadership, hypernationalism, mass movement, stress on voluntarism and activism, rejection of Marxism and the idea of necessary class struggle, elitism, antiparliamentarism, statism, the single-party regime, imperialism, rejection of materialist and positivist doctrines. Oriented in this way, the European fascist movements in the period 1919–45 "cannot be described as 'counter-revolutionary,' for they did not seek to replace something overthrown by a previous revolution. They were essentially revolutionary movements." [27] Perhaps it is better to say that European fascists "were or wanted to be revolutionaries." [28] The difficulty in making a definitive characterization of fascism is that wherever it appeared, it presented something of a split personality.

Hugh Trevor-Roper has suggested that "behind the vague term 'fascism' there lie, in fact, two distinct social and political systems. . . . These two systems are both ideologically based. Both are authoritarian, opposed to parliamentary liberalism. But they are different; and the confusion between these essentially different systems is an essential factor in the history of fascism." [29] Trevor-Roper calls these two elements "clerical conservatism" and "dynamic fascism." [30] Nearly every fascist movement was made up of these two elements, "but in varying proportions; and the variety of the proportions bears some relation to the class structure of the society concerned." [31] This variability is the point of departure for any truly comparative study of fascism. Unfortunately, this means that each fascist movement (or pseudofascist movement [32]) "had and maintained such peculiarities that it appears difficult, historically speaking, to talk of an effectively unitary phenomenon." [33] Though the authentic core of fascism contains a truly revolutionary dynamic, in the majority of cases it was neutralized or suspended through the strength of traditional conservatism either in the global society or in the movement itself. Thus fascism was compelled to tread a variety of paths. Since the Italian, German, and Spanish cases are somewhat exemplary and intrinsically important, the next section will attempt a brief interpretative sketch of Italian Fascism, German National Socialism, and Spanish Falangism. Only thus can we get a firmer grasp of the balance between conservative, counterrevolutionary, and revolutionary factors in the history of fascism.

Three Paths of Fascism

The nature and fate of the "fascist revolution" in various European countries depended on highly idiosyncratic conditions. Important variables included the extent of the threat of Marxist revolution; the organizational strength of Leftist trade unions and political parties; the intensity of fascist anticlericalism; the attitude of the military; the strength of fascism vis-à-vis conservative social forces such as the Church, the aristocracy, big business, the government bureaucracy, and the monarchy; the level of national integration; leadership and factionalism within the fascist movement; and so on. The most crucial consideration was the balance of power between "dynamic fascism" (i.e., its revolutionary core) and "clerical conservatism," both within the fascist movement and within the polity as a whole. Could fascism retain its initial revolutionary impetus or would it be partly or wholly commandeered and denatured by conservative, reactionary, or counterrevolutionary tendencies? Everywhere compromises were made, and only in Germany, Hungary, and Romania did fascism conserve a substantial share of its revolutionary élan. In Italy, compromises with the Church, the army, and business were serious enough to restrain—though not completely to suppress—revolutionary tendencies. With Falangism in Spain, the conservative and counterrevolutionary forces inundated, overwhelmed, and transformed the movement so that only a tiny spark of its original "dynamism" remained.

Germany. There is an abundance of explanations of the rise of National Socialism in Germany. Some Marxist explanations maintain that "German fascism" is merely a special case of the tendency of the bourgeoisie, because of the "general crisis" of capitalism, to shunt aside the nineteenth-century ideological props of liberalism and parliamentarism that disguised class rule and resort to a regime of blatant terrorism and repression. Whatever its national form, the content of fascism is a capitalist weapon to quell the workers' and revolutionary movement; thus it is inherently reactionary and counterrevolutionary. Another interpretation, the so-called cultural theory, looks back in German cultural history and finds that certain anti-Western features were associated with the growth of romanticist nationalism during and after the Napoleonic Wars. Such trends as irrationalism, antiliberalism, an ethnic or "folkish" concept of nationalism, an atavistic longing for the tribal Germanic past have borne their fruit in the ideology of National Socialism.[34] Still another approach sees the development of a mass society fostered by modern industrialism and accelerated by World War I as largely responsible for the rise of National Socialism[35]: "The National Socialist Party was, from the beginning, the expression of a crowd; Hitler himself realized that he could offer propaganda only to masses, that he could win and keep power only if he reduced the whole people to a crowd. And that he did." [36] Some students less enamored with the grand hypotheses mentioned have looked to more narrow political factors such as the Versailles Treaty, the rise of Bolshevism, the breakdown of the German multiparty system and thus of parliamentary government, the political impact of the Great Depression, etc., as important strands of a complex explanatory network.

National Socialism presented conservative and reactionary elements in Germany with a classic dilemma: on the one hand, here was a movement with potential mass appeal willing to do the dirty work apparently required by modern politics; on the other hand, the movement was plebeian and vulgar, with little regard for important traditions and with a disturbing, if demagogic, taste for social radicalism. German and other European conservatives were convinced that they could eventually check the verbal and activist excesses of the youthful fascist movements.[37] This was a gamble that had different results in different places. In Spain the conservatives won hands down; in Italy they both won and lost; in Germany their eventual loss had disastrous results for themselves, their country, and the modern world.

What the fascist movements needed from the conservative forces was money, some intellectual and social respectability, and a lessening of police harassment. Hitler did deliver certain points of the *quid pro quo* arrangement at the outset of his regime: (1) he abandoned some of the anti-big business tenets of early Nazi ideology; (2) he reached some understanding with the churches, as exemplified in the Concordat with the Pope (July 8, 1933); (3) he did not formally destroy the bureaucracy and the judiciary—two institutional sources of conservatism; (4) to placate the army, he attacked the "revolutionary" storm troopers (SA) and their leader Colonel Roehm in the famous "night of the long knives" (June 30, 1934). As the officer corps of the army was largely made up of the Prussian military "caste," Hitler seemed to offer something to each one of the conservative social forces on the German scene. Despite some misgivings German conservatives after the first year and a half of the Nazi regime must have congratulated themselves on their good fortune or good strategy. In foreign policy Hitler had begun to "revise" the hated Versailles "Diktat," and at home "order" had been restored and the Left reduced to impotence.

However, the history of the Third Reich from the mid-1930's to 1945 is largely a history of Hitler's reneging on his explicit and implicit promises to his erstwhile allies. Though business remained in private hands, economic decisions increasingly followed the decrees of a "command economy" supported by the political might of the Nazi regime.[38] Sporadic persecution of the Catholic and Protestant churches portended an even gloomier future for them if Hitler had not become embroiled in World War II.[39] Alongside the traditional bureaucratic and judicial structures there developed new Nazi political and coercive institutions: "This is the area in which the revolution actually took place, not in the changes of the traditional machinery of state; only in the build-up and encroachment of the police and SS state did the leader dictatorship prove to be a truly revolutionary system of rule." [40] In the case of the army we find increasing humiliation and purges of the officer corps, and a climax in the abortive plot to kill Hitler in June, 1944.

This is not simply a question of broken promises: the twelve years of the Third Reich represent a definite revolutionary thrust towards a kind of society that no German conservative true to his principles could approve.[41] Furthermore, it now seems clear that had Hitler won World War II, he would have sought a "final solution" regarding the church, the state, the army, and the economy.[42] The racism of National Socialism is a revolutionary doctrine because it envisages a radically new society: it did not wish the restoration of the Bismarckean Reich, to say nothing of earlier political forms. Its pan-Aryan aims carried beyond nationalism. To build a racially pure Aryan folk community led by a new elite of "blond beasts" requires such a reconstruction of society that one cannot withhold the label "revolutionary." The extermination of millions of Jews and others is only the most dramatic and tragic instance of measures directed to this end. That the Nazi revolution was at first more a political and a cultural revolution than an economic and social one does not make it the less a true revolution. Because of the Nazi defeat we have been spared further confirming evidence of this. What Hugh Seton-Watson says of fascist movements in general is true *a fortiori* of National Socialism: "The fact that their aims and policies were distasteful to me entitles me to call them evil revolutions, but not to deny their revolutionary character." [43]

Italy. It must be with some hesitation that one includes German National Socialism and Italian Fascism under the generic category of fascism. The ideological and organizational differences are manifold and deep, as are those between Chinese, Soviet, and Yugoslav "communism." Italian Fascism was never racist in the sense of National Socialism and its political system was far less totalitarian. However, there are real affinities: activism, elitism, the charismatic leader, dictatorship, militarism, etc. In political terms, the overriding difference was that the "fascist revolution" in Italy was forced to make and live up to more and greater compromises with the conservative social forces. The revolutionary impulse was considerably curtailed. Residues of parliamentarism lingered on, and the balance between legality and terrorism veered in different directions in Italy and Germany. Mussolini, for example, was never "head of state": since the monarchy was retained (fascism abandoned its early republicanism), he was merely "head of government." [44] Hitler soon absorbed both positions, and conservative hopes for a monarchical restoration were quickly shattered. Since Church-state relations were actually better under the Italian Fascist than under the previous liberal regime, it is evident that the Fascists lived up better to their own Concordat with the Pope (1929) than the Nazis to theirs. The Church's position was stronger in all respects than under the Nazis. Similarly, the "fascistization" of many aspects of Italian life proved more of a thin veneer than a real transformation. Thus the much-heralded "corporate state" was more of a formal reorganization than a distinctive alternative to capitalism or socialism.

Among the reasons why Italian Fascism proved less revolutionary than National Socialism, despite a head start (as a political regime) of more than a decade, are the nature of the respective parties and their relationship to the state. It must be recalled that Mussolini began his political career as a militant Anarcho-syndicalist leader of the revolutionary wing of the Italian socialists. He broke with his party because he favored Italian entry in World War I on the Allied side. After the war he formed the *fasci di combattimento,* paramilitary groups made up of ex-soldiers, students, and other malcontents. The early (1919) fascist program promised that they "would put an end to the monarchy; abolish the Senate, the aristocracy, compulsory military service, banks and stock exchanges; confiscate unproductive revenues; attack the money power; decentralize government; protect and educate the poor." [45] Had these measures come to pass, they would have constituted a revolution by almost anybody's standards. They could not have been "peacefully" introduced in the Italy of 1919. But fascism began as a numerically and financially weak movement; to achieve power required compromises and concessions to somebody. When the fascists counteracted increasing socialist militancy, the possessing classes and non-Leftist intellectuals saw the movement as a dike against the revolutionary flood. As Ernst Nolte (somewhat rhetorically) puts it: "Within a few months a few hundred squads of young men, supported by almost all the established forces of society, in a ruthless, naked class war destroyed with fire and sword . . . all these hard-won institutions in which the process of the people's self education had taken place, but which after the attempted impossible revolution seemed to large sectors of the middle classes an intolerable threat." [46]

This association with conservative social forces shifted the political center of gravity of Italian Fascism towards the right. The best indication of this development is the fusion of the Fascist and Nationalist parties in February, 1923, some months after the installation of Mussolini as premier in the previous October. Though this fusion diluted some of the socially radical aspects of the nascent fascist movement, the new merged party was always more than the tool of conservatives and vested interests: there was an obverse side to the compromise. "In securing conservative support, Fascism did not itself become conservative; rather, it obliged the men of the Old Right who joined Fascism to give actual or feigned approval to a political order which in its extremist practices had little in common with traditional conservatism. . . . The repressive dictatorship and one-party rule Fascism established after 1925 made it preeminently authoritarian, permanently disassociating it from the political position of the Old Right." [47] This was, however, a more gradual and less definitive political rupture than took place in Germany. Mussolini's compromises always weighed more heavily upon him than did Hitler's—a fact he would bitterly resent in the last eighteen months of his life.

Further blunting and retarding the revolutionary impetus of Italian Fascism is the relationship of the party to the state. While it is not necessarily the case, revolutionary militancy in a modern revolutionary regime tends to be centered more in the ruling party than in the government bureaucracy. The latter may harbor elements hostile or indifferent to the revolutionary movement and is addicted to that bureaucratic routine so alien to revolutionary enthusiasm. The Italian Fascist concept of the state—we owe the term "totalitarian" to them—differs substantially from that of National Socialism. As the ex-Nationalist Alfredo Rocco put it, "The force of the State must exceed every other force; that is to say, the State must be absolutely sovereign and must dominate all the existing forces in the country, coordinate them, solidify them, and direct them towards the higher ends of national life." [48] National Socialism had a less exalted, more instrumental view of the state. Hitler wrote in *Mein Kampf* that the "precondition for the existence of a higher humanity is not the state, but the nation possessing the necessary ability." [49] Thus "the state is a means to an end. Its end lies in the preservation and advancement of a community of physically and psychically homogeneous creatures." [50] States which do not obey the racial principle are "misbegotten, monstrosities in fact. The fact of their existence changes this no more than the success of a gang of bandits can justify robbery." [51]

In fascist Italy the state tended to absorb the party and perhaps unwittingly to impose its bureaucratic norms over the revolutionary norms of the latter. Just the opposite relationship has tended to prevail in the Soviet Union, though bureaucratization has increased since Stalin's death. Party-state relations in Nazi Germany fell vaguely somewhere in between the Soviet and Italian Fascist extremes. [52] Thus, under National Socialism

> where traditional and revolutionary elements continued to exist partly fused and partly as rivals, the primacy of the party was established only in specific instances; at times it almost seemed as if the opposite was the case. . . . The party did not issue orders to the state but rather gained quasi-governmental privileges and pushed through the total claims of the system in the social sphere as well by carrying out the extra-governmental functions of 'education,' coordination and control, and recruitment of youth. [53]

Thus, the greater autonomy of the party vis-à-vis the state meant that National Socialism could act in a more revolutionary way than Italian Fascism, but perhaps less so than Soviet or Chinese communism.

Spain. Spanish Falangism gives us a different rendition of the relationship between conservative ideas and social forces, and a professedly revolutionary fascist movement. Spanish fascism emerged on the political scene with the unification of two splinter groups to form the JONS or Juntas de Offensiva Sindicalista. Henceforth the movement was bifurcated into a more moderate, traditionalist tendency and a more radical, revolutionary one. Fascism in Spain, however, became a force to contend with only when José Antonio Primo de Rivera, son of the dictator of the 1920's, merged his own movement, the Falange, with the JONS to produce the Falange Espanola de Offensiva Nacional-Sindicalista. This merger further beclouded the ideological character of the movement.

In the early 1930's, the JONS and the Falange, first separately and then together, stridently proclaimed that theirs was a truly revolutionary movement. The Falange asserted its considerable sympathy with revolutionary socialism, but rejected its internationalism, its doctrine of class struggle, and virulent anticlericalism. Nevertheless, as in Germany and Italy, the Falange seemed a proper vehicle to serve the interests of those whose desires were the opposite of revolutionary. Like the related movements in their early days, the Falange suffered from a shortage of members and money. This allowed conservative elements to gain a foothold in it by enrollments and subventions. Even so, the protestations of José Antonio against this gambit have the ring of authentic indignation: "They suppose that we, too, are reactionaries, for while they murmur in their casinos and long for their lost privileges, they nourish the vague hope that we are going to be the shock troops of the reaction, that we are going to snatch their chestnuts from the fire and exhaust ourselves in re-establishing those who now contemplate us so comfortably. . . ." [54]

José Antonio tried with mixed success to keep clericals, monarchists, militarists, and other rightist elements at arms distance, but the very weakness of the Falange enjoined some flexibility. Thus, there came working agreements with the most hidebound conservative, indeed reactionary, group in Spain, the Carlists who were monarchists and clericals to a man. Of decisive importance for his movement and his country, José Antonio found himself in jail four months before the actual outbreak of the civil war. Other top Falangists were seized or slain not long after and the chief himself was executed on November 20, 1936. José Antonio's incarceration and execution removed the one personality that might have halted, if not reversed, the conservative drift of the movement. During the civil war, more and more conservative elements joined the movement, further watering down its "revolutionary" ideology and élan. The Falange was divided into a radical faction centering around Manuel Hedilla, a centrist faction that tried to follow the path of José Antonio but without his leadership, and a rightist group of newcomers of various conservative persuasions. [55]

But the *coup de grace* to the revolutionary hopes of Spanish fascism occurred when civilian and military supporters of General Francisco Franco saw the need for some sort of ideological and nonmilitary orientation to the Nationalist regime. After suitable plastic surgery to the movement (purge of radicals, influx of conservatives), April 19, 1937, marked the emergence of the Falange Espanola Tradicionalista y de las Juntas de Offensiva Nacional-Sindicalista, which to say the very least was "a clumsy title reflecting its eclectic composition." [56] From that point onward, the Falange despite occasional protests, was the thoroughly domesticated beast of the Francoist regime, and so it remained for over three decades. With its take-over by and subordination to the more conservative forces in Spain, the Falange could not be properly described as revolutionary or even fascist, though a few of the early members still cherished such illusions. Its role as the only legal political party in Spain masks its complete submission to the regime and its supporters. It is only one—and not necessarily the most important—of the power blocs including the Church, the army, business, and landowners, whose equilibrium is deftly managed by Franco. It is not "single-party" in the Soviet, Nazi, or even Italian sense: "Instead of a select, energetic political movement, the Falange had become a grand national honorary society." [57]

Just a brief survey of the German, Italian, and Spanish experiences should show that the question about the revolutionary nature of fascism is not easy to answer. That fascist ideology is more ambiguous than some of its competitors is no disqualification, if we recall the ideological vagueness of the early English, Cuban, and Mexican revolutions. In any case, a fascist or racist ideology in its specific context may promise and seek a society so different from the present one that its realization would be a truly revolutionary transformation. So long as the patterns of social stratification are significantly altered without restoration of the recent past, our criteria of revolutionary change seem to be met. Fascism as a social movement attracts true revolutionaries (especially youthful ones), as well as conservatives, counterrevolutionaries, and careerists. We have seen how the balance of these elements is of crucial moment in determining the final outcome of the movement. The revolutionary quality of the fascist regime is a resultant of the internal composition of the party and the relation of the latter to the state and to the Church, the army, the aristocracy, business, landowners, etc. All of these things worked out differently in Germany, Italy, and Spain. The revolutionary process went furthest in the first country, some distance in the second, and virtually nowhere in the third.[58]

FINAL CONCLUSIONS

The Study of Revolution

If one thing has clearly emerged from our comparative survey of revolution, it is the complexity and particularity of each historical revolution. For a certain type of historian this finding would seem to preclude the possibility of a rigorous "sociology of revolution" or even of a more modest comparative study of revolutions. This is an unduly pessimistic conclusion. In fact, there is some interconnection between discovery of certain common features of different revolutions and the full appreciation of their peculiar characteristics. Historians have rightly protested that many schemes and models of revolution ill accord with the actual complexity of particular historical revolutions. On the other hand social scientists have a point when they complain that the antitheoretical bias of certain historians is imported into their work from extrinsic considerations and is not simply the result of dispassionate historical inquiry. The wisest historians have always had one eye on the developments of the social sciences, while many social scientists have never lost sight of the historical fundament of their abstractions. The study of revolution seems one of the most promising areas for mutual aid between cautious fact-finders and unabashed theorists: it demands that the former look up and around from their narrow object of study and that the latter descend to the realm of facts to test the viability of their theoretical position.

This complexity of revolutions forced us very early to look to multiple causation as the best approach to studying the causes of revolution. The conclusion of Chapter IV that dissynchronous change in the social, cultural, and technological subsystems can produce revolutionary sentiments in certain crisis strata implies that only a broadly based interdisciplinary approach can begin to grapple with the multilateral totality of the revolutionary process. Two major methodological suggestions follow from this. First, specialists in anthropology, economics, and psychology should join historians, political scientists, and sociologists and study revolution from the particular perspective of their discipline. Second, all social scientists interested in revolution should acquaint themselves with how the insights and methods of the various disciplines can illuminate specific revolutions and aid general theory. At this stage the problems of the revolutionary personality, the relationship between population growth and revolution, and the economic history of revolutions are the areas that require the greatest research. The end result should be a theory (or group of theories) that is neither so streamlined as to lack empirical reference nor so complicated as to be inoperable.

If complexity is the primary methodological issue in the study of revolution, then the problem of objectivity runs it a close second. Much debate has developed on the very possibility of objectivity in the social sciences.[59] Probably no subject in the social sciences arouses such passionate disagreements as the study of revolution. Whether revolutions in general or specific revolutions are involved, moral and political values obtrude themselves at nearly all stages of analysis. Books on the French Revolution by Frenchmen or on the Spanish Civil War by Spaniards almost always double as political tracts. Foreign studies are often no less polemical. Perhaps complete objectivity in social science or the study of revolution is in principle unattainable, but this has unfortunately been taken as a license for the worst sort of ideological indulgence. Because we cannot achieve unsullied perfection is no good reason to abandon the quest for excellence or improvement. We have seen how issues such as spontaneity and conspiracy, the rationale of terror, the nature and role of the revolutionary crowd, or the meaning of the revolutionary personality are seen through the prism of ideology. The student of revolution must be aware of these tendencies in himself and others: it is not enough, as is sometimes held, to openly acknowledge one's ideological prejudices at the outset and then let them run rampant through his analysis. Unless there is a difference in principle between science and ideology, both notions lose their significance. The fact that science and ideology are often intermixed does not change this at all. In all the issues we have covered, we have implied that radicals or conservatives might be closer to the truth on this or that specific issue. Sometimes both have seemed equally wide of the mark; but there is a mark. The greatest analysts and historians of revolution have had their ideological predilections, but one soon senses that their accounts are subtle and nuanced and make more concessions to opposed viewpoints than their coreligionists can bring themselves to do. Passion may have its place in politics: in the study of politics it is often counterproductive.

The Future of Revolution

Though social science rightly warns against prophecy and facile prognostics, the argument of Chapters III and IV assumes that explanation and prediction are essentially similar operations. Prediction proves enormously more difficult, however, not so much because of some metaphysical principle, but because the information necessary to make decent predictions is either too little or too much. It is too little when we lack knowledge about a country's economic condition because of government control of information, or about the plans of a revolutionary group which follows norms of secrecy. Too much information means that there is insufficient time to cull through and evaluate what we know so that some predictive guess can be ventured before events supersede our study. Prediction also runs into the problem of the "self-negating" prophecy, in which the very prediction of event X causes the actors involved to take steps to make sure that X does not happen. Our emphasis on the specific features in the explanation of particular revolutions carries over to all talk of the future: rigorous prediction would descend to a country-by-country analysis. Thus, what follows is to be taken rather as broadly suggestive than as definitive.

Leaving countries that have recently experienced revolution totally out of consideration, we must divide the remaining countries into two crude categories: the prospects for revolution in what we have come to call "advanced industrial societies" are slight, while those for "underdeveloped societies" are considerably greater. Advanced industrial societies include the United States, Canada, Japan, and Common Market countries; other West European states; and countries of the "white" British Commonwealth. We can exempt various communist countries from this category, because they consider themselves revolutionary regimes. Advanced industrial societies are not hospitable to the development of a serious full-scale revolutionary movement. They can, of course, harbor a number of professedly revolutionary sects and cliques—what the French call *groupuscules* (minigroups). These do not constitute a serious revolutionary threat, because the mass basis of the historic Western movements is lacking to them. And yet, there was more talk of revolution in Western countries in the late 1960's than at any point since the close of World War I. The works of revolutionary anarchist theorists, out of print for nearly half a century, came out in cheap editions. Does all this thought and activity betoken the buildup towards an authentic revolutionary situation, at least in the more "vulnerable" Western countries?

In order to evaluate this problem, we should examine briefly a theory that sees revolutionary possibilities in advanced industrial societies. The works of Herbert Marcuse [60] qualify as one of the more coherent expressions of the philosophy of the New Left, a heterogeneous movement not all of which is revolutionary. We are not concerned with Marcuse's multilateral critique of "advanced capitalist society," but rather with his portrayal of how a revolutionary situation could come about. For Marcuse, certain aspects of nineteenth-century revolutionary thought have been superseded by new sources of apparent strength that modern technology contributes to the capitalist economic system. The "immiseration" of the Western proletariat has been checked and reversed by technological advance and by the surplus gleaned from exploitation of the Third World by classic colonialism and neocolonialism. Furthermore, the masses have been conditioned to a new set of artificial needs which they can only gratify under the aegis of the existing socioeconomic order. The consumer society deludes them into thinking that they never had it so good, whereas in fact the gap between richer and poorer groups and that between what is and what could be continues to widen. A truly nonrepressive society is now technologically possible, but this fact is obscured for us by the monotone message of the mass media. The contradictory nature of modern society is mirrored nowhere better than in the dual nature of the working class: "By virtue of its basic position in the production process, by virtue of its numerical weight and the weight of exploitation, the working class is still the historical agent of revolution; by virtue of its sharing the stabilizing needs of the system, it becomes a conservative, even counterrevolutionary force. Objectively, 'in-itself,' labor is still the potentially revolutionary class; subjectively, 'for-itself,' it is not." [61]

The ultimate prospects for revolution thus depend on ridding the working class of its false consciousness. While Lenin saw the answer to this problem in the vanguard party, Marcuse sees hope in the "militant intelligentsia," especially its student sector. Also important is the spontaneous protest of the lowliest strata such as slum-dwellers, blacks in the United States, and various minorities who benefit far less than the organized working class from the bread and circuses of the "welfare-warfare state." The intelligentsia and the subproletariat reject the existing order for different reasons, yet their conjunction will start the snowball effect that will eventually bring in the bulk of the traditional working class. The radical intellectuals reject the system because of a moral-aesthetic value syndrome that stresses the ugliness, wastefulness, hypocrisy, and repressiveness of advanced capitalist society; the abjectly poor reject it because of elemental human misery.

While Marcuse does not conceal his pessimism about early deliverance from the system he condemns root and branch, he sees basic structural weaknesses that could worsen and produce an authentically revolutionary situation. Opposition to imperialism at home and abroad could make things difficult for the big capitalist countries. Protest against United States involvement in Viet Nam strengthened the radical forces in many countries. Economic problems such as inflation, unemployment, and huge defense outlays would sap the foundations of the system. When the hoped-for collapse occurs, the radical intelligentsia would be there to guide the transition to a form of socialism untainted by Stalinist bureaucratism and military exigency. That this would mean provisional rule by an elite does not deter Marcuse for two reasons: (1) what we already have is rule by an elite; and (2) the new elite would be freely judged by a majority liberated from the ideological fetters of advanced capitalism. "To be sure," he adds, "this has never been the course of a revolution, but it is equally true that never before has a revolution occurred which had at its disposal the present achievements of productivity and technical progress." [62] Apparently these will be enough to ensure that *this* revolution will give us true majority rule, though why a new elite capable of managing this sophisticated technology would not arise out of the ashes of capitalism is never made clear.

There are several major weaknesses in Marcuse's analysis. In the first place, the working class upon which so much hope is placed is highly differentiated and its most powerful groups are committed to the survival of the system. It must be recalled, for example, that only a small fraction of the French workers supported the Student Revolt of 1968 and workers' demands had precious little to do with the utopianism of their temporary allies. Inflation, unemployment, and taxation are problems whose gravity is not likely to reach dimensions conducive to revolution. The success and recent expansion of the Common Market and the continued strength of the American economy despite temporary and chronic problems suggest stabilization rather than the sharp ups and downs associated with many revolutionary breakthroughs.

Secondly, the repressive capacity of the modern state is more than adequate to handle riots and demonstrations that seem a true revolutionary threat to the authorities. More individualized acts such as bombings and assassinations may hit their targets without endangering the social or political order. "Propaganda by deed" may have a catalytic effect in deeply divided societies whose nerve centers are afflicted by political paralysis, but in advanced industrial societies it may have no appreciable effect or one directly counter to the aims of its practitioners. The disorders of the 1960's have served to strengthen rather than to weaken the repressive apparatus of the modern state.

Finally, the massive American military intervention in Viet Nam has been terminated. There is no doubt that the Viet Nam conflict was the single greatest stimulus to the resurgence of radicalism in the United States and Europe in the 1960's. For many this radicalization was a three-phase process: (1) rejection of the specific Viet Nam policy of the United States, (2) followed by rejection of the whole tenor of American foreign policy since the end of World War II, and finally (3) rejection of the system ("the military-industrial complex") that produces such allegedly evil foreign policy. The roots of the American involvement in Viet Nam were to be found in the type of socioeconomic system characteristic of all Western capitalist countries. With the catalyst of Viet Nam removed (and barring the appearance of new "Viet Nams" in the mid-1970's), protest against foreign and domestic policy is likely to remain "within the system." In short, we will not even have the illusion of the kind of revolutionary situation that captivated so many imaginations in France in 1968. Strikes, riots, violence, and disorder do not necessarily mean a revolutionary situation.

As a group, the countries of the Third World present a different and somewhat more favorable picture of the prospects of revolution. One reason for this simply applies our conclusions of Chapter IV that dissynchronous social change is conducive to the emergence of revolutionary situations and movements. In many studies the greater susceptibility of Third World countries to revolution or to various forms of collective violence is naturally linked to the process of modernization. Most of these countries are at some point between full-scale traditionalism and full-scale modernity: thus we call them "transitional," "developing," or "modernizing" countries. S. N. Eisenstadt has emphasized the connection between transitional societies and revolutionary and collective violence: "The very fact that modernization entails continual changes in all major spheres of a society means of necessity that it involves processes of disorganization and dislocation, with the continual development of social problems, cleavages and conflicts between various groups, and movements of protest, resistance to change." [63]

A complementary line of attack introduces the variable of the *rate of modernization:* "the more rapid the process of change, the greater the likelihood of opening new perspectives of modernity, that is, of creating higher and higher levels of aspiration, thus inevitably increasing the gap between aspiration and achievement, at least in the early stages." [64] If we recall the notion of relative deprivation in the social psychology of revolution (Chapter IV), the implication would be that revolution would be most likely where modernization is most rapid (i.e., in transitional societies).

This conclusion is formally correct, but masks several difficulties. At the end of Chapter IV we noted the resemblance between the seven "long-term causes of revolution" [65] and the components of many notions of modernization. However, we declined to make the simple connection between revolution and modernization for several reasons. In the first place the seven phenomena of change often proceed in an extremely dissynchronous manner, a fact whose importance is neglected or underestimated by simplistic theories of modernization. Moreover, as the historian Perez Zagorin points out, modernization is "merely a name for an ensemble of complex processes. Unless these are disentangled and their effects separately tested and verified, it is difficult to see how reliable conclusions can be drawn as to their connection with revolution." [66] Thus, it is not so much rapidity of change that leads to revolution, but rather the disharmony, indeed the cacophony, of the processes lumped under the generic term "modernization" that is causally important. In addition, the causal nexus of revolution includes certain middle-term factors, some of which may not be simple results of the long-term or modernizing trends, but may be cyclic or random in their operation.[67]

Another difficulty is the number and variety of societies placed under the "transitional" label. There is broad agreement that since all societies contain modern, traditional, and transitional elements, their precise rank in a classification depends on the basis of which syndrome (modern, traditional, or transitional) predominates at a given time. Accordingly, transitional societies would be those most divided and incoherent because neither the old or the new ways have the complete upper hand. Neglecting the problem of borderline cases between traditionalism and transitionalism, or between the latter and full modernity, one is still struck by the vast array of societies grouped under the umbrella of transitional systems. Highly urbanized, fairly industrialized countries such as certain ones in Latin America are cast into the same bag as predominantly peasant or tribal societies of Southeast Asia, Africa, or elsewhere in Latin America. No doubt all of these societies are more or less exposed to currents of change from the West and the East: it is intellectually irresponsible to neglect or underestimate the structural and cultural, economic and political differences between these countries, however.

One difference between Third World countries is that separating those still under colonial domination, as in Portuguese Africa, and those with formal political sovereignty. However, this distinction is somewhat blurred because many believe that the independence of certain countries is vitiated by the neocolonialist presence of the United States or Western European powers. Even if the notion of neocolonialism casts more heat than light on world politics and certain countries retain greater autonomy than sometimes thought, the fact remains that many Third World radicals and revolutionaries are convinced that their country's leaders are "lackeys of imperialism" and have convinced others that this is so. With a strong United States or Western economic or military visibility, the convincing is substantially easier. Thus, even if the colonial situation in its classic form is lacking, many of its features may be artificially reproduced to the benefit of revolutionaries.

Another point of difference is the level of urbanization reached by various states: Argentina, Brazil, Uruguay, and Venezuela are so highly urbanized that the first and third are often classified as modern rather than transitional; while Peru, Turkey, or Nigeria rank lower on urbanization. While urbanization is sometimes equated or associated with modernization, the process of urban growth can outstrip elements of modernization such as industrialization. It is with this in mind that Samuel P. Huntington concludes that Third World countries may be opened up "to the possibility of new types of social revolution absent from the history of the early modernizers." [68]

The demographic, socioeconomic, and geographic diversity of Third World countries obviously presents a diversity of chances and settings for revolution. From the standpoint of revolutionaries (and counterinsurgency doctrine) this diversity is reflected in debate about the general and particular suitability of different models of revolutionary strategy. In other words, predicting Third World revolutions has become largely enmeshed with the questions of how to make or break revolutionary insurrection. Though deep analysis of revolutionary strategy has not been and is not now a chief preoccupation of this study, it becomes necessary to inspect certain proposed revolutionary strategies to sharpen our insight into possibilities of Third World revolutions.

The central concept of Third World revolutionary strategies is guerrilla warfare, and the three versions of it to be discussed have certain points in common. In 1943—well before the strategic writings of Mao, Giap, Guevara, Debray, and others were written or won prominence—Katharine Chorley laid down the conditions necessary for a guerrilla insurgency to overcome a modern conventional army.[69]

(1) For various reasons the conventional army is unable to exert its full strength.
(2) The general population is sympathetic to the insurgents to the point of secretly aiding them.
(3) The insurgent organization has good discipline and is able to faithfully execute a strategic plan.
(4) Operations are long-term and will escalate in scope, while destroying the will to resist of the incumbent forces, and topography and terrain allow the hit-and-run tactics essential to guerrilla warfare.

These four points need some slight elaboration in the light of later theory and practice. (1) The conventional army is unable to deliver a knockout blow against the revolutionary insurgents because the latter (at first) refuse to fight on terms that could prove truly decisive. As Mao Tse-tung puts it: "enemy advances, we retreat; enemy halts, we harass; enemy tires, we attack; enemy retreats, we pursue." [70] These tactics are supposed to demoralize and incapacitate the counterrevolutionary forces over the long haul. (2) Though the widespread popular sympathy for the guerrillas is a condition for success in theories, as well as in certain specific insurrections, it would be wrong in general to confuse compliance with complicity. The lack of affection and allegiance of remote rural populations for the central government and its minions is not automatically translated into unbridled enthuasism for the revolutionary insurgents. Hindsight all too often converts the negative into the positive. Furthermore, even if revolutionary terror is *selectively* meted out to government officials or the rich, the ordinary peasant may get the feeling that he may be next, without that message being fully intended by the guerrillas. (3) Without strong organization devoted to a definite revolutionary strategy (a party?), guerrilla bands can be readily contained or degenerate into pure and simple bandit formations.[71] (4) According to General Vo Nguyen Giap, "the long-term revolutionary war must include several different stages: stage of contention, stage of equilibrium, and stage of counter-offensive." [72] In the first stage, hit-and-run tactics with relatively small numbers involved is the basic operation. Later, the guerrillas are able to withstand pitched battles against their adversaries before leaving the scene. Finally, there is the stage of mobile war with virtually conventional forces supported by some heavy equipment. The counterrevolutionary enemy passes from the strategic offensive to the strategic defensive.

The three main models of revolutionary guerrilla warfare in Third World countries are (1) the classic Maoist doctrine of "people's war" with the development of a party-state; (2) the rural guerrilla *foco,* ostensibly based upon the Cuban experience and expounded by Che Guevara and Regis Debray; and (3) the urban guerrilla "vanguard" elaborated by Abraham Guillén among others. The Maoist model of people's war is intended for countries with a vast peasant population. It also applies to the colonial or what Mao called the "semicolonial" situation (countries dominated by foreign economic or political interests). Operations commence with the retreat of revolutionary cadres from the cities into the countryside. There the first job is to avoid attempts of government troops to "encircle and annihilate" them. This involves the usual ambushes, hasty retreats, and so forth. But in the Maoist or Viet Minh vision, military considerations must always be subordinated to political ones. Thus, as the guerrilla movement gains strength, it increasingly couples its purely military operations with ideological and organizational work to set up base areas in the countryside and remote areas. Eventually the dual power situation emerges, with a countergovernment and counteradministration headed by the revolutionaries. This state within the state can often hold its own against government troops or can temporarily dissolve itself if government pressure becomes too great. Clearly this stage is well beyond the elementary guerrilla strategy of destroying the enemy's troops in numerous small engagements, because a whole political infrastructure is imposed upon a given *territory.*

Following the Maoist logic, the protracted quality of people's war will undermine the old regime in two ways. In the first place, the revolutionary army will *outfight* the government's army; in the second and more important place, the revolutionary infrastructure will *outadminister* the government's bureaucracy.[73] From this point of view party, army, and (new) state are three sides of the same triangle, with the proviso that in the Maoist framework the party "commands the gun."

> The rebels must build an administrative structure to collect taxes, to provide some education and social welfare, and to maintain a modicum of economic activity. A revolutionary guerrilla movement which does not have these administrative concerns and structures to fulfill its obligations to the populace would degenerate into banditry. Even in clandestineness, the parallel government must prove its efficacy.[74]

In the end the revolutionary movement will be the real government of most of the national territory.

The theory of the rural guerrilla *foco,* as elaborated by Regis Debray, is an attempt to evaluate and to generalize the course of Castro's victory in Cuba. While denying that this new revolutionary strategy involves a mechanical imposition of the Cuban model, the notion of the guerrilla *foco* stresses features that differentiate the Cuban from the Chinese or Vietnamese guerrilla experience. The common elements include the protracted nature of revolutionary warfare and the basically (though not exclusively) rural theater of operations. In an early work, "Castroism: The Long March in Latin America," Debray was at pains to stress that the rural guerrilla *foco* must be subordinated to an overall strategy including urban components: "The *centre* is installed as a *detonator* at the least guarded position, and *at the moment* most favorable to the explosion. In itself, the *foco* will not overthrow a given social situation nor even, through its own struggles, reverse a given political situation." [75] Even here, however, the implication is clear that urban activities are *ancillary* to the main military effort in the countryside. First of all, "social contradictions," according to Debray, "are . . . not as explosive in the cities because even the least favoured strata are integrated into modern society." [76] Furthermore, from the tactical standpoint the urban guerrilla has only limited mobility and hence is more liable to capture or destruction than his rural counterpart.

The main differences between the rural guerrilla *foco* and the Maoist people's war lie in the rather scanty numbers in the guerrilla bands, the absence (as we saw in Chapter VII) of a strong revolutionary party or of close relationships to professedly revolutionary parties, and the reluctance to build up a political-administrative structure going beyond the immediate logistical needs of the military effort. As a leftist critic of Debray points out:

> this view leads to the reversal of the stages of development not only in the military but also in the political and organizational aspects of revolutionary warfare. The incumbent government is outfought before it is administered. The military factor takes precedence over the political. Tactical considerations must precede questions of overall strategy. Political parties cannot initiate the guerrilla movement; rather the guerrillas galvanize into a party, and establish a socialist state.[77]

In *Revolution in the Revolution?* Debray presents the *foco* theory in a starker and less qualified form. Where previously he formally acknowledged the primacy of politics over military considerations, he now virtually identifies the two: "under certain conditions, the political and the military are not separate, but form one organic whole, consisting of the people's army, whose nucleus is the guerrilla army." [78] Likewise the co-ordinate action of urban revolutionary elements is reduced to providing the *coup de grace* to the tottering regime with eleventh-hour general strikes or mass demonstrations. The real, active "overthrow" of the government is the work of the rural guerrilla struggle as it grows and flourishes.

The theory of the urban guerrilla has certain resemblances to the rural guerrilla *foco* theory. It too rejects the need or feasibility of semi-permanent base areas in the hinterland and concedes that urban guerrilla warfare must be placed within a broader strategic panorama that includes a rural dimension. However, the thrust now is to make rural guerrilla activity ancillary to the purposes of urban-oriented revolution. The theory of the urban guerrilla is a response to the high level of ur-banization achieved by certain Latin American countries such as Chile, Argentina, and Uruguay. While allowing the propriety of a rural em-phasis in some revolutionary contexts, Abraham Guillén, a theorist of the urban guerrilla, maintains that in countries with more than 50 per-cent urban population "the revolutionary battle should preferably be not in the mountains and countrysides but in the urban areas. For the revolution's potential is where the population is. . . ." [79] But Guillén's position is in truth much stronger than allowing a 50 percent thresh-old to determine the character of revolutionary warfare. Though he admits that a rural emphasis might be appropriate to Brazil, he re-proves the failure of a lengthy rural insurrection in Colombia. Because this insurrection was "without massive support from the urban popula-tion, without an urban guerrilla force," it proved incapable not only of winning but of even advancing beyond the "second phase of revolu-tionary war" with base areas in the power of the guerrillas.[80] It is thus clear that the *foquismo* of Guevara and Debray, and the theory of the urban guerrilla are not simply exclusive alternatives applicable to dif-ferent situations: they are to some extent *competitive* strategies.

Despite its urban focus, the theory of the urban guerrilla does not revert to the mass insurrectionary motifs of French and Russian his-tory. The techniques of the general strike or the barricades are aban-doned: "If the urban masses find themselves without work and are dis-content, it is not a question of encouraging them to demonstrate in the streets just to be trampled by the horses of the police. They should be placed in guerrilla units. . . ." [81] Since acute urban disorders along the lines of the French Student Revolt of May, 1968, are likely to involve mass action such as barricades and street fighting, Guillén stipulates that victory "will depend on the combination of a guerrilla force of sev-eral hundred men who will attack everywhere in order to disarm and weaken the enemy, giving cover to the regular formations of the people deployed on semi-mobile fronts. . . ." [82]

The main protagonists of the urban guerrilla revolution would seem to be two distinct crisis strata: the urban intelligentsia—especially of academic, professional, or civil service background—and the *lumpenproletariat* of unemployed or underemployed people who live crowded on the outskirts of many Third World cities. The preconditions for an alliance between these two groups were suggested by a study whose implications go far beyond its concern with India:

> Growing slums, worsening sanitary conditions, lowering living standards, and unemployment concentrate misery visibly, not in inaccessible villages, but in areas which are the habitat of writers, social reformers, artists, poets, teachers, religious preachers, humane societies, dreamers, city planners, sociologists, journalists, and economists. They arouse the concern and the ire of these and other socially sensitive and articulate individuals and groups. . . . Believing that they are bystanders, not participants, in processes of social change, many intellectuals become angry men—young and old. [83]

Recruits from the intelligentsia will loom large in the "vanguard" of professional revolutionaries. According to Guillén, the revolution's ultimate aim—socialism—will have to be kept in the far background. In the foreground should be nationalism, concrete issues, and propaganda by deed. [84] This constitutes one of the frankest avowals in modern revolutionary thought of the distinction between esoteric ideology for the elite and exoteric ideology for the masses.

Though the dissynchronous patterns of change, the strident nationalism, the massive population growth, the "urbanization without industrialization," and other factors characteristic of Third World countries make revolution there a more likely event than in advanced industrial societies, there are also a number of countervailing forces at work. [85] Some of these affect all three forms of revolutionary warfare. A major weakness is the disunity of revolutionary elites themselves, partially indeed over which of the three revolutionary strategies is appropriate for *their* revolution. When one faction decides to go it alone in the hopes of shocking the others into action, it is often disappointed with the result. This infighting and the resulting polemic hamstrings the tight strategic control so many deem essential to victory. Also, popular support and the capability of waging protracted conflict are bound to suffer from disunity. Another major factor is that recently there has occurred "a quantum jump in the effectiveness of counter-insurgency weapons, techniques, and doctrines." [86] Part of the reason for Guevara's debacle in Bolivia in 1967 was that crack government troops had received the latest training under United States auspices. These technical and doctrinal improvements allow the government army to translate its (on paper) strategic advantage into the concrete reality of tactics. Finally, thaw in the Cold War and a reorientation of American foreign policy after Viet Nam have allowed Third World governments to take a more convincingly nationalist posture and thus to take some of the neocolonialist wind out of the sails of radicals and revolutionaries.[87]

Some particular factors militate against further successes of the Maoist-style people's war. This type of revolutionary strategy applies best to countries with high rural population, low economic development, and colonial or semicolonial dependency. The revolutionaries transform nationalist sentiment and desire for reform into radical revolution. Urbanization by siphoning off surplus population from the countryside may deprive the rural guerrilla movement of much of its rationale and support. Conditions may improve for those peasants who choose to remain in the countryside. Furthermore, successful land reform could alleviate rural discontent and thereby deprive revolutionaries of the degree of active support or benevolent neutrality necessary for successful insurrection. Given the dismal results of so many land reforms, Samuel P. Huntington stipulates that their antirevolutionary potential depends on such factors as genuine government commitment, available funds to implement the reform, and the ability of the government to force compliance of groups hostile to the reform.[88] While a relatively successful land reform would affect the fortunes of the guerrilla *foco*, it would seem to operate more strongly against the people's war because of its greater dependence on popular response.

As we have seen, the theory of the guerrilla *foco* is an interpretation and generalization of the Cuban experience. This raises two immediate problems: (1) There is an element of misinterpretation involved because the apotheosis of the guerrilla *foco* leads to undervaluing the urban and "collapse" aspects of the Cuban Revolution. (2) There is an element of overgeneralization because the weight of uniquely Cuban features is underestimated. The combined result of these misperceptions is to overestimate the general chances of revolution in countries with a superficial resemblance to Cuba and to endow the guerrilla *foco* in particular with almost magical virtues. For this reason, any improvement of repressive techniques—even more than "diversions and concessions" such as nationalism and land reform—is likely to prevent the *foco* from detonating a revolutionary conflagration. As Abraham Guillén points out rather pithily, *foquismo* in reality is an "insurrectional movement for piling up cadavers, for giving easy victories to the repressive generals trained by the Pentagon." [89]

The revolutionary strategy of the urban guerrilla is obviously less affected by countervailing factors such as land reform and some counterinsurgency techniques that are rurally oriented. On the other hand Third World urbanization, which seems in the short run to have stabilized both the cities and the countryside, may in the long run promote urban-centered revolution. Bakunin, Frantz Fanon, and others have extolled the revolutionary potential of the *lumpenproletariat,* especially when teamed up with the elite of professional revolutionaries.[90] Nevertheless, up to now the *lumpenproletariat,* when its active elements have not been rightist in political tendency, has responded more to the themes of the classic urban mob or of millenarian social movements than to those of a "socialist" revolution. (This may, of course, change.) Furthermore, there are clear limits to how much popular support urban guerrillas can generate. As John H. Hoagland points out:

> The anonymity imposed by terrorist activities is really not conducive to the establishment of a leadership that can become known and admired by the population or of a clear alternative to the government in power. Furthermore, the operating methods of the urban guerrillas fail to create an image of either benevolence or leadership. Castro, leading his small band in the Sierra Maestra could present himself . . . as a popular and heroic figure. Those who murder, kidnap, rob banks, and plant explosives are in a far less favorable position.[91]

Ironically, it may well be those Third World countries that depart most from the pattern of low economic development and preponderant rural population, such as Argentina and Chile, which have the greatest potential for revolution as distinct from other forms of political violence and instability. The return of Juan Perón to power has lessened for the time being the chances of revolution in Argentina, while Chilean politics presents a scenario that resembles nothing more than the situation in Spain in the mid-1930's, though the rightist military coup of September, 1973, may prove a successful preemptive counterrevolution. If revolution comes to these countries, urban as well as rural guerrillas may end up playing the same marginal role as in the great Western revolutions.

The Effects of Revolution

It has often been remarked that far more attention has been devoted to studying the causes, phases, and protagonists of revolution than to studying the effects—especially the long-term effects—of revolution. What follows is not an attempt to remedy this apparent deficiency, but to show why the problem is such a difficult one.

As we have frequently seen, divergent moral and ideological outlooks color judgments on nearly all aspects of revolution. Nowhere is this clearer than in attempts to gauge and evaluate the effects of revolution—what revolution has meant for societies that have passed through a revolutionary crisis. An obvious and immediate conclusion that follows from our stress on the highly idiosyncratic causal pattern and trajectory of various revolutions is that each revolution produces a different impact on the society it has transformed. "Political" revolutions change different things from those revolutions which we call "social." The more "radical" revolutions change more things more profoundly than do the milder ones. But when one goes beyond these somewhat superficial generalities, one becomes caught in a welter of moral and ideological issues. Both the historiography of particular revolutions and philosophical attempts to deal with revolution in general have usually adhered to one of two fundamental paradigms or interpretive molds. One approach is that of *melodrama,* the other is that of the *balance sheet.*

Theatrical melodrama is noted for a clear simplicity in characterization: the protagonists are good *or* evil, noble *or* base, cowardly *or* courageous. In popular melodrama the hero or heroine is virtually unblemished by the defects of human nature, while the villain and his henchmen embody the bulk of them. The plot consists of the hero's overcoming the villain or general adversity so that he "gets the girl and lives happily ever after." However, another type of melodrama which can be called the "literature of disaster" has the reverse of a happy ending and is thus sometimes confused with true tragedy.[92] Despite their different endings, popular melodrama and the literature of disaster assume a Manichean universe: "man is pitted against some force outside of himself—a compact enemy, a hostile group, a social pressure, a natural event, an accident, or a coincidence." [93] Whether the heroes overcome the villains or adversity, or whether adversity or the villains overcome the heroes, it is still melodrama.

One of the difficulties in using the historiography of revolutions to measure the effects of revolution is that so much of it is either conservative or radical melodrama. For sympathizers of the French Revolution, for example, the enduring meaning of the revolution is encompassed by a set of melodramatic antitheses: the people vs. the aristocracy; democracy vs. absolutism; enlightenment vs. superstition; progress vs. backwardness; economic growth vs. economic stagnation; industrialism vs. agrarianism; capitalism vs. feudalism; science vs. obscurantism; and so on. The results of the revolution are seen as the victory of the first term over the second in each antithesis.

For the defeated counterrevolutionary or his conservative sympathizer, the successful revolution also has an essentially melodramatic significance. But now it is the "literature of disaster" that can serve as an analogy: evil triumphs over good. The conservative sets of melo-dramatic antitheses include: quantity vs. quality; disorder vs. order; equality vs. liberty; centralization vs. localism; uniformity vs. diversity; irreligion vs. piety; abstract rationalism vs. tradition; philistinism vs. chivalry; and so on. The results of the revolution are seen as the defeat of the second term by the first term in each antithesis. Whatever its other qualities, Burke's *Reflections on the Revolution in France* betrays the essential features of the literature of disaster.

With either conservative or radical melodrama we get a rather simple rendering of the meaning and results of revolution. The revolu-tionaries and their works are either good or evil, and the same follows for their opponents and their works. But surely this constitutes an abridgement of the true historical process: all the good or evil that emerges in the postrevolutionary society is attributed to the primordial conflict. Depending on the context, we can probably uncover many fea-tures of the new society that existed in the old or that emerged in ways that had little or no connection with the revolution.

One response to this simplistic vision is the ostensibly more objec-tive, and certainly more nuanced, "balance-sheet" approach to revolu-tion. There is even the possibility that someone using the balance-sheet approach might come up with a positive evaluation for some revolu-tions and a negative one for others. Revolutions involve both benefits and costs, the problem in each case being to compare both sides of the ledger. Barrington Moore even suggests that the "costs" of revolution must be weighed against the "costs of going without a revolution." [94] Societies that have not experienced revolution tend to produce a myriad of less visible, but perhaps more destructive, forms of human suffering than revolutionary societies. Certain societies that have had modernization without revolution have taken the path of fascism, with its disastrous domestic and international consequences. Others, like India, have avoided both revolution and fascism, but at the price of lingering misery of the masses and a snail's pace of modernization. Fur-thermore, the vaunted social peace and democratic institutions of France, England, or the United States were baptized in the fires of rev-olution and violence.

In another work Moore suggests three criteria by which to mea-sure whether revolutions are worth the trouble. First, the old regime must be shown to be "unnecessarily repressive" (i.e., "the essential work of society could continue with less suffering and constraint").[95] Second, the situation must be "ripe" for revolution in the dual sense that "the destructive aspects of the revolution will enjoy enough support to carry them out" and that "there are realistic prospects for introducing a bet-ter system. . . ." [96] Third, "there has to be good reason to believe that the costs in human suffering and degradation inherent in the continuation of the status quo really outweigh those to be incurred in the revolution and its aftermath." [97] Though these criteria are future-directed, they help us to understand how Moore would apply the balance sheet to past revolutions. In fact, Moore has little difficulty in seeing much more on the credit than the debit side for both the English and French revolutions. He is much more circumspect about the Russian and Chinese revolutions, especially when he complains that "in general one of the most revolting features of revolutionary dictatorships has been their use of terror against little people who were as much victims of the old order as were the revolutionaries themselves, often more so." [98]

Though Moore's use of the balance sheet leads to some different evaluations of different revolutions, his analysis of the "costs" of the French Revolution shows how partisanship can slip into this approach. One salient issue is the cost in human lives associated with the revolution. The figure Moore chooses to place on the debit side of the ledger is the "35,000 to 40,000" persons who "lost their lives as a direct result of revolutionary repression." [99] From this he moves on to argue in the following terms:

> That this blood bath had its tragic and unjust aspects no serious thinker will deny. Yet in assessing it, one has to keep in mind the repressive aspects of the social order to which it was a response. The prevailing order of society always grinds out its tragic toll of unnecessary deaths year after year. It would be enlightening to calculate the death rate of the *ancien régime* from such factors as preventable starvation and injustice if that were at all possible. Offhand it seems very unlikely that this would be very much below the proportion of .0016 which [the] figure of 40,000 yields when set against an estimated population of around 24,000,000. . . . I think it would be vastly higher.[100]

But Moore's choosing victims of the Terror as the debit figure in this calculation constitutes a kind of double-entry bookkeeping. The Reign of Terror proper lasted less than a year, and the number of deaths attributable to the revolution is enormously higher than 40,000 or so. *All* deaths directly attributed to the political convulsion we call the French Revolution must be added to the list: such deaths would not have occurred at the time and in the way they did if the revolution had not taken place. Thus, we must add those lost in the wars of the French Revolution and of Napoleon.[101] These wars would not have occurred, or would have occurred on a greatly reduced scale typical of eighteenth-century warfare, had there been no revolution. Furthermore, the victims *on both sides* of all clashes between the revolution and the counterrevolution in the West or South of France must also be brought in. This follows if our argument above that counterrevolution is an integral part of revolution is valid. Likewise, we would have to add the deaths due to starvation and disease in the harsh middle years of the 1790's if, as is likely, these exceed the average of the old regime. In short, even if we subtract those people "saved" by the revolution, the figure is many, many times higher than the 40,000. There is no more (or less) reason to limit the "victims" of the revolution to those consciously executed as enemies of the people than to limit "victims" of the old regime to those executed for *lèse-majesté*.[102]

Though the balance sheet is a clear improvement over melodrama and is useful as far as it goes, writers such as Moore feel a certain unease about it. Such hesitations suggest the possibility of another paradigm to help appraise the effects of revolution. In 1931 Herbert Butterfield lay siege to the "Whig interpretation of history" as essentially melodramatic and inadequate. His insight can be applied to both conservative and radical melodrama:

> Instead of seeing the modern world emerge as the victory of the children of light over the children of darkness in any generation, it is at least better to see it emerge as the result of a clash of wills, a result which often neither party wanted or even dreamed of, a result which indeed in some cases both parties would equally have hated, but a result for the achievement of which the existence of both and the clash of both were necessary.[103]

Butterfield is suggesting the rudiments of a tragic conception of history. In tragedy as opposed to melodrama, the protagonists are mixed in character: they are neither purely good, nor purely evil. The tragic situation contains an irony or paradox absent from melodrama: "not only is everyone in the right, but . . . each person and power in the struggle presents an equally superior right, or appears to fulfill an equally superior duty." [104] This rightness of the contestants, however, is rightness within a certain sphere, rightness from a certain point of view. In the confrontation between revolution and counterrevolution, neither side has a monopoly on virtue or vice—especially when we examine behavior rather than slogans. Courage, loyalty, self-sacrifice, patriotism can occur on either side, as do recklessness and wanton cruelty. As Max Scheler points out: "In general, . . . the quality of the tragic is lacking when the question 'Who is guilty?' has a clear and definite answer." [105]

Tragedy further differs from melodrama in that it involves "an uncompromising inevitability of the destruction of a value." [106] If it is necessary to destroy in order to create, the destruction remains an absolute loss. To the radical, any destruction pales into insignificance before the sublimity and majesty of the "creative revolutionary act"; for the conservative, actions which in quieter times he could tolerate or even approve are obscured by the revolutionary penumbra surrounding them. Scheler describes the underlying reality of tragedy as emerging because "the course of the causal events disregards completely the value of things." [107] In other words, the movement of history does not follow the dictates of anyone's value system: a world uniformly and consistently friendly to one's value scheme would be as incapable of tragedy as one always and unequivocally hostile. We have already encountered something like this, but in the parlance of modern sociology. The Mertonian distinction between "manifest" and "latent" functions contains implicitly the tragic message that what we intend to happen by our conscious acts and what often transpires are two largely different things.[108]

The tragic dimension of revolution emerges clearly from this point of view. In the first place is the destruction of so many of the original revolutionaries: this facet of the Terror in France, of the Purges in Russia, of the succession of civil wars between revolutionary factions in Mexico does not need rehearsal here. But perhaps the most tragic feature of revolutions is their failure in terms of the conscious ideological objectives of the original enthusiasts. England under the Protectorate and later under the Restoration was a far cry from what Cromwell and others more militant than he had wanted. Nineteenth-century France bore little resemblance to the "republic of virtue" envisaged by Robespierre. Soviet society after Lenin has gotten further and further away from the utopian expectations of *State and Revolution*. The Great Leap Forward and the Cultural Revolution show among other things that Chinese society has yet a distance to travel to reach the Maoist ideal. This is far, however, from embracing the "vulgar Realist" position that revolutions bring only superficial changes or from denying that anyone benefits substantially from revolutionary change. It is just that things do not change in ways wholly anticipated by the revolutionary founding fathers.

No doubt we are forced to invoke the balance sheet to see if the elevation of some is worth the destruction or denigration of others. But even here the tragic vision seems superior. Some balance-sheet accounts suggest that the suffering endured by people at the time of the revolution and for a time afterwards is justified because later generations will reap the blessings of the democracy or progress or industrialization or modernization or "socialism" that has been produced or furthered by the revolution. In this context three questions obtrude themselves. (1) How legitimate is it to trade off one generation's well-being for that of others? (2) Are the blessings themselves so blessed?

Are modernization, industrialism, a somewhat nebulous "socialism" un-alloyed boons to mankind? We are now in the West addressing our-selves to some of the human and aesthetic costs of unbridled tech-nological change. (3) Even accepting, as we must, that some of the results of revolution are beneficial, is it wholly ruled out that some of these results might have come about without a revolution? Is the speed-up of certain trends worth the trouble? Russia was modernizing in many ways before the revolution, and only a few doubt that had there been no revolution it would have continued to do so.[109] In fact, in agri-culture, though not in industry, the revolution, as well as Soviet institu-tions and ideology, have been a serious brake on modernization.

However, these queries are a reversion to the balance sheet, and it should now be clear that very often the balance sheet is no more than a more subtle rendition of the melodrama. Thus, to interpret the results of revolution exclusively in terms of the balance sheet is to lose consid-erable in the translation; for both the revolutionary side and the coun-terrevolutionary are complex in nature, as is the protagonist in tragedy. Each side has perhaps a part of the truth: things demand change and yet there are values worth preserving. But each side inflates its partial perspective into an exclusive principle: one has to accept the revolution or reject it *en bloc*. Passions are unleashed and there are those on both sides for whom the conflict and extirpation of the adversary become ends in themselves. And yet, it would be an unconscionable case of "in-sight through hindsight" to suggest that revolution is due to misunder-standing, that value differences are composable, or that conflicting in-terests are easily reconcilable. As with classic tragedy there is a species of necessity, a point of no return in the revolutionary process that leads to the denouement.

Though melodrama and the balance sheet have their proper place in trying to assess the results of revolution, neither is adequate. The continuing appeal of the tragic motif since it was developed two and a half millennia ago in classical Greece suggests that it evokes something about the permanent condition of mankind. Revolution as one of the most dramatic acts a human collectivity can undertake is not the poorest illustration of this principle.

NOTES

[1] Jacques Godechot, *The Counter-Revolution: Doctrine and Practice* (New York: Howard Fertig, 1971).

[2] Obviously, the most basic distinction is between extreme or "integral" counter-revolutionaries, who want a total restoration of the old regime, and moderate counter-revolutionaries, who accept the need for some reforms.

[3] Austin Woolrych, "The English Revolution: An Introduction," in *The English Revolution 1600–1660*, ed. E. W. Ives (New York: Harper Torchbooks, 1971), p. 21.

[4] Charles Tilly, *The Vendée* (New York: John Wiley, 1967), p. 12. Tilly's notion of urbanization is roughly equivalent to what others call "modernization."

[5] *Ibid.*, p. 36.

[6] Edward E. Malefakis, *Agrarian Reform and Peasant Revolution in Spain* (New Haven: Yale University Press, 1970), p. 5.

[7] Hugh Thomas, *The Spanish Civil War* (New York: Harper Colophon Books, 1963), p. 172.

[8] There are limitations and variations to the success of this approach. William H. Chamberlin points out that despite the virulent Soviet attacks on religion, the "efforts of the Whites to impart a kind of religious fervor to their cause by arousing the fanaticism of the masses met with scanty success." *The Russian Revolution*, Vol. II (New York: Grosset & Dunlap, 1965), p. 355.

[9] A simple fact often goes unmentioned when the "upper class" flavor of the emigration is emphasized: to emigrate under revolutionary conditions may be so difficult and costly that only the wealthier citizens can afford it.

[10] Tilly, *Vendée*, p. 281.

[11] *Ibid.*, p. 227.

[12] Carlism preaches the restoration of the traditional "legitimate" monarchy and the extirpation of all forms of liberalism from Spanish life.

[13] Robert Redfield, *Peasant Society and Culture* (Chicago: University of Chicago Press, 1965), p. 140.

[14] Katharine Chorley, *Armies and the Art of Revolution* (London: Faber & Faber, 1943), p. 243.

[15] Chamberlin, *Russian Revolution*, Vol. II, p. 32.

[16] Ricardo de la Cierva y de Hoces, "The Nationalist Army in the Spanish Civil War," in *The Republic and the Civil War in Spain*, ed. Raymond Carr (London: Macmillan, 1971), pp. 188–89.

[17] Chamberlin, *Russian Revolution*, Vol. II, p. 32.

[18] Stanley Payne, "The Army, the Republic and the Outbreak of the Civil War," in Carr, ed., *Republic and Civil War*, pp. 84–85.

[19] This typology is more simplified than the scheme of Arno J. Mayer, who distinguishes seven varieties of counterrevolution: (1) preemptive, (2) posterior, (3) accessory, (4) disguised, (5) anticipatory, (6) externally licensed, and (7) externally imposed. *Dynamics of Counterrevolution in Europe, 1870–1956* (New York: Harper Torchbooks, 1971), Chap. IV. The weaknesses of Mayer's typology stem from his inclusion of conservative, fascist, and other movements under the broad label of "counterrevolution." His interest, then, is really more with rightest movements than with counterrevolution in the strict sense. His typology will be acceptable only to those who interpret politics from the ideological standpoint of the extreme left.

[20] For an analysis of the *discontent* which along with such other factors as ideology, Nazi strategy and tactics, and Hitler's charismatic leadership helped to bring National Socialism to power in Germany, see the classic study by Theodore Abel, *The Nazi Movement: Why Hitler Came to Power* (New York: Atherton Books, 1966).

[21] To minimize confusion, Clinton Rossiter preferred to capitalize "Conservatism" when referring to one of the great political traditions of the West and to retain the lowercase letters when referring to an attitude favorable to the preservation of the status quo as with "American conservatism." *Conservatism in America* (New York: Vintage Books, 1962).

[22] Just what should be included in a Conservative syndrome is disputed. Most

authorities would include such notions as the organic theory of the state; an aristocratic or hierarchical view of politics and society; a pessimistic theory of human nature, authoritarianism, traditionalism, and clericalism. For a denial that Conservatism can be anything other than a *situational* defense of existing institutions, see the (Mannheimian) analysis of Samuel P. Huntington, "Conservatism as an Ideology," in *Political Thought Since World War II*, ed. W. J. Stankiewicz (New York: The Free Press, 1965), pp. 356–76; and for a different approach, M. M. Auerbach, *The Conservative Illusion* (Ithaca: Cornell University Press, 1959).

[23] Fritz Stern, *The Politics of Cultural Despair* (Garden City, N.Y.: Anchor Books, 1965), p. 7. Stern, of course, is using the term "revolution" loosely, about equivalent to social movement.

[24] John R. Harrison, *The Reactionaries* (New York: Schocken Books, 1967).

[25] See, for example, discussion of Rauschning's thesis, Chapter VI, "Esoteric and Exoteric Ideology."

[26] A. James Gregor, *The Ideology of Fascism* (New York: The Free Press, 1969), p. 12.

[27] Hugh Seton-Watson, "Fascism, Right and Left," in *International Fascism 1920–45*, ed. Walter Laquer and George L. Mosse (New York: Harper Torchbooks, 1966), p. 191.

[28] Eugen Weber, "The Men of the Archangel," in *ibid.*, p. 104.

[29] Hugh Trevor-Roper, "The Phenomenon of Fascism," in *European Fascism*, ed. S. J. Woolf (New York: Vintage Books, 1969), p. 25.

[30] For an approach that virtually identifies rather than distinguishes these two elements, see John Weiss, *The Fascist Tradition* (New York: Harper & Row, 1967).

[31] Trevor-Roper, "Phenomenon," p. 25.

[32] As Trevor-Roper points out: "Much of the 'fascism' of the interwar years was factitious: an artificial 'fascist' colour temporarily imposed on native conservative movements by the example or domination of Germany or Italy." *Ibid.*, p. 35.

[33] Renzo De Felice, *Le interpretazioni del fascismo* (Bari: Laterza, 1969), p. 20.

[34] See Peter Viereck, *Metapolitics: The Roots of the Nazi Mind* (New York: Capricorn Books, 1961).

[35] See Sigmund Neumann, *Permanent Revolution* (New York: Praeger, 1965); William Kornhauser, *The Politics of Mass Society* (New York: The Free Press, 1963); and Hannah Arendt, *The Origins of Totalitarianism* (New York: Harcourt, Brace & World, 1966).

[36] Emil Lederer, *The State of the Masses* (New York: Howard Fertig, 1967), p. 108.

[37] The youthfulness of fascist movements was remarked in every country in which they emerged.

[38] Hitler even developed a kind of welfare state that must have chagrined some sectors of German business. See David Schoenbaum, *Hitler's Social Revolution* (Garden City, N.Y.: Doubleday, 1966).

[39] See Edward N. Peterson, *The Limits of Hitler's Power* (Princeton: Princeton University Press, 1969) for the wide local variations in anti-Church activity in Nazi Germany.

[40] Karl D. Bracher, *The German Dictatorship* (New York: Praeger, 1972), p. 351.

[41] On this problem, see Klemens von Klemperer, *Germany's New Conservatism* (Princeton: Princeton University Press, 1968).

[42] Albert Speer, *Inside the Third Reich* (New York: Avon Books, 1971).

[43] Seton-Watson, "Fascism, Right and Left," p. 191.

[44] King Victor Emmanuel was instrumental in the fall of Mussolini in July, 1943; technically speaking, the king simply fired his premier.

[45] Eugen Weber, *Varieties of Fascism* (Princeton: Van Nostrand, 1964), p. 26.

[46] Ernst Nolte, *Three Faces of Fascism* (New York: Holt, Rinehart & Winston, 1966), p. 198.

47 Salvatore Saladino, "Italy," in *The European Right,* ed. Eugen Weber and Hans Rogger (Berkeley: University of California Press, 1965), p. 255.

48 Alfredo Rocco, "The Transformation of the State," in *What is Fascism and Why,* ed. T. Sillani (New York: Macmillan, 1931), p. 18.

49 Adolf Hitler, *Mein Kampf* (Boston: Houghton Mifflin, 1943), p. 392.

50 *Ibid.,* p. 393.

51 *Ibid.*

52 Franz Neumann, *Behemoth* (New York: Octagon Books, 1963), p. 67.

53 Bracher, *German Dictatorship,* p. 235.

54 Quoted in Stanley Payne, *Falange* (Stanford: Stanford University Press, 1961), p. 56.

55 *Ibid.,* pp. 150–51.

56 *Ibid.*

57 *Ibid.,* p. 201.

58 Another way to envisage this is to recall that most authorities consider Nazi Germany more truly "totalitarian" than Fascist Italy. Our own conclusion is that the former was more truly revolutionary than the latter. A linkage between these two views is provided by Sigmund Neumann's formulation of the nature of modern dictatorship: "The first aim of totalitarianism is to perpetuate and to *institutionalize revolution.* Paradoxical though it is to put revolution on a permanent basis, the conscious creation of quasi-instutional structures is the most significant feature of modern totalitarian rule." *Permanent Revolution,* p. xxii.

59 See Max Weber, *The Methodology of the Social Sciences* (New York: The Free Press, 1949); Arnold Brecht, *Political Theory* (Princeton: Princeton University Press, 1967); and Herbert Marcuse, *One-Dimensional Man* (Boston: Beacon Press, 1966) for contrasting views on this problem. For a "radical" critique of the social scientific study of revolution, see Sheldon S. Wolin, "The Politics of the Study of Revolution," in a special issue of *Comparative Politics* on "Revolution and Social Change," V (April, 1973), pp. 343–58.

60 See also Herbert Marcuse, *Eros and Civilization* (New York: Vintage Books, 1962); and *Five Lectures* (Boston: Beacon Press, 1970); as well as *An Essay on Liberation* (Boston: Beacon Press, 1969) and *One-Dimensional Man.*

61 Marcuse, *Essay,* p. 16.

62 *Ibid.,* p. 70.

63 S. N. Eisenstadt, *Modernization: Protest and Change* (Englewood Cliffs, N.J.: Prentice-Hall, 1966), p. 20.

64 Ivo K. Feierabend and Rosalind L. Feierabend, "Systemic Conditions of Political Aggression: An Application of Frustration-Aggression Theory," in *Anger, Violence, and Politics,* ed. I. K. Feierabend, R. L. Feierabend, and T. R. Gurr (Englewood Cliffs, N.J.: Prentice-Hall, 1972), p. 149.

65 These are economic growth, technological innovation, scientific advance, democratization, secularization, growth of the modern state, growth of nationalism.

66 Perez Zagorin, "Theories of Revolution in Contemporary Historiography," *Political Science Quarterly,* LXXXVII (March, 1973), 48–49.

67 That is, economic depression, alienation of the intellectuals, division and ineptitude of the rulers, war, and government financial crisis.

68 Samuel P. Huntington, "Civil Violence and the Process of Development," *Adelphi Paper No. 83* (London: The International Institute for Strategic Studies, 1971), p. 10.

69 Chorley, *Armies and the Art of Revolution,* p. 61.

70 Anne Fremantle, ed., *Mao Tse-tung: An Anthology of his Writings* (New York: Mentor Books, 1963), p. 99.

71 William J. Pomeroy, "Questions on the Debray Thesis," in *Regis Debray and the*

Latin American Revolution, ed. Leo Huberman and P. M. Sweezy (New York: Monthly Review Press, 1969).

[72] General Vo Nguyen Giap, *The Military Art of People's War* (New York: Monthly Review Press, 1970) p. 101.

[73] Eqbal Ahmad, "Revolutionary Warfare and Counterinsurgency," in *National Liberation,* ed. N. Miller and R. Aya (New York: The Free Press, 1971), p. 145.

[74] *Ibid.,* p. 157.

[75] Regis Debray, "Castroism: The Long March in Latin America," in *Struggles in the State,* ed. George Kelly and C. W. Brown (New York: John Wiley, 1970), p. 454.

[76] *Ibid.,* pp. 468–69.

[77] Eqbal Ahmad, "Radical but Wrong," in *Debray and the Latin American Revolution,* p. 76.

[78] Regis Debray, *Revolution in the Revolution?* (New York: Grove Press, 1967), p. 106.

[79] Abraham Guillén, *The Philosophy of the Urban Guerrilla* (New York: Morrow, 1973), p. 238.

[80] *Ibid.,* pp. 234–35.

[81] *Ibid.,* p. 240.

[82] *Ibid.,* p. 249.

[83] Shanti Tangri, "Urbanization, Political Stability, and Economic Growth," in *Political Development and Social Change,* ed. J. L. Finkle and R. W. Gable (New York: John Wiley, 1971), p. 221.

[84] Guillén, *Urban Guerrilla,* p. 260.

[85] See Harry Eckstein's discussion of the facilities of the incumbents, effective repression, and diversions and concessions in "On the Etiology of Internal War," in *Why Revolution?* ed. C. T. Paynton and R. Blackey (Cambridge, Mass.: Schenkman, 1971), pp. 139–45.

[86] Huntington, "Civil Violence," p. 6.

[87] *Ibid.*

[88] *Ibid.*

[89] Guillén, *Urban Guerrilla,* p. 269.

[90] According to Fanon, "It is within this mass of humanity, this people of the shanty towns, at the core of the *lumpenproletariat,* that the rebellion will find its urban spearhead. For the *lumpenproletariat,* that horde of starving men, uprooted from their tribe and from their clan, constitutes one of the most spontaneous and the most radically revolutionary forces of a colonial people." *The Wretched of the Earth* (New York: Grove Press, 1968), p. 129.

[91] John H. Hoagland, "Changing Patterns of Insurgency and American Response," in *Revolutionary War: Western Response,* ed. D. S. Sullivan and M. J. Stattler (New York: Columbia University Press, 1971), p. 141.

[92] Robert B. Heilman, "Tragedy and Melodrama," in *Tragedy: Vision and Form,* ed. R. W. Corrigan (Scranton, Penn.: Chandler Pub. Co., 1965).

[93] *Ibid.,* p. 254.

[94] Barrington Moore, *Social Origins of Democracy and Dictatorship* (Boston: Beacon Press, 1968), p. 505.

[95] Barrington Moore, "Tolerance and the Scientific Outlook," in R. P. Wolff, B. Moore, and H. Marcuse, *A Critique of Pure Tolerance* (Boston: Beacon Press, 1965), p. 75.

[96] *Ibid.,* p. 76.

[97] *Ibid.*

[98] Moore, *Social Origins,* p. 507. Cf. Stanley Rothman's critique of Moore, which maintains that "the difference between Moore's view and one which emphasizes the irony

of Chinese development is a difference between a view of history as involving genuine tragedy and one which sees it as a conflict between heroes and villains. Despite Moore's explicit disclaimers, it is quite clear that the latter is his perspective." "Barrington Moore and the Dialectics of Revolution: An Essay Review," *American Political Science Review,* LXIV (March, 1970), p. 64. While certain of Moore's rhetorical flourishes have overtones of melodrama, his formal analysis retains the basic criteria of the balance sheet.

[99] Moore, *Social Origins,* p. 103.

[100] *Ibid.,* p. 104.

[101] The rise of Napoleon and the prowess of French arms, two notable factors in the warfare from 1800–15, are both attributable to the French Revolution.

[102] Cf. D. W. Brogan, *The Price of Revolution* (New York: Grosset & Dunlap, 1966), where the author uses a balance-sheet analysis informed by a different political outlook from Moore's. For example, Brogan argues that "there are in politics no necessarily good solutions; there may only be a choice of evils, and of great evils [p. 17]." Though Brogan admits certain benefits flowing from the French Revolution and concedes that it may have been a lesser evil than continuance of the old regime, he is highly critical of the Terror: "if it be answered that revolutions cannot be made with rosewater and that the tree of liberty must be lavishly watered with blood, well that is a part of the book-keeping of revolution that should not be neglected [p. 11]."

[103] Herbert Butterfield, *The Whig Interpretation of History* (New York: W. W. Norton, 1965), p. 28.

[104] Max Scheler, "On the Tragic," in *Tragedy,* p. 6.

[105] *Ibid.,* p. 13.

[106] *Ibid.,* p. 7.

[107] *Ibid.,* p. 10.

[108] See Chapter II, "Conclusion," above.

[109] One of these seems to be Robert L. Heilbroner; see his article "Counterrevolutionary America?", *Commentary Magazine,* (April, 1967), reprinted with a different title in *Struggle Against History,* ed. N. D. Houghton (New York: Simon & Schuster, 1968), pp. 106–24.

SUGGESTIONS FOR
FURTHER READING

The suggestions for further reading which follow are selected and arranged according to each of the eight chapters. Readers who desire a more specialized bibliography should check the chapter footnotes carefully. More comprehensive bibliographies on revolution and related themes are to be found in the following books: David V. J. Bell, *Resistance and Revolution* (Boston: Houghton Mifflin, 1973); Crane Brinton, *The Anatomy of Revolution* (New York: Vintage Books, 1960); Peter Calvert, *Revolution* (New York: Praeger, 1970); Ted Robert Gurr, *Why Men Rebel* (Princeton, N.J.: Princeton University Press, 1971); Carl Leiden and Karl M. Schmitt, *The Politics of Violence: Revolution in the Modern World* (Englewood Cliffs, N.J.: Prentice-Hall, 1968); Mostafa Rejai, *The Strategy of Political Revolution* (Garden City, N.Y.: Anchor Books, 1973); Neil J. Smelser, *Theory of Collective Behavior* (New York: Free Press, 1971); Clifford T. Paynton and Robert Blackey, eds., *Why Revolution?* (Cambridge, Mass.: Schenkman, 1971). Journals most helpful to the author in English include *Past and Present, The American Historical Review, The American Journal of Sociology, The American Sociological Review, World Politics,* and *Comparative Studies in Society and History.*

CHAPTER I

ANDREWS, WILLIAM G., and RA'ANAN, URI, eds. *The Politics of the Coup d'état.* New York: Van Nostrand, 1969.

COHN, NORMAN. *The Pursuit of the Millennium.* New York: Oxford University Press, 1970.

ELLUL, JACQUES. *Autopsy of Revolution.* New York: Alfred A. Knopf, 1971.

EMERSON, RUPERT. *From Empire to Nation.* Boston: Beacon Press, 1963.

FORSTER, ROBERT, and GREENE, JACK P., eds. *Preconditions of Revolution in Early Modern Europe.* Baltimore: Johns Hopkins University Press, 1970.

HARRISON, JAMES P. *The Chinese Communists and Chinese Peasant Rebellions.* New York: Atheneum, 1971.

HARTZ, LOUIS. *The Founding of New Societies.* New York: Harcourt, Brace & World, 1964.

HOBSBAWM, E. J. *Primitive Rebels*. New York: W. W. Norton, 1965.

HUNTINGTON, SAMUEL P. *Political Order in Changing Societies*. New Haven, Conn.: Yale University Press, 1970.

LANTERNARI, VITTORIO. *The Religions of the Oppressed*. New York: Mentor Books, 1965.

LUTTWAK, EDWARD. *Coup d'État*. Greenwich, Conn.: Fawcett Publications, 1969.

MANNONI, O. *Prospero and Caliban*. New York: Praeger, 1964.

MICHAEL, FRANZ. *The Taiping Rebellion*. Seattle: University of Washington Press, 1972.

MOUSNIER, ROLAND. *Peasant Uprisings in Seventeenth Century France, Russia, and China*. New York: Harper & Row, 1971.

TILLY, CHARLES. "Collective Violence in European Perspective." In *Violence in America: Historical and Comparative Perspectives*, edited by Hugh D. Graham and Ted R. Gurr. New York: Bantam Books, 1969.

WALLACE, ANTHONY F. C. "Revitalization Movements." *American Anthropologist* 58: 264–80.

WOMACK, JOHN, JR. *Zapata and the Mexican Revolution*. New York: Vintage Books, 1969.

CHAPTER II

ARENDT, HANNAH. *On Revolution*. New York: Viking Press, 1963.

CALVERT, PETER. *Revolution*. New York: Praeger, 1970.

FINER, S. E., ed. *Vilfredo Pareto: Sociological Writings*. New York: Praeger, 1966.

HUNTINGTON, SAMUEL P. *Political Order in Changing Societies*. New Haven, Conn.: Yale University Press, 1970.

JOUVENAL, BERTRAND DE. *On Power*. Boston: Beacon Press, 1962.

MARX, KARL. *On Revolution*. Edited by S. K. Padover. New York: McGraw-Hill, 1971.

MARX, KARL, and ENGELS, FRIEDRICH. *Selected Works*. 2 vols. Moscow: Foreign Languages Publishing House, 1958.

PARETO, VILFREDO. *The Mind and Society: A Treatise on General Sociology*. New York: Dover Books, 1963.

STONE, LAWRENCE. "Theories of Revolution." *World Politics* 18: 159–76.

TAINE, H. A. *The Ancient Regime*. Gloucester, Mass.: Peter Smith, 1962.

TOCQUEVILLE, ALEXIS DE. *The Old Regime and the French Revolution*. New York: Anchor Books, 1955.

CHAPTER III

ARISTOTLE. *The Politics*. Translated by E. Barker. New York: Oxford University Press, 1950.

ASTON, TREVOR, ed. *Crisis in Europe*. Garden City, N.Y.: Anchor Books, 1967.

BALANDIER, GEORGES. *Political Anthropology*. New York: Vintage Books, 1972.

BÉTEILLE, ANDRÉ, ed. *Readings in Social Inequality*. Baltimore: Penguin Books, 1969.

COX, OLIVER C. *Caste, Class and Race*. New York: Modern Reader Paperbacks, 1970.

DAHRENDORF, RALF. *Essays in the Theory of Society*. Stanford, Calif.: Stanford University Press, 1968.

EASTON, DAVID. *The Political System*. New York: Alfred A. Knopf, 1963.

ECKSTEIN, HARRY. "On the Etiology of Internal Wars." In *Why Revolution?*, edited by C. T. Paynton and R. Blackey. Cambridge, Mass.: Schenkman, 1971.

ENLOE, CYNTHIA. *Ethnic Conflict and Political Development*. Boston: Little, Brown, 1973.

HUNTINGTON, SAMUEL P. *Political Order in Changing Societies*. New Haven, Conn.: Yale University Press, 1970.

JOHNSON, CHALMERS. *Revolutionary Change*. Boston: Little, Brown, 1966.

KUPER, LEO. "Race, Class, and Power: Some Comments on Revolutionary Change." *Comparative Studies in Society and History* 14: 400–21.

MARSHALL, T. H. *Class, Citizenship and Social Development*. Garden City, N.Y.: Doubleday, 1964.

MOSCA, GAETANO. *The Ruling Class*. New York: McGraw-Hill, 1939.

MOUSNIER, ROLAND. *Social Hierarchies*. New York: Schocken Books, 1973.

PALMER, R. R. *The Age of Democratic Revolution*. 2 vols. Princeton, N.J.: Princeton University Press, 1969.

PETTEE, GEORGE. *The Process of Revolution*. New York: Harper & Row, 1938.

WEBER, MAX. *Economy and Society*. 3 vols. New York: Bedminster Press, 1969.

ZAGORIN, PEREZ. *The Court and the Country*. New York: Atheneum, 1970.

CHAPTER IV

BRINTON, CRANE. *The Anatomy of Revolution*. New York: Vintage Books, 1960.

BRODBECK, MAY, ed. *Readings in the Philosophy of the Social Sciences*. New York: Macmillan, 1968.

CHORLEY, KATHARINE. *Armies and the Art of Revolution*. Boston: Beacon Press, 1973.

DAVIES, JAMES C. "Toward a Theory of Revolution." In *When Men Revolt and Why*, edited by James C. Davies. New York: Free Press, 1971. Article first published in the *American Sociological Review* 27: 5–19.

EDWARDS, LYFORD P. *The Natural History of Revolution*. Chicago: University of Chicago Press, 1970.

GARDINER, PATRICK, ed. *Theories of History*. New York: The Free Press, 1959.

GOTTSCHALK, LOUIS. "Causes of Revolution." *The American Journal of Sociology* 50: 1–8.

GURR, TED ROBERT. *Why Men Rebel*. Princeton, N.J.: Princeton University Press, 1971.

HEMPEL, CARL G. *Aspects of Scientific Explanation*. New York: The Free Press, 1965.

KOHN, HANS. *The Idea of Nationalism*. New York: Macmillan, 1961.

KORNHAUSER, WILLIAM. *The Politics of Mass Society*. New York: The Free Press, 1963.

KRAMNICK, ISAAC. "Reflections on Revolution: Definition and Explanation in Recent Scholarship." *History and Theory* 11: 26–63.

MacIver, R. M. *Social Causation*. New York: Harper Torchbooks, 1964.

Neumann, Sigmund. *Permanent Revolution*. New York: Praeger, 1965.

Olsen, Mancur. "Rapid Growth as a Destabilizing Force." In *When Men Revolt and Why*, edited by James C. Davies. New York: The Free Press, 1971.

Paynton, Clifford T., and Blackey, Robert, eds. *Why Revolution?* Cambridge, Mass.: Schenkman, 1971.

Pettee, George. *The Process of Revolution*. New York: Harper & Row, 1938.

Shils, Edward. "The Intellectuals and the Powers: Some Perspectives for Comparative Analysis." In *On Intellectuals*, edited by Philip Rieff. Garden City, N.Y.: Anchor Books, 1970.

Sorokin, Pitirim. *The Sociology of Revolution*. New York: Howard Fertig, 1967.

CHAPTER V

Brinton, Crane. *The Anatomy of Revolution*. New York: Vintage Books, 1960.

―――. *The Jacobins*. New York: Russell & Russell, 1961.

Capp, B. S. *The Fifth Monarchy Men*. London: Faber & Faber, 1972.

Daniels, Robert V. *The Conscience of the Revolution*. New York: Simon & Schuster, 1969.

Edwards, Lyford P. *The Natural History of Revolution*. Chicago: University of Chicago Press, 1970.

Palmer, R. R. *Twelve Who Ruled*. Princeton, N.J.: Princeton University Press, 1970.

Pettee, George. *The Process of Revolution*. New York: Harper & Row, 1938.

Schapiro, Leonard. *The Origins of the Communist Autocracy*. New York: Praeger, 1965.

Schurmann, Franz. *Ideology and Organization in Communist China*. Berkeley: University of California Press, 1971.

Soboul, Albert. *The Sans Culottes*. Garden City, N.Y.: Anchor Books, 1972.

Talmon, J. L. *The Origins of Totalitarian Democracy*. New York: Praeger, 1970.

Timasheff, Nicholas. *The Great Retreat*. New York: E. P. Dutton, 1946.

Trotsky, Leon. *Permanent Revolution*. New York: Pioneer Publishers, 1965.

CHAPTER VI

Bury, J. B. *The Idea of Progress*. New York: Dover Books, 1955.

Christenson, Reo M., et al. *Ideologies and Modern Politics*. New York: Dodd, Mead, 1971.

Cox, Richard H., ed. *Ideology, Politics, and Political Theory*. Belmont, Calif.: Wadsworth, 1969.

Draper, Theodore. *Castroism: Theory and Practice*. New York: Praeger, 1965.

Eliade, Mircea. *Myth and Reality*. New York: Harper Torchbooks, 1967.

Friedrich, Carl J. *Man and His Government*. New York: McGraw-Hill, 1963.

Germino, Dante. *Beyond Ideology: The Revival of Political Theory*. New York: Harper & Row, 1968.

Hsiung, James C. *Ideology and Practice*. New York: Praeger, 1970.

MacIver, R. M. *The Web of Government*. New York: Macmillan, 1963.

Mannheim, Karl. *Ideology and Utopia*. New York: Harcourt, Brace, n.d.

MANUEL, FRANK, ed. *Utopias and Utopian Thought*. Boston: Beacon Press, 1967.

MARX, KARL, and ENGELS, FRIEDRICH. *The German Ideology*. New York: International Publishers, 1960.

MERTON, ROBERT K. *Science, Technology and Society in Seventeenth-Century England*. New York: Harper Torchbooks, 1970.

MULLINS, WILLARD A. "On the Concept of Ideology in Political Science." *The American Political Science Review* 66: 498–510.

PLEKHANOV, GEORGE. *Fundamental Problems of Marxism*. New York: International Publishers, 1969.

SCHURMANN, FRANZ. *Ideology and Organization in Communist China*. Berkeley: University of California Press, 1971.

SOREL, GEORGES. *Reflections on Violence*. Glencoe, Ill.: The Free Press, 1950.

WAXMAN, CHIAM, ed. *The End of Ideology Debate*. New York: Simon & Schuster, 1969.

CHAPTER VII

ALAVI, HAMZA. "Peasants and Revolution." In *The Socialist Register 1965*, edited by R. Miliband and J. Saville. New York: Monthly Review Press, 1965.

BROWN, ROGER W. "Mass Phenomena." In *Handbook of Social Psychology*, edited by Gardner Lindzey. Reading, Mass.: Addison-Wesley, 1956.

BYCHOWSKI, GUSTAV. *Dictators and Disciples*. New York: International Universities Press, 1969.

DOWNTON, JAMES V., JR. *Rebel Leadership*. New York: The Free Press, 1973.

ERIKSON, ERIK. *Young Man Luther*. New York: W. W. Norton, 1962.

FEUER, LEWIS S. *The Conflict of Generations*. New York: Basic Books, 1969.

FREUD, SIGMUND, and BULLITT, WILLIAM C. *Thomas Woodrow Wilson*. Boston: Houghton Mifflin, 1967.

HOFFER, ERIC. *The True Believer*. New York: Mentor Books, 1958.

HOOK, SIDNEY. *The Hero in History*. Boston: Beacon Press, 1967.

KORNHAUSER, WILLIAM. *The Politics of Mass Society*. New York: The Free Press, 1963.

LASSWELL, HAROLD D. *Psychopathology and Politics*. New York: Viking Press, 1960.

LEBON, GUSTAVE. *The Crowd*. New York: Viking Press, 1960.

LEFEBVRE, GEORGES. *The Great Fear of 1789*. New York: Vintage Books, 1973.

MALEFAKIS, EDWARD E. *Agrarian Reform and Peasant Revolution in Spain*. New Haven, Conn.: Yale University Press, 1970.

MAZOUR, ANATOLE. *The First Russian Revolution, 1825*. Stanford, Calif.: Stanford University Press, 1965.

RUDÉ, GEORGE. *The Crowd in the French Revolution*. New York: Oxford University Press, 1969.

SHANIN, TEODOR, ed. *Peasants and Peasant Societies*. Baltimore: Penguin Books, 1971.

SHILS, EDWARD. "The Intellectuals in the Political Development of the New States." In *Political Change in Underdeveloped Countries*, edited by John H. Kautsky. New York: John Wiley, 1964.

SMELSER, NEIL J. *Theory of Collective Behavior*. New York: The Free Press, 1971.

TOCQUEVILLE, ALEXIS DE. *Recollections*. New York: Meridian Books, 1959.

WOLF, ERIC R. *Peasant Wars of the Twentieth Century*. New York: Harper & Row, 1969.

WOLFENSTEIN, E. VICTOR. *The Revolutionary Personality*. Princeton, N.J.: Princeton University Press, 1971.

CHAPTER VIII

AHMAD, EQBAL. "Revolutionary Warfare and Counterinsurgency." In *National Liberation*, edited by N. Miller and R. Aya. New York: The Free Press, 1971.

BRACHER, KARL D. *The German Dictatorship*. New York: Praeger, 1972.

CHORLEY, KATHARINE. *Armies and the Art of Revolution*. Boston: Beacon Press, 1973.

DEBRAY, REGIS. *Revolution in the Revolution?* New York: Grove Press, 1967.

FANON, FRANTZ. *The Wretched of the Earth*. New York: Grove Press, 1968.

GREGOR, A. JAMES. *The Ideology of Fascism*. New York: The Free Press, 1969.

GODECHOT, JACQUES. *The Counter-Revolution: Doctrine and Practice*. New York: Howard Fertig, 1971.

HUNTINGTON, SAMUEL P. "Civil Violence and the Process of Development." *Adelphi Paper No. 83*. London: The International Institute for Strategic Studies, 1971.

JOHNSON, CHALMERS. *Autopsy on People's War*. Berkeley: University of California Press, 1973.

MARCUSE, HERBERT. *An Essay on Liberation*. Boston: Beacon Press, 1969.

MAYER, ARNO J. *Dynamics of Counterrevolution in Europe, 1870–1956*. New York: Harper Torchbooks, 1971.

MOORE, BARRINGTON, JR. *Social Origins of Dictatorship and Democracy*. Boston: Beacon Press, 1968.

PAYNE, STANLEY. *Falange*. Stanford, Calif.: Stanford University Press, 1961.

TILLY, CHARLES. *The Vendée*. New York: John Wiley, 1967.

NAME INDEX

SUBJECT INDEX